Joseph Wright of Derby, *The Dead Soldier* (1789). ©University of Michigan Museum of Art, oil on canvas, 165.1 cm × 198.12 cm × 12.7 cm, museum purchase made possible by the W. Hawkins Ferry Fund and anonymous individual benefactors, 2006/1.156.

Civilians and War in Europe,
1618–1815

Eighteenth-Century Worlds

SERIES EDITORS:
Professor Eve Rosenhaft (Liverpool) and Dr Mark Towsey (Liverpool)

Eighteenth-Century Worlds promotes innovative new research in the political, social, economic, intellectual and cultural life of the 'long' eighteenth century (c.1650-c.1850), from a variety of historical, theoretical and critical perspectives. Monographs published in the series adopt international, comparative and/ or interdisciplinary approaches to the global eighteenth century, in volumes that make the results of specialist research accessible to an informed, but not discipline-specific, audience.

Civilians and War in Europe, 1618–1815

EDITED BY

Erica Charters, Eve Rosenhaft and Hannah Smith

LIVERPOOL UNIVERSITY PRESS

First published 2012 by
Liverpool University Press
4 Cambridge Street
Liverpool
L69 7ZU

This paperback edition published 2014

British Library Cataloguing-in-Publication data
A British Library CIP record is available

ISBN 978-1-84631-711-8   *cased*
ISBN 978-1-78138-012-3   *paperback*

Typeset in Caslon by R. J. Footring Ltd, Derby
Printed and bound by CPI Group (UK) Ltd, Croydon CR0 4YY

Contents

Contributors

David A. Bell is the Sidney and Ruth Lapidus Professor in the Era of the North Atlantic Revolutions at Princeton University. He is the author of *The Cult of the Nation in France* (2001) and *The First Total War: Napoleon's Europe*

and the Making of Warfare As We Know It (2007).

Horst Carl is Professor of Early Modern History at Justus-Liebig-University, Giessen. His current research project is on early modern mercenaries and the function of violence for the cohesion of social groups. Recent publications include *Kriegsniederlagen. Erfahrungen und Erinnerungen* (2004) and *Europäische Wahrnehmungen 1650–1850. Interkulturelle Kommunikation und Medienereignisse* (2008).

Erica Charters is University Lecturer in the History of Medicine at the University of Oxford. She is the author of *Disease, War, and the Imperial State: The Welfare of the British Armed Forces during the Seven Years War, 1756–63* (forthcoming) and is working on a study of French forces during the Seven Years War.

Stephen Conway is Professor of History at University College London. He is the author of *The War of American Independence, 1775–1783* (1995), *The British Isles and the War of American Independence* (2000), *War, State, and Society in Mid-Eighteenth-Century Britain and Ireland* (2006) and *Britain, Ireland, and Continental Europe in the Eighteenth Century* (2011).

Gavin Daly is Senior Lecturer in Modern European History in the School of History and Classics, University of Tasmania. He is the author of *Inside*

Napoleonic France (2001) and has published widely on Britain and France during the Napoleonic Wars. He is currently writing a history of British soldiers' cultural encounters in Spain and Portugal during the Peninsular War.

Barbara Donagan is an independent scholar at the Huntington Library, California. She has published articles relating to the codes, conduct and conditions of the English civil war and also on aspects of puritan lives. *War in England 1642–1649* (2008) dealt primarily with the soldiers' war. She is now working on a book on the civilian experience of civil war.

Alan Forrest has been Professor of Modern History at the University of York since 1989. He has published widely on French Revolutionary and Napoleonic history and the history of modern warfare. His recent books include *The Legacy of the French Revolutionary Wars: The Nation-in-Arms in French Republican Memory* (2009) and *Napoleon* (2011).

Melanie Harrington received her BA from the University of Liverpool and her MPhil in Early Modern History from the University of Cambridge, where she is currently completing her doctorate. Her thesis examines the Restoration period and the long-term legacies of the mid-seventeenth-century crisis in England, particularly the social, cultural and political consequences of royalist disappointment after 1660.

Leighton James is a Lecturer at the University of Swansea. His current research is focused on the social and cultural history of warfare in the eighteenth and early nineteenth centuries. He has just completed a book on the experience of the Revolutionary and Napoleonic wars in German central Europe, entitled *Witnessing War*.

Matthew McCormack is Senior Lecturer in History at the University of Northampton. He works on 'public' manifestations of masculinity, particularly in the arenas of politics and the military. His publications include *The Independent Man: Citizenship and Gender Politics in Georgian England* (2005) and, as editor, *Public Men: Masculinity and Politics in Modern Britain* (2007).

Colm McKeogh is a lecturer in political science at the University of Waikato, New Zealand. He studied political science at Trinity College Dublin and strategic studies at Aberystwyth University. His previous publications include *The Political Realism of Reinhold Niebuhr* (1997), *Innocent Civilians* (2002) and *Tolstoy's Pacifism* (2009).

Markus Meumann is a researcher at the University of Halle-Wittenberg in Germany. He is currently preparing a book on the effects of war and the establishment of standing armies on the political and legal culture of seventeenth-century Europe, with a special focus on France and the Holy Roman Empire.

Eve Rosenhaft is Professor of German Historical Studies at the University of Liverpool. She has published on aspects of labour, gender and ethnicity in German history of the eighteenth to twentieth centuries. Her work in eighteenth-century studies focuses on cultures of money, insurance and popular financial practices, especially on the part of women.

Philip Shaw is Professor of Romantic Studies in the School of English at the University of Leicester. His most recent publications include: *The Sublime* (2006), *Waterloo and the Romantic Imagination* (2002) and, as editor, *Romantic Wars: Studies in Culture and Conflict, 1789–1822* (2000). At present he is working on a book-length study entitled *Suffering and Sentiment in Romantic Military Art*.

Hannah Smith is a Tutorial Fellow and University Lecturer in History at St Hilda's College, Oxford. She has published *Georgian Monarchy: Politics and Culture, 1714–1760* (2006). She is currently working on a study of the British army and society from 1660 to 1750.

Mark Towsey is Lecturer in Modern History at the University of Liverpool, having previously held fellowships at Harvard, Yale and the IHR. He is the author of *Reading the Scottish Enlightenment: Books and their Readers in Provincial Scotland, 1750–1820* (2010) and has published extensively on reading experiences and the cultural history of libraries in the eighteenth and nineteenth centuries.

Peter H. Wilson is GF Grant Professor of History at the University of Hull, having worked previously at Sunderland and Newcastle universities. He has written or edited fifteen books on European history including *Europe's Tragedy. A History of the Thirty Years War* (2009).

Acknowledgements

Many of the chapters in this volume are versions of papers presented at the 'Civilians and War in Europe, c.1640–1815' conference held at the University of Liverpool in June 2009. The editors wish to thank all who participated in the conference; the Eighteenth-Century Worlds Research Centre, University of Liverpool and the Centre for Early Modern British and Irish History, University of Oxford, for providing financial, administrative and intellectual support which ensured that the conference took place; and the Royal Historical Society for the award of a grant that facilitated graduate attendance at the conference. The editors additionally wish to thank Tim Blanning, Val Fry, Felicity Heal, Malasree Home, Holger Hoock, Stephanie Jenkins and Guy Rowlands for their invaluable help, advice and encouragement with various aspects of the conference; the readers for Liverpool University Press for their incisive, careful and supportive responses to the text; and Alison Welsby at Liverpool University Press for her assistance with the volume's publication. Thanks are also due to the John Fell OUP Research Fund and the Leverhulme Trust for sponsoring periods of research leave for Erica Charters and Hannah Smith respectively, which very much assisted with the completion of the volume.

The editors gratefully acknowledge the University of Michigan Museum of Art for permission to reproduce Joseph Wright of Derby, *The Dead Soldier* (1789, oil on canvas, 165.1 cm x 198.12 cm x 12.7 cm, museum purchase made possible by the W. Hawkins Ferry Fund and anonymous individual benefactors, 2006/1.156); the Trustees of the British Museum, London for permission to reproduce James Gillray, 'Supplementary Militia, turning out for Twenty-

Days Amusement' (1796), 'The 2 H. H.'s' (March 1756), 'The Church Militant' (September 1779), 'The Chymical Macaroni, Capt Ludgate' (November 1772), 'Capt Jessamy learning the Proper Discipline of the Couch' (1782), 'He Leads the Van Again' (26 August 1780), 'Advance Three Steps Backwards, Or the Militia Heroes' (c. 1779), 'A Trip to Cocks Heath' (28 October 1778), and Charles Williams, 'After the Invasion – The Levée en Masse – or Britons Strike Home' (August 1803); and the National Portrait Gallery, London for permission to reproduce George Townshend, unpublished sketch of the Duke of Cumberland (1750s).

Illustrations

Abbreviations

ADN	Archives départementales de France
ANF	Archives nationales de France
BL	British Library, London
BM	British Museum, London
BnF	Bibliothèque nationale de France
Bod.	Bodleian Library, Oxford
CAM	*Calendar of the Proceedings of the Committee for the Advance of Money, 1642–1656*, 3 vols. (Eyre and Spottiswoode for HMSO, 1888)
CCC	*Calendar of the Proceedings of the Committee for Compounding, 1643–1660*, 5 vols. (Eyre and Spottiswoode for HMSO, 1889–92)
CRO	Cheshire Record Office, Chester
DTA	Deutsches Tagebucharchiv, Emmendingen
ERO	Essex Record Office, Chelmsford
HRO	Hampshire Record Office, Winchester
HStaS	Hauptstaatsarchiv Stuttgart
NAS	National Archives of Scotland, Edinburgh
NMM	National Maritime Museum, Greenwich
NPG	National Portrait Gallery, London
ODNB	*Oxford Dictionary of National Biography*
OED	*Oxford English Dictionary*
ÖKA	Österreichisches Kriegsarchiv, Vienna
SBA	Scottish Border Archives at the Hawick Heritage Hub

SHDAT   Service historique de la défense, armée de terre, Vincennes
TNA   The National Archives, Kew
WiltSHC Wiltshire and Swindon History Centre, Chippenham
WSRO   West Sussex Record Office, Chichester

Introduction

ERICA CHARTERS, EVE ROSENHAFT and
HANNAH SMITH

THE EXPERIENCE of civilians in wartime has received new and productive attention in recent years, with scholarship on war and the military
being enriched by impulses from social and cultural history. As a result, the
penetration of everyday life by the business of war, and the implication of
civilians in military action, have become central to the history of warfare. Such
approaches have spotlighted the complex situation of the civilian between
1618 and 1815, a period that saw shifting understandings of the treatment that
civilians could expect and the rights that they could claim.[1] This concern has
also been integral to the recent historical literature that locates the beginnings
of the modern phenomenon of 'total war' in the French Revolutionary and
Napoleonic periods.

A long-standing perception that the French Revolutionary and Napoleonic
wars were the first modern wars has come to be articulated as a statement that
they represent the first 'total war', anticipating Carl von Clausewitz's pioneer-
ing conceptualisation and its adoption into general use to characterise the great
wars of the twentieth century. In the case of the French Revolutionary and
Napoleonic wars, 'total war' refers specifically to their ideological objects and
the ways in which wars waged in the name of extirpating error tendentially
legitimated hostilities against civilian populations. The term has also been

---

1   See Best, *War and Law*, pp. 18–44; Childs, *Armies and Warfare*; Anderson, *War and Society*;
    Corvisier, *Armies and Societies*; Grimsley and Rogers, eds., *Civilians in the Path of War*;
    Tallett, *War and Society*.

deployed to describe the mobilisation of civilian populations for the prosecution of war (the *levée en masse* on the one hand, the 'war of liberation' involving guerrilla action and calls for public sacrifice for the nation on the other). For this period, a number of in-depth studies of local and national experiences have illuminated how social practices and political and social values were shaped and shaping in the interaction between civilian and military life over almost a quarter of a century of conflict.[2]

At the same time, the findings of scholars working on the seventeenth century challenge – or at least complicate – the notion that this was the first 'total war'. Contemporary accounts of the sufferings of civilian populations in the Thirty Years War have long attracted the interest of historians. Recent research on the English Civil War has moved from a primarily political or military focus to foreground the violent and traumatic qualities of that conflict, which marked the lives of ex-soldiers and nominally non-combatant civilians for generations.[3] And new studies of the armed conflicts that seethed in Europe throughout the eighteenth century, finding an initial climax in the Seven Years War, have shown how non-combatants were constantly involved with, and exposed to, the exigencies of war. Mass mobilisation; the extensive scope and prolonged length of campaigns; the traffic of refugees, hostages and prisoners of war; and garrisoning and the military pressure for supply ensured that few civilians remained untouched by warfare.[4]

This collection of essays explores the impact of war on civilians as 'victims' of armed conflict. It also approaches civilians as active agents in situations of conflict and as contributors to a 'war effort'. More particularly, it reconsiders the status of the conflict of 1792 to 1815 as 'total war' (and indeed the notion of 'total war' itself) by situating it within the *longue durée* of seventeenth- and eighteenth-century civilian–military relations, thus allowing developments in values and practices to be traced and elements of continuity to be identified, as well as pointing to authentic moments of change.

---

2   See Bell, *First Total War*; Forrest, *Conscripts and Deserters*; Forrest, *Revolution in Provincial France*; Esdaile, *Fighting Napoleon*.

3   Carlton, *Going to the Wars*; Donagan, *War in England*; Youngman, 'Our Dear Mother Stripped'; Stoyle, 'Memories of the Maimed'.

4   For example, Conway, *War, State, and Society*; Lynn, *Women, Armies and Warfare*; Hochedlinger, *Austria's Wars of Emergence*.

1. TOTAL WAR

THE GENEALOGY of the concept 'total war' suggests a fertile seed. Its origin lies in Clausewitz's *On War*, the Prussian officer's collection of writings on war, which drew on his experience of Napoleonic warfare.[5] Hew Strachan and others have pointed to how Clausewitz's thought, when carefully placed in historical context, develops a concept that should more accurately be called 'absolute war', an ideal state never grasped, and not within reach.[6] Regardless, the notion of a total war has proved a useful and appealing way of exploring conflict in the modern world. Most widespread is the characterisation of the First and Second World Wars as total wars and, as such, they are often studied together.[7] Indeed, Ian F. W. Beckett's seminal essay on the concept of total war focuses almost exclusively on the application of the term to these wars.[8] In American historiography, the American Civil War has long been analysed as a total war, beginning with J. B. Walters's article from 1948 entitled 'General William T. Sherman and Total War'.[9] Most recently, David A. Bell has argued the case for the French Revolutionary and Napoleonic wars as being the first total war: a fundamental transformation in warfare and how it was understood, which marked the beginning of Western society's modern sensibilities of war and military culture.[10]

Given the concept's wide application, it is unsurprising that its definition is elastic.[11] As an ideal-type, total war is associated with a war of unprecedented intensity. Restraints imposed by the laws of war are cast aside as battle rages everywhere. The entire population is mobilised into the war effort. Its aim is unlimited – the complete destruction of the opposing side. As Beckett points out, the First and Second World Wars were global in scope, with leaders demanding not just dynastic settlements but the destruction of states and

---

5 The seminal English edited translation is Michael Howard's and Peter Paret's Clausewitz, *On War* (1976).

6 Strachan, *Carl von Clausewitz's On War*.

7 For example, Marwick, *Britain in the Century of Total War*; Chickering, Förster and Greiner, eds., *World at Total War*; Chickering and Förster, eds., *Great War, Total War*; Wright, *Ordeal of Total War*; Marwick, ed., *Total War and Social Change*; Beckwith, *Total War*; Buckley, *Air Power in the Age of Total War*; Dreisziger, *Mobilization for Total War*.

8 Beckett, 'Total War', pp. 26–44.

9 Walters, 'General William T. Sherman and Total War'.

10 Bell, *First Total War*, Introduction.

11 Even beyond academia the concept of total war seems widely deployed, as indicated by the popular video game series *Total War*, which demands not only tactical decisions but also resource management and long-term strategy to ensure victory. The series has a number of games, including 'Empire: Total War' (mid-eighteenth-century and early nineteenth-century British amphibious colonial warfare) and 'Napoleon: Total War'.

peoples. Through the use of aerial bombardment and genocide, civilians were deliberately targeted. Moreover, historians have been keen to demonstrate that these wars led to widespread social change, most notably by mobilising sections of the population who were otherwise uninvolved in warfare – whether women into the workforce or minority groups and colonial subjects into the armed forces.[12] Indeed, the concept of total war evaluates the interaction between military and civilian spheres. More specifically, total war suggests the erosion of the difference between the civilian and the soldier, either through widespread mobilisation or the inclusion of civilians as legitimate targets as direct extensions of the state under attack.[13] In determining whether or not the American Civil War was a total war, Mark E. Neely concludes, '[t]he essential aspect of any definition of total war asserts that it breaks down the distinction between soldiers and civilians, combatants and non-combatants'.[14]

In all of its defining features, the concept of total war rests on the proposition that it is a new type of war. Total war is fundamentally different from what came before, and hence often conflated with modern war.[15] As to what makes it novel, the terminology shows that it is the antithesis of limited war, war that is controlled and restrained in its aims, scope and intensity. In other words, total war relies on a narrative, the inexorable progression from limited warfare towards unlimited, total war. The events in France in 1792 along with industrialisation led to the American Civil War, and finally, '[t]he plot culminates in the "Century of Total War"', with the Second World War as the quintessential total war.[16] As many have pointed out, the narrative of total war obscures the variety and nature of war in the modern period. By the same token, it also distorts the variety and nature of war in the period preceding it.

The language of totality implies that late seventeenth- and early to mid-eighteenth-century warfare was restrained, a situation that has been viewed as a response by contemporaries who looked back in horror at the devastation of the Thirty Years War. Warfare was conducted by state-funded professional armies that followed practised manoeuvres on battlefields. The activities of these armies only infrequently spilled over into civilian life, not least because state funds and the officially organised extraction of resources from civilian populations ensured that indiscriminate, disorderly plunder had a reduced role in the military economy. There were clear demarcations between soldiers and civilians, with the latter being generally well treated. In comparison to the Thirty Years War, the ideological, confessional impetus

---

12 Beckett, 'Total War', pp. 31–35, 37–41.
13 Mulligan, 'Review Article: Total War', pp. 213–14.
14 Neely, 'Was the Civil War a Total War?', p. 458.
15 For a thoughtful analysis, see Strachan, 'On Total War and Modern War'.
16 Chickering, 'Total War: The Use and Abuse of a Concept', p. 14.

was less apparent in these 'cabinet wars', which were fought, in the main, by the princes rather than peoples of Europe to maintain the balance of geo-political power. This almost nostalgic assessment is central to the construction of the concept of total war.[17]

Support for the characterisation of late seventeenth- and early to mid-eighteenth-century warfare as 'limited' can be found in the writings of contemporaries, who stressed the need for restraint and humanity in warfare, both between combatants and between combatants and non-combatants. Robert Parker related how, during the War of the Spanish Succession, William Cadogan, a senior British army officer, sent some of the best surgeons and physicians in the British army to tend a badly wounded, captured enemy officer who had treated Cadogan 'with great civility' when he had taken Cadogan prisoner several years earlier. Once the officer had fully recovered, Cadogan released him. 'This humane and generous treatment is for the most part the practice of all European nations, when once the heat of action is over', commented Parker approvingly in his military memoirs, published in 1746–47.[18]

The destruction of cities and towns, and thus the lives, livelihoods and property of civilians, was seen as departing from civilised norms and likely to incur international outrage. 'The pain of having to destroy cities as considerable as Worms and Speyer leads me to put before His Majesty the bad effect that such a desolation would have on his reputation and his *gloire* in the world', declared the French commander, Marshal Duras, in 1689 during the devastation of the Palatinate.[19] A decade and a half later, in 1704, the English general John Churchill, Duke of Marlborough, was anxious to explain the reasons behind his part in the concerted destruction of settlements in the Elector of Bavaria's territories. Such a policy 'is so uneasy to my nature that nothing but an absolute necessity could have obliged mee to consent to itt, for these poor pepel suffers onely for their master's ambision, there having been noe war in this country for above 60 yeares'.[20]

---

17 Eric Robson, for example, remarked that '[a] note of leisure characterised eighteenth-century warfare, both on land and at sea, until the Revolutionary wars, first of America, then of France, introduced a sense of energy such as the preceding years had never known, and began that ideological warfare characteristic of the nineteenth and twentieth centuries': Robson, 'Armed Forces and the Art of War', p. 163. See also Chandler, *Marlborough*, pp. 62–68.

18 Chandler, ed., *Robert Parker and Comte de Mérode-Westerloo*, p. 109; Childs, *Armies and Warfare*, p. 100. Of course, not all prisoners of war were treated with such consideration during the War of the Spanish Succession. For the sufferings of prisoners of war during that period see Scouller, *Armies of Queen Anne*, pp. 310–21.

19 Cited in Lynn, *Wars of Louis XIV*, p. 197. See also Lynn, 'Brutal Necessity?', p. 87.

20 Snyder, ed., *Marlborough–Godolphin Correspondence*, p. 344.

Strikingly, however, when Winston Churchill came, in his interwar biography of his ancestor's career, to deal with this particular episode, he reached for comparisons with 'the destruction wrought by the Germans in their withdrawals from France and Belgium in our own times'.[21] The research of historians working on the late seventeenth and early to mid-eighteenth centuries has demonstrated what Winston Churchill sensed, the inadequacy of conceptualising warfare in this period as 'limited', in terms of both military strategy and civilian–military relations.[22] As John Childs has remarked:

> Napoleon's vast armies living off the countryside and based upon a homeland that was organised for an approximation of 'total war' after the edict of 1793 did not come sweeping down on Europe as a barbaric novelty. Every war of the later seventeenth and eighteenth centuries, ending with the climax between 1756 and 1763, had prepared the populations and governments of the continent for the formal return to unlimited martial contests.[23]

Warfare in this period took a material and physical toll on civilians and the communities in which they lived in various ways although, as Frank Tallett has noted, the impact of war was socially differential, a conclusion buttressed by Christopher R. Friedrichs's study of the early modern German city of Nördlingen, which suggested that the city's poor were harder pressed by wartime taxation than the rich.[24] War disrupted trade and communications and brought poverty, famine, disease and mortality in its wake to communities still recovering from the Thirty Years War. Refugees put urban government infrastructures under further financial and social pressure.[25] Civilian facilities, such as hospitals and their medical staff, were employed to serve the needs of injured soldiers.[26] Throughout the period, plunder remained an important motivation for all ranks, including the senior officer corps.[27] Marlborough adorned his new mansion, Blenheim Palace, with a bust of Louis XIV that he had removed from the Porte Royale, Tournai, as well as angling for paintings appropriated from the collection of his enemy, the Elector of Bavaria.[28]

Moreover, as the examples of the devastation of the Palatinate and Bavaria indicate, although commanders decried involving non-combatants in the mêlée of war, their stance was ultimately dictated by military necessity. This was

---

21   Churchill, *Marlborough*, p. 409; Best, *Churchill and War*, pp. 265–66.
22   Black, *European Warfare*, pp. 67–86.
23   Childs, *Armies and Warfare*, p. 144.
24   Tallett, *War and Society*, pp. 158–60; Friedrichs, *Urban Society*, pp. 293–94.
25   Tallett, *War and Society*, pp. 148–65; Friedrichs, *Urban Society*, p. 34.
26   Arni, *Hospital Care*, esp. pp. 92, 126–29, 141; Friedrichs, *Urban Society*, pp. 33–34.
27   Childs, *Armies and Warfare*, pp. 161–68.
28   Avery, 'Duke of Marlborough', pp. 427–28.

particularly the case where a city or town housed a garrison. One consequence of early modern developments in siege warfare was that cities and towns grew to become expensively and elaborately fortified, notably in north-eastern France, the Dutch Republic, and the Spanish Netherlands. In peacetime, this had a decided impact on domestic urban expansion and the routines of every-day life.[29] In wartime, the impact could be devastating. The most celebrated military architect of his age, Sébastien Le Prestre de Vauban, criticised the practice of bombarding cities and towns as well as their garrisons, believing it to be a waste of military resources and destructive of the potential for effective working relations with civilian inhabitants after the siege.[30] However, such a view was not widespread. As Jamel Ostwald comments, 'time-pressed commanders frequently erased the distinction between combatant and non-combatant in their attempts to put a quick end to the war'.[31] Commanders took little interest in attempting to limit destruction within besieged cities and towns (despite the appeals of their civilian inhabitants). They were also more than prepared to specifically target civilians and civilian property to try to drive a wedge between civilians and the garrison, as Douai, Ghent, Lille and Mons found to their cost during the War of the Spanish Succession.[32] Indeed, in 1708 Marlborough blamed the citizens of Ghent for the city's capture by the French, and was unsympathetic to their plea to spare the city from destructive bombardment: 'since they had brought this misfortune upon themselves by their own folly or negligence, they must either assist us against the garrison or expect we should use all manner of extremity to reduce them to their duty'.[33]

The traditional characterisation of combat in this period becomes even more problematic when the practice of irregular warfare in the late seventeenth and early eighteenth centuries is examined. While historical interest in irregular warfare has focused on the French Revolutionary and Napoleonic era, including the activities of guerrillas, irregular warfare in the preceding century has received much less sustained attention.[34] Yet it is clear that irregular warfare in its various forms – involving detachments of professional soldiers, militia units and groups of armed peasants and other non-professional fighters – was a crucial element in the conduct of earlier wars.[35] George Satterfield has drawn attention to the significance of partisan warfare in the Dutch War of

29 Childs, *Armies and Warfare*, pp. 145–47; Pollak, *Cities at War*.

30 Ostwald, *Vauban under Siege*, p. 290.

31 Ibid., p. 293.

32 Ibid., pp. 291–93.

33 Cited in Ostwald, *Vauban under Siege*, p. 292.

34 Satterfield, *Princes, Posts, and Partisans*, pp. 2–8. For discussion of the evolution of the terms *guerrilla* and *petite guerre* see Scotti-Douglas, 'Regulating the Irregulars', pp. 137–39.

35 Black, *European Warfare*, pp. 231–33.

the 1670s. Although printed definitions of *petite guerre* or *kleiner Krieg* only came into wider usage in the eighteenth century, 'the tactics of light troops in the eighteenth century was fully developed by the Dutch War, if not before', Satterfield concludes.[36] Partisan warfare was a feature of other military campaigns of the era. Peasants attacked French troops in the Palatinate in 1674 and 1689.[37] The war in Spain during the War of the Spanish Succession was marked by the activities of militias and *miquelets*, and retaliatory measures against civilians.[38] As a form of combat, irregular warfare had a particular impact upon civilians. It not only transformed civilians into unofficial combatants, but since the acquisition and extraction of material resources and the taking of hostages was a key aim of partisan warfare, it involved – one might say targeted – civilians from the outset.

Additionally, while the period after the Peace of Westphalia (1648) saw the decline of the confessional, ideological impetus to warfare (often given as a reason for the emergence of 'restraint' in this period), it needs to be recognised that this depended on the specific region in which fighting took place.[39] The Nine Years War and the War of the Spanish Succession, for instance, contained a strong confessional and denominational angle, including the use of disaffected French Protestants in the Allied armies. While the religious idiom in which war was defended and celebrated became less strident, it did not disappear. Eighteenth-century diplomacy operated within confessional contexts, and even in the late 1750s, the British soldiery still possessed a confessionalised, or at least anti-clerical, outlook that was particularly pronounced when they encountered Catholic clergy.[40]

The conduct of war after 1648 undoubtedly became more regulated but the label of 'limited' or 'restrained' fails to convey the complex range of military experiences and civilian–military relations that can be found in the period between the end of the Thirty Years War and the start of the French Revolutionary and Napoleonic wars. Indeed, it may well be unproductive to conceive of this period as a single bloc of time. John A. Lynn has suggested how warfare between 1661 and 1715 can be seen as a distinct period in relation to the years before and after. Lynn also points to how the widely condemned

---

36 Satterfield, *Princes, Posts, and Partisans*, p. 323.
37 Lynn, *Wars of Louis XIV*, p. 130; Lynn, 'Brutal Necessity?', p. 81.
38 Dickinson, 'Earl of Peterborough's Campaign', pp. 35–52.
39 Parker, 'Early Modern Europe', p. 54; Lynn, *Wars of Louis XIV*, pp. 174–81.
40 Childs, 'Laws of War', pp. 283–300; Claydon, *William III*; McLay, 'Blessed Trinity', pp. 103–20; Thompson, *Britain, Hanover and the Protestant Interest*; Hopkin, Lagadec and Perréon, 'Experience and Culture of War', p. 210.

devastation of the Palatinate in 1688–89 may have influenced the desire to make eighteenth-century warfare more restricted in scope.[41]

Despite a recognition that warfare between 1648 and 1792 cannot be satisfactorily described as 'limited', fundamental assumptions about the narrative of total war are retained in traditional periodisation. Histories of modern warfare begin with 1792, while histories of eighteenth-century wars tend to focus overwhelmingly on the transformations found in Napoleonic warfare. By the same token, the wars of the early to mid-seventeenth century – central to the shaping of eighteenth-century warfare – are hardly ever included alongside assessments of late seventeenth-century and early to mid-eighteenth-century wars. By bringing together scholarship on the Thirty Years War and the English Civil War with that on the key wars of the late seventeenth century, eighteenth century and the French Revolutionary and Napoleonic wars, this volume encourages fresh ways of thinking about the changing nature of warfare during the early modern and modern periods.

In many ways, the contour of the contributions here remains traditional. The focus is on western European land warfare from circa 1618 to 1815. The fact that this volume neglects eastern European, naval and colonial warfare serves as recognition that these represent three fundamental challenges to the accepted periodisations of warfare. Warfare and military action in eastern Europe could be strikingly brutal, both for soldiers and civilians.[42] At sea, where commerce was armed and the difference between piracy and privateering negligible, distinctions between civilians and the armed forces were generally irrelevant. Instead of distinguishing between merchants and sailors, naval law and custom was more concerned with deciding whether individuals belonged to enemy or neutral vessels.[43] In colonial warfare, too, it is clear that what came to be called 'guerrilla warfare' was common in the period before the outbreak of the French Revolutionary and Napoleonic wars, drawing on the European tradition of light troops. As Jeremy Black has pointed out, the myopic focus on Frederician linear warfare is in part because military historians of this period insist on considering colonial warfare separately from, and on the periphery of, eighteenth-century European military operations.[44] Detailed archival research has not only demonstrated the Europeanised nature of colonial warfare but

---

41 Lynn, *Wars of Louis XIV*, pp. 366–67; Lynn, 'Brutal Necessity?', p. 88. For a recent challenge to traditional periodisation see Chickering and Förster, eds., *War in an Age of Revolution*.

42 Black, *European Warfare*, pp. 116, 231; Stevens, *Russia's Wars of Emergence*, pp. 241–43, 283–85.

43 For example, Marsden, ed., *Documents Relating to Law and Custom of the Sea*.

44 Black, 'A Military Revolution?', pp. 107–11.

has also underlined the vibrancy of eighteenth-century European warfare.[45] Since the nineteenth century it has typically been continuing engagements in colonial and ex-colonial theatres – 'wars' or 'police actions' against colonial subjects or against the forces of other metropolitan powers or their proxies – that have constituted the everyday, taken-for-granted war-making against the background of which it became possible to imagine that war in Europe was or could be exceptional.

2. THE USEFULNESS OF TOTAL WAR

WHAT, THEN, of the fertile seed of total war? In the opening chapter, Peter H. Wilson perceptively argues that evaluating the nature of the Thirty Years War by applying the concept of total war demonstrates the emptiness of the concept. At the same time, this exercise is not without its uses, as it also reveals much about changing perceptions of war. For the earlier period, the notion of total war is empty partly because it relies on anachronistic categories, not least that of 'civilian'. Similarly, measuring the mobilisation of state and society for war in the early modern period has limited utility for an era in which mobilising for war was the state's *raison d'être*. The profusion of writings on the rise of the fiscal-military state and the military revolution show how early modern European state formation was fundamentally tied to the waging of war. Whereas analysts of total war are impressed by proportions of 20 to 25 per cent of a modern state's economy devoted to warfare, it is possible to find at least 75 per cent in the case of an early modern state.[46]

Moreover, perceptions and records of warfare between 1618 and 1789 make evaluations of its novelty and intensity inconclusive. There is far more surviving material for the late eighteenth and early nineteenth centuries than for the preceding century and a half.[47] Yuval N. Harari points out in his recent study of military memoirs from 1450 to the present that early modern writers often did not bother to record their experiences of war, let alone publish them. Service in the armed forces was common and the experience of war ubiquitous, making such commentary uninteresting. By contrast, modern memoirs, grounded in Romantic sensibilities, saw war as necessarily exceptional and transforming,

---

45   For example, Chet, *Conquering the American Wilderness*; Pargellis, *Lord Loudoun in North America*; Lenman, 'Transition to European Military Ascendancy in India'. For an explanation of the interest in colonial-style warfare, specifically in the American context, see Lee, 'Early American Ways of War'.

46   For example, Parker, *Military Revolution*, esp. pp. 61–63.

47   Forrest, Hagemann and Rendall, 'Introduction: Nations in Arms', pp. 2–3.

breaking free of the everyday, often a sublime, individual experience.[48] It seems that total war is an irrelevant framework for the earlier period, as it is formed of inapplicable categories.

Yet, as this volume clearly demonstrates, applying the framework of the concept of total war is still useful, not only to show where the two do not match, but also to suggest an explanation for this incongruity. This is especially the case for the fundament of total war, civilian–military relations. The modern usage of the term 'civilian' had yet to come into fully fledged existence. In England, 'civilian' originally denoted one who studied and practised civil law. By the mid- to late eighteenth century it had started to be used to mean a non-military employee of the East India Company, and by the early nineteenth century the word had come to describe a non-military man. This idea of distinguishing between the military and the non-military, however, had a longer history via the concept of the 'civil'. 'Civil' encompassed the more abstract idea of citizens, community and authority, the frequently evoked 'civil magistrate'. A similar development in terminology can be traced in France, while in Germany the development began somewhat earlier.[49]

Although the term 'civilian' did not exist, it was understood that there was a distinction between soldiers and civilians, and that within the latter category this distinction was created by location, occupation and social status, as well as by gender and age. When soldiers wrote about civilians, it was, unsurprisingly, often in terms of the (military) rural or urban context in which they encountered them, as 'country people' and 'peasants', or as 'inhabitants' and 'magistrates'.[50] In early modern terms of surrender, soldiers and sailors were treated differently from so-called inhabitants, wives, children and followers. This sense of difference between soldiers and civilians manifested itself even when soldiers were stationed on their own home soil. Friction, which might turn into physical violence, was common between civilians and soldiers – especially as soldiers were frequently used to police crowds, and were quartered or garrisoned in locations where they acted more like an occupying force than as compatriots.

Terminology is thus not restrictive if the concepts underlying the terms are examined in detail. Likewise, a productive approach to opening up the dialogue between the 'total war' paradigm and an understanding of what came before it

---

48 Harari, *Ultimate Experience*.
49 Bell, *First Total War*, Introduction; Conway, 'British Soldiers at Home', below; Forrest, Hagemann and Rendall, 'Introduction: Nations in Arms', pp. 4–5; entries for 'civil' and 'civilian' in the *OED*.
50 Snyder, ed., *Marlborough–Godolphin Correspondence*, p. 357; Chandler, ed., *Robert Parker and Comte de Mérode-Westerloo*, pp. 23–24, 118; Withington, 'Citizens, Soldiers and Urban Culture in Restoration England'.

is to analyse the vision of the French Revolutionary and Napoleonic wars as a conjuncture of material and cultural developments, and ask whether and where elements of that conjuncture can be found in the centuries that preceded it. An approach to the history of warfare that goes beyond the chronology of military engagements or the cataloguing of changes in the 'art of war' will take account of developments in the realm of ideology – what in the nineteenth century came to be articulated as a set of 'isms'. This includes changing visions of war and society themselves. Thus David A. Bell, considering the Napoleonic period in the light of its character as the 'first total war', acknowledges a new kind of 'nationalism' as one element in the conjuncture – giving a name to the purpose of combat and arguably justifying its brutalisation. But he prefers to emphasise the way in which the Napoleonic crisis marks the beginnings of 'militarism'. In Bell's use, 'militarism' denotes a paradoxical and characteristically modern process: war and the preparation for war, he proposes, were indeed a continuous presence and a part of everyday life in pre-Napoleonic Europe. The crisis of 1792 to 1815 inaugurated a development in which the civilian and military spheres first came to be viewed as distinct from one another, and in which war came to be understood as an exceptional state of affairs (while at any given time over the two centuries that followed soldiers of nearly every nation state were in fact engaged in combat somewhere in the world). But this made possible a transaction in which the values of the military or the purposes of waging war could be imposed on or made to structure civil society in new ways – by informing political culture and by enabling the kinds of general mobilisation that characterised the two World Wars.[51]

From this point of view an understanding of the ways in which civil and military experience are related in warfare in any period should take into account not only the developing forces of material production – the technological, logistical and subsistence issues implicit in the notion of 'industrialised warfare' and its contraries – but also what might be called the forces of cultural production. An awareness is needed of the technologies, materials and practices that constitute a public sphere in which individuals see themselves as part of a common project, of which the waging of war is one manifestation.[52] The 'total war' paradigm emerged in Germany, and it did so in the context of a developing narrative of national identity. One feature of this was the self-conscious engagement in the struggle against Napoleon of women, who were

---

51 Bell, *First Total War*, pp. 12–13; Bell, 'Limits of Conflict in Napoleonic Europe', below. Bell's is an idiosyncratic use of a 'keyword' that has been used in various ways in political rhetoric and historical analysis since it emerged around 1800. See Berghahn, *Militarism*; Conze, Stumpf and Geyer, 'Militarismus'.

52 For a synthesis of the voluminous work on the public sphere see Melton, *Rise of the Public*.

celebrated as moral examples by their contemporaries and expressly emulated by German women in subsequent conflicts.[53] The engagement of women in the French Revolution and Napoleonic crisis bespeaks the power of discourses about individuality, family and nation whose gendered aspects had been the object of intense and explicit reflection and debate for a generation.[54] More broadly, the voluntary mobilisation of sections of society for whom military service had hitherto been at best a formal duty and at worst an imposition depended on the circulation of information, argument and imagery made possible by the development of the periodical press and the growth of a reading public beyond the educated elites – as well as on the kinds of arguments and images in circulation. And only the continued expansion of these 'forces of cultural production' could sustain the translation of testimony and action into myth as the basis for renewed commitment to a vision of shared effort and sacrifice in subsequent wars. This way of understanding 'total war' situates it as a phenomenon at the intersection of developments in cultural and material life and the articulation of social values that have had distinct historical rhythms.

3. The Volume

As a method of deconstructing modern assumptions contained in the notion of total war, the essays here examine in detail the shifting contours of the military and civilian spheres, showing how and when they were created, crossed and transgressed. They provide a history of the practice of war during the seventeenth and eighteenth centuries, demonstrating war's broader significance to areas in which warfare is usually considered irrelevant, and challenging accepted understandings about the chronology and development of early modern and modern warfare. In order to trace the relationship between civilians and soldiers over the course of these two centuries, it is necessary to shed modern presumptions about the categories of 'civilian' and 'soldier'.

This volume uses an interdisciplinary approach to studying combatants and non-combatants. Contributors include political and legal theorists, scholars of literature and visual arts, and military, political, social and cultural historians. Civilians and their relationship to military conflict are discerned through legal

---

53 Hagemann, *"Männlicher Muth"*, pp. 374–93. For later developments in Germany see Quataert, *Staging Philanthropy*. See Hopkin, 'World Turned Upside Down', and Ross, 'La femme militaire', for cases of women combatants in the French Revolutionary armies.

54 For the German case see Gleixner and Gray, eds., *Gender in Transition*. On women and politics in the late eighteenth century more generally see Applewhite and Levy, eds., *Women and Politics*.

texts and theory, written memoirs, visual representations and the bureaucratic archival record. The volume is thus an examination of a broad variety of military and civilian experiences of warfare, an examination that crucially illuminates the historical limitations of concepts such as 'total war'. As such, it is not the volume's objective to present a uniform, or linear, account of the development of western European warfare and civilians from 1618 to 1815. Indeed the variances in perspective and emphasis that should be expected from a conversation among 17 individual scholars reveal the difficulties – and debunk the merits – of attempting such a task.

The volume is organised on a chronological axis, but is structured thematically. Each of the four sections is introduced by a short essay considering that section's theme, thereby providing an induction for non-specialists, whether by period or discipline. The first section focuses on the experience of warfare in the seventeenth century, examining perceptions and reactions. In the sectional introduction, Peter H. Wilson reflects on the concept of total war, arguing that it cannot be evaluated through material or demographic considerations. Instead, his analysis focuses on the role of perception in shaping how the Thirty Years War and later wars were remembered, viewed and assessed. Colm McKeogh's chapter explores how contemporary military conflicts profoundly shaped Hugo Grotius's arguments for restraint in warfare. McKeogh traces the framework of Grotius's arguments, demonstrating that Grotius took a pragmatic approach in order to reconcile theory and Christianity with the realistic practice of warfare. Barbara Donagan and Melanie Harrington examine how civilians reconciled their brutal experience of warfare to peacetime society after the English Civil War. Donagan presents a detailed study of civilian responses and understandings of plundering practices and civilian attempts to recover the property taken during wartime. Harrington applies the emerging field of transitional justice theory to post-civil war England as a way of comprehending the decisions made by the Restoration regime in its attempts to reconcile a divided post-war society with contemporary expectations of justice and retribution.

The second section focuses on the administration of war, with a particular emphasis on warfare in the late seventeenth and early and mid-eighteenth centuries. In the sectional introduction, Erica Charters discusses the historiography on the relationship between war and state administration, before examining the nature of the British administration of French prisoners of war during the Seven Years War (1756–63), a case that demonstrates the centrality of state administration to the waging of war. Likewise, Markus Meumann outlines the workings of French military justice for civilians under Louis XIV, using rich archival material that exposes the state's difficulties in administering and maintaining the military discipline needed to protect civilian populations from the depredations of soldiers, even after Louis XIV's reorganisation of military jurisdiction early in his reign. Horst Carl examines the German territories during the mid-eighteenth century, studying the administration of occupation. His study contrasts the development of a regulated system of payments, billeting and political intervention with examples of arbitrary violence during occupation. Stephen Conway also finds variety in the nature of civilian–military interaction in his essay on British soldiers on British soil during the mid- to late eighteenth century. While there were benefits to having home soldiers quartered nearby, who might be welcomed by civilians, civilians also complained of the presence of troops, not only because of the soldiers' material demands but more frequently because of their disorderly and threatening behaviour.

In the third section, the focus is the fluidity between the categories of civilian and soldier from the mid-eighteenth to the early nineteenth centuries. With his analysis of Joseph Wright of Derby's painting *The Dead Soldier*, Philip Shaw's sectional introduction is a reminder not only of the central role that civilians played in artistic commentary on the nature of war, but more particularly of the *category* of a civilian, and its transformation during this period. Matthew McCormack examines how this transformation happened, looking at images of the British militiaman during the mid- to late eighteenth century, a figure who occupied an uneasy place between the civilian population and the professional army. His chapter shows that the militia was a project that drew on potentially radical notions of a popular patriotic struggle as early as the 1750s. But his account of this uneasiness – the militiaman as a liminal or even subversive figure and an object of ridicule – suggests that in England the birth of the citizen in arms who would come to populate the Continental memories of the French Revolutionary and Napoleonic wars was slow and painful. Where McCormack finds that these men were considered potentially dangerous in their ability to undermine categorisation, Alan Forrest focuses on the men (and sometimes women) who clearly contravened the boundaries between civilian and soldier: insurgents and counter-insurgents who wreaked such havoc in Europe between 1792 and 1815. As Forrest rightly argues, civilians were not necessarily passive victims, but were responsible for some of the bloodiest war actions.

The final section of the volume opens up the ambiguities and varieties of civilian–military interactions during the French Revolutionary and Napoleonic wars. David A. Bell urges in his sectional introduction that this variety should not obscure historically significant trends. The French Revolutionary and Napoleonic wars were clearly seen as different in kind by those who experienced them, not only because of their enhanced size and scope but also because of the transformation in ideology that accompanied them. Viewed in detail, episodes in these wars reveal not so much a clean break from the past as moments of asynchrony and transition. Gavin Daly examines the nature of plunder by British soldiers in the Peninsular War, demonstrating that while the practice became routine to some extent, there also developed new forms of plunder, shaped by both cultural perceptions and the specific experience of the Peninsular War. In his detailed study of civilian–military experiences in German central Europe, Leighton S. James challenges the traditional nineteenth-century narrative of the wars in which subjugation and occupation solidified German nationhood. Instead, he notes that perceptions of the war varied widely, and many civilians managed to profit from the conflict. Mark Towsey explores an aspect of the Napoleonic Wars that demonstrates how good relations might flourish between soldiers and civilians: French officers stationed in a Scottish border town as prisoners of war. The reading practices of these prisoners reveal divergent national interests alongside cultural likenesses. The latter two chapters particularly draw attention to the importance of print culture in sustaining and propagating identity in wartime and beyond, though taken together they underline the ambiguous power of the public sphere; cosmopolitan reading reconciles those who would be enemies while national publication patterns preserve the memory of conflict.

While each section provides insights into a specific period of war, along with a particular approach to the study of warfare, these chapters are also illuminating when heard as conversations across time periods. Peter H. Wilson's observations on the Thirty Years War have surprising similarities with and differences from David A. Bell's summary of the significance of the French Revolutionary and Napoleonic wars. Barbara Donagan's examination of plunder during the English Civil War of the 1640s read together with Gavin Daly's and Leighton S. James's analyses of plunder carried out by soldiers in the 1800s suggests continuities alongside changes in attitudes, if not practices. Prisoners of war are found across time periods, and in different physical circumstances, yet reactions towards them in many ways remain the same over the course of the period under scrutiny, as Erica Charters's and Mark Towsey's chapters demonstrate. The soldier's self-perception of being different, even superior, in status to the 'civilians' around him transcends the divide between old regime and Revolutionary Europe as the essays by Stephen Conway, Gavin Daly and Alan Forrest suggest.

One of the volume's two principal aims is to reconsider European warfare across two hundred years by stepping back from established historiographical categorisations and narratives. The second objective is to emphasise the problematic classification of 'the civilian' as the passive victim of war. Nearly all the essays in this volume chart the anguished sufferings of civilians. What also emerges from these essays, however, is the agency of the civilian, either as an individual, group or community. Civilians fought back with violence, refusing to accept their 'non-combatant' designation – to the anger, terror and bewilderment of military personnel. Civilians might gain from war, which provided them with commercial opportunities to operate as small-time war profiteers. Even in the aftermath of a conflict, civilians might fashion narratives of their sufferings as a way of negotiating material and social redress. But if this is a history of civilian agency in times of war, it needs to be remembered that within this history is another: of civilians profiting from the sufferings of others (both civilians and soldiers), and of more socially and economically vulnerable members of civilian communities being sacrificed, or at least feeling the brunt of military depredations and burdens, to ensure that their neighbours escaped relatively unscathed.

The introduction to this volume has emphasised how the modern terminology of 'civilian' had yet to become fully formulated in the seventeenth and eighteenth centuries and, as a result, there existed a range of contemporary understandings as to how to treat the range of groups of people who were not soldiers. To comprehend the complex, complicated nature of civilian experiences and actions in the eras from the Thirty Years War to the Napoleonic War, the civilian cannot be viewed as a single category but must be analysed in terms of socio-economic, demographic and gendered status and capital. If warfare was a generally negative experience for most civilians, how well the civilian survived its depredations might indeed depend on social and economic capital – as well as good fortune.

PART I

Suffering, Reconciliation and Values
in the Seventeenth Century

2

Was the Thirty Years War a 'Total War'?

PETER H. WILSON

1. Introduction

THE CONCEPT of 'total war' has exercised a powerful influence on the history of conflict. There is no firm agreement on what it means, or to which conflicts it can be applied. Nonetheless, most commentators emphasise three defining characteristics. To be total, a war must entail the complete mobilisation of a belligerent's society and economy, as well as their rejection of any outcome other than the complete destruction of the enemy's resistance and way of life, while its conduct will erode the boundaries between soldiers and civilians. These elements have been detected in a range of major wars by many commentators. However, attempts to refine this definition have merely exposed the concept's serious shortcomings. It is the contention of this chapter that these deficiencies are so fundamental as to invalidate the concept as a means of exploring civilians' relationship to war.

First, it has proved impossible to escape from the concept's origins as an ideological construct emerging from the controversy surrounding the German General Staff's management of their country's effort during the First World War. Though the term appeared during 1917, it was not articulated until 1935 when the former commander, Erich Ludendorff, tried to justify his policy both to his countrymen and outsiders. While presented as based on rational, material criteria, the idea is in fact highly emotive and this subjectivity has hindered definition ever since. For instance, Ludendorff presents total war as a necessity in which all the negative elements are off-loaded on to the enemy, while his own side preserves a more honourable character associated with previous forms of war-making.[1]

Secondly, it has proved impossible to rid the concept of an implicit comparison between the era of its own origins and the era to which it is applied for analysis. Each fresh area of investigation is compared with the First World War and, especially, the Second World War – the only conflict consciously regarded as total by its participants. As a result, total war is defined in relation to a Eurocentric modernisation thesis that (depending on interpretation) emphasises a fairly narrow range of military and political factors. War is presented as developing along a linear path that can be labelled a 'progress of destruction' as weaponry seemingly becomes ever more potent. This is a technologically determinist view, often closely related to the belief that industrialisation defines modernity.[2] The political elements also relate to this definition of modernity. Revolutionary ideology, nationalism and democracy are all highlighted as elements facilitating the complete mobilisation of human and material resources for total war, as well as legitimating or even necessitating the enemy's complete destruction.

This has been applied recently to the French Revolutionary and Napoleonic wars (1792–1815), where the French Revolution of 1789 allegedly initiated a political dynamic driving belligerents to ever more extreme measures aimed at the systematic destruction of their enemy's society. The French *levée en masse* of August 1793 has been identified as 'the first declaration of total war' and compared directly with Joseph Goebbels's famous speech of 1943 intended to rally support for the Nazi war effort.[3] Similar claims have been made for the American Civil War (1861–65) and the Franco-German war of 1870–71, even if those making them have been rightly cautious of drawing a direct line between these conflicts and those after 1914.[4] Nonetheless, drawing these connections, however indirect, constructs, no doubt unintentionally, an Atlantic thesis of the United States and major western European states as forging models that the rest of the world then adopts. This distracts attention from other conflicts that possibly have better claims to the dubious honour of being termed 'total wars', such as the war of Argentina, Brazil and Uruguay

---

1   Ludendorff, *Der totale Krieg*. Further discussion in Strachan, 'On Total War and Modern War'.
2   For example, Gillis, ed., *Militarization*.
3   Blanning, *French Revolutionary Wars*, p. 101. The case for the French Revolution initiating the world's first true total war has been developed by Guiomar, *L'invention de la guerre totale*; Bell, *First Total War*.
4   Förster and Nagler, eds., *On the Road to Total War*; Boemeke, Chickering and Förster, eds., *Anticipating Total War*; Chickering and Förster, eds., *Great War, Total War*.

against Paraguay in which the latter lost over 70 per cent of its population between 1864 and 1870.[5]

Relating total war to modernisation obscures the fact that many earlier wars often appear more total than those of modernity.[6] It also make it difficult to distinguish between 'modern' and 'total' war – at what point along this linear path to modernity do we cross from one to the other? Further, where do we go once total war is reached? Is total war a one-off, time-specific event (perhaps restricted to Europe between 1914 and 1945) or is it relative to other factors? Indeed, it is doubtful whether total war is necessarily related to modernity at all: 'modern war is not necessarily total (no matter how this is defined), and total warfare is not necessarily modern'.[7]

Thirdly, like all absolute concepts, the entire idea is fundamentally flawed because totality can never be reached. A nuclear war might entail the enemy's total destruction, but it does not require total mobilisation on the part of an advanced industrialised nation. We are forever consigned to debating 'thresholds of totality', or what constitutes a level of war-making beyond the norm. This problem also bedevils the closely related concept of 'social militarisation', which some political scientists have defined as occurring when 10 per cent of a population is under arms or engaged in supporting military preparations.[8] The selection of such percentages lends a spurious precision to analysis without satisfactorily answering how these thresholds can be determined.

It is clear that, at best, we are dealing in degrees rather than absolutes. Perhaps a look at an early modern example will help, since debates on total war concentrate on the period after 1792 and often rest on the assumption that previous struggles were more limited. The Thirty Years War (1618–48) is a useful starting point because of its benchmark character in the history of war. It has become a yardstick by which to measure the destructiveness of later conflicts, and has been woven into other historical grand narratives, such as the culmination of the age of 'Religious Wars' beginning with the Reformation, or as the epicentre of a much wider 'General Crisis of the Seventeenth Century'.[9] Above all, it has entered popular perception as an 'all-destructive fury'; a conflict

5   Whigham and Potthast, 'Paraguayan Rosetta Stone'.
6   For example, those of archaic and classical Greece; see Wees, *Greek Warfare*.
7   Black, *War in the Nineteenth Century*, p. 9. For arguments that the French Revolutionary and Napoleonic wars and those of German unification were less than total see Showalter, 'Retaming of Bellona'; Showalter, 'The Prusso-German RMA'; Kanter, 'Exposing the Myth'; Kühlich, *Deutschen Soldaten*.
8   Regan, *Organizing Societies for War*. Further discussion of this and 'militarism' in Wilson, 'Defining Military Culture', pp. 39–41.
9   Further discussion of the historiography in Wilson, 'Causes of the Thirty Years War'.

waged with unprecedented ferocity that inflicted widespread devastation across the Holy Roman Empire and neighbouring countries.[10]

Research on the war has also developed a new approach that perhaps offers a way out of the impasse on total war. Debates on the level of destruction have moved beyond quantitative assessments to consider how the war was experienced by those caught in its maw. Investigations concentrate on accumulated experience (*Erfahrung*) that is written down and reflected upon, rather than the fleeting momentary experience (*Erlebnis*) of events as they occur.[11] This approach is not without its problems, but it does draw attention to the question of perception, which is an aspect largely overlooked in the total war debate. Perhaps we can go beyond debating when totality is reached in material terms, and investigate how contemporaries experienced certain conflicts as more extreme than others.

The rest of this chapter will assess the Thirty Years War through the three aspects identified in the 'classic' definition of total war: total mobilisation, the objective of the enemy's total destruction and the alleged fusion of soldiers and civilians. It will conclude with a brief examination of how the war was perceived by its participants and later generations. My point is not to prove that the Thirty Years War was a total war, but to suggest that any correspondence with the conventional criteria merely underlines the problems of that concept. I wish to stress that 'total war', as far as it serves any analytical purpose, cannot be defined in material terms but instead through perceptions, and is thus relative to each conflict's context rather than its position along any linear progress of destruction.

2. MOBILISATION

TOTAL WAR implies the maximum possible direct mobilisation of human resources through universal military service. This is usually discussed in terms of the French Revolutionary ideal of 'citizens-in-arms', whereby all able-bodied males were required to fight for republican liberty and national defence.[12] On surface, the Thirty Years War matches the standard criteria for a total war: the obligation for universal military service already existed well before the French *levée en masse* of 1793. Denmark and Sweden employed conscription systems that enrolled most of their rural populations. Men were selected for infantry and cavalry regiments that formed the core of both kingdoms' forces. The German lands all had territorial militias that were reorganised

10   Cramer, *Thirty Years War*.
11   Nowosadtko, 'Erfahrung'; Munch, ed., *'Erfahrung'*.
12   Moran and Waldron, eds., *People in Arms*.

and expanded in the four decades preceding the war. Around one in ten able-bodied males were actually engaged in these militias, representing 2.5 per cent of the total population. The rest were theoretically liable in a dire emergency.[13]

Actual practice fell short of the theory, but later conscription has also proved far from truly universal. Even in the nineteenth century, most European systems allowed substitution and retained exemptions on social or economic grounds. The Bohemian rebels called up one man in ten in June 1618, followed by a general levy in September. Both failed to produce either the desired numbers or quality and though termed 'militia' in many secondary works, the bulk of the rebel forces in fact consisted of professional soldiers recruited by the various provincial Estates of the Bohemian lands.[14]

The performance of militias was generally poor, but just how poor has been exaggerated, and militias did fight well on occasion. Militias continued to be used throughout the war, often as a disguised form of conscription to find men to keep units of professionals up to strength. Meanwhile, large numbers of volunteers, usually known by the misleading label 'mercenaries', joined the regular forces. For example, 10 per cent of adult Scottish males fought on the continent during the war, mainly in the Danish and Swedish forces, but also in the imperial army as well as additional Scots serving France, Poland and the Dutch. Whereas the economic factors stressed by the older literature were certainly important motives behind enlistment, recent research has highlighted the significance of politics, culture and religion in the decisions to join particular armies.[15]

The total number of combatants in the Empire reached 250,000 in 1632 and there were still probably around 183,000 men under arms when the war ended sixteen years later. The peak represented about 1 per cent of the Empire's pre-war population, or considerably less both in overall and proportional terms than the French army at its height during the reign of Louis XIV, which was the largest single force in Europe since the Roman Empire. However, the size of the forces during the Thirty Years War is still significant, especially when the numerous additional supporting personnel are factored in. There was probably at least one non-combatant camp follower for every soldier in Germany. The largest single group were women, but there were also some adult males and numerous teenagers in this 'military community' of camp followers providing

---

13 Overviews of these systems and the associated historical literature in Glete, *War and the State*, pp. 34–35, 202–06; Wilson, *Europe's Tragedy*, pp. 142–44, 173–74, 186–87.

14 Winkelbauer, 'Nervus belli Bohemici'.

15 Examples include Murdoch, *Britain, Denmark-Norway*; Worthington, *Scots in Habsburg Service*.

logistical support.[16] Large numbers of peasants were periodically conscripted as pioneers and transport personnel, while others fought as guerrillas – a significant, but neglected aspect of the war.[17] Furthermore, the duration of the conflict must be considered since these numbers were sustained for a generation at a time of considerable population displacement and loss. Around 1.8 million military personnel were killed, while total war-related deaths in the Empire were probably about 5 million, or 20 per cent of the pre-war population (compared to 5.5 per cent in the First World War and 6 per cent in the Second World War). Danish intervention, though lasting only eleven of the thirty years, resulted in the deaths of 20 per cent of all adult males, while Swedish involvement killed 30 per cent of that country's adult males. The overall impact of such losses was magnified by the fact that they occurred in an age of labour-intensive agrarian society considerably less able to spare manpower than later industrialised societies.[18]

Sweden was only able to absorb such losses thanks to the decentralised character of most of its farming, which allowed women to substitute for the missing male labour. This draws our attention to the importance of indirect mobilisation whereby non-combatants provide food, fodder, arms and other military material and, above all, the money needed to sustain war. Unlike the two World Wars and other later conflicts, there was little attempt to organise a war economy during the Thirty Years War. Spain and the Dutch used some forms of economic warfare in their separate struggle from 1568 to 1648, including trade embargoes, blockades and a Spanish attempt to dig a canal to divert trade from the Rhine into its possessions in the southern Netherlands. The imperial general Wallenstein organised a form of 'command economy' in his own lands from 1625 to 1634, but this played only a subordinate role in sustaining the emperor's war effort.[19] Instead, the real impact was felt through taxation and other forms of resource extraction, especially those entering the literature as 'contributions'. These have been widely misunderstood as either indiscriminate plundering or a deliberate attempt to deny resources to the enemy. While both were elements of war-making, contributions essentially

---

16 Lynn, *Women, Armies and Warfare*. There has been considerable debate on the size of this wider 'military community'. Contemporary commentators were often hostile to their presence and greatly exaggerated the numbers of camp followers. While they did outnumber soldiers in some units, most reports from the Thirty Years War suggest a ratio of one soldier to every woman or child.

17 More detail in Wilson, *Europe's Tragedy*, pp. 278, 310, 401, 500, 533, 688, 769, 784, 792, 837–38.

18 Research on Danish and Swedish losses is more advanced than for German casualties, thanks to a considerably better source base. Findings are summarised in two essays by Lindegren, 'Politics of Expansion', and 'Men, Money and Means'.

19 Ernstberger, *Wallenstein*.

involved commandeering existing taxes in occupied areas and diverting them to sustain the army.[20] As with the direct mobilisation of manpower, these methods made a major impact on what were inflexible economic structures. War probably consumed a far higher proportion of surplus production than during twentieth-century conflicts, yet still fell far short of total mobilisation.

3. The Objective of Total Destruction

THE CONCEPT of total war maintains that the purpose of this effort is the total destruction of the enemy and their way of life. Again, the Thirty Years War superficially fulfils these criteria, but on closer inspection a more complex picture emerges. The objective of total destruction is usually thought to require a fusion of political and military command. It was precisely this issue that Ludendorff sought to justify, following the effective seizure of political power by the German General Staff in 1916.[21] Much to his frustration, Kaiser Wilhelm II failed to live up to the ideal of the warrior king – an ideal unquestionably embodied by Gustavus Adolphus of Sweden and Christian IV of Denmark during the Thirty Years War: the former was killed at the head of his troops at the battle of Lützen in 1632, while the latter lost an eye commanding the Danish fleet. Other rulers accompanied their armies, like Frederick V of the Palatinate, and could take command on occasion, as did Emperor Ferdinand III, Johann Georg of Saxony and Maximilian of Bavaria. A royal presence was hardly unusual in early modern European warfare and features in other conflicts that have never been presented as candidates for total war; for example George II led the British and allied army at the battle of Dettingen in 1743 during the War of the Austrian Succession (1740–48).

Far more significant than unified command is the purpose for which war was being waged. As with mobilisation, the belligerents of the Thirty Years War already possessed a theory of war that implied totality. Military operations were legitimated through the Christian concept of a Just War defined as promoting good and combating evil. The justice of any cause, like religious truth itself, was regarded as singular, not plural. Thus, only one side could be right and have divine support. One consequence was the widespread condemnation of neutrality as immoral since it allowed an injustice to go unpunished. At the most, belligerents would only accept benevolent neutrality, whereby a state might avoid direct involvement, but was still expected to allow one side's troops to cross its land, as well as providing food and other supplies. Contemporaries

---

20   Further discussion with reference to the debate in Wilson, *Europe's Tragedy*, pp. 399–408.
21   Kitchen, *Silent Dictatorship*.

also recognised a right of conquest that allowed a victor to do as he pleased with captured lands and resources. This was expressly invoked by the Swedes when they landed in the Duchy of Pomerania in June 1630 at the start of their invasion of the Empire.

Concern to avoid alienating allies and other considerations meant that practice fell far short of the theoretical totality. While the Swedes confiscated part of the Duke of Pomerania's personal possessions, they refrained from annexing his duchy until the final peace, preferring instead a treaty disguised as an alliance that obliged his subjects to feed and accommodate the Swedish army.[22] Other forms of more equal neutrality were tolerated from mutual convenience. Hamburg, Bremen and Lübeck functioned as would Switzerland during the World Wars as venues for diplomacy and financial transactions for all the major belligerents. Europe's various wars remained distinct despite the efforts of diplomats and religious militants to rally support for alleged common causes. Spain's Dutch War and the Franco-Spanish war beginning in 1635 were treated separately from the struggle in the Empire in negotiations at the Westphalian peace congress of 1644–48, despite the participation of some belligerents in more than one conflict simultaneously. Above all, war remained an instrument of policy, considered an expression of orderly power (*potestas*), not illegal violence (*violentia*).[23] Contrary to both contemporary and later perceptions, the soldiers alone did not rule and operations remained linked to diplomacy as a means to put pressure on opponents, not destroy them.

Importantly, there was no blanket demonisation of the enemy. Of course, the war was not short on violent sectarian invective, but there was also no clear split among belligerents along ethnic, linguistic or even religious lines. Most criticism was selective and there were degrees of enmity. For example, the Protestant Union and Bohemians at the start of the conflict distinguished between a few evil-minded Catholics, usually identified as 'Spanish Jesuits', whom they blamed for causing the war, and the majority whom they had no intention of harming 'when they merely abide peacefully and blamelessly by the constitution'.[24]

The distinction between friend and foe was further blurred by the concept of the enemy within. Unlike later conflicts, this was not an alien fifth column, but literally within the population. Clergy of all confessions continually reminded the population that they were to blame for the conflict through their sinfulness. Regular days of prayer and penance were organised from the outset, and

---

22 Rydberg and Hallendorf, eds., *Sveriges traktater*, Vol. V, part 1, pp. 395–98.

23 Excellent discussion with references to the extensive literature on this issue in Kaiser, 'Maximilian I. von Bayern'.

24 Frederick V, *Unser Friderichs*.

became widespread in both Catholic and Protestant lands after 1620. The population was expected either to pray and fast for up to 40 hours, or set aside two hours for this purpose on a designated day each month. While this represented an element of ideological mobilisation, its target was the enemy within each parishioner's heart, not invaders actually threatening their homes. Decrees and sermons exhorted individuals to reflect on their own consciences and effect a change of heart that would manifest itself in external public moral improvement and deflect God's wrath.[25]

The war's conduct was undoubtedly brutal and accompanied by numerous atrocities, including the massacre of fleeing soldiers and wounded in the closing stages of many battles, as well as the slaughter of civilians during the sack of cities, most notably at Magdeburg in 1631 where four-fifths of the 25,000 inhabitants died. While commanders generally justified their soldiers' behaviour by reference to the prevailing 'laws of war', they did so in order to excuse what was still considered shocking to contemporaries, rather than to trumpet their success in killing large numbers of the enemy. The line between legitimate and illegitimate violence remained contested, but all parties subscribed to common assumptions about acceptable behaviour.[26]

While none of the belligerents aimed at the physical extermination of the enemy, some did seek to destroy their opponents' way of life. This is best illustrated through an examination of the Habsburg dynasty which governed Bohemia, where the war broke out, as well as ruling the Empire through their possession of the imperial title. The dynasty's immediate goal was to eliminate the hostile aristocratic elite they blamed for the conflict. While they remained opposed to Protestantism in principle, they had no intention of attacking the nobles of their hereditary lands purely on religious grounds. Instead, they concentrated on those who refused to submit to their authority and who took up arms after 1618. Their physical extermination was unimportant, and only 27 Bohemian rebel leaders were eventually executed in June 1621. Far more significant was the designation of the opposition as 'rebels', since this allowed the Habsburgs to rescind political and religious privileges, and to confiscate property. While driven in part by financial expediency, this also removed the leadership and material basis for a whole way of life. This policy was extended to the rest of the Empire after 1622 in the wake of further victories, where more 'rebel' property was expropriated and redistributed to men considered

---

25 Contemporary Protestant and Catholic examples include Barich, 'Nachrichten', pp. 38–39, 41, 47, 52; Friesenegger, *Tagebuch*, p. 14. Further examples and discussion in Asche and Schindling, eds., *Das Strafgericht Gottes*. Days of prayer and penance were a standard response in the face of 'natural' disaster as well: Jakubowski-Tiessen and Lehmann, eds., *Um Himmels Willen*.

26 Kaiser, 'Ärger als der Türck'; Wilson, 'Atrocities'.

loyal to the Habsburgs. The process culminated in the Edict of Restitution (1629) which demanded the return of all former Catholic church land taken by Protestants since 1555. This still fell far short of totality: Protestant nobles who remained loyal or at least passive during the revolt generally kept their lands and freedom of worship, while no attempt was made to extend these measures at this point into Habsburg Hungary. However, the scale was still impressive. The land expropriation represented the largest transfer of property prior to the Communist seizure of power after 1945, with, for instance, half the Moravian population changing landlord in the 1620s.[27]

The Habsburgs' opponents pursued similar policies. The Bohemians were defeated before they could implement much, but they had already begun to confiscate property of Catholic opponents in 1619. The Swedish redistribution of captured land (known as euphemistically as 'donations') was more significant and affected large parts of Germany in 1631–34, though much of it was reversed after the imperial victory at Nördlingen in 1634.[28]

The Habsburgs' long-term objective was to enforce Catholicism throughout their possessions as the basis for more stable political authority. Again, they were not alone in pursuing this goal which clearly lay behind the policy of the French crown against its Huguenot minority, and found its mirror in Bohemian and Swedish promotion of Protestantism in areas under their control. Having first beheaded the Protestant movement by expelling the pastors, school teachers and aristocratic patrons, the Habsburgs issued a series of 'Reformation Mandates' in 1625–28 ordering the population to convert or leave. Around 350,000 people were driven from the Bohemian lands and Austrian provinces, representing about 9 per cent of their populations. The measures really did entail the destruction of a way of life: whereas three-quarters of the population had embraced some form of Protestantism at the end of the sixteenth century, virtually all were at least officially Catholic by the later seventeenth century.[29]

All of this needs to be set into context, however. The Habsburgs did not seek conflict to achieve these goals; rather the war radicalised their existing policy of restricting crown appointments and patronage to loyal Catholics. The rest followed from the dynasty's interpretation of the war as a rebellion – a view largely accepted by Lutheran, as well as Catholic German princes. Anyone taking up arms identified themselves as a rebel, and thus forfeited their rights under the territorial and imperial constitutions. This legitimised the confiscation of their property (and theoretically their execution, though

---

27 Louthan, *Converting Bohemia*; MacHardy, *War, Religion and Court Patronage*; Pörtner, *Counter Reformation*.

28 Deinert, 'Schwedische Epoche'; Goetze, *Politik*; Weber, *Würzburg und Bamberg*.

29 Winkelbauer, *Ständefreiheit und Fürstenmacht*, Vol. II, pp. 27–28, 51, 182.

the emperor almost invariably pardoned his opponents). Thus, the enemy was identified using the existing legal framework – a framework they did not dispute: most of those suffering confiscation did not contest its legal basis, but rather claimed mitigating circumstances when appealing against it. The war was about the interpretation of the Bohemian and imperial constitutions. Neither side intended to overthrow those constitutions; merely to return them to their 'proper' state. Danish, Swedish and French intervention was justified in relation to the constitution, with each claiming to uphold the 'right' interpretation. In short, all parties remained within a common framework.

The language of religious militancy, with its view of the war as Armageddon, did not translate into political practice. Diplomacy and strategy were intended to achieve peace with honour, not annihilate the enemy. Each belligerent sought to boost its prestige and position relative to rivals within a common Christian international framework. Though they had serious disagreements, including over faith, all adhered to the early modern concept of an inclusive peace that required honour for both sides – a true compromise that would ensure lasting amity. This is linked to the prevailing concept of a just war: the enemy might be heretics, but they were still Christians. War was an acceptable means to achieve the immediate objectives of defeating rebellion and stabilising authority, but the longer term goal of confessional conformity was to be secured through patient persuasion.[30]

4. Fusion of Civil and Military Spheres

THE ALLEGED fusion of civil and military spheres of life is the third element in the standard definition of total war. This has several aspects, three of which relate to mobilisation. The high level of mobilisation of human resources inherent in the *levée en masse* places a significant proportion of civilians in uniform. Indirect mobilisation promotes the militarisation of society by advancing military requirements before other social needs. Both factors produce the third aspect: militarism, defined as military values superseding civilian ones. Two further factors relating to the objectives of total war also break down barriers between soldiers and civilians. The war zone is expanded, destroying the physical distinction between battleground and civilian areas, while the latter and their inhabitants become legitimate targets alongside military personnel and equipment. The exclusive association of these elements with wars after 1792 lies in a superficial understanding of pre-modern war as 'limited'. This applies

---

30 A distinction that is clear from Trevor Johnson's detailed case study, *Magistrates, Madonnas and Miracles.*

in particular to warfare in Europe during the so-called 'age of absolutism' (1648–1789) which is widely regarded as having 'tamed Bellona', reducing conflict to 'cabinet wars' intended to advance narrow dynastic objectives and waged without popular involvement.[31] These assumptions make the alleged fusion of civil and military spheres the least satisfactory aspect of the customary definition of total war.

Seventeenth-century Europeans drew legal distinctions between soldiers and civilians, or rather recognised soldiers as one distinct legal group within a society of many groups. However, non-combatants could also fall under martial law through their association with soldiers, as in the case of the numerous camp followers. Further, as we have seen, there was a relatively high level of mobilisation that placed many civilians in the ranks. Participation was most pronounced among the social elite, where aristocratic martial values enjoyed considerable prestige.

There was already what might be dubbed a 'home front' during the Thirty Years War where the population provided taxes and other material support, as well as praying for victory. While not on the scale claimed by many nineteenth-century historians, the war still caused considerable destruction and few people escaped its effects entirely. The scale of the devastation is indicated by the environmental impact felt increasingly from the early 1630s through the destruction of valuable resources such as prized oak trees and the plagues of rodents and wild animals infesting much of the countryside.[32] However, civilians were rarely deliberately targeted; it was their proximity to operations that placed them at risk, notably during sieges where they were killed indirectly during operations to capture a town, and only directly during the search for plunder if the place was subsequently sacked. Arguably the idea of distinct home and military fronts only emerged during the classic age of total war from 1914 to 1945, while the situation in the seventeenth century corresponded more closely with the conceptual model, as there was no such distinction between civil and military areas, and armies moved across the entire Empire as need dictated.

5. PERCEPTIONS

THE SCALE and scope of military operations, together with the rapidity of changes of fortune for the main belligerents, fostered a general sense of limitless, unending conflict that had spiralled out of control. The repeated flight

---

31   For example, Fiedler, *Kriegswesen und Kriegführung*.

32   Examples in Friesenegger, *Tagebuch*, pp. 60, 66, 69, 74–75, 79.

of rulers in advance of the enemy's approach heightened a sense that order had disintegrated leaving only soldiers in charge. Pictures of drunken soldiers fighting over spoils featured prominently in contemporary art, and one of the most striking images of the war is of a monster devouring whole towns, while skeletal figures cut down civilians and snakes slither in the overgrown fields.[33]

This perception was heightened by the prior absence of major conflict in the Empire for over sixty-five years. The last war of 1546–52 comprised only two significant campaigns, affecting parts of central and southern Germany. Thereafter there had been intermittent, limited fighting on the Rhine during the disputes over the electorate of Cologne and bishopric of Strasbourg (1584–92), followed by a much more intense conflict against the Ottoman Empire that was waged outside the Empire in Hungary (1593–1606), and two further brief struggles over the Jülich-Cleves inheritance at the Empire's north-western extremity. These conflicts certainly contributed to the Empire's political problems and to a sense of impending trouble, yet the Bohemian revolt took contemporaries largely by surprise and most expected it to be resolved quickly. The prolonged absence of major warfare inside the Empire before 1618 contributed to the subsequent lasting impression of a flourishing land left despoiled.

This aspect is something that the Thirty Years War shares with most of those conflicts that have been presented as total wars. The French Revolutionary and Napoleonic wars followed the longest period of general peace experienced in eighteenth-century Europe and began against a backdrop of Enlightened discussion suggesting that war could be tamed, if not eliminated. The American Civil War was the first conflict fought within the USA for forty-six years, during which the republic had waged only one, brief and spectacularly successful war entirely in neighbouring Mexico. The conditions were different for the war of 1870–71 which followed two wars in central Europe during the 1860s, as well as conflict associated with the 1848 revolutions. Likewise, France had fought a major war in 1859. However, all were relatively brief struggles that followed relative tranquillity in Europe since 1815. The First World War also began after more than four decades of peace in Europe during which the main belligerents such as Britain or France had pursued only distant 'colonial' wars far from home. In all cases, hopes that this new war would prove short, decisive and, naturally, successful were dashed as combatants found themselves locked in prolonged, bloody and anxious struggles. This was doubly true of the Thirty Years War, which proved longer than these other cases and where the sense of its impact was clearly heightened by its duration. Only two of the principal

---

33 Reproduced as plate 23 in Beller, *Propaganda*.

players at the outset still ruled in 1648 (Maximilian of Bavaria and Johann Georg of Saxony), and a whole generation grew up knowing only conflict.

As in the case of wartime objectives, these perceptions need to be put into context. The conflict's length made it just one among several elements in daily life, indicating the ambiguity of contemporary experience. The war certainly features prominently in contemporary memoirs, yet it is possible to find examples where it is scarcely mentioned, or indeed makes no appreciable impact on the writer's life. Encounters with soldiers were not invariably bad. One Catholic nun remarked 'Though the Swedes visited us daily, they always behaved correctly and honourably towards us. Though they had appeared terrible, as soon as they saw us and talked to us, they became patient, tender little lambs.'[34] In short, individual perceptions often do not correspond with the general view, or the historical analysis of the conflict's demographic and material impact. However, the overall legacy was a sense of fear and loss and the war was remembered as a true disaster. This was reworked in the light of later experience and concerns, not least the debate over Germany's future in the nineteenth century.

6. CONCLUSIONS

IT IS clear that the Thirty Years War does not match all the standard criteria for a total war, yet it was perceived by many participants of the world wars as far more destructive, and it has been remembered even into the twenty-first century as Germany's greatest national catastrophe. These perceptions are underpinned to an extent by recent research on the war that reaffirms the scale of its material impact.[35]

Rather than making a case that the Thirty Years War might be yet another total war, the partial correspondence with the standard definition returns us to the opening discussion of the concept. Any attempt to define a single, absolute model is doomed to fail as totality cannot be reached, and remains relative, condemning us to debate endlessly on what constitutes a threshold for totality. Thus, we are directed to the world of perceptions. Rather than debating the threshold with material criteria such as the proportion of a population mobilised, a war's magnitude is revealed through the extent to which it is considered to exceed past precedents and break accepted norms. While the Thirty Years War might not have been a true total war, it was certainly a major conflict perceived as having a profound impact and lasting consequences.

---

34 Sister Maria Anna Junius, 'Bamberg im Schweden-Kriege', pp. 220–21.
35 Hippel, *Herzogtum Württemberg zur Zeit des Dreißigjährigen Krieges*.

Some of these conclusions are supported by the chapters that follow. Whereas historians have defined total war by looking back from twentieth-century experience, early modern Europeans viewed their own and potential future conflicts through past experience. The Thirty Years War assumed a prominent place within this experience. Hugo Grotius, the seventeenth century's foremost expert on international law, wrote with knowledge, and to an extent direct experience, of the war's opening stages, as well as the violent civil wars in the Netherlands and France. As Colm McKeogh argues, Grotius sought to limit war's excesses by attacking the legal and moral arguments used to justify killing civilians. Rather than propose a normative approach derived abstractly or from Scripture, Grotius engaged with the reality of power politics – he was, after all, a Swedish envoy during the Thirty Years War. A pragmatist, Grotius sought to change behaviour by providing clearer statements of existing norms to curtail their use to legitimise violence.

Numerous pamphlets, newsletters and sermons had kept the inhabitants of the British Isles informed of events on the continent before their own lands slid into civil war after 1638. There was a widespread fear of 'England becoming Germany', something that reinforced efforts to contain conflict within acceptable bounds.[36] Barbara Donagan explores one aspect through a detailed study of military plundering during the English Civil War. She shows that, just as in the Thirty Years War, plundering was widespread and contributed to perceptions of war spiralling out of control. In practice, however, soldiers and civilians still shared ideas of individual rights and entitlements that were used by victims to claim compensation. Perceptions of victimhood complicated post-civil war reconciliation, as Melanie Harrington argues in her chapter on England in the 1660s. There was a tension between perpetuating memory as legitimation for revenge, and the desire to consign painful experiences to oblivion in the interests of post-war reconciliation. Diverging interpretations of justice were major factors in causing early modern wars. Fear of reopening these wounds prompted the restored monarchy to refuse its supporters' demands for restorative justice at the Parliamentarians' expense, a factor contributing to lasting Royalist bitterness and perceptions of the war as cruel and unjust.

36 Roy, 'England Turned Germany?'; Donagan, 'Codes of Conduct'.

3

Grotius and the Civilian

COLM McKEOGH

An enemy, then, who wishes to show respect not for what human laws permit him to do but for what is his duty and what is right and godly, will spare the blood of his adversary. He will sentence no one to death unless by so doing he escapes death himself or something like it, or because his enemy has committed crimes which measure up to capital offences. And even to some who deserve such punishment he will extend pardon, either in full or from the death penalty, moved perhaps by the promptings of humanity, perhaps by other good reasons...

As for the killing of persons who are slaughtered incidentally, without intention, we must maintain what we said above, that mercy, even if not justice, requires that except for grave reasons affecting the safety of multitudes, nothing should be done that may threaten the destruction of innocent people.[1]

Hugo Grotius (1583–1645) has long been regarded as a founding figure of modern international law.[2] In particular he is credited with the secularisation of the natural-law approach: 'Grotius finally excised theology from international law,' writes Shaw, 'and emphasised the irrelevance in such a study of any conception of a divine law.'[3] More recently he has been studied as a seminal political theorist of the early modern period who began

---

1 Grotius, *Law of War and Peace*, Book 3, ch. 11, ss. 7 and 8, p. 353.
2 See, for example, Lauterpacht: 'Grotius did not create international law. Law is not made by writers. What Grotius did was to endow international law with unprecedented dignity and authority by making it part not only of a general system of jurisprudence but also of a universal moral code'; 'The Grotian Tradition', p. 51.
3 Shaw, *International Law*, p. 23.

the investigation of violence and accountability that was to be continued by Thomas Hobbes and John Locke: 'seventeenth-century social contract theory is better seen as a conversation among Grotian thinkers than as a quarrel between "Leviathan" and constitutionalism', suggests Baumgold.[4] A consequence of such views of Grotius's contribution to international law and political theory is that the role that Christianity plays in his outlook is downplayed. This chapter has two aims. First, it sets out the ideal as regards the treatment of civilians in war as enunciated by Grotius in the early years of the Thirty Years War. Secondly, this chapter pays attention to the role that Christianity plays in Grotius's endeavour to limit the harm of war through the construction of a multi-faceted pro-peace ideology.

Grotius died in 1645 with the famous last words 'By understanding many things I have accomplished nothing.'[5] What he had wished to accomplish were the immense and intertwined political and religious goals of restraining war and restoring Christian unity. What he had understood was that Christian peacemaking efforts could most profitably be directed, not into a sectarian pacifism that stood aside from society, but rather into a persuasive political engagement and propagandising that sought to minimise bloodshed. Spurred on by his Christian faith and his horror at the scale and savagery of the wars of religion in Europe, Grotius set out in his great work *De Jure Belli ac Pacis* (1625, hereafter *JBP*) to restrict warfare and to protect people from its harm. The Dutch lawyer had already established his legal skills when he had argued for freedom of navigation in *Mare Liberum* (The Free Sea) of 1609 and had achieved the office of Pensionary of Rotterdam in 1613. However, a theological controversy between Arminians and strict Calvinists had ended Grotius's political career in the Netherlands (and led to his imprisonment in 1619 on treason charges) and he sought to sidestep all disputed elements of Christianity in *De Jure Belli ac Pacis*. On his escape from Loevenstein Castle in 1621 (by hiding, at his wife's suggestion, in a chest of books that was being removed from the prison) he had fled to Paris where he was granted a royal pension under Louis XIII. This patronage allowed Grotius to resume his scholarly work and it was to the French king that he dedicated *JBP*. The intended audience for this work in Latin was the educated classes of Europe as a whole, both Catholic and Protestant. Religiously he was motivated to bridge the gaps between Christians in Europe. Intellectually he wanted Europe to hold together in the face of the centrifugal forces unleashed by the Reformation. Practically his concern was to limit and moderate the war that was being waged in Europe. He attempts this by putting forward in *JBP* a persuasive and multi-layered argument about the

---

4   Baumgold, *Contract Theory*, p. 29.
5   Knight, *Life and Works*, p. 289.

legality and morality of war. Grotius claims to be constructing a comprehensive jurisprudence and his treatment of every issue does indeed start from natural law and the law of nations, but it is not primarily through natural law or the law of nations that *JBP* seeks to attain its ends.[6] Rather, Grotius seeks to restrain war by restraining natural law and the law of nations; he does this by strongly espousing principles of humanitarianism and Christian charity. Many of these Christian and humanitarian principles relate to the civilian.

Assessments of Grotius's contribution to the cause of the civilian in war vary greatly. Colonel G. I. A. D. Draper lambasts Grotius's acknowledgement that neither natural law nor the law of nations at the time afforded protection to the civilian. This, Draper claims, amounts to an 'abandonment of the main purpose with which the author set out, namely, the humanization of the law of war'. Grotius's concession that contemporary cruelties were permitted by natural law and the law of nations meant that his passionate pleas for moderation and restraint were 'spent and wasted', Draper complains.[7] In contrast, Geoffrey Best lauds Grotius as having taken the most significant step in the civilian's cause: 'It was above all Grotius who brought the non-combatant firmly onto the stage of warfare and set the pattern for that categorization of "protected persons" which provides the *dramatis personae* of international humanitarian law. It must be doubtful whether any greater single stroke has ever been struck on the non-combatant's behalf.'[8] Grotius did promote a pro-civilian ideology in *JBP* but that great work is as much political propaganda as a legal text.

Both Draper and Best approach Grotius as a foundation figure in modern international law even though the Dutchman looks, not at every field of international law, but only at those relevant to war. Certainly Grotius was more modern and humanistic than legal predecessors such as the Spanish Catholics Francisco de Victoria and Francisco Suárez, whose *De Jure Belli* of 1532 and *De Legibus* of 1612, respectively, applied scholastic methods and Thomistic theology to issues of war.[9] Grotius does, however, adopt Suarez's distinction between natural law, on the one hand, and positive and customary law, on the other, as well as the Jesuit's acknowledgement that the law of nations was of the latter type. Grotius builds too on *De Jure Belli Libri Tres* of 1598 by the Protestant Italian jurist Alberico Gentili, but adopts a more orderly, methodical and

---

6   Grotius himself presents *De Jure Belli ac Pacis* as a legal tract. His aim, he writes in the Preface, was to be the first to treat 'in a comprehensive and systematic way' the 'law that exists between peoples, or between the rulers of peoples, whether based upon nature, or established by divine decree, or grown out of custom and tacit agreements': Grotius, *Law of War and Peace*, Preface, s. 1, p. 3.

7   Draper, 'Grotius's Place', pp. 197–98.

8   Best, 'Place of Grotius in the Development of International Humanitarian Law', p. 105.

9   McKeogh, *Innocent Civilians*, pp. 75–97.

systematic approach than is found in Gentili's medieval-style catalogue of the laws of war.[10] Grotius's work also had an overarching normative intent that was absent from the Italian's work. It is this all-embracing normative intent that distinguishes Grotius from more positivist successors such as Emmerich de Vattel, the Swiss jurist whose *Le Droit de gens* was published one hundred and thirteen years after Grotius's death.[11] The materials Grotius refers to are far broader than those admissible by international lawyers: in addition to the positive and customary law of nations, he looks also at natural law and Christian ethics. But it is Grotius's practical concern and ideological aims that distinguish his work. His goal in *JBP* was to counter 'reason of state' and to restrain war and massacre. For this reason Grotius's great work is best termed a pro-peace ideology. There may be multiple layers to Grotius's normative approach but there is only one aim. Natural law and the law of nations are the first and second layers to Grotius's approach but he does not wish these to determine the resort to and the conduct of war. Rather it is the third layer that Grotius hopes will limit and motivate people in conflict. He wishes to change law and practice in order to make it better reflect Christian ethics and humanitarian principles.

Grotius tackles violence using law and religion in a work of politics and propaganda. Because it is a work of politics and propaganda, Grotius never sets out the Christian assumptions that underlie his anti-war endeavours in *JBP*. Politics requires one to be unclear and imprecise in order to build coalitions and to maximise the number of people with whom a common platform can be built. Making clear his religious assumptions would only have impeded the achievement of Grotius's political and legal ends. Nonetheless, Grotius clearly had an optimistic view of human nature and of states, a view very similar to that of Aquinas and very different to that of Augustine.[12] He built up his ideas about law on the foundation of a belief in the rationality of human beings and in their sociable and altruistic impulses. Their common rational and social nature is the primary bond between human beings.[13] Relations between states and peoples can be based on reason, trust and shared interest.[14] Such was his faith in truth and justice that he believed that people could and would continue to act rationally and justly even after the outbreak of war. He was a Christian pragmatist and a practical idealist who promoted a comprehensive and persuasive

---

10 Haggenmacher, 'Grotius and Gentili', p. 161.

11 McKeogh, *Innocent Civilians*, pp. 99–122.

12 Grotius's most significant opening towards Catholicism remained always his adoption of natural law, an approach that was associated with Thomas Aquinas and the Catholic tradition and that was excoriated by the Protestant reformer Martin Luther as founded on the work of the 'the blind heathen teacher Aristotle': Skinner, *Foundations*, p. 16.

13 Remec, 'Position of the Individual in International Law', p. 241.

14 Wight, *International Theory*, p. 232.

pro-peace ideology. After Grotius, the most important Christian opposition to war would take the form, not of pacifist sectarianism, but of attempts to moderate violence. With his focus on humanitarian principles of restraint in war, Grotius pointed the way for subsequent legal efforts to restrain war, moving the legal focus from the *ad bellum* to the *in bello* level of war. But he also pointed the way for subsequent Christian peacemaking efforts, marking a shift from pacifism to humanitarianism. While their opposition to violence often led post-Reformation pacifist sects to stand outside society, Grotius showed how Christian peacemaking efforts could endeavour to moderate violence through constructive engagement.

1. LAW AND WAR

IN *JBP* Grotius tries to limit war by accommodating it in law, morality and Christianity. By claiming that law and war are not irreconcilable, he stops the fact of war undermining the claims of law. The phenomenon of war does not win the case for 'reason of state' in its battle with law, as a place can be found for war within law. Likewise a place can be found for it in Christian morality. Grotius had accepted in *On the Truth of the Christian Religion*, written in prison and published in 1622, that Christ commands pacifism:

> But the Law of Christ wholly forbids us, to return an injury that is done us either in words or deeds; lest the wickedness, which we condemn in others, we should again allow, by imitating. It wills that good be done, to the good indeed, chiefly, but to the wicked also; after the example of God, from Whom we have the sun, the stars, the air, the winds, the showers, as gifts common to all men whatsoever.[15]

However, for Grotius to have proclaimed pacifism as binding on Christians in *JBP* three years later would have marginalised him as a Christian thinker and resulted in his work having very little impact. Instead he sides with the majority opinion but tries to nudge it towards greater restraint on violence. His rejection of Christian pacifism in *JBP* is straightforwardly Augustinian:

> If then it had been the intention of Christ to introduce such an order of things as had never been heard of, he would undoubtedly, in the most clear and explicit language, have forbidden all capital punishment and all bearing of arms, which

---

15 Grotius, *On the Truth of the Christian Religion*, Book 2, s. 14, p. 31. One cannot reconcile *On the Truth of the Christian Religion*'s pacifism with *JBP*'s acceptance of violence by seeing the former as addressing the Christian's private life while the latter looks at their public role, for *JBP* deals with both public and private wars. Wars of defence, restitution and even punishment may be waged privately, according to Grotius in *JBP*, as the right to punish arises from the law of nature and therefore the right to punish belongs to all persons.

we never read that he did. For his words which are quoted to support such an idea are either very general or obscure. Both justice and common sense tell us not only that general expressions should be taken in a limited sense, and ambiguous sayings given a suitable meaning, but that there may even be some departure from the precise significance and ordinary use of words, to avoid an interpretation that would lead to great disturbance and harm.[16]

To strengthen his case, Grotius (craftily but inaccurately) presents his approach as the middle way and he dismisses both pacifism and unbridled realism as extremes. Both Machiavellian realists (those who claim that 'for a king or a free city nothing is wrong that is to their advantage'[17]) and Christian pacifists are dismissed in that famous section of the Preface to *JBP*:

> Throughout the Christian world I have seen a lawlessness in warfare that even barbarian races would think shameful. On trifling pretexts, or none at all, men rush to arms, and when once arms are taken up, all respect for law, whether human or divine, is lost as though by some edict a fury has been let loose to commit every crime. Confronted by this hideous spectacle, many of our best men have concluded that all armed conflicts must be forbidden to Christians, whose chief duty it is to love everyone [...] But their very effort to force a thing back too far toward the other extreme frequently does more harm than good, because the exaggeration in it is easily detected and detracts from the influence of what else they say that is actually true. A remedy must therefore be found for both sets of extremists, that men may neither suppose that nothing in the way of war is lawful, nor that everything is.[18]

Though he dismisses pacifism as extremism, Grotius is clearly in favour of peace and the purpose of *JBP* is the restraint of war. On issues such as the resort to war and the killing of civilians, Grotius initially accepts a realist stance as the one permitted by natural law and the law of nations but he then urges political leaders towards peacefulness on the basis of moral justice, charity and humanitarianism. He accepts the state's right to resort to war but then tries to restrict it. He accepts that the enemy, civilian as well as combatant, may be killed in war but then furnishes manifold reasons why they ought not be. There are thus three different types of law in Grotius's schema: natural law, the law of nations and a Christian and humanitarian law that includes the law of the Gospels and the law of Christian love (*lex caritatis, lex dilectionis, caritatis regula*). The former two determine what political and military leaders may do, the last what they ought to do.

---

16 Grotius, *Law of War and Peace*, Book 1, ch. 2, s. 7, p. 32; in seeking to preserve *pax* and *ordo* from Christian pacifism, Augustine too relies on a narrow interpretation of the words of Jesus: 'In the case of the centurion [...] Christ gave due praise to his faith; He did not tell him to leave the service': Augustine, *Political Writings*, pp. 164–65.

17 Grotius, *Law of War and Peace*, Preface, s. 3, p. 3.

18 Ibid., Preface, ss. 28–29, pp. 10–11.

2. NATURAL LAW

NATURAL LAW is intended to be a law independent of religious revelation, societal norms and the express or tacit consent of states. Instead such laws are said to have their source in the human instinct towards social, tranquil and reasonable living. Following Aquinas, Grotius claims that they can be discerned by reason. Of them, Grotius writes:

> Among these traits peculiar to man is his desire for society, that is, for life in a community; not any sort of life, but one that is peaceful and organized to suit the measure of his intelligence, with persons of his own kind. [...] He also, alone among animals, has the special instruments of speech, and the faculty of understanding and conducting himself in accordance with general rules. [...] This care to preserve society [...] is the source of all law which is properly so called. From it come the rules that we must not take something belonging to another, must restore whatever we have that is another's with the profit we made from it, must keep our promises, and must make good a loss incurred through our fault; and also that it is right to punish men who deserve it. [...] Evidently, then, it is part of human nature, as far as the capacity of the human mind allows, to follow in these matters well-framed judgments, and not be led astray by fear or temptation of present pleasure, or be carried off by reckless impulse. Whatever we do that is plainly contrary to good judgment is contrary also to the law of nature, that is to say, of the nature of man. And what we have just said would have validity, even if we granted what cannot be granted without great wickedness, that there is no God, or that he has no care for human affairs.[19]

Grotius describes a natural law as 'a dictate of right reason, showing the moral necessity or moral baseness of any act according to its agreement or disagreement with rational nature'.[20] The achievement of personal well-being and social tranquillity requires personal security, property and contracts. No society, including international society, can function without the preservation of rights. Natural law bestows a right to use force to preserve our rights. In international society, war is waged only to vindicate rights and is to be carried on within the limits of rights.[21]

Grotius's famous claim that natural law would have validity 'even if we granted [...] that there is no God, or that he has no care for human affairs' is often seen as moving natural law to a secular basis.[22] But, four centuries earlier, Thomas Aquinas had given primacy to natural law in the debate with non-Christians and non-Jews. Aquinas had aimed to convince Muslims with natural law:

---

19   Ibid., Preface, ss. 7, 8, 9, 11, pp. 4–5.
20   Ibid., Book 1, ch. 1, s. 10, pp. 20–21.
21   Vincent, 'Grotius, Human Rights, and Intervention', p. 244.
22   Grotius, *Law of War and Peace*, Preface, ss. 7, 8, 9, 11, pp. 4–5.

Muslims and pagans do not agree with us in accepting the authority of any Scripture we might use in refuting them, in the way which we can dispute against Jews by appeal to the Old Testament and against heretics by appeal to the New. These people accept neither. Hence we must have recourse to natural reason, to which all men are forced to assent.[23]

Grotius gave primacy to natural law in the new era of Christian division and strife. He intended to use it to gain agreement among Christians of all denominations and also to counter the moral and political scepticism exemplified by Machiavelli.[24] Grotius declared natural law to be independent of God, not in order to alter its content, but to maintain its impact in the post-Reformation age. His aim was to separate it from religion and to make it tenable by all parties in the religious and intellectual disputes of his era. However, Grotius keeps the content of natural law to a minimum in order to establish it as applicable to all peoples in all times. Natural law therefore does little to restrain war.

3. LAW OF NATIONS

THE LAW of nations has its origin in consent between states and its *raison d'être* is the common interest of nations. The law of nations is distinguished from the law of nature in that, while the latter can be deduced from self-evident principles, the former cannot.[25]

A rule that cannot be deduced from fixed principles by a sure process of reasoning and that is yet apparently everywhere observed must have originated in the free will of mankind [...] [T]he law of nations [...] derives its forceful authority from the will of all, or at least of many nations [...] The proof of a law of nations is the same as that of unwritten civil law, long custom, and the testimony of experts.[26]

To establish the content of the law of nations, Grotius quotes extensively from classical authors, both Greek and Latin. Poets, philosophers, playwrights, jurists, historians, orators and grammarians are cited in *JBP* as well as the fathers of the Church. Grotius refers to the events of antiquity for all his illustrations of the practices of warfare, of the treatment of prisoners, of the declaration of war, of the conclusion of treaties, and of the rights of ambassadors. There is, as Geyl observes, 'hardly an allusion to any event later than the downfall of the

---

23 Kenny, *Aquinas*, p. 2.
24 Harrison, *Hobbes, Locke*, pp. 132–34; Jeffery, *Hugo Grotius in International Thought*, pp. 36–37.
25 Grotius, *Law of War and Peace*, Preface, s. 40, pp. 13–14.
26 Ibid., Preface, s. 40, pp. 13–14, Book 1, ch. 1, s. 14, p. 23.

Roman Empire'.[27] In referring only to classical and biblical stories Grotius is following the humanist fashion, but doing so also serves his purposes in that the principles and norms encapsulated therein were the subject of agreement in a way that more recent events were not. Protestant and Catholic Europeans could not agree on the principles and events of their own times; they were more likely to agree on those of an earlier age.

4. CHRISTIAN AND HUMANITARIAN LAW

THE THIRD layer of Grotius's pro-peace project is more variegated. It includes divine law, which does not apply to all people but only to those to whom it has become known. The divine law of the New Testament supersedes that of the Old Testament but not all of Christ's precepts in the New Testament are divine law binding on Christians. Grotius writes of divine law:

> We find three occasions on which it was given by God to the human race, the first immediately after the creation of man, the second, on the restoration of mankind after the Flood, and the third on that more glorious restoration of mankind through Christ. These three bodies of divine law are undoubtedly binding on all men, as soon as they come to a sufficient knowledge of them […] [T] his most holy law requires a greater holiness on our part than the law of nature alone demands.[28]

Grotius uses the divine law to argue for much greater restraint and moderation in war than are demanded by the natural law and the law of nations. But the divine law applies only to Christians and so Grotius always furnishes many arguments for moderation including arguments that will apply to non-Christians. He argues for such moderation with appeals to the duty of Christians (*officium Christiani homini*) but also to the precepts of humanity (*regulae humanitatis*), natural equity (*aequitas naturalis*), an undefined notion of internal justice (*interna justitia*) and the rules of prudence (*regulae prudentiae*).[29] Grotius even appeals to honour and reputation and to considerations of utility and long-term expedience in his comprehensive arguments for peace and moderation. Legal positivists may criticise Grotius for mixing law, religion and morality, but the law on its own was insufficient to his task. A pro-peace ideology based on either law or religion alone would be too narrow to succeed.

---

27 Geyl, 'Grotius', p. 92.
28 Grotius, *Law of War and Peace*, Book I, ch. I, s. 15, p. 23, Preface, s. 50, p. 15.
29 Jeffery comments, 'Although it appears on numerous occasions in his work, particularly Book III of *De Jure Belli ac Pacis*, Grotius did not clearly or consistently define precisely what "internal justice" entailed': Jeffery, *Hugo Grotius in International Thought*, p. 45.

It could not restrain the behaviour of states in war, and so Grotius adds the appeals to moral, ethical and religious norms, to Christianity, civilisation and humanitarianism, to charity, gender and innocence, and to honour, reputation and utility.[30] Uncertainty and doubt are put to practical use by Grotius too: in matters of justice and war, doubt rather than certainty is usually appropriate. Uncertainty should lead to moderation and doubt should temper extremism.

5. CIVILIANS IN WAR

IN APPLYING his three-layered approach to the issue of the protection of civilians in war Grotius uses what Furukawa Terumi calls a retractive method of argument in which the freedom to wage war is granted on one level but retracted on another.[31] Grotius seeks as broad a consensus as possible at the start: he casts the net of natural law and the law of nations wide so as to exclude no one. A wide range of acts in war are established as permitted by natural law and the law of nations. But Grotius then draws the net back, introducing restrictions and limitations on the conduct of war, and urging moderation. He starts by allowing that natural law and the law of nations permit war to be waged against the enemy population but then goes on to forward arguments of love, humanity and utility to reduce the bloodshed in war. As Furukawa observes, 'Grotius never tires of devising means of avoiding the occurrence of war and mitigating its consequences, even at the risk of occasionally contradicting himself.'[32]

First, Grotius allows that natural law does not yield much in the way of restrictions on the conduct of hostilities. At beginning of Book 3 Chapter 1, Grotius asserts that, under natural law, all things necessary for attaining the purpose of the war (whether that purpose is defence, restitution or punishment) are permissible in the war: 'we have a right to do whatever is necessary to the end of maintaining our right'.[33] The restoration or realisation of justice is the key to Grotius's concept of just war and there is no principle of natural law that requires a war, once it is commenced, to be stopped until such justice is achieved.[34]

Secondly, Grotius acknowledges that the law of nations does not yield much in the way of restrictions on the conduct of hostilities either. Indeed,

30 For an analysis of how, for Grotius, the woman is the civilian *par excellence* see Kinsella, 'Gendering Grotius', pp. 161–91.

31 Furukawa, 'Punishment', p. 242.

32 Ibid., p. 243.

33 Grotius, *Law of War and Peace*, Book 3, ch. 1, s. 2, p. 269.

34 Kasai, 'Laws of War', p. 248.

the law of nations gives great license to the parties in war: 'How far this rule of license extends may be gathered from the fact that the slaughter of infants and women too is committed with impunity and sanctioned by the same law of war.'[35] Grotius allows that the law of nations as then recognised sanctioned the killing or wounding of all persons found in enemy territory whether they bore arms or not. Grotius affirms the right to kill or wound infants and women, captives, those who surrender unconditionally or whose surrender is not accepted, and hostages.[36] The same applies to foreigners who enter the enemy's territory after the outbreak of war or who fail to leave. It also applies to enemy citizens abroad: according to the law of nations, citizens of an enemy country are enemies wherever they may be found and may be killed with impunity. It is for these admissions that Draper sharply criticises Grotius. By allowing that civilians may lawfully be killed without restriction, complains Draper, Grotius undermines his own attempts to save them.[37] But Grotius is here reporting the law of nations as it existed and he cannot be censured for the lack of contemporary constraints on the treatment of civilians. Grotius cannot locate the protection for civilians within the law of nations as recognised and practised by states of the time.

Thirdly, Grotius seeks to anchor restrictions on war in the final layer of his pro-peace project, that composite of Christian religion, morality, virtue, humanity, sound judgment and good sense. Natural law and the law of nations are where Grotius always starts from, but never where he finishes. On all issues relating to war, he urges rulers to go beyond natural law and the law of nations. Having accepted in Book 3 Chapters 3–9 that the law of nations permits indiscriminate devastation, pillage and capture of property, the enslaving of captives, and the killing of enemy subjects regardless of age or sex, Grotius then moves in Book 3 Chapter 10 to limit the law, using arguments of Christianity, love, mercy, honour, fairness and utility.

> I must now retrace my steps, and must deprive the warmakers of almost all the privileges I may seem to have conferred, but did not confer, on them. For when first I started to explain this part of the law of nations, I declared that many things are said to be lawful or permissible because they may be done with impunity; in part too because coercive courts sanction them with their authority. There are things, however, that either are far from the rule of right – whether that rule is based on law strictly so called, or on the dictates of other virtues – or at least, with more piety and more applause from good men, they would be left undone.[38]

---

35   Grotius, *Law of War and Peace*, Book 3, ch. 4, s. 9, p. 297.
36   Ibid., Book 3, ch. 4, ss. 9–14, pp. 297–99.
37   Draper, 'Grotius's Place', pp. 197–98.
38   Grotius, *Law of War and Peace*, Book 3, ch. 10, s. 1, p. 342.

In Book 3 Chapters 10–16 (known as the *temperamenta belli*), Grotius seeks to reverse his position and to withdraw many of the rights he had earlier granted, under the law of nations and natural law, to both parties waging a formal war. He introduces the notion of *temperamenta belli* (moderation in war) and urges restraint in a just war. Grotius advances many different arguments in order to limit war and massacre. He draws on the principles of love and charity to recommend humanity in warfare, although love and charity go beyond what reason requires in social conduct and are therefore not binding. Women ought not to be killed in war (unless they had committed a crime or were fighting in place of men).[39] Children ought to be spared and also 'men whose way of life is opposed to warmaking' (Grotius lists clergy, religious, novices, penitents, agricultural workers, merchants, workmen, artisans and men rather like himself 'who devote their time to literary studies, which are honourable and useful to the human race').[40] They were to be spared in principle because they did not bear arms. Grotius does not base their immunity from harm in natural law though he artfully suggests as much when he quotes, in reference to the sparing of children in war, Livy's phrase 'the laws of war, that is, the laws of nature'.[41] Grotius upholds the customary prohibitions on poison, rape and assassination. Rape, he claims, could never contribute to attaining the purposes of the war: acts of rape are of 'no help toward establishing security or determining punishment. Consequently rape should not go unpunished in war any more than in peace. But this last is not law among all nations but among the better.'[42] Though the killing of prisoners of war is permitted both by natural law and the law of nations, Grotius points out that a 'sense of shame, that is, a respect for justice, forbids us to put a captive to death'.[43] Even their enslavement would deviate from natural equity. As regards sacred buildings, Grotius strongly urges against their destruction. Needless destruction would be madness, impiety, an offence against God and a contempt of humanity.[44] He also points to the practical benefits of moderation.[45] Moderation deprives the enemy of despair. Clemency reduces enmity. Ferocity will only provoke resistance.[46] He even claims that a reputation as an impious Christian will be detrimental to a king as a matter of *realpolitik*.[47] The perception of a just cause and honourable action

---

39 Ibid., Book 3, ch. 11, s. 9, p. 354.
40 Ibid., Book 3. ch. 11, ss. 10–12, p. 355.
41 Ibid., Book 3, ch. 11, s. 9, p. 354.
42 Ibid., Book 3, ch. 4, s. 19, p. 303.
43 Ibid., Book 3, ch. 11, s. 13, pp. 355–56.
44 Tanaka, '*Temperamenta* (Moderation)', p. 285.
45 Onuma, ed., *Normative Approach to War*, pp. 347–51.
46 Grotius, *Law of War and Peace*, Book 3, ch. 7, s. 8, p. 364.
47 Onuma, ed., *Normative Approach to War*, p. 347.

will benefit one by permitting the soldiers to wage war more effectively and the ruler to forge alliances more easily. In short, Grotius will go so far as to claim that one ought to do the Christian thing because it looks good and it allows one to promote one's self-interest more effectively.

Doubt and uncertainty are also reasons for moderation in war. A case in point occurs in the *temperamenta belli* when Grotius looks at desert of punishment on the individual level. This is striking because Grotius has already accepted that natural law and the law of nations permit punitive war. Punishment of wrongdoing is one of the three just causes of war for Grotius.[48] Punitive war can be waged with regards to the same catalogue of substantive rights as are listed in Book 2 with respect to wars of restitution. This punitive war is waged against the ruler and his people:

> As for those who are actually subjects of the enemy, that is, on a permanent basis, the law of nations permits injuring them in their persons wherever they are. For when war is declared on anyone, it is declared at the same time on the persons of his people [...][49]

Nonetheless, in the *temperamenta belli* Grotius distinguishes three levels of guilt. Outright wrongdoing (*injuriae*) occurs when the outcome of an action could have been foreseen and there was an evil intention. Culpable errors (*culpae*) occur when the outcome was foreseeable but there was no evil intention. Pure misfortunes (*infortuniae*) occur when the outcome of an action was unforeseeable and evil intention was absent.[50] Grotius proclaims:

> No one can lawfully be killed intentionally save as a lawful punishment, or when necessary to protect our lives and property [...] To make the punishment lawful it is required that the man who is put to death should himself have committed an offense, and one so serious that by any fair judge he would be sentenced to the death penalty.[51]

It is clear that most civilians cannot be tainted even with the mildest form of guilt as regards the cause of their ruler or his conduct of war. Indeed, in war, few will deserve punishment. This distinction of *injuriae, culpae* and *infortuniae* leads to his famous assertion that collective guilt is a 'fiction':

---

48 Grotius sets out three just causes of war in *JBP*: the first is defence against an injury to life, body, property or other legal rights or entitlements, actual or threatening, but not anticipatory (Book 2, ch. 1, ss. 3–18); the second is recovery of what is legally due, the restitution of things or enforcement of debts (Book 2, chs. 2–19); the third is the infliction of punishment (Book 2, chs. 20–21).

49 Ibid., Book 3, ch. 4, s. 8, p. 297.

50 Ibid., Book 3, ch. 11, s. 4, p. 348.

51 Ibid., Book 3, ch. 11, s. 2, p. 347.

> A fair reprisal, properly so-called, should be inflicted on the very person who committed the wrong […] In war, on the contrary, what is called reprisal results very often in suffering by persons who are guiltless of the wrong […] But the law of nature does not allow inflicting reprisals, except on the actual persons who committed the offense. Not is it enough that by a kind of fiction the enemy may be regarded as forming a single body.[52]

Though it appears in the *temperamenta belli*, this distinction between *injuriae*, *culpae* and *infortuniae* is not based on love, charity or humanitarianism. It is very much a distinction based on natural justice. How does this distinction between three levels of desert of punishment on the individual level sit with the natural-law right of rulers to wage punitive war against other rulers and their peoples? Grotius does not seek a theoretical reconciliation of these two issues. Is it contrary to natural justice to kill civilians in a punitive war? No such argument is made in *JBP* but uncertainty is planted in the reader's mind. Grotius's treatment of the just cause of punishment on the political and collective level is in tension with his treatment of guilt and innocence on the personal and individual level. Grotius does not seek to resolve this tension. He offers no solution to the inconsistency but simply uses it to urge restraint and moderation in war. He highlights the tension to encourage rulers to moderate punitive war. His aim is not the theoretical justification of war but the practical limitation of it. He successfully sows seeds of doubt about the justice of killing civilians in war by suggesting that the right to kill civilians in punitive war is not solidly grounded.

6. Conclusion

Grotius's *JBP* is best seen as a work in which he promotes a pro-peace and pro-civilian ideology. His method is an eclectic one, drawing on natural law, positive law and a great range of values. Positive law changes and that change can be driven by values. Promoting such changes in custom and practice is precisely what Grotius is doing in *JBP*. The work is better seen as propaganda for moderation and peace rather than as law. Those commentators who approach it as law are struck by its flaws; Draper sees it as a defect that

> Grotius informs his reader of the position under Divine Law, natural law, and the *jus gentium*, but it is often impossible to ascertain his views of what the law actually is or was on any given case […] In much of the treatise it is uncertain whether Grotius is concerned with law or morals.[53]

---

52 Ibid., Book 3, ch. 4, s. 13, p. 299; Book 3, ch. 11, s. 16, p. 357.
53 Draper, 'Grotius's Place', p. 193.

JBP is poor law in that Grotius departs from strict standards of evidence as regards the consent of states. He admits a variety of rules without providing criteria for choosing between them. He deals with morals and values that are, at best, 'soft law'. It leads, Hedley Bull complains, to a 'blurring of the distinction between what is international law and what is not'.[54] Geoffrey Best is struck by the 'ambiguity' of *JBP*, Tanaka Tadashi by its 'inconsistency'.[55] But *JBP* is better seen as a goal-focused political work in which Grotius is concerned to motivate, inspire and cajole military and legal practice to move in the direction of moderation and peace. For that reason, as Tanaka points out, 'it matters little if Grotius's theory of *temperamenta* is criticized for its inconsistency. It is sufficient for Grotius that his readers clearly understand his practical intention of specifying the people and property that ought to be spared.'[56]

What did Grotius achieve for the civilian? We have Grotius's own assessment of what he accomplished: nothing. Grotius's dim assessment of his achievements may seem at odds with the immediate impact and enduring fame of his work on the laws of war. The influence Grotius sought is to be found in the *temperamenta belli*, those chapters of Book 3 of *JBP* in which he put his case for moderation in war based on divine law and charity and honour; however, the main impact of *JBP* was to come, not from his pleas based on his third type of law, but from his orderly account of the other two types of law. His systematic outline of the requirements of natural law and the law of nations were valued by subsequent legal thinkers and Grotius was credited with moving the laws of war and peace from their medieval theological basis on to a more solid foundation in natural and voluntary law. This is not the effect he sought. His aims had been pressing and practical: to moderate war and to foster a bridge between Christians in Europe. Neither had been attained. Indeed, Draper can lament that it is a 'sad reflection upon the influence of Grotius that in the later stages of the [Thirty Years] war the cruelties committed increased at a time when further editions of his treatise were being published and his reputation as a jurist stood as high as ever'.[57]

For over two centuries after Grotius's death, it was reason of state rather than international law or Christian humanitarianism that continued to be the dominant force in matters of war. The conduct of war continued to be determined primarily by military necessity rather than by a *jus in bello* anchored in international law. It was not until the second half of the nineteenth century that humanitarian principles akin to Grotius's *temperamenta* began to be

---

54 Bull, 'Importance of Grotius in the Study of International Relations', p. 80.
55 Onuma, ed., *Normative Approach to War*, p. 301; Best, *War and Law*, p. 29.
56 Tanaka, '*Temperamenta* (Moderation)', pp. 300–01.
57 Draper, 'Grotius's Place', p. 198.

incorporated into the law of nations through written agreements on the laws and customs of war.[58] The humanitarian principles he had espoused concerning civilians, prisoners of war, poisons and sacred buildings would come to be accepted by belligerents and many of the acts he forbade would come to be forbidden in international law. But too much time elapsed between *JBP* and the introduction of *in bello* laws of war to claim the former as a cause of the latter.

When developments to lessen the harm done to civilians in war did occur, they came in part through the political, legal and moral efforts of campaigners taking the same pragmatic approach that Grotius had taken. For Grotius had foreshadowed the approach to war, not only that international law was to take, but also Christianity. Grotius did not initiate Christian efforts for civilian immunity in war but he did move those efforts from the field of canon law to that of international law.[59] He also focused those efforts on the pragmatic achievement of a goal. In his attempt to be 'as shrewd as a serpent and as innocent as a dove', Grotius's approach marks a significant development in the history of Christian attitudes to politics and law.[60] In his *JBP* we see a Christian putting his energies into promoting, not what he believes to be Christ's commands, but what he believes to be a realistic ideal that is achievable in practice and that most people can agree on in principle. The ideal he promotes in *JBP* is thus a contrived ideal, constructed on time-honoured religious and societal norms, not directly reflective of Grotius's own values and beliefs, and designed to be achievable in practice. After Grotius would come many more Christians working 'within the system', and motivated by values that they kept out of sight, in order to promote public and political acceptance of legal and humanitarian restraints on the conduct of hostilities.

---

58 Ibid., p. 199.
59 For an account of the 'Peace of God' movements over six hundred years before see McKeogh, *Innocent Civilians*, pp. 32–36.
60 Matt. 10:16 NIV.

4

War, Property and the Bonds of Society: England's 'Unnatural' Civil Wars

BARBARA DONAGAN

God allowed Israel to take what they did win in their iust wars; therefore they
[…] took the *Midianites* Prisoners, carried away infinite spoyle, & burnt their
towns and Cities with fire. David spoyled the Nations which he subdued. It is
accounted by the law of Nations a lawfull purchase and the practice of all people
in time of warre. For nothing is proper by nature, but either by ancient possession
of seis[in], or victory.[1]

So wrote Richard Bernard, a fierily Protestant preacher, in 1628, at a time
when English men and women were familiar with the battles that ravaged
continental Europe. After England's brief and undistinguished interventions in
continental wars in the 1620s, however, the English enjoyed a decade of peace,
but they followed the course of the Thirty Years War and were shocked by its
vividly reported horrors. They congratulated themselves on England's halcyon
days even as many Englishmen fought abroad and, at home, knowledge of
the laws and conditions of war was widespread. That knowledge was of many
kinds – Bernard, for example, linked his biblical examples to the law of nations
as recognised in his own day – but until 1639 its application remained comfort-
ably distant from everyday English life. The multiple domestic tensions of the
1630s – religious, constitutional, financial and social – were contained, if with
increasing strain, until war and its associated costs and taxation forced a crisis.

---

1 Bernard, *Bible-Battells*, pp. 71–72; 'proper' here has the now largely archaic sense of
'owned as property' (*OED*).

In 1639 and again in 1640 England found itself at war with its sister king-dom of Scotland, and suffered humiliating defeat. In 1641 rebellion erupted in Ireland and was reported in England in terms reminiscent of the worst atrocities of the Thirty Years War. These crises and their ensuing financial demands forced the calling of parliaments to authorise taxation, and at the same time fostered fierce public concern, popular demonstrations and a thirst for scapegoats, whether Irish Catholics, the king's advisor the Earl of Strafford, or the purportedly crypto-Catholic Archbishop Laud. By the summer of 1642 the breach between King Charles I and his increasingly combative parliament could not be healed and their respective armies faced each other in the field. Unlike the conflicts with the Scots and the Irish, this was a war between Englishmen. It lasted until, in the summer of 1646, parliament was decisively victorious; it was briefly renewed in 1648, and evolved into a new war with Scotland in 1650–51. In the 1650s the divisions and instability of parliamentary rule were replaced by the protectorate of Oliver Cromwell, but in 1660 the wheel came full circle and Charles II, the son of the executed Charles I, was restored to the throne.

In these decades of war and unsettled peace the boundaries between sol-diers and civilians were fluid. In recent years the study of war has come to encompass its social histories as well as traditional narratives and analyses of campaigns, commands and the political consequences of victory or defeat. It now also investigates the ways in which war has affected the societies provid-ing the soldiers and the dislocations of established patterns of law, politics and social relations. England's experience in the civil war years demonstrates the difficulty of divorcing studies of the military conduct of war from the domestic experience of civilians. As in other early modern conflicts soldiers fought and lived among civilians, on whom they depended not only ultimately for their pay but also for lodging, food and drink, and a host of services from intelligence to nursing care. Status was shifting: civilians became soldiers and when, after this civil war, they became civilians again, their military pasts sometimes caught up with them in local feuds or legal proceedings. If they were lucky, enemies and friends found a way to live together, but one of the factors that often complicated such a happy outcome was the wartime fate of civilians' property.

The years of war, change and disorder left few English men and women unaffected. Early in the civil war King Charles observed, with notable modera-tion, that 'the residence of an army is not normally pleasant to any place'.[2] War's unpleasantnesses were of many kinds, and they were not always the consequence of the immediate residence of an army. They affected all ranks of society and they befell civilians as plentifully as they did soldiers. Soldiers were,

2   'His Maiesties Speech at Shrewsbury', p. [6].

obviously, the primary victims of battle casualties, although civilians were not immune, and both suffered from such wartime evils as epidemic disease and hunger. Civilians were also the victims of a whole roster of further evils: their houses were burned or pulled down and they themselves set adrift; they were subject to unremitting and vastly increased financial demands, both legal exactions and more questionable impositions that included extortion; their lands were subject to confiscation or to sequestration until fines were paid, while rents became a volatile and often vanishing commodity; and their goods, from cows to plate, from shirts to tubs of butter, from stools and iron pots to treasured tapestries, were vulnerable to legal, quasi-legal and plain predatory seizures. In an intimate civil war in which enemies were not neatly divided by regional, linguistic or social barriers, harms might as easily be inflicted by neighbours and former friends as by strangers. Material loss, social estrangement and pervasive uncertainties multiplied the anxieties of the 1640s and 1650s.

This chapter will concentrate on property loss and its connection to one of the standard 'institutions' of this and many other wars, namely plunder. It will look particularly at the loss of chattel goods, broadly defined to include movable goods generally. The fate of chattel goods has had less attention than, for example, the consequences of civil war for landed property, and when they have been studied the focus has usually been on luxury goods such as paintings, hangings and jewels. Yet the loss of commonplace objects spread the impact of war through all ranks of society.

Richard Bernard's explanation, quoted above, of the right to spoil and 'takings' that accompanied success in just war (and virtually all wars are just in the eyes of their proponents) was characteristic of the representations of war with which early seventeenth-century English men and women were familiar. Its implications were deeply subversive. It suggested that the right to property was not 'natural' but instead derived either from 'ancient possession of seisin' (that is, established legal possession) or from 'victory', and that in war 'victory' challenged and trumped 'ancient possession': victorious force endowed the victor with the right to spoils regardless of the provisions of pre-existing law, and by the 'law of Nations' their acquisition counted as 'a lawfull purchase'. Such views were not presented as a kind of amoral Machiavellianism offering a guide to policy, but as regretful conclusions drawn from empirical observation of the facts of wars both biblical and modern, conclusions that appeared to have divine sanction.[3]

---

3   Bernard distinguished between laws of nature, that is, the basic rules that universally apply to human conduct, and the law of nations, that is, internationally recognised conventions of conduct governing relations between nations.

Plunder and destruction of property were a boon to civil war propagandists, who eagerly exploited a vein of frightening polemic already familiar in England from accounts of the Thirty Years War and, more recently, the Irish rebellion of 1641. When property rights lost the protection of the law, ordered society was endangered. Without legal security of tenure – not only of real property but also of the products of labour and land, of livestock, of household possessions – the foundations of society were undermined. Accounts of loss of property in England's civil wars thus had a dual character. They partisanly trumpeted personal hardships, but they gained much of their fervour and their resonance from their exploitation of fears of a return to a lawless, predatory, pre-civilised, non-Christian condition in which social order would be overturned along with property rights. The greatest and most socially disturbing threat to movable property came from plunder, which while it was sometimes relatively orderly and official, was too often violent, even frenzied, and made more dangerous by the fact that civilians as well as soldiers actively engaged in it. Not only were legal rights to property over-ridden but habits of degree and order were, in the eyes of property-holders, threatened by these mob actions. The symbiotic relationship between plunder and chattel property placed heavy strains on the social fabric.

A few preliminary points need to be made. First, when losses were enumerated the lists, often obsessively detailed, tended to mix indiscriminately several kinds of loss – for example, from fire, vandalism and plunder, and of cash, household goods, rents and assorted kinds of potential income. Secondly, such lists need of course to be taken with several grains of salt. The tendency of losers to exaggerate their losses and of takers to minimise them is not unfamiliar. And thirdly, many of the 'takings' – including plunder – about which complaints abounded were in fact 'legal', at least in origin, a point to which we shall return.

One unremarkable example illustrates the multiple and intertwined losses that civilians might sustain. In 1649 Sir John Harrison, a royalist and former customs farmer, prepared a characteristically miscellaneous and aggrieved calculation of losses.[4] Harrison's calculations were those of a man with a strong sense both of financial privilege and of ill usage. His list included loss of rents, the cost of the loan (including interest) borrowed to support himself and his family while his land was sequestered, the composition he paid parliament, bad-tempered notes of claims paid for 'pretended debt' or pretended aid in presenting his cases, and damage done to his house and grounds. It also revealed

---

4   BL Stowe MS 184, fos. 136, 161–162, Stowe MS 185, fo. 28. Harrison joined the king in Oxford in 1643. His lands were sequestered, and even after he paid his fine his income was slow to recover (*CAM*, Vol. III, p. 1187; *CCC*, Vol. II, pp. 1206, 1523).

his anger at his parliamentarian son John. His final total, which included a loss of £50,000 from expected profits from the customs, was £97,574. Mingled with his more grandiose claims were a number for straightforward material loss. His two houses were plundered of bedding, linen, hangings, pewter and assorted household goods that he valued at £5,000 and books valued at £300. Losses of corn, hay, wood, horses, cows, sheep and 'other cattle' accounted for another £2,000. By the time he had added six years' interest (from 1643 to 1649) his total losses from plunder had reached nearly £11,000. The combined loss from material goods is thus a little less than one-ninth of the ingenious overall total of £97,000 plus, but in its range it is characteristic of the miscellaneous losses recorded again and again in the papers of propertied families.

Such losses were not confined to the rich, however. More modest house-holds and the poor were equally vulnerable. One woman's list of 'extraordinary payments' in 1644 totalled £20 9s. 10d. Seventeen entries noted small sums for various military exactions (such as 6s. 7d. for provisions for Waller's army) while twenty-three weekly contributions of 4s. 7d. accounted for £5 5s., but £10, just under half of the total, was accounted for by 'losses [...] violently taken away'.[5] After Bradford fell to the royalists young Joseph Lister was twice sent by his master to the fair where the soldiers sold their plundered goods, with instructions to buy back a cow to provide milk for his family; and twice, within hours, the soldiers reclaimed the cow 'and carried her back to camp'. After the second loss his master gave up. Meanwhile the soldiers had already 'emptied all the town of what was worth carrying away', and in their rampage they had slit sacks and mattress ticks so that the streets were filled with meal and feathers that the women of the town tried to gather up.[6] Sir William Brereton had to remind his troops that indiscriminate plunder of the Welsh, for no better reason than that they were Welsh, was both counterproductive and would incur severe penalties.[7] A parliamentarian soldier returning home after years of service found that the enemy had passed through his Cheshire village of Kettleshulme and taken all his goods, leaving his wife and children destitute.[8] The London house of Edward Pitt, an Exchequer official who wanted nothing more than to be an invisible 'neuter' in the conflict, was that of a prosperous man, but when he lamented that he was left with 'the mere carcass of a house' in which 'there was nothing left' he described the condition of many men and women of all

---

5   Derbyshire Record Office, Gell MSS, D. 258, 31/10 (ma).
6   Lister, *Autobiography of Joseph Lister*, pp. 26–27. Meal sacks and mattress ticks were useful for carrying off other plunder.
7   BL Add. MS 11331, fo. 25v.
8   CRO, QJF/74/1, # 71.

classes.[9] Phrases such as 'the soldiers [...] plundered my house' and 'our house [...] was ransacked and plundered, over and over again' are among the clichés of reports of experience of the civil war.[10] What was ransacked and taken away were the movable 'goods and chattels' – along with equally movable provisions and livestock – that constituted a large part of the wealth of most households.

So far the word 'plunder' has been used without modification or explanation, but its implications were protean. It was not completely uncontrolled, for there were laws, both written and customary, civilian and military, designed to protect civilians and their property, and commanders' attempts to force their soldiers to observe them were frequent if only marginally successful. Like most of the other kinds of 'takings' of property prevalent in the civil war, plunder had both a legal and an illegal side. The quartering of troops on civilian households, for example, was one of the commonest forms of takings from which civilians suffered and both sides in the war assumed its legitimacy, but it was obviously open to abuse. Civilians were, nominally, paid for their costs in food, fodder for horses and general lodging, but the payments frequently went unpaid and soldiers' demands and depredations went beyond strict military need. So we find a proclamation forbidding soldiers from demanding more expensive food – food that was, in effect, above their station – and complaints that soldiers killed and ate landlords' game and felled their woods. We also see that armies found it necessary to forbid quartered soldiers from abusing, beating or frightening landlords and their families, or extorting money or victuals by violence.[11] Thus if quarter was not strictly plunder, it too fell into the category of potentially illegal takings and threatened material loss and violence to civilians. Similarly property – most notably horses – might be legitimately commandeered when needed by the army and when ordered by an officer. Yet horses remarkably often ended up being sold privately by the commandeering soldiers while

---

9 Pitt's country house was also plundered (BL Add. MS 29974.2, fo. 381). Lucky concealment or the connivance of friends sometimes meant that losses were not quite as comprehensive as victims suggested. After his wife's death Pitt assumed that she might still have had 'keys, gems, money, writings, papers, or table book' in her possession; in reply his sister-in-law wrote that papers and the table book were being delivered to him, and that she would send a note of his wife's things in her possession (see BL Add. MS 29974.2, fos. 392, 395 v).

10 For example, Shaw, 'Life of Master John Shaw', p. 137; Priestley, 'Some Memoirs Concerning the Family of the Priestleys', p. 9.

11 *Lawes and Ordinances of Warre*, p. C2v.; for similar royalist provisions see *Military Orders And Articles Established by His Maiesty*, pp. 10–11, 18. In January 1646 a Cheshire man complained that royalist soldiers had threatened to kill him if he did not produce better provisions (CRO, QJF/74/1, # 64). There may be minor deviations between different printings of the same set of military orders. The citations above are taken from copies in the Bodleian Library, Oxford.

original owners vociferously challenged the pretended legality of the seizure or vainly sought for redress.[12]

Plunder was the most widespread and most reviled kind of taking. It was a favourite accusatory word of the mid-seventeenth century, closely followed by pillage. 'Loot', we may note, was a nineteenth-century import into English, and 'prize' and even 'booty' have a more respectable aura. Yet if the connotations of 'plunder' are now universally bad, the practice was not, in the seventeenth century and for long before and after, necessarily illegitimate.[13] According to the unwritten laws of war, for example, a town that refused to surrender could be plundered when it fell, and it was recognised that both the lives and the property of the defenders and citizens were at the mercy of 'the enraged soldiers in their spoil'. So were the pickings to be found by the victors on the bodies of dead men and horses on the battlefield. Revenge for a perceived atrocity or breach of faith or unwarranted killing excused retributive plunder.[14] In such cases the spoils were part of the traditional winnings of war ('To the victor the spoils'), but legitimacy often lay in the eye of the beholder.

Army regulations contained provisions against damage to and seizure of civilian property but their reach was circumscribed. They forbade destruction of crops, wood or barns, for example, *unless* it was ordered by a commander, but the purpose was military rather than humanitarian: namely, as in the original biblical injunction, the preservation of supplies and materials of which the army might itself have need. The prohibition of plunder *until* permitted by a commander also had a long and pragmatic history. When Shakespeare wrote, 'Cry "havoc," and let slip the dogs of war' he was literally recalling late medieval army regulations that mandated death for the soldier who, by an unauthorised cry of 'havoc', unleashed troops to plunder and kill before their

---

12   See, for example, the case of Thomas Chrymes, husbandman, who had 'lent' a gelding and its 'furniture' – saddle, bridle, holsters, pistols – at the request of an ensign, with a promise that all would be returned. Instead the gelding was sold and Chrymes was unable to obtain any compensation. When he demanded satisfaction he was attacked with a drawn sword, wounded in his head and arm, and left unconscious. Furthermore, he had witnesses to prove it (CRO, QJF/74/1, #81).

13   For the survival of a morally neutral use of 'plunder' into the nineteenth century, note the comment of the future General Gordon on the burning of the palaces of Peking in 1860. Such was their 'beauty and magnificence […] [i]t made one's heart sore to burn them; in fact, these palaces were so large, and we were so pressed for time, that we could not plunder them carefully'. Cited in Sullivan, 'Restoring the Summer Palace', and compare A. E. Housman's lines, 'Soldier from the wars returning, / Spoiler of the taken town'.

14   In 1645 a Yorkshire gentleman complained that his house was taken and plundered by parliamentary soldiers 'upon pretence that a soldier was slain near the house, but it was not by any that had relation to him' (*CCC*, Vol. II, p. 1012).

commander had given permission.[15] (The cry of 'a town, a town' had a similarly liberating intention as parliamentary troops surged towards Chester in 1645.)[16] Armies tried to regulate both the act of plunder and the distribution of its spoils, but they did not attempt to eliminate it. When Newcastle fell to the Scots in 1644, for example, plunder was officially permitted for twenty-four hours, but it was also regulated and common soldiers were restricted, at least in theory, to the goods of the common people, to 'household stuff'.[17] Although English armies of the 1640s were no longer organised on entrepreneurial principles, by which the 'wynnynges of warre' were both a major incentive to and the legitimate profits of military service (as seen in the legislation for their distribution in Henry VIII's articles of war), controlled plunder remained one of war's legitimate rewards.[18]

Nevertheless, for manifest reasons, plunder could not be uncontrolled. Its attractions for soldiers were many, ranging from simple profit to the pleasures of vandalism and destruction for their own sakes and to the satisfaction of subversive and retaliatory acts against the popish and the propertied, but it had obvious military disadvantages. Soldiers caught up in the frenzy of plunder were deaf to military duty: they preferred plunder to attacking the enemy or keeping their place in the ranks, or they straggled abroad looking for prey.[19] If they did obey an order to desist they might, like the disgruntled horse after the battle of Naseby, be 'very leisurely' in their pursuit of the fleeing enemy.[20] Furthermore, commanders were well aware that uncontrolled plunder alienated civilian populations: the depredations of Colonel George Goring's troops in Cornwall had, by 1646, turned a county once strongly royalist to one that welcomed the parliamentarian advance.[21]

---

15 'Ordinances of Warre' of Henry V, in Grose, *Antiquities of England and Wales*, Vol. I, p. 36: the 'beginner' of the cry was to die, his followers were to have 'horse and harneses' confiscated until they paid a fine and to be imprisoned at the king's pleasure. Richard II's articles had specified that all involved were to be beheaded (Grose, *Military Antiquities Respecting a History of the English Army*, Vol. II, p. 62). Henry V's provision remained in Henry VIII's *Statutes and Ordynances for the Warre* of 1544, p. B ii v. See William Shakespeare, *Julius Caesar*, III.i.273.

16 BL Harl. MS 2155, fo. 113.

17 Although restricted, they were thorough, even to plundering the pockets of guests at a christening. Officers provided safeguards for the houses of the rich – in their own interests, it was said (Lithgow, *Siege of Newcastle*, pp. 30–31).

18 *Statutes and Ordynances for the Warre*, p. [B v], and preceding sections on division of profits from prisoners; also see generally Keen, *Laws of War*, Redlich, *De Praeda Militari*.

19 Corbet, *Historicall Relation*, p. 107, on 'stragling plunderers'.

20 Wogan, 'Proceedings of the New-Moulded Army', p. 129.

21 [J.R.], *Letter Sent To the Honble William Lenthal*, p. 4.

The charms of plunder can hardly be exaggerated, and their attraction was not confined to soldiers. For soldiers it was part of their way of life. As General Robert Venables complained of the civil war veterans in his rag-tag army in Jamaica in 1655, they expected 'Pay and Plunder both (which they had in England)', and when pay failed, as it often did in both countries, 'to be denied Pillage much exasperated their Spirits'.[22] At the fall of Sherborne Castle in Dorset in 1645 one observer noted that 'five shillings gotten in the way of spoil from the Enemy gives [the soldiers] more content than twenty shillings by way of reward in an orderly manner'; they were 'zealous to be their own Carvers'. One parliamentarian officer told his men, apparently without rancour, that 'they were as good fighters, and as great plunderers, as ever went to the field': 'valiant acts,' he concluded, were 'done by contemptible instruments'.[23]

Yet as already noted plunder and other forms of seizure of property were not purely military activities. Armies sometimes had scavenging camp followers, but local civilians also shared in battlefield pickings, whether stripping the bodies of the dead or joining with soldiers in making off with the detritus of battle.[24] After one engagement the field yielded up to a thousand muskets and pikes, barrels of powder, tools, knapsacks and portmanteaus (and presumably their contents), 'Swedes' feathers' (stakes used against cavalry attack), armour and clothing: 'All these the souldiers and countrey people adjacent made pillage of'.[25] Plunder indeed was often a co-operative venture shared between civilians and soldiers. In 1643 eminent parliamentarians felt compelled to write to their general the Earl of Essex:

> The soldiers are grown so outrageous that they plunder every place. Even this morning 5 or 6 gentlemen's houses have been ransacked by them of which we conceive [one] great cause to be the malignity of the country people who instigate & direct the soldiers in what places they should exercise this insolency.[26]

One of the strong attractions of plunder was the money to be made from other people's property. It was not just a matter of seizure by individuals carried

22 Venables, *Narrative of General Venables*, pp. 14, 17. Given the appalling conditions of the expedition it is not surprising that 'Men [...] rambled up and down for Pillage': ibid., p. 27.

23 The account of Sherborne is cited in Bayley, *Great Civil War in Dorset*, p. 288; Hodgson, 'Memoirs of Captain John Hodgson', p. 119.

24 The draft of a royalist order against plunder included a provision against 'persons no way listed or employed in our service [...] but following the same for spoil and pillage' (BL Harl. MS 6804, fos. 79–79v).

25 *Most True Relation Of Divers Notable Passages*, p. 6.

26 They warned that '[if] this go on awhile the army will grow as odious to the country as the cavaliers' (Bod. MS Tanner 62 1/A, fo. 115).

away after the heat of battle or of the mob frenzies in which both soldiers and civilian shared, nor of the pleasures of personal acquisition or of destruction. It could also be a matter of commercial forethought. Adam Martindale, of modest yeoman stock, reported that his father's house 'was plundered of every thing they thought worth carrying away, in cartes which they brought to his doore to that purpose'.[27] There was a market for plunder, and the buyers of its bargains were often the neighbours of the plundered victims.[28] For some neighbours moreover the pleasures of plunder went beyond profit and mob action: there were echoes of old quarrels, while tenants' resentment against landlords was expressed not only in refusals to pay rents but in triumphant destruction of 'writings' that recorded their obligations.

What did plunder mean for the victims when houses were ransacked and 'plundere[ed] [...] to the bare walls' and to merchants and travellers whose goods were seized en route?[29] For one thing, in an age before insurance, it meant that loss of property was terminal unless the former owners could achieve some kind of legal redress, and indeed the indemnity cases of the post-war years reveal both continued English faith in the processes of law and the difficulties encountered by plaintiffs. In general, though, as one official remarked when asked for a reckoning, '(Fortune de la Guerre) they are gone'.[30] It is, as usual, harder to find details of the condition of the poor than of the prosperous – their losses tended to be comprehended in a larger whole, as when Shrewsbury was described as 'exceedingly plundered'. But what is striking about so much of the recorded loss is its ordinariness. One parson's wife lost her 'Child-bed Linnen'; Mrs Venables was 'plundered on the Lord's day' (which made it worse) when 'they took all they could lay their hands on; some cheese, all kinds of Provisions, Beds and clothes'; Edward Pitt's man of business reported that '[t]here was not left in my house so much as a stool nor for myself [wife] or children so much as a suit of clothes.'[31] Richard Congreve, a Staffordshire gentleman, made lists of the 'payments and plunder' he had suffered 'by pretended warrant'; in one, from early 1645, the value of goods lost, although individually modest, totalled

---

27 Martindale, *Life of Adam Martindale*, p. 39.

28 For the cut-rate bargains available, note royalist complaints about the sale of the spoils of Wardour Castle: the parliamentarians cut down the noble 'Oakes and Elmes' in the grounds and sold them 'for four pence, six pence, or twelve pence a piece, that were worth Three, Foure, or Five pound a Tree', while the lead conduit that brought water to the house was 'cut up [...] and sold ([...] [like] bone lace) at six-pence a yard' (*Mercurius Rusticus*, pp. 44–45).

29 Corbet, *Historicall Relation*, p. 143.

30 TNA, State Papers 28/160, fo. 188.

31 CRO, DDX 428 (24-2-1645); *Mercurius Rusticus*, p. 28; Venables, *Some Account of General Robert Venables*, p. 21; BL Add. MS 29974.2, fo. 387.

over £300. They included – to give only a small selection of items – eight nightcaps at £2, three hats and a hat case at £6 10s., three shirts at £1 16s., a pair of brass compasses at 8 shillings, and four bands and cuffs at 10 shillings. There were also larger collective sums, such as £40 for six horses and £15 for his wife's and children's clothes. Such inventories of loss reveal how comprehensively households were gutted. They also, as in Congreve's case, reveal the preciseness of the records not only of what was taken but also of the names of the takers.[32] The consequences of loss, furthermore, went beyond the purely material. They mingled with anxieties about safety and violence and, for many, seemed to threaten status by the taking away of its outward signs. Loss of gold or, more commonly, silver plate was particularly painful, and indeed plate fell into a special category, for it was not only a movable asset and a realisable form of capital (which, once melted down, was unidentifiable) but also a visible assertion of status, success and identity. Edward Pitt sometimes seemed more anguished over the loss of his plate (in his case by forced contribution rather than plunder) than over other losses.[33]

Not only were civilians plunderers as well as plundered, the market in plundered goods could not have operated without them, and it was the predatory opportunities that civil war gave to the general populace and the mob disorders that accompanied plunder that exacerbated social anxieties. As Sir Simonds D'Ewes observed in 1642, 'all right and property, meum and tuum, must cease in a civil war and they knew not what advantage the meaner sort also may take to divide the spoils of the rich and noble amongst them'.[34] 'Babel [...] [was] now in building' towards 'the destruction both of Church and State', and law was no protection when a jury could allegedly declare that 'they did not thinke PLUNDERING (a new name for an old Theft) to be Felony by the Law'.[35] Homely examples led to similar conclusions about the overturning of the principles of law and the right to property. A kinswoman wrote to Edward Pitt's wife about the 'stuff' intended to make clothes for a young cousin: it was, she said, 'otherwise disposed of by some, who had least right and interest in it, such who account all they can lay either hand or eye on as justly their own by the new claim of Plundering as we formerly did by the old titles of purchase or inheritance'.[36]

---

32 William Salt Library, Salt MSS 47/1/1. The costliness of Congreve's hats is explained by the fact that two were 'beavers'.
33 BL Add. MS 29974.2, fos. 379–81.
34 Cited in Morrill and Walter, 'Order and Disorder in the English Revolution', pp. 149–50.
35 *Mercurius Rusticus*, pp. 28–29.
36 BL Add. MS 29974.2, fo. 383.

Loss of property, both modest and luxurious, through plunder fed the multiple anxieties aroused by this intimate war. The threat to the sanctity of property and fear of undisciplined plundering troops merged with long-standing fears of popular violence that had been intensified by reports of outbreaks by civilian mobs before the civil war actually began. Of these the most notorious were the attack on the Lucas family and its property in Colchester, brilliantly dissected by John Walter, and the frightening destruction by an enthusiastic crowd of Countess Rivers's houses, where estimates of her losses ranged from £50,000 to £150,000.[37] Law, whether military or civilian, offered very imperfect protection. Its bounds, as we have seen, were uncertain and its operation variable.

Nor could the bonds of society and community be relied on. The frequency with which takers' names were recorded indicates how often they were known to the plundered. Furthermore, it suggests that the victims nourished a hope of future redress, and the post-war indemnity cases indicate that some at least, if they did not regain their property, got other satisfaction. Social bonds were also strained by the rich new opportunities for informers, who were already in normal times the initiators of much legal and administrative action. Disputes over plunder, like accusations of tax evasion and subversion, could be a tempting source of profit for informers, who won a cut of proceeds recovered in such cases, but the practice also contributed to the mistrust between neighbours, between landlords and tenants, even between family members, that was readily ignited in a civil war.

A well-documented case history incorporates many of the features already discussed.[38] In 1635 Sir John Bankes, recently appointed Charles I's Attorney General, bought Corfe Castle in Dorset. The office brought him some £10,000 a year, and he and his wife furnished lavishly. When the war came Bankes – by now Lord Chief Justice of Common Pleas – followed the king to Oxford, where he died in 1644. Lady Bankes and her children had moved from London to Corfe Castle, and in 1643 their parliamentarian neighbour Sir Walter Erle led an unsuccessful siege. After several months of alarums and excursions, the parliamentarians returned for a more serious siege in late 1645, led by Colonel John Bingham. After nearly seven weeks the castle fell, not to surrender or

---

37 Walter, *Understanding Popular Violence*; *Mercurius Rusticus*, p. 14: the mob was also said to have 'pull[ed] downe, cut in pieces, and carr[ied] away the costly Hangings, Beds, Couches, Chaires, and the whole furniture of her house, rob[bed] her of her Plate and Monies'. The total estimates of loss included a second attack on her house at Melford.

38 The following information is derived from the Bankes MSS at Kingston Lacy, bound in 'Autograph Letters. I', unpaginated; some of this material is printed in *Corfe Castle*. See also *ODNB* for Sir John and Lady Bankes.

attack, but to subterfuge. There was therefore no treaty of surrender with protective clauses that might conceivably have safeguarded the castle and its contents, and in the days that followed it was gutted.

Colonel Bingham, a tenant of the Bankes family, was the leader in the proceedings, but he was not alone. We know what was lost through the obsessive records of Lady Bankes and her agents as they listed the vanished contents of room after room and also of innumerable trunks (the castle seems to have been a repository for papers and for a great store of textiles). We are here in a different world of material goods from that of the poor or of Richard Congreve or even Sir John Harrison. A list attributed to Lady Bankes contained many sets of tapestry hangings – among them one of eight large tapestries telling the story of Astraea and Calydon – and proceeded (to give a small sample) to 'furniture' for a bed, quilts of embroidered green cloth, scarlet and gilt leather hangings, Turkey carpets and numerous trunks of initialled linens. There was also a very large ebony cabinet, a large trunk inlaid all over with mother of pearl, six very fine and large down beds with bolsters, valances and blankets – and so on and on. They were valued at £1300 and were 'all very new and good' – a reminder that the losses were those of a successful man and his houseproud wife whose new house and furnishings asserted success and status. There were also lists of less elevated items: 'ordinary' linen; 'lumber' such as tables and stools; iron shovels; tongs, bellows and racks for the kitchen; and a variety of brass and pewter objects such as pots, skillets and kettles. A marginal note estimated the value of this list of lesser items at £300 – equal to the total value of Richard Congreve's goods.

The lists are interesting, but what happened to the goods afterwards is more interesting. Some stayed in the neighbourhood: six locals acquired 14 tubs of butter between them; another had two of Lady Bankes's chairs and, when he married, acquired more that were in his future wife's possession; still others made off with loads of stone and lead. Sir Walter Erle took timber. The great beneficiary, however, was Colonel Bingham. Some goods he kept, but he sent much of his booty to 'Stone the broker in Barbican' for a total of £600 odd. A year later Lady Bankes's agent listed what he had seen there, although Stone had already sold much, including one batch to Mr Beck, a Dutch merchant, for two or three hundred pounds, and 'the story of Astraea and Callidon, […] for 150 l. odd money to the Earl of Manchester'. He was, in effect, running an outlet store.

Lady Bankes and her son spent much of the rest of the Interregnum engaged in various proceedings by which they tried to protect their landed property, reduce their financial obligations and keep track of their chattel goods. A lawsuit involving Sir Anthony Ashley Cooper, who had invested the castle in a loose and desultory way between the two sieges, was conducted in terms of civility, in which Cooper expressed the hope that they might 'be still friends and hearty neighbours there being in this no difficulty but that 'tis out of fashion'. At the Restoration those who had made off with the castle's contents could expect less forbearance. Colonel Bingham was harried for the goods in his possession, and from his prudent retirement he wrote to Sir Ralph Bankes offering to return the large bed, single red velvet chair and set of hangings in his possession, and concluded with the abject hope that 'a continual gale of happiness may yet blow on you here below the stars and that you may enjoy heaven hereafter'. A damning list of Bankes items seen in Bingham's house was vastly more extensive, and in another letter Bingham's own list was expanded, but he assured Sir Ralph that the table linen was 'but once used by me, but whited once in 2 years'. We do not know whether this care mollified Bankes, yet there is a suggestion of grudging acceptance of Bingham's past. Sir Ralph seems sensibly to have advised his tenant to 'live retired and keep at home'.

No such tolerance was extended to Sir Walter Erle, whose pickings had been less domestic and extensive than others' but who, according to Sir Ralph Bankes, had been 'instrumental in destroying the Castle' (it was slighted after the siege). The terms of their exchange are suggestive of the tensions between former enemies who, at one level, were forced to accept a *modus vivendi* – Sir Ralph and Sir Walter were neighbours and sat together in parliament. Erle tried conciliation. He had meant to bring up the subject of return of Bankes's goods as they sat side by side in the House of Commons, but 'some business or other intervened', and he had then planned to bring the matter up in the country. Nevertheless he denied that he was under any legal obligation to make restitution. Besides, Bankes had been misinformed: the goods had not been taken on his directions, nor were they worth as much as was claimed (a mere 'five or six load of timber and stone', he said dismissively). Nevertheless, in view of the 'honour and respect' of the Bankes family and 'in respect of neighbourhood and civility' he hoped that tolerable relations could be restored. Sir Ralph was unmoved, and in 1661 he wrote:

> It may perhaps seem strange to you after such an intermission that I should now demand of you that which belongs to me [...] I incline to believe want of memory occasions this failure in you [to make restitution] and that it is rather the defect of your age than of your will. The timber and other materials for building you had from Corfe Castle (which you have since employed in your own fabrick) you musts needs acknowledge are mine, and what in law as well as justice ought to be restored to me [...] one of the great pieces of timber (if not the greatest) in your house came from the Castle [...] The Scripture which you profess [...] to make the rule of our actions cannot justify you in such proceedings, nor can you bring any text from them which allows you to build with my timber [...] Many throughout England [...] have thrown from them that which, belonging

to others, would have proved a moth and canker in their estates [...] I hope your conscience will be as just to you as theirs have been, and that you will be ruled by it: and, by making me a just satisfaction, you will oblige me to be,

Sir,

Your friend and servant,

R.B.

This was not very conciliatory, and Erle was only intermittently conciliating in return. But the three cases suggest the range of possible responses to the intimate violence of the war years. If Cooper stressed legal process, civility and neighbourliness, and Bingham may have obtained grudging acquiescence, the rift with Erle was unhealed. Bankes asserted that time had not annulled his property rights as original owner ('that which belongs to me') and rejected all overtures for reconciliation. According to local legend (at least as regaled to tourists) the cannon on the ha-ha at his new house at Kingston Lacy in Dorset was trained on the Erle estates.

The picture was not all black. Some neighbours helped neighbours; kin protected kin – Edward Pitt's family was aided by his parliamentarian brother William; some family breaches were healed, as in the case of Harrison and his son; some officers successfully restrained their troops; law may have been bent but was not irretrievably broken; on occasion, goods were even recovered. Nevertheless the losses of common, everyday property, which threatened the 'meum and tuum' not only of the gentry but of all ranks of society; the 'Contempt and derision' that often accompanied these takings – in, for example the mock processions in which cheeses on pikes' heads became the triumphal symbols of defiance of established order and its rituals; and the violence and disorder that came with plunder – taken together, these accompaniments of civil war increased the sense that civil society was in danger, and that threat to property entailed threat to order. It surely contributed to what Derek Hirst has called the de factoism of the 1650s and the acceptance, even when unenthusiastic, of Restoration settlements.

If the fact of civil war rather than war between nations (of the kind envisioned by Richard Bernard) on the one hand embittered social relations, on the other it facilitated a return to old legal and property relations. To Sir Ralph Bankes, possession conferred no right to property taken without legal sanction: it still 'belong[ed]' to its initial owners. Restitution may have been patchy and partial, but the rejection of a right to goods plundered and violently taken under colour of victors' spoils signalled not only perpetuation of property rights but also rejection of the popular violence that had frightened many English men and women. This may have provided little comfort to those whose goods and chattels had gone for good, and it clearly did not entail the forgetting of past wrongs and a return to universal benevolence. What Bankes appealed to, however, was a return to the conjunction of 'law as well as justice' and the protection of property rights in a properly ordered society. The fate of commonplace household goods had a political dimension, for the fear that chaos could come again was, then as now, a powerful political argument.

England's civil war, it is clear, was not confined to conflict between soldiers or between ideologies or religious beliefs. Nor were its consequences confined to areas that saw marching armies or battles or garrisons. Regions traditionally regarded as having a 'quiet war' saw episodes of local violence and could not escape demands for the sinews of war in money and goods. Everywhere rich and poor experienced new levels of taxation, new threats to their property and new dangers to the bonds of family and neighbourhood as civilians joined soldiers in destruction and predation, informers flourished, and the language of partisan division escalated. Many before the war had feared that the skin of civil society was fragile and that, once it was broken, mob violence would overwhelm the institutions of civil society. Among those threatened institutions was property in all its forms, and the destruction and appropriation of houses and seizures of landed property that followed 1642 all seemed evidence of such breakdown. Loss of ordinary chattel goods was less dramatic than the destruction of a great house and its contents, but actual loss, or the fear of it, of such commonplace items as shirts and stools, pots and mattresses, was a widespread experience of the war years. Such goods constituted a major part of the wealth of poor and middling families. In their memories as much as in the memories of their richer fellow countrymen, civil war had brought loss of property as well as loss of life. Losses of both kinds contributed to a national reluctance, in the decades that followed the war, to resolve political divisions by the 'arbitrament of war'.

5

Transitional Justice Theory and Reconciling Civil War Division in English Society, circa 1660–1670[1]

MELANIE HARRINGTON

THE CIVIL wars that raged across England, Ireland, Scotland and Wales from 1638 to 1651 began with conflict between King Charles I and his parliaments over the scope of royal authority and the direction of the post-Reformation Church of England. There were multiple and complex causal factors that led to war, including the personalities of the king and his chief advisors. One consequence was the king's execution in front of a crowd of thousands on a cold January morning in 1649. But this was a bloody revolution for Charles I's subjects as well as for the king himself. Direct and indirect total war dead from the civil wars in England has been estimated at 180,000 (3.6 per cent of the population) with estimated proportions higher still in Scotland and Ireland.[2]

1   I would like to thank the convenors of the conference 'Civilians and War in Europe, 1640–1815' for their interest in my research, and the attendees for their helpful questions and comments. Grateful thanks are also due to the Arts and Humanities Research Council which has have funded the PhD research from which this article is taken. I would also like to thank Dr Matthew Clark, Professor John Morrill and Dr Jacqueline Rose for their helpful and insightful comments on both the conference paper and this essay, and also Dr Mark Goldie and Rob James for conversations that first brought transitional justice theory to my attention.
2   Carlton states that his figure of 180,000 in England is erring 'on the side of caution', suggesting that numbers may have been higher. Carlton acknowledges the problems of trying to calculate the number of civil war dead and concedes that any estimates of those who perished as a result are 'extremely rough': Carlton 'Impact of the Fighting', p. 20. The estimates for Scotland are 6 per cent and for Ireland 41 per cent of the total population: Carlton, *Going to the Wars*, p. 214.

The civil wars created widespread turmoil and destruction that spread far beyond the battlegrounds. It is thought that one out of every four adult males took up arms,[3] representing the departure of many fathers, brothers, uncles and nephews who were gone to kill or be killed. Contemporaries perceived that the conflict tore through the fabric of society to the very core of the family unit. Sir John Oglander wrote for posterity in his commonplace book, 'Thou wouldest think it strange if I should tell thee there was a time in England when brothers killed brothers, cousins cousins, and friends their friends [...] When thou wentest to bed at night, thou knewest not whether thou shouldest be murdered afore day.'[4] As Barbara Donagan's chapter has shown, the civil wars created a dynamic in which victims were all too familiar with their assailants.[5] Thus, after the conflict was over, a desire for revenge was often personal and closely felt.

Parliament's victory over the Stuart monarchy led to the establishment of a republic between 1649 and 1660, during which a succession of regimes attempted to create a lasting political settlement through various constitutional experiments.[6] The most durable of these were the Protectoral governments beginning in 1653, which were led by a monarch-in-all-but-name, Oliver Cromwell as Lord Protector. When Oliver died in 1658, and his son Richard failed to rally even the passive support that had sustained his father, the edifice quickly crumbled. In early 1660 George Monck, the Commonwealth's general in Scotland, gathered his forces and moved south to confront the collapsing military regime in London. Monck and his supporters returned those MPs who had been purged from parliament in 1648 because they desired to negotiate a settlement with the king, and then forced an election.[7] The return of these MPs ensured a more favourable basis of support for monarchical government and the new Convention Parliament duly voted for the return of the Stuart monarchy in May 1660 in the person of Charles I's eldest son, Charles II, who had spent the last decade in impoverished exile on the continent.

Charles II realised that he owed his restoration to the sudden surge of support from erstwhile enemies such as Monck. The Declaration of Breda dated 4 April 1660 was designed to consolidate this sea change in political sympathies. Charles chose to compose the Declaration with the advice of his closest confidants and ministers at the time, Sir Edward Hyde, Chancellor, Secretary of State Sir Edward Nicholas, and James Butler, Marquis of Ormonde.[8] The Declaration attempted to allay the fears of those who had acted against

---

3   Carlton, *Going to the Wars*, p. 340.
4   Bamford, ed., *Royalist's Notebook*, p. 103.
5   See Barbara Donagan's chapter in this volume.
6   Smith, 'Struggle for New Constitutional and Institutional Forms', pp. 15–34.
7   Underdown, *Pride's Purge*.
8   Hutton, *The Restoration*, p. 108.

Charles and his father by offering a general pardon.[9] A promise was made that
'no crime whatsoever committed against us or our royal father before the publication of this shall ever rise in judgement or be brought in question against any
of them', other than those whom parliament chose to except.[10] Their desire was
to appease old enemies and reconcile a society still fractured by the divisions of
the civil wars.[11] To do so, however, they would need to incorporate the support
of all Charles's subjects, a task that proved far more complicated than pacifying
only that section of society represented by his erstwhile opponents.

Charles II's wish to forgive and forget was in contrast to the hopes of many
of those who, either through their own acts of loyalty to the House of Stuart
or their attempts to avoid getting involved, had been labelled as royalist during the conflict.[12] The last thing on many of their minds was clemency. The
eighth Earl of Derby, for example, whose father became a royalist martyr after
his execution by the Commonwealth powers in 1651, made clear his desire 'to
revenge a father's bloud'. His belief was that after rebellion society must be
'purified by the blood of the most heinously guilty', as a 'fitting sacrifice'.[13]
Many royalists had endured years of persecution prior to 1660 and wanted to
settle old scores. That in general their treatment by the Long Parliament and
the Protectoral regimes during the 1640s and 50s had been motivated less by
vengeance and more by the necessity of raising money made little difference.[14]
Beginning in 1643, royalists' lands were sequestered for their 'delinquency'
or 'malignancy', the former (in more than 3,000 cases) resulting in heavy
composition fines before they were released, the latter (in 780 cases) leading
to permanent confiscation and sale. To add to their penury, in 1655 they had
been penalised with the decimation tax (a 10 per cent income tax) to fund the
Protectorate's militia, and this came on top of all the other taxes needed to
maintain armies in all three kingdoms of up to 60,000 men. Dignity and the
means of making a living were also forfeited when convicted royalists had been
purged from their lay and clerical offices. The banning of the Book of Common

9 Miller, *After the Civil Wars*, pp. 161–62.
10 The Declaration is printed in *Journal of the House of Lords: Volume 11: 1660–1666*, pp. 6–9;
   Keeble, *The Restoration*, pp. 69–70.
11 For further details on the making of the Declaration, the subsequent Act of Indemnity
   and the roles played by Charles II and his advisors see my forthcoming PhD thesis,
   'Disappointed Royalists in Restoration England and Wales', University of Cambridge.
12 The term 'royalist' is a problematic one as, by 1660, it was used by a wide variety of people,
   many of whom had actually fought against the king in the civil wars. For the purpose
   of this essay, however, it is used to define those who were labelled as royalist delinquents
   by the parliamentary and Commonwealth regimes for the purpose of prosecution.
13 'Mandate of Charles Earl of Derby for the Trial of William Christian', pp. 1–2.
14 Gentles, 'Sales of Crown Lands', p. 614.

Prayer even prevented them from openly worshipping as they had done, and would again.[15] In the 1650s Cromwell had aimed for the 'healing and settling' of a society divided by civil war, but failed to achieve reconciliation and to prevent continued tensions or royalist plots prior to 1660.[16]

Charles II was thus faced with the dilemma of either pleasing his loyal supporters or appeasing his erstwhile enemies. To grant royalists their hopes and expectations would potentially alienate those who had brought about the dissolution of monarchy in 1649. Returning land forfeited for royalism, for example, would be to take it out of the hands of purchasers, many of whom had been supporters of the parliamentarian regimes.[17] The dilemma was exacerbated by the fact that soon after the Restoration rumours of plots and risings were rife, leaving Charles and his ministers feeling decidedly nervous that the potential for renewed conflict and upheaval was simmering under the surface of society. Assisted by this state of heightened suspicion, the government was effective in discovering and quashing plans for rebellion. Several conspiracies were exposed before they had chance to become reality, such as the Tong Plot in 1662, and a planned revolt by Thomas Blood and his co-conspirators in 1663, which was brought to an abrupt end the day before it was due to take place. Risings that actually got underway, such as Venner's rebellion in January 1661, never posed a serious challenge to the new regime because of the rebels' lack of strength and the efficiency of the government's response.[18] However, the presence of these plots made the new regime even more cognisant of the need to placate erstwhile enemies, often at the cost of disappointing old friends.

Questions of retribution or compromise similar to those faced by Charles II and his ministers have been deliberated by scholars of post-conflict resolution in the present-day context. The legal theory that defines this field is known as transitional justice. It was first developed in the 1990s among legal scholars, and within a few years had grown into a new field of scholarship.[19] The concept has proved somewhat 'slippery' to define,[20] yet an enduring definition

---

15 Not that the ban prevented clandestine Anglican worship from continuing: Hardacre, *Royalists during the Puritan Revolution*, p. 131.

16 Davis, *Oliver Cromwell*, pp. 169–70, 180; Hardacre, *Royalists during the Puritan Revolution*, pp. 120–22.

17 Thirsk, 'Restoration Land Settlement', pp. 315–16.

18 Greaves, *Deliver Us From Evil*, pp. 6–7, 50–53. For a more detailed discussion of Restoration plots and risings such as Venner's Rebellion see Greaves, *Deliver Us From Evil*.

19 Bell, 'Transitional Justice, Interdisciplinarity', p. 7.

20 Roht-Arriaza and Mariezcurrena, eds., *Transitional Justice in the Twenty-First Century*, p. 1. Bell has very recently noted the need to clarify the concept's definition: Bell, 'Transitional Justice, Interdisciplinarity', p. 23.

offered in 2000 by Ruti Teitel, a legal scholar, is 'the conception of justice in periods of political transition'.[21] Theorists of transitional justice have deliberated over how governments can move societies forwards from a traumatic past towards a peaceful and reconciled future. A particular focus has been the role of law and the political choices of governing bodies during these periods of transition. Attention was originally focused on twentieth-century regime changes, beginning in response to transitions towards democratic forms of government in Eastern Europe and Central America during the late 1980s and early 1990s.[22] In recent years the term has been used more broadly to consider a wider range of political and cultural transitions and social goals, and has expanded to incorporate the insights of a broad range of disciplines including ethics, philosophy, political science, psychology, sociology, theology and history.[23] The social scientist Jon Elster has drawn attention to how historical study can inform transitional justice theory in his recent work, *Closing the Books*. Elster offers a comparative analysis of historic transitional justice using over thirty case studies of regime changes, from Athens in the fifth century BC to the present.[24] The Restoration of 1660, in its attempt to make a transition between two radically different regimes after a period of conflict, is discussed briefly as one of Elster's case studies.[25] His work, however, is oriented more towards informing transitional justice scholarship than historical knowledge. By contrast, this chapter will take the historian's perspective, exploring the Restoration of 1660 and its relationship to transitional justice theory as a way of testing how an interdisciplinary approach towards early modern post-conflict resolution may benefit historical scholarship. The chapter's conclusions will also point more broadly towards what can be gained from a dialogue between legal scholars and historians.

There are, of course, many potential pitfalls to applying a modern legal theory to an early modern case study, such as the danger of reading historical evidence inappropriately in an attempt to make it fit with a theoretical model at the cost of letting the evidence itself drive interpretation. Another danger is that of anachronism. Scholars of transitional justice working on modern-day case studies have argued that each case should be viewed in its local context

---

21 Teitel, *Transitional Justice*, p. 3.
22 Bell, 'Transitional Justice, Interdisciplinarity', p. 7.
23 Bell, for example, has recognised the shift to a broader conception of 'transitional justice as a tool for a range of political and social goals beyond accountability': Bell, 'Transitional Justice, Interdisciplinarity', pp. 8–9; Leebaw, 'Irreconcilable Goals', p. 103; Lutz, 'Transitional Justice', p. 326.
24 Elster, *Closing the Books*.
25 Ibid., pp. 49–51.

and treated as unique, based upon factors such as culture, custom and history.[26] Such sensitivity is required to an even greater degree when we are exploring a case study that occurred 350 years ago. For example, the issue of religion in conflict resolution has not been a significant focus of transitional justice literature, yet religion was central to the civil wars and integral to the Restoration settlement. We are also dealing with transitions between very different forms of government: changes between republics and monarchies in the early modern period are not the same as transitions between authoritarian and democratic forms of government in the modern era. Moreover, historians do not encounter the past in the same way as those who are implementing and theorising transitional justice for purposes in the present. Nevertheless, it will be argued here that there are benefits to be found in a dialogue between historical research and current legal theory. If used carefully, this approach has the potential to raise new questions with which to study the past. It can provide a new appreciation of the complexity of conflict resolution, point to continuities in the human response and highlight the central role played by civilians.

Ruti Teitel has defined the forms that law takes during periods of transition as 'punishment, historical enquiry, reparations, purges, and constitution making'.[27] Although it might be argued that all these elements could be applicable to the Restoration settlements of 1660–61, this chapter will focus on the issue of reparation as a case study to highlight the complex role of civilian participation in conflict resolution.[28] Reparatory justice focuses on restorative measures for those who consider themselves victims of conflict or a preceding regime,[29] making it an appropriate aspect from which to study the royalist response to the Restoration settlement. In this way, transitional justice theory offers a new perspective on Restoration historiography. While historians have acknowledged the disappointment felt by parts of society towards the Restoration settlements, there is still more work to be done on their consequences.[30] For the purpose of this chapter, England will be central

---

26 Teitel, 'Transitional Justice Genealogy', p. 76; Leebaw, 'Irreconcilable Goals', p. 117; Lambourne, 'Transitional Justice and Peacebuilding', p. 47.

27 Teitel, *Transitional Justice*, p. 6.

28 For an example of how other elements may relate to the Restoration of 1660 see James, 'The Trials of the Regicides: Transitional Justice, Memory, and Law in Restoration England'. James's dissertation studies the trial of the regicides from the combined perspectives of collective memory studies and the criminal justice debates within transitional justice literature.

29 Teitel had described its diverse forms as 'reparations, damages, remedies, redress, restitution, compensation, rehabilitation, tribute': Teitel, *Transitional Justice*, p. 119.

30 For examples of historians' discussion of royalist disappointment see Miller, *After the Civil Wars*; Keeble, *The Restoration*.

to the discussion although the questions raised could equally be applied to Ireland, Scotland and Wales. The chapter will focus on the position of royalists in order to highlight how conceptions of the war and its aftermath held by some sections of civilian society in 1660 played a formative role in attempts to reconcile a society in the transition from conflict to peace. Royalist civilians are defined here as those who did not hold a military office after 1660. Although after the Restoration a number of royalists placed great emphasis on their previous military service for Charles I and his son, for many their position had shifted in post-conflict society from military to civilian. This transition, and the way in which it was encountered and experienced, is in itself an important element of post-conflict resolution.

1

S HORTLY AFTER Charles II was restored to the throne a bill was introduced to make good on the king's promises from Breda. The bill passed into law on 29 August 1660 as the 'Act for free and general pardon, indemnity and oblivion'. It offered a comprehensive pardon for all crimes since 1638, in order to encompass the start of the civil wars with Scotland. This was a sweeping gesture of royal clemency targeted at reconciling the civil war divisions that still fractured society. Charles II was clear from the start that he wanted as few people as possible excepted from pardon. 'It will make them good subjects to me,' he told parliament, 'and good friends and neighbours to you.'[31] The regicides who had signed the death warrant for the execution of Charles I were the principal exceptions to the more general royal clemency. Charles had previously offered pardon to all but seven, and when Monck introduced the bill on 9 May he proposed only five men.[32] Out of a list of around 60 originally debated, only 33 were finally excepted. Twenty-nine regicides were put to trial and ten were executed: the scapegoats for a nation's crimes.[33] Charles's greatest desire was that the old civil war differences and animosities between his subjects could be peaceably smoothed over and forgotten, led by the example of the new regime's acts of clemency. The Convention Parliament as a whole did nothing to overtly contest this. Their moderation may partly be explained by the fact that the Commons was relatively balanced between members with parliamentary and royalist backgrounds. Although some areas, such as deciding on who should be excepted from pardon, were hotly debated, in general the two groups tended

31 *Journal of the House of Lords: Volume 11: 1660–1666*, pp. 107–09.

32 Keeble, *The Restoration*, p. 72.

33 Hutton, *The Restoration*, pp. 132–34; Keeble, *The Restoration*, p. 55.

to cancel each other out. Many members were also strongly influenced by the king's desire for mercy.[34] To avoid stigmatising Charles's former enemies, the Act of Indemnity declared that 'no crime whatsoever committed against his Majesty or his Royal Father shall hereafter rise in judgment or be brought in question against any of them'. Furthermore, it stated that for the space of three years if any person should 'presume maliciously to call [...] any name or names, or other word of reproach anyway tending to revive the memory of the late differences or the occasions thereof' they would be fined.[35] The fines, however, were mild, and would not have provided much incentive to informers who would have expected to face the wrath of their Cavalier neighbours.[36]

Charles and his advisors also sought to appease the king's old enemies by attempting to settle the question of land ownership and through the provision of Crown appointments. The new Privy Council, for example, represented a mixture of Cromwellians, parliamentarians and royalists.[37] A mixed and balanced appointment of advisors made political sense for the new regime, but ensured frustration and bitterness for many royalists. Allen Apsley wrote to the Earl of Clarendon, the king's Lord Chancellor, in June 1660 to warn him of 'the language of very many of the kings party who think his enemys have much more favour at Court then his friends'.[38] Charles passed the land question on to parliament, but they could find no easy solution to the fundamental problem that returning land to its original royalist owners would mean taking it out of the hands of many purchasers who had supported the Commonwealth and Protectorate. What made things still more problematic was that while all legislation lacking the royal assent (ie. all laws passed since 1641) were deemed null and void, 'The Act of Confirmation of Judicial Proceedings', passed in 1661, judged all sales that had not been made directly by the Interregnum regimes as legal.[39] So all land acquired under Acts of Sale were void, but those sales made by royalists in order to raise money to pay fines to release property or buy back part of estates were now legally binding. The status of all those sales that had since been made on royalist property to second- and third-hand buyers was left ambiguous. Ironically enough, many royalists had bought back land taken from them by the state, and they now found the crippling mortgages they had taken out were legally enforceable. The parliament passed no specific legislation after the Restoration to help royalists regain their land.

---

34 Miller, *After the Civil Wars*, pp. 162, 165.
35 'An Act of Free and Generall Pardon Indemnity and Oblivion', pp. 226–34.
36 Seaward, *Cavalier Parliament*, p. 74. Hutton has noted only one prosecution under it: Hutton, *The Restoration*, p. 135.
37 Keeble, *The Restoration*, p. 82.
38 Bod. Clarendon MS v. 73, fos. 63–64.
39 Keeble, *The Restoration*, p. 81.

While some of the more influential managed to regain estates through private Acts in parliament, many were left without remedy except via the problematic and expensive recourse of pursuing their cases privately in the law courts.[40]

A further problem was that the Crown did not have enough resources of its own to repair all the losses sustained by royalists.[41] It was thus not the case that Charles II was ungracious or unsympathetic to those who had served him faithfully, and indeed there were certainly some of those who had stood loyal to the House of Stuart who benefited from the king's bounty. High-profile royalists close to the king who had been in exile with him were well rewarded, such as James Butler and Edward Hyde, who were granted estates and made Duke of Ormonde and Earl of Clarendon, respectively. Charles also used his patronage in the formation of the new professional army to provide for some who had fought in royalist armies with posts, although many were still left disappointed.[42] In general, however, there were simply not enough available resources to satiate all those who had remained loyal to the Stuart cause while achieving the balance necessary to pacify old enemies.

As royalists witnessed their old enemies being treated with forgiveness and patronage, a joke became popular that said that the king granted indemnity to his enemies and oblivion to his friends.[43] Like most decent jokes, it had some truth in it. There existed a widespread impression that those who had fought against the king had done better out of the Restoration than those who had supported him. Some contemporaries believed that justice, and God's will, had not been done. John Evelyn, for example, noted that during a sermon in January 1662 the Dean of Windsor judged the current unseasonable weather, which prevented the fleet from leaving for Portugal to collect Charles II's new queen, Catherine of Braganza, as evidence of punishment by God for 'the neglect of exacting justice on offenders' regarding the decision to reprieve some of the regicides from execution.[44] Sir Richard Bulstrode reflected in his memoirs that Charles had been all too willing 'to disoblige his old Friends, in hopes of getting new ones' and that 'they who suffered for his late royal Father, were not the better for all his immoderate Bounties'.[45] The aggrieved royalists were even identified as a type in Restoration society. Samuel Pepys referred to them in 1665 as the 'discontented Cavaliers that thinks their Loyalty is not considered'.[46]

---

40 Thirsk, 'Restoration Land Settlement', pp. 318–20.
41 Hutton, *The Restoration*, p. 138; Keeble, *The Restoration*, p. 83.
42 Childs, *Army of Charles II*, pp. 18–19. Childs, *Army of Charles II*, pp. 18–19.
43 Burnet, *History of My Own Time*, Vol. I, p. 289.
44 Evelyn, *Diary of John Evelyn*, p. 434.
45 Bulstrode, *Memoirs and Reflections*, pp. 224–26.
46 Pepys, *Diary of Samuel Pepys*, p. 303 (19 Nov. 1665).

Scholars of transitional justice have recognised the impossibility of compensating all who have been the victims of warfare and regime change, not just because of factors such as limited resources but because of its impact on reconciliation and state-building. Crucially, where the line is drawn by those in authority is seen as a key factor in the creation of a new social identity for the new regime.[47] It could be argued that Charles's attitude towards fully addressing the material losses of royalists in the Restoration settlements reflects a similar theme. If Charles had provided full reparation to a broader section of royalist society the new social identity may have been divided along the same lines as the civil war, rather than nurturing the healed society that he so desired. But do the problems of material reparation fully explain the depth of royalist disappointment in reparatory justice?

Scholarship on transitional justice has suggested new ways of understanding how justice is perceived by members of society during periods of transition between regimes. Ruti Teitel has researched descriptions of reparatory justice in periods of transition that occur in the Bible. Since biblical references were well known in mid-seventeenth-century England, an intensely Bible-literate society, they may also shed light on how those who had suffered as royalists during the wars conceptualised reparation after 1660. Teitel explores the story of the Israelites' Exodus from Egypt in the Old Testament.[48] After four hundred years of being enslaved to the Egyptians, God, through Moses, offered the Israelites the prospect of freedom. At the same time he told them to take (or borrow, depending on interpretation) the gold and jewellery belonging to the Egyptians and dress themselves in these along with the Egyptians' clothes.[49] Thus, in addition to financial reparation in the form of gold, the freed slaves took on the trappings and identity of their erstwhile oppressors. Teitel suggests that this reversal of roles is linked to the word 'redress', which links 'attire, status, and the restoration of dignity'.[50] The word's original sense and usage relate to an outward show of restoration – to set something upright once more to a restored position.[51] Thus, in the seventeenth century, reparation or redress may have been associated with the establishment of public dignity and identity as well as economic restoration through material sources. It was also seen as God's will, or providence.

The story of Moses and the Israelites' exodus from Egypt was a particularly resonant one in mid-seventeenth-century England. Cromwell's supporters

---

47 Teitel, *Transitional Justice*, p. 137.
48 Ibid., pp. 120–21; Exodus 3.
49 Teitel, *Transitional Justice*, pp. 120–21.
50 Ibid., p. 120.
51 *OED*.

referred to him as a Moses figure leading them from oppression into a promised land in which political and religious liberty thrived.[52] Royalists felt their
own affinity with the Exodus story, and indeed it may have shaped their
expectations of justice and redress in the deliverance of the Restoration. Sir
John Oglander described life in the 1650s thus: 'instead of our former joy, comfort & true liberty we have now as bad as Egyptian slavery'.[53] Gilbert Ironside,
soon to be Bishop of Bristol, preached a sermon to mark the Restoration in
which he likened the royalist experience of the civil wars and Interregnum to
the persecution of the Israelites. 'What Peace had *Israel* in *Egypt* for near 200
yeares together, or in *Babylon* for 70', stated Ironside, 'I am sure our Jerusalem
complaines, *that the plowers made long furrowes upon her back* [...] and we our
selves have lived to see, and feel, and smart under this Truth'.[54]

Furthermore, legal theorists have argued that restoring the public dignity
of members of society who have been victims of previous regimes, which they
refer to as 'moral reparation', plays an important public and symbolic role in
repairing shame and humiliation after conflict. Teitel gives as an example the
modern-day Truth and Reconciliation Commissions in Chile, which held a
mandate for 'moral reparation' to 'publicly restore the good name of those who
perished from the stigma of having been falsely accused as enemies of the state'.
In Chile the names of the victims were flashed onto a stadium's electronic
scoreboards for public viewing while they were read out.[55] Teitel also argues
that moral reparation can take the form of 'symbolic trappings' such as titles
and medals, or be applied to acts of collective memory such as the naming of
streets or the building of monuments.[56] In early modern society, where dignity
and honour were valued so highly, surely this form of reparatory justice must
have been crucial?

Certainly, there were plans in the early 1660s to honour the king's loyal supporters in this way through new orders of knighthood. One was the Order of
the Royal Oak, which below the surface appears to have been mainly a money-
making exercise to boost the king's coffers. However, another, the Esquires
of the Martyred King, does seem to have had a genuine objective to benefit
suffering royalists as it proposed that the members of the order would receive
an office in addition to title and membership of the order. It was specifically
designed to recognise the royalist who had faithfully suffered. A canton of their
family shield would include a heart and crown signifying that their hearts had

---

52 Morrill, 'Cromwell, Oliver'.
53 Bamford, ed., *Royalist's Notebook*, p. 132.
54 Ironside, 'Sermon Preached at Dorchester in the County of Dorcet', p. 15.
55 Teitel, *Transitional Justice*, p. 126.v
56 Ibid., pp. 137–38.

been fixed to the crown through the worst of times.[57] Neither of these orders came to fruition, probably because of the new regime's fear of alienating old enemies and re-opening civil war divisions.[58] There was no explicit, public or symbolic move to restore the dignity and honour of many royalists.

Why did Charles II proceed in such a restrained and moderate way towards his former enemies? Historians such as Ronald Hutton have credited it to Charles's lack of a personal grudge against them. Hutton contrasts this with the king's actions in Scotland, where Charles's experiences in that kingdom during his problematic alliance with the kirk party in 1650–51 'left him with livid animosities'. These animosities are seen by Hutton as a key motivation behind the execution of certain individuals such as Archibald Campbell, Marquis of Argyll, in May 1661.[59] Charles remained offended and infuriated by Argyll's 'uselessness to him in 1650–1' and for his decision to join the Cromwellians in 1654 rather than support the Earl of Glencairn's rising for the royalist cause. In none of his kingdoms, however, would Charles seek revenge 'unless public opinion permitted it'.[60] This has led historians to view Charles's choice to forgive his old enemies as a cynical move of self-interest, calculated to appease whichever groups in society were the most likely to turn against him. Others have labelled it as conservative pragmatism on the part of the king and his advisors.[61] Perhaps there were more complex considerations, however.

2

RECENT DEVELOPMENTS in transitional justice literature have linked reparative and restorative justice to a new emphasis on building long-term stability in societies after conflict.[62] Integral to this goal is civilian participation which, it is argued, can achieve goals of community reconciliation.[63] These objectives incorporate psychological and emotional aspects of reparative and restorative justice and emphasise the shift to viewing civilians as 'subjects rather

---

57 Both these orders are usefully discussed in Matikkala, *Orders of Knighthood*, pp. 67–76, and are further studied in my forthcoming PhD thesis.

58 Matikkala, *Orders of Knighthood*, p. 76. The 1811 publication of Dugdale's list of those intended for the Order footnotes that it was abandoned because 'it was thought proper to lay it aside, lest it might create heats and animosities, and open those wounds afresh, which at that time were thought prudent should be healed': Dugdale, *Antient Usage*, pp. 160–72.

59 Hutton, *Charles the Second*, pp. 141–42, 171.

60 Ibid., pp. 80–81, 142.

61 For example, Miller, *After the Civil Wars*, pp. 164–65; Hutton, *The Restoration*, pp. 137–38.

62 For example, Lambourne, 'Transitional Justice and Peacebuilding', pp. 28–48.

63 Lambourne, 'Transitional Justice and Peacebuilding', pp. 35, 47.

than objects' of transitional justice.[64] Wendy Lambourne has recently written about the importance of overcoming 'the psychological barriers between people created by experiences of war' in order to transform societies from conflict to peace, stressing that this must be based on the participation of all members of society.[65] It has been acknowledged that in order to come to terms with the past, societies benefit from the 'public airing' of personal narratives such as can be facilitated through bodies such as the Truth and Reconciliation Commissions, and the opportunity for dialogue that reaches across political and social divisions.[66]

Yet Charles II and his ministers tried to remove the Restoration's troubled past through a selective approach to silence and forgetting. Charles was always eager to relive for posterity his escape from the battle of Worcester in 1651 when he attempted to claim his crown using military force. Neither did he deter the commemoration of the regicide with an annual day of fasting and prayer to take place on 30 January, or the commissioning of a mausoleum for his martyred father in 1678.[67] The more divisive elements of the past, however, represented in some part by those royalists who wished to settle old scores, were largely stifled by the enforced emphasis on forgiving and forgetting. In general the Restoration styled itself on an attempt to turn back the clock and erase the years of war, exile and parliamentary rule, save only for selected events such as the regicide to warn against future rebellion. Even Charles's reign was dated as beginning directly after the death of his father in 1649, obliterating the intervening period. This ethos, which was manifest in the Act of Indemnity and Oblivion, was at odds with a society that was still fractured by animosity resulting from the memory of civil war. Teitel has argued that desire for reparation lingers rather than diminishes with time, while Lambourne has noted that where lack of material and psychological reparation remains, it is far harder for societies to forget and move forward.[68] From the perspective of transitional justice theory, then, Charles's attempt to heal society had a long-term flaw.

The restoration of the French monarchy in 1814 and 1815 provides an informative analogous case study.[69] The issue of *biens nationaux*, land that had been

---

64 Ibid., p. 47.
65 Ibid., pp. 34–35. The participation of society as a whole is also stressed by others as a direction for the future. See, for example, Lutz, 'Transitional Justice', pp. 325–26.
66 Roht-Arriaza and Mariezcurrena, eds., *Transitional Justice in the Twenty-First Century*, p. 4. Leebaw, 'Irreconcilable Goals', p. 111.
67 Lacey, *Cult of King Charles the Martyr*, pp. 129–71.
68 Teitel, *Transitional Justice*, pp. 9, 140; Lambourne, 'Transitional Justice and Peace-building', p. 42.
69 Elster also features this case study in his book and briefly notes the similarity with the restoration of the Stuart monarchy: Elster, *Closing the Books*, pp. 24–46, 49.

assimilated and transferred by the French Revolutionary state, became a lingering issue in society after the restoration.[70] Parish priests, for example, were known to deny last rites to purchasers unless they had given up the property.[71] As with the royalist land settlement in England, some of the purchasers of the *biens nationaux* were supporters of the preceding regime, creating the dilemma of how to restore land while maintaining political stability. In France, as in England, one solution was silence and forgetting. The French government made it a crime to question the legitimacy of the new purchasers' ownership of *biens nationaux* property.[72] The bitterness over the settlement of property after the French Restoration lingered into the twentieth century. Lefebvre highlighted how the heirs of *biens nationaux* property were still the source of hostility in local communities prior to the First World War.[73] Moreover, after the second restoration of the French monarchy in 1815, which took a more rigorous approach to punishment than the first restoration in 1814, 'ultra-royalists' took revenge into their own hands on a widespread scale. The illegal 'white terror' saw mass atrocities committed by ultra-royalists in a wave of revenge during which several hundreds were killed and many more injured.[74] The newly restored French king abhorred this wave of vengeance, and by its occurrence effectively lost control of authority over justice.[75] If Charles II had offered a free rein to royalist desires for revenge and retribution, it is possible that conflict on a broad scale might have resumed.

3

THE PURPOSE of this interdisciplinary approach which incorporates transitional justice theory is not to judge as right or wrong the choices of Charles II and his ministers to prioritise the appeasement of the king's old enemies, some of whom had made his restoration possible, or to criticise their attempts at reconciliation. Indeed it has further highlighted the complexity of the issues they faced. Although Charles II and his advisors would, of course, have had no concept of transitional justice, an engagement with the theory has emphasised complicated factors that may have influenced their decision making: their fear of re-opening civil war division, or encouraging widespread

---

70　Price, *Perilous Crown*, pp. 52, 70, 116–17.

71　Elster, *Closing the Books*, p. 38.

72　Ibid., p. 39.

73　Georges Lefebvre, *Les paysans du Nord pendant la Révolution Française* (Paris: Armand Colin, 1924), cited in Elster, *Closing the Books*, p. 44.

74　Price, *Perilous Crown*, p. 84; Elster, *Closing the Books*, pp. 32–33.

75　Price, *Perilous Crown*, p. 84; Elster, *Closing the Books*, p. 46.

acts of revenge and renewed conflict; their need to create a new social identity for the purpose of state-building that marked a clear break from the past; and the lack of means to compensate all, which meant that only some who had suffered as royalists received the benefit of the king's patronage, leaving the rest to question whether justice had been done. There was no correct answer between pacifying old enemies or rewarding loyal friends. It was a decision based on the contingencies and values of the day. In this sense, a drawback of transitional justice theory in an historical context is that its modern-day perspective makes any counterfactual judgement on the legitimacy of decision making in the historic past anachronistic and unhelpful. What transitional justice can offer historians, however, is a different perspective from which to ask new questions of the past, questions that might otherwise be overlooked. In terms of the Restoration in 1660, a challenge awaiting historical enquiry is to fully explore whether continued loss of dignity through lack of symbolic reparation was one reason why royalist bitterness may have festered in society after 1660.[76] As the story of the Exodus suggests, some royalists may have seen their reparation as something which, by God's will, should have restored their good name as well as their fortunes.

An interdisciplinary approach to understanding early modern post-conflict resolution suggests the benefit of dialogue between legal scholars and historians: it may increase our knowledge of the past while informing our future. For legal scholars the approach offers fruitful case studies for the forward-thinking objectives of transitional justice. For the historian, exploring the Restoration of 1660 from the perspective of transitional justice theory not only brings about new questions, but differs from a traditional historical approach by placing greater emphasis on the implications and consequences of political choices rather than the causes behind them. This has helped to highlight the fundamental political role played by Restoration society in the process of transition. The new regime chose to impose a culture of selective forgetting and silence on civilians in an attempt to reconcile a traumatic past. By doing so the participation and support of all sections of society, a mandate at the heart of current transitional justice theory on long-term peace-building, was forfeited for the purpose of perceived political necessity. This had consequences for how people viewed the Restoration. The ordinary men and women who had been labelled as royalist delinquents by the Interregnum regimes for the purpose of prosecution, for example, may have felt that the new emphasis on clemency and moderation towards past actions, and selective forgetting and silence, disenfranchised their perspective on the past and their expectations for the future. Troubled memories of the past could not so easily be swept under the

---

76 This is a question addressed by my forthcoming PhD thesis.

carpet, however. Although renewed civil war was avoided, and Charles II kept his throne, the trauma of civil war continued to haunt Restoration society. Its legacy is evident in the Exclusion Crisis of 1678–83 when successive parliaments sought to exclude Charles II's Catholic brother and heir from succession to the throne. As Jonathan Scott has suggested, contemporary responses to the troubles of 1678–80 and of 1681–83 were an 'extended, and troubled, rumination upon the nation's own past'.[77] The crisis focused its demonology on the Irish rebellion of 1641 and the onset of the civil wars,[78] and it was partly through the use of public memory that the government eventually quelled it. This re-remembering played on the threat that the war could come again, bringing with it the potential for material and physical loss, and social and religious chaos that cut to the heart of the family unit. Instead of a thing of the past, people saw the potential for civil war to be very much in the present. Its enduring, festering presence in Restoration society emphasises the pivotal role that public memory and opinion, and thus the perspective of civilians, play in making a successful transition from post-conflict instability and insecurity to concord and peace. The new regime may have avoided another civil war, but this was a nervous state that perceived itself to be vulnerable – contemporaries continued to be disturbed and discomforted by a threat of renewed conflict and chaos simmering just below the surface of Restoration society. The lack of material and psychological reparation towards royalists, limiting the extent of civilian participation in the transition to secure peace, may have been a contributing factor.

---

77 Scott, 'England's Troubles', p. 126.
78 Ibid., pp. 122–23.

PART II

The State, Soldiers and Civilians

6

The Administration of War and French Prisoners of War in Britain, 1756–1763

ERICA CHARTERS

THE INTIMATE relationship between warfare and political administration in early modern Europe has been extensively detailed through the debates regarding the military revolution. First outlined by Michael Roberts in 1955 and thoroughly expanded by Geoffrey Parker, the concept of the military revolution explains the growth of the armed forces during the early modern period, and fundamentally links it to the expansion of state power. While historians continue to debate the extent of this revolution, as well as its timing, geographical location and causality, its widespread influence demonstrates the energy of investigations into the relationship between war and the development of the early modern European state.[1]

As noted in the general introduction, one of the main issues with which the concept of 'total war' is concerned is the extent of the mobilisation of state and society. In this respect, the administration of war is clearly relevant to the concept of total war. As Parker's thesis of the military revolution suggests, the development of the early modern state was the direct result of the demands of warfare. These demands led early modern states to devote a majority of their resources to war. By the same token, the administration of war provides various insights into the nature of civilian–military relations, the fundamental aspect of total war. A focus on the logistics of war and the management of state resources demonstrates how extensively the demands of war reached into early modern

---

1   Rogers, ed., *Military Revolution Debate* reprints the initial arguments of Roberts and Parker, as well as seminal responses.

civil society. Yet the administration of war also demonstrates the inapplicability of 'total war' to the early modern period, as it collapses in on itself: the early modern European state was, by definition, concerned with war-making.

As an introduction to the following chapters, which explore, in various ways, the connections between warfare and the state, this essay analyses war administration in seventeenth- and eighteenth-century Europe via a case study of administration in practice: British management of French prisoners of war during the Seven Years War (1756–63). Such a study illustrates the variety of civilian–military interactions during this period and the relationship between war, civilians and the state's administrative structures.

1. WAR AND THE STATE

WHILE HISTORIANS and political scientists have long recognised the funda-mental role of war in the formation of the state, the thesis of the military revolution revitalised early modern military history, not least by demonstrating the relevance of warfare to areas beyond military history. In general, Roberts, Parker and other writers on the military revolution are concerned with the transformation of European armed forces from small groups of independent and mostly mercenary forces to large-scale, complex, disciplined and increasingly permanent and professional forces. Roberts pointed out that such transforma-tions – especially the prodigious increase in the size of the armed forces – had profound effects on the authority of the state. Not only did states increasingly have a real military monopoly (including naval power) but also, 'This develop-ment, and the new style of warfare itself, called for new administrative methods and standards; and the new administration was from the beginning centralised and royal.'[2] Clearly, the growth in army size also intensified the impact that war had on society, and not simply through the experience of larger battles.

As Parker remarked, 'The greater destructiveness, the greater economic costs, and the greater administrative challenge of the augmented armies made war more of a burden and more of a problem for the civilian population and their rulers than ever before.'[3] Although Parker challenged Roberts's thesis to some extent, he also built extensively upon its foundations, most notably through his in-depth analysis of the role of innovations in defensive fortifica-tions, and by tying the revolution to the rise of the West's global dominance. Parker's argument has received much attention, not least from historians and political theorists challenging and modifying various aspects, based on their

---

2   Roberts, 'Military Revolution', p. 20.
3   Parker, *Military Revolution*, p. 2.

own areas of expertise. Jeremy Black, for example, has pointed to the details of warfare beyond Europe, claiming a different chronology and arguing that it was not simply superior technology or tactics that drove the West's dominance but also techniques and practices such as financial institutions.[4]

Likewise, various historians have modified Parker's thesis through detailed research of areas and regimes other than Parker's own area of speciality, the Spanish army in the sixteenth and seventeenth centuries. France, considered the paradigm of absolutist bureaucracy and army expansion during the seventeenth century, has been studied in detail. As a result, earlier estimates of army growth have been modified downwards, while factors other than military technology – such as the growth in France's population and wealth – have been suggested as the engine behind expansion.[5]

Approaching the military revolution from another angle, historians have undermined the assumption that expansion of the state necessarily results in state rationalisation or centralisation.[6] One of the key issues regarding the role of warfare, these studies point out, in the expansion of the state is the nature of the war administration, not only because expansion does not always result in centralisation, but also because centralisation is not always the most efficient method of extracting resources for war. The eighteenth-century fiscal-military state of Britain, for example, is taken as exemplar, if not exceptional, in terms of its ability to extract resources to fund warfare and yet remain comparatively decentralised.[7] This did not mean that the British state lacked administrative structures; as various studies of the Royal Navy demonstrate, warfare during this period depended on extensive administration.[8]

The nature of administration can thus be discerned through military success and failure. At the same time, it is the impact of war on civilian society that most clearly demonstrated differences between systems of administration. Although poorly fed and poorly clothed, soldiers could, if pushed, win victories; it was civilian populations who then suffered from the depredations of ill-disciplined

---

4   Black, 'Military Revolution?', p. 103. See also his *Military Revolution?*

5   Lynn, 'Recalculating French Army Growth'; Lynn, '*Trace italienne* and the Growth of Armies'; Parrott, 'Strategy and Tactics'.

6   Most notable here is Parrott, *Richelieu's Army*, but see also Gunn, Grummitt and Cools, 'War and the State in Early Modern Europe'.

7   For Britain see Brewer, *Sinews of Power*; Jones, *War and Economy*; Braddick, *State Formation*. For beyond Britain see Glete, *War and the State*; Bonney, ed., *Rise of the Fiscal State*; Downing, *Military Revolution and Political Change*; Storrs, ed., *Fiscal–Military State in Eighteenth–Century Europe*.

8   See especially Baugh, *Naval Administration in the Age of Walpole*. For an examination of French naval administration see Pritchard, *Louis XIV's Navy*.

and hungry soldiers, even though these soldiers were officially on their side.[9] Civilians thus experienced the administration of warfare not only through the civil service and taxation, but also through exposure to the ravages of warfare, especially if administration broke down. The case of French prisoners of war held in Britain during the Seven Years War demonstrates this relationship, as the French government stopped its payments for the upkeep of its prisoners at the same time that French forces began to lose on the battlefield.

2. The Administration of Prisoners of War

ALTHOUGH THE practice of taking enemy soldiers and sailors prisoner during and after combat had been long established among early modern European armed forces, modern historians have paid little attention to details regarding enemy prisoners during the early and mid-eighteenth century. In contrast, much attention has been paid to the fate of prisoners during the Revolutionary and Napoleonic wars, so much so that it often appears as if that era established conventions regarding prisoners of war.[10] With regard to eighteenth-century British warfare, prisoners of war have been discussed only with reference to the American War of Independence (1775–83) and the treatment of prisoners, or captives, by non-European populations (especially Native Americans) during imperial warfare. Consequently, these studies are interested in prisoners of war precisely because the treatment of these prisoners challenged standard conventions.[11] A detailed examination of French prisoners held in Britain during the Seven Years War establishes both the theoretical conventions

---

9   See, for example, Lynn, 'How War Fed War'. Lynn's *Women, Armies and Warfare* also examines how the logistics of war influenced the role of women in war.

10 See, for example, Daly, 'Napoleon's Lost Legions'; Pierard, 'Un dépot de prisonniers de guerre anglais'; McKibbin, 'Citizens of Liberty, Agents of Tyranny'; Dupont, *Les prisonniers de guerre anglais en France au 18e siècle*; Bernard, *Les prisonniers de guerre du Premier Empire*. Many are local in focus: see Bennett, *French Connections: Napoleonic Prisoners of War on Parole in Leek*; Biddell, *Napoleonic Prisoners of War in and around Bishop's Waltham*; Crane, *Napoleonic Prisoners of War in Ashby de la Zouch*; James, *Prisoners of War in Dartmoor Towns*.

11 Studies of American prisoners of war during this period stress how the experience of imprisonment helped foster American identity, with little attention paid to the general context of prisons during the eighteenth century. See, for example, Cogliano, 'We All Hoisted the American Flag'; Cohen, *Yankee Sailors in British Gaols*. For attempts to redress this balance see Ranlet, 'The British, Their Virginian Prisoners, and Prison Ships of the American Revolution'; Sampson, *Escape in America*. For Europeans taken prisoner by Native Americans see Steele, 'Surrendering Rites: Prisoners on Colonial North American Frontiers'.

regarding what European powers thought they owed to captured enemy combatants as well as the standard practices regarding prisoners of war. This, in turn, demonstrates that modern European conventions regarding prisoners of war were developed prior to the Revolutionary and Napoleonic wars.

Standard conventions, or treaties, stated that enemy soldiers and sailors taken during combat were to be held prisoner for a short period of time (during the Seven Years War, this was limited to fifteen days), before being exchanged in return for an equal number of equivalent rank. During their captivity, prisoners were to be fed, accommodated and treated much as were one's own troops. They were not allowed to be recruited into one's own forces, or punished for simply being part of the enemy's forces.[12] However, such straightforward measures were difficult to establish during the realities of war. In part, this was due to the hectic nature of warfare, where accurate records and precise exchanges were difficult to maintain. But more specifically, unequal numbers of enemy prisoners were commonly taken, resulting in prisoners requiring longer-term accommodation. Alongside this, warfare during the late seventeenth and eighteenth century increasingly took place beyond the bounds of Britain and Europe. As a result, in practice during the late seventeenth and early eighteenth century, exchanges were most often loosely organised and conducted at the local level. If at sea or in the colonies, prisoners were left in neutral ports where they could be recruited into those fleets, obviating the necessity of officials taking material responsibility for enemy troops, and in theory avoiding the possibility that prisoners would immediately re-join their own forces.[13]

With the increasingly global scope of warfare during the eighteenth century, involving larger numbers of armed forces, and the recognition that this ad hoc system encouraged unequal exchanges and the return of prisoners to immediate service in their original forces, new practices emerged. Most significantly, prisoners were more regularly sent back to the captors' home country, held prisoner for longer periods of time and, overall, captured in larger numbers. Not surprisingly, the administration of these prisoners also gradually developed, and responsibilities became standardised. In Britain, the board responsible for this was the naval Sick and Hurt Board, also referred to as the Sick and Wounded Commissioners, and otherwise known as the medical department of the Admiralty.

The exact reason why the Sick and Hurt Board, partly composed of medical men, was made responsible for the care of prisoners of war is unknown. It

---

12 See, for example, Savory, 'Convention of Écluse, 1759–1762'.
13 Anderson, 'Impact on the Fleet of the Disposal of Prisoners of War'. See also Scouller, *Armies of Queen Anne*, pp. 310–21.

is most probable that the care that sick troops required, and their status as non-combatants, made them most like enemy prisoners of war. Regardless of the reasons, by 1761 the Sick and Hurt Board was responsible for overseeing 20,000 enemy prisoners stationed throughout England, not counting those on parole or in the colonies, and over 5,000 that were exchanged each year. The Commissioners of the Board decided where incoming prisoners should be stationed and monitored their care via correspondence from local authorities, often referred to as the local 'agent for prisoners' of war. The Commissioners, as officials on a navy board, reported to the Lords of the Admiralty. At the highest level, the prisoners of war were officially the responsibility of the Secretary-at-War (predominantly Viscount Barrington during this period), although their basic care was financed by the French state. Exchanges were coordinated through the French Commissaire for Prisoners (Monsieur de Moras) and the British Commissioner (Guiguer). These Commissioners had a small number of officials stationed in the other country, who were responsible for overseeing the details of prisoner exchanges (including transportation) and provided some information regarding the welfare of the prisoners.[14]

In Britain, the prisoners were stationed in various towns, most often near ports. This made use of ports' pre-existing infrastructure for sailors and other vagrant populations, such as those in Portsmouth, Plymouth, Liverpool and Exeter. Kinsale, Ireland (Cork Harbour) was also used to accommodate the prisoners, it being one part of the British Isles with barracks. Overall, more prisoners were stationed in southern towns, although locations were spread throughout Britain. In 1761 the 20,000 rank and file prisoners of war in England were stationed in Portsmouth, Winchester, Plymouth, Sissinghurst, Deal, Bristol, Liverpool, Exeter, Bideford, Falmouth and Yarmouth. Numbers varied, with Plymouth housing near 5,500 and Deal having fewer than 50.[15] At other times during the war, Penrhyn, Edinburgh and Aberdeen held prisoners, as did Guernsey, Jersey and North Shields.[16]

The daily life of prisoners was regulated similarly in extent to that of soldiers. Rank and file prisoners had fewer liberties than did officers. While the men were generally restricted to quarters, officers were allowed to go on parole (from the French for giving their word of honour that they would not use their liberty to escape). Regulations stated that officers were only allowed to travel a few miles while on parole, but complaints sent to the Sick and Hurt Board

---

14 See, for example, SHDAT, Series A 3569, letters 41, 53, 104, 220. TNA also contains various petitions regarding the condition of prisoners; see, for example, ADM 97/118.

15 NMM, ADM F/21, Sick and Wounded to Admiralty, 28 May 1761.

16 NMM, ADM F/15, Account of Prisoners of War in Great Britain and Ireland, 22 June 1757.

regarding officers travelling without guard over 20 miles to go to the horse races suggest that these were not always followed.[17] As during war, opposing European officers treated each other with respect and with gifts; this deference to rank was clearly maintained for prisoners as well.

Rank and file prisoners, like rank and file soldiers, were given less responsibility and enjoyed fewer pleasures. Their food was standard rations, although the amount provided was carefully regulated. Following official guidelines, the victualling table was posted, in French, in each prisoner of war institution.[18] Complaints from British prisoners of war held in France often concerned a lack of medical attention and the poor quality, or lack, of food.[19] The amount and type of victuals provided to prisoners was similar to that supplied on campaign, consisting of salted meats, bread and cheese. Also similar to soldiers on campaign, sutlers sold supplies to prisoners and were the source for additional necessaries, such as fruits and vegetables. Prisoners also bought their clothes from sutlers, just as soldiers paid for their uniforms, albeit through a regimental or state bounty. In the case of prisoners of war, the funds used to buy clothes and extra foodstuffs came from the Royal Bounty, the fund officially supplied by the French government, following regulations on how much was to be supplied according to the number of prisoners (the British paid three pence per day for every prisoner in France).

Local populations generally did not welcome the arrival of prisoners of war, in part because of problems finding accommodation and food, and also because the men were in poor condition, having been transported back from a losing battle and thus ill-clothed, hungry and very sickly.[20] Once settled for some time, however, it appears that prisoners could peacefully integrate, with inhabitants making money from the market that the prisoners created and benefiting from French labour. During the coronation celebrations in 1761, with Britain's victory seemingly close at hand, various provincial newspapers noted that free ale was given not only to the local poor, but also to French prisoners.[21] In times of danger, however, the prisoners were clearly seen as a threat, especially during the French invasion scares. Prisoners at Dundee were

---

17 NMM, ADM F/16, Commissioner Bell to Sick and Wounded, 22–23 August 1757. See also Morieux, 'Ordre social versus ordre national'.

18 See, for example, NMM, ADM F/16, Joseph Knight to Sick and Wounded, 22 July 1757; ADM F/15, Sick and Wounded to Admiralty, 11 June 1757.

19 See, for example, NMM, ADM F/17, Sick and Wounded to Admiralty, 28 March 1758.

20 See, for example, NMM, ADM F/19, Agent for prisoners at Dover to Sick and Wounded, 15 January 1759; NMM, ADM F/18, Captain O'Brien of HMS *Colchester* and Agent for prisoners at Corke to Sick and Wounded, 6 November 1758.

21 See, for example, *The London Chronicle, or, Universal Evening Post*, 26–29 September 1761, 'Country News' regarding Liverpool, Cumberland, Norwich, Lynn and Yarmouth.

moved to Edinburgh Castle, and those stationed in Ireland were moved away from the coasts.[22] Although prisoners were paid for by central state authorities, through French or British government funds, it was local civilian populations that had to administer to various details – such as carriages and horses for the transportation of prisoners – during wartime, when shortages were already widespread. The local agents for prisoners thus occupied a contentious position, often enforcing unpopular state orders upon an unwilling local population with its own local civil authorities, and representing to the Commissioners the difficulties of enacting official regulation.

The prisoners of war at Winchester proved particularly problematic for both the local population and the Commissioners of the Sick and Hurt Board, requiring one Dr Maxwell (very likely James Maxwell, one of the four Commissioners) to be sent by the Board in 1759 to report on conditions and practices and act as a mediator between civilian authorities and the local agent. Winchester at mid-century was not a particularly large city, with a population of less than 5,000.[23] Its location near Portsmouth, and its infrastructure, with one of the earliest British provincial infirmaries (1738) and other large buildings such as the King's House (an abandoned royal palace built for Charles II on the site of the former Winchester castle) appear to have made it a promising location in which to quarter prisoners of war.[24]

Prisoners were first sent to Winchester late in 1757, the Commissioners requesting that the King's House be prepared to house 3,000 prisoners.[25] This also required quartering the guarding regiments. When there were 3,600 prisoners of war housed in Winchester in 1761, for example, at least 300 soldiers were stationed there as guards. While the prisoners were housed together in the King's House, these soldiers were quartered among the civilian population, for the most part in pubs and alehouses, as was common for quartering other British soldiers.

The local population, and more specifically the publicans, objected to quartering these soldiers because of the cost. N. P. Smith, the local agent for prisoners at Winchester, wrote repeatedly to the Sick and Hurt Commissioners throughout 1759, requesting additional funds so that those in Winchester would agree to quarter the soldiers necessary for guarding the prisoners. The

---

22 NMM, ADM F/20, Dr James Walker, Agent for prisoners at Edinburgh to Sick and Wounded, 22 September 1759; NMM, ADM F/19 enclosure in Sick and Wounded to Admiralty, 16 June 1759.
23 Chalklin, 'South–East'.
24 Page, ed., 'Winchester Castle', pp. 9–12.
25 NMM, ADM F/16, Sick and Wounded to Admiralty, 7 December 1757, and see turn-over-note, 9 December 1757, for Admiralty's agreement.

Admiralty refused, as did Winchester's Mayor and Aldermen.[26] Some sort of inducement for the publicans may have been envisaged when the city's Common Assembly agreed to the proposal from the Mayor's Brethren that ten guineas be paid towards one of the subscription plates for the 1759 Winchester Races. This was done to ensure that the races would run for their usual duration, as otherwise they might have been shortened by a day, the assembly noting that this 'would have been a great detriment to the City in General and to the Publick House Keepers in particular who for a longtime past have been excessively Burthened with soldiers'.[27] Despite this measure, a month later in June 1759, the innkeepers of Winchester announced that they were refusing to house the guards, shutting their premises and renouncing their licenses. Even Pitt was aware of this problem and, under his and Barrington's advice, the guarding troops encamped nearby.[28] The city also paid its clerk five pounds and five shillings in September of the same year:

> For a vast number of attendances in Mr King's time of office and drawing several petitions & writing a great number of letters to Lord Barrington, Mr Secretary Pitt, Ld Marquiss of Winchester & Mr Penton and drawing & [illeg] petition to the Parliamt about the great Burthen of Soldiers on the Publicans & also for several attendances & letters [...] about employing the poor of the City.[29]

Clearly, accommodating the prisoners – specifically, their guards – caused problems in Winchester.

Winchester felt burdened by the prisoners in ways other than funds. Indeed, the correspondence of the local agent demonstrates that negotiating the demands of the civic authorities, who wished to ensure that the prisoners' establishment was under their control, along with those of the regiment guarding the prisoners was beset with difficulties. Smith repeatedly complained to the Sick and Wounded Commissioners about the regimental guards' officers. The Commissioners wrote directly to the Admiralty regarding these problems at Winchester, while the Admiralty in turn referred the problem to the Secretary-at-War, Barrington.[30] The frictions in Winchester were complicated by the fact that the colonel of the militia guards was also the local MP, Lord Bruce, who had complained to Lord Ligonier (commander-in-chief of the British forces and master-general of the ordnance) about Smith, the

26 NMM, ADM F/19, Mr Smith to Sick and Wounded, 5 July 1759.
27 HRO, WB/1/11, Common Assembly of 22 June 1759, fo. 183.
28 WiltSHC, 9/34/134, Pitt to Barrington, 3 July 1759.
29 HRO, W/K5/8, A Retrospect of Civic Manners and Customs (Jacob Scrapbooks), 29 September 1759, fo. 150.
30 NMM, ADM F/20, Smith to Sick and Wounded, 9 August 1759; see also that of 6 August 1759; NMM, ADM F/20, Sick and Wounded to Admiralty, 10 August 1759.

local agent. Smith, in turn, again complained to the Commissioners about the continuing obstructions to his care of the prisoners. Significantly, Smith recognised that while this was in some ways the conflict between a military and civilian authority, it was also a battle over local authority. He wrote to the Commissioners, 'in short, I am under so great restraint by the military, that the business is but half done, and I see plain enough that the point aimed at is, that, myself and Clerks and every other person and thing relating to this prison, should be under their absolute direction and countroul'.[31] This problem was temporarily resolved when Dr Maxwell, sent by the Sick and Wounded Commissioners, visited Winchester in September 1759, and issued orders to both the agent and the guards, which both sides agreed to follow. Yet only a month later the Commissioners were displeased to discover that Colonel Berkley, officer of the militia guarding the prisoners at Winchester, had again contravened their direct orders.[32]

For Winchester, where the number of enemy prisoners during wartime equalled two-thirds of its civilian population, the quartering of prisoners of war created sites of tension between local and central state authority, and between civil and military authority. Yet these tensions were also successfully, and relatively quickly, resolved by making use of urban civil administration alongside non-state organisations. With friendly societies and other voluntary associations a significant part of urban provincial community life in eighteenth-century Britain, it is hardly surprising that the official care given to the prisoners of war was supplemented by that collected through voluntary charities.[33] This was especially the case once the French government defaulted on its bounty, necessary for the French prisoners to buy such additional necessities as clothes. Local agents and local populations were well aware of the problems this created for the French prisoners. The Sick and Wounded requested additional funds for the prisoners in these circumstances from the Admiralty, reporting in December 1759, 'particularly, as their King having withdrawn the Allowance formerly made them which enabled them to purchase Cloaths &c, vast numbers of those poor People are now in all Our prisons becoming almost naked, which may very reasonably be expected to encrease

---

31 NMM, ADM F/20, Smith to Sick and Wounded, 6 August 1759; see also Sick and Wounded to Admiralty, 24 August 1759.
32 NMM, ADM F/20, Sick and Wounded to Admiralty, 2 November 1759.
33 On friendly urban societies see Morris, 'Voluntary Societies and British Urban Elites'; Gorsky, 'Growth and Distribution of English Friendly Societies'; on voluntary societies and philanthropy see Clark, *British Clubs and Societies*; Andrew, *Philanthropy and Police*; and on the mixture of state welfare and charity in urban centres see especially Innes, 'Mixed Economy of Welfare'.

the number of sick'.[34] One of the best-known visitors to the prisoners of war was John Wesley, who described their miserable condition and want of necessities. In his journal entry recording his visit to them just outside Bristol, on 15 October 1759, he noted that a fund was immediately begun that collected £24 in two days.[35] With no clothes for many of the prisoners in the winter of 1759–60, increasing sickness, and with the Admiralty unable to pay any additional funds, British civilians indeed raised money to pay for these enemy combatants. The largest organisation was the Committee on French Prisoners, which first met in London in December 1759, raising more than £4,000 by June 1760, the money being spent on shirts, coats, caps and shoes.[36]

Alongside these charities, it was the British state that overwhelmingly provided for prisoners of war. By the last year of the war, due to the French government's financial default, the Commissioners supplied £15,000 a month for the upkeep of French prisoners stationed in Britain.[37] Upon the conclusion of the Seven Years War, the French state was to reimburse these costs, which totalled over £1,000,000. In the face of France's financial failure, in 1765 British officials had no choice but to agree to a repayment of only £670,000, spread out over 13 instalments.[38] The remainder was absorbed by the British state within its overall debt of £133 million. The ability to administer such financial debts was fundamental to the British victory; this was tangibly demonstrated through the state's capacity to provide food, clothing and accommodation to its own and its enemy's armed forces. Likewise, French failure to do so both hastened and signalled French defeat. British contemporaries were aware that the ability to help French prisoners attested to the strength of the British nation. French prisoners were without clothes because 'the glorious successes of his Majesty's arms has so distressed the French in general, that they cannot assist their friends and relations in England'.[39] The British victory was thus not only that of having won campaigns through the exertions of its armed forces, but also of having secured the welfare of the people living in its country, enemy or not, through the sound and responsive management of its resources. Efficient administration was thus directly related to victory, even off the battlefield.

34   NMM, ADM F/20, Sick and Wounded to Admiralty, 29 September 1759.

35   Wesley, *An Extract of the Rev. Mr John Wesley's Journal*, pp. 81–82.

36   *Proceedings of the Committee Appointed to Manage the Contributions.*

37   TNA, ADM 106/1130, fo. 102, Sick and Wounded, 2 May 1763.

38   The final settlement can be found in Parliamentary Archives, London, HL/PO/ JO/10/7/183, House of Lords Papers, fo. 5010, 15 January 1765. On negotiations for the payment see TNA, SP 78/256, fos. 284, 287; SP 78/262, fos. 33, 144, 169–183, 217–34.

39   *London Chronicle*, 29 January 1760.

3. CONCLUSION

SEEN WITHIN the context of the overall British war effort, in which close to 200,000 troops were deployed in four continents simultaneously, the administration of 20,000 French prisoners of war was a relatively minor concern. However, the ability of the British state to answer such constant demands in such various contexts demonstrates its efficient administrative structure, especially when compared with the breakdown of the French finances. This was achieved in part because central authority negotiated with, and accommodated, local demands.[40] Although military victory was intertwined with efficient administration, it was not tied to centralisation. Even though Britain was far away from the fields of battle, warfare was still a presence through its underlying organisation. Mainland Britain experienced little more than invasion scares during the Seven Years War, and its territory was probably the least directly affected of any nation or colony involved in this wide-ranging conflict. However, tracing the details of the administration of war efforts offers a reminder that warfare affected civilians in a variety of ways.

Prisoners of war are not quite civilians, but neither are they fully soldiers. They are administered by an enemy government and population while being funded by a government that does not enjoy their fighting power, an expensive demand on systems already strained during wartime. As historians have long acknowledged, the administrative differences between Britain and France accounted for their differing military outcomes during the eighteenth century. The state of prisoners of war makes this comparison explicit, with the British state ably caring for thousands of French prisoners who could not be maintained by the prisoners' own government. The British administration supported an enormous long-term debt while implementing and coordinating the details of wartime logistics, thanks to the willingness of central authorities to negotiate and use local authority. The administration of war also involved patriotic discourse: British civilians accepted the administration of French prisoners as part of the British war effort. War was, therefore, a tangible experience to British civilians, even when no fighting took place on British soil.

The following three chapters raise similar questions about the state, administration, warfare and civilians. They emphasise the extensive and thoroughgoing demands made by the so-called limited wars of the late seventeenth to mid-eighteenth century. Markus Meumann examines the locus of civilian–military relations and state administration: military justice regarding the protection

---

40 On the British state's partnerships and negotiations with the localities throughout the eighteenth century see footnote 33; Conway, *War, State and Society*, esp. ch. 2; Mackillop, 'Political Culture of the Scottish Highlands'.

of civilians. His research demonstrates not only the extent to which military justice had long been developing in response to this problem, but also how discipline, or lack thereof, reflected changing campaign situations and regional differences. Similarly, Horst Carl looks at how military occupation functioned during the eighteenth century, noting in particular how this process combined efficient and orderly administration – often even providing an opportunity for a state to increase its powers – with military conquest. This is not only about the state, however. Carl points out how the experience of occupation was also significant in patriotic publications, which in turn signalled a kind of nascent nationalism. Stephen Conway's analysis of the reactions of British civilians to their own soldiers during the mid- to later eighteenth century finds similar developments. Like Meumann and Carl, Conway notes the importance of locality and the difficulty of making general statements, but nevertheless suggests that attitudes had broadly changed by the end of the Seven Years War, an indication of the transformation of civilian attitudes to the armed forces made apparent during the Revolutionary and Napoleonic wars. These chapters challenge the traditional periodisation of the cataclysmic birth of modern warfare with the Revolutionary and Napoleonic wars. In its stead, they trace a longer term development, demonstrating that late-seventeenth to mid-eighteenth-century warfare made extensive demands on the state through a variety of means. These authors illustrate how mutually responsive war-making and civil administration were in the early modern era, presenting an image of war as a process that allowed – indeed, demanded – continual refinement.

7

Civilians, the French Army and Military Justice during the Reign of Louis XIV, circa 1640–1715

MARKUS MEUMANN

How MILITARY justice functioned is central to our understanding of the relationship between civilians and warfare, since – at least in theory – an army's judicial apparatus is not only concerned with prosecutions for violations of military discipline but also with the protection of the civilian population from assaults by soldiers and any infringements of the laws of war. This is particularly true of the period spanning the second half of the seventeenth century until the death of Louis XIV, the '*roi de guerre*',[1] in 1715, when the nature of warfare in its turn dictated the nature of military–civilian relations. Rather than being directly involved in hostilities such as battles and sieges, civilians in early modern Europe were most frequently affected by war as the result of military logistics, army provisioning and associated consequences such as contributions and billeting.[2] These encounters were particularly detrimental to the civilian population not only because of the financial and material burdens that they imposed, such as the demands for quarters, food and fodder, but also because they often went hand in hand with robbery and plunder or, even worse, personal assault and violence. As a consequence, military discipline and its maintenance were questions of crucial importance to the civilian population.

Whereas the protection of civilians in war had been guaranteed by Christian natural law since the late middle ages, its effectiveness depended on the existence of a working military justice system, which did not emerge until the early

---

1   Cornette, *Le roi de guerre*.
2   For a general survey see Childs, *Warfare*.

modern period.[3] In this context, the 'long' seventeenth century – marked by a number of geographically extensive and long-lasting conflicts such as the Thirty Years War, the wars of Louis XIV or the Northern Wars from 1654 onwards – is of special interest for at least two reasons. First, the burden on the civilian population increased significantly as the growth in number and size of armies and tactical units intensified their supply problem, a situation that was only resolved in part during the late eighteenth century. Secondly, a significant increase in the constraints of warfare as well as in the institutions of military justice and police can be observed for nearly all European armies and warring powers from the second half of the Thirty Years War. One obvious reason for this development was that the increasing size of armies required stricter discipline to control them. Furthermore, the growth of European public opinion increased the importance of a functioning military judiciary to the rulers because it became an important criterion for the reputation and approval of a prince's rule and its legitimacy in the eyes of the prince's own subjects, as well as of the inhabitants of newly conquered or occupied territories.[4] In this context, Jacques Callot's well-known series of images of the *Misères de la guerre* (1633), which has usually been understood as a realistic depiction of the horrors of warfare, can be read as a piece of propaganda promoting the just reign of Louis XIII of France. The latter interpretation provides support for the view that a functioning military justice was not only important for the civilian population but also for warring powers already sensitive to public opinion during the Thirty Years War.

Nonetheless, historians usually proceed on the assumption that a 'taming of Bellona' (as a result of which the civilian population was in the main kept out of the hostilities) only occurred during the course of the eighteenth century.[5] This notion goes along with the fact that the maintenance of discipline and the functioning of justice in the European armies of the early modern period remain essentially unexplored despite their immense importance to historical analyses of the impact of war and violence on civilian populations. As a result of older studies dating mostly from the late nineteenth and the early twentieth century, we do have some picture of the rules and institutions of military justice since the sixteenth century. However, the practice of military justice, at least before the eighteenth century, remains largely obscure. Current views of seventeenth-century military discipline are predominantly influenced by particularly notorious incidents of unbridled violence committed against civilians during the Thirty Years War or the English Civil War, which are hardly compatible with the idea of a functioning military justice system. This

---

3   For example, Keen, *Laws of War*; Howard et al., eds., *Laws of War*; McKeogh, *Innocent Civilians*.

4   Cf. Parrott, *Richelieu's Army*, p. 527.

5   For example, Schindling, 'Krieg und Konfession im Alten Reich', p. 266.

corresponds with our limited knowledge of the procedures and practices of military jurisdiction, particularly during this period. At best we have evidence of individual incidents but, a few exceptions aside, we still lack systematic and comparative studies on the subject.[6]

Even for France, the most important military power of the period, whose army, the so-called 'giant of the *grand siècle*' (John A. Lynn) is probably the best-researched of the seventeenth century, there are no systematic studies regarding military jurisdiction. As a result, assessments of French military justice and its effectiveness vary significantly depending on the author's point of view. Rather surprisingly, and somewhat at odds with the prevalent image of seventeenth-century warfare, the majority present a predominantly positive picture of the French army's discipline especially after 1661, the year in which Cardinal Mazarin died and Louis XIV assumed personal rule, a period when the French army increasingly came into contact with the civilian populations of various neighbouring countries through conquests and temporary occupations.[7]

In this chapter I will evaluate this positive assessment by contrasting it with examples primarily drawn from the French conquests in the southern Netherlands between circa 1640 and the beginning of the eighteenth century. First, I will briefly outline developments in military law and justice in France up to the mid-seventeenth century, and the nature of the protection it offered to the civilian population. Secondly, I will consider military discipline and military jurisdiction during the Thirty Years War and Franco-Spanish War between 1635 and 1659. Finally, I will address in greater detail the reforms made to military justice at the beginning of the reign of Louis XIV and see whether, and to what extent, military discipline improved in the wake of the wars conducted by the *roi de guerre* himself and what that meant for the civilian population. In this context, the chapter will appraise the proposition that some sort of 'taming of Bellona' can be seen as beginning in the later seventeenth century.[8]

1. The Protection of Civilians and the Development of Military Justice in France up to the Mid-Seventeenth Century

It is well known that the early modern period did not know of a codified law of war in the sense of an internationally binding convention, or set of conventions, to which the warring parties had signed up. The first signs of

6   Lorenz, *Rad der Gewalt*; Storrs, 'Giustizia militare'.
7   See below, footnote 61.
8   Étienne Rooms even speaks of a 'humanisation of warfare' from the middle of the seventeenth century: Rooms, 'Contributions', p. 86.

such regulation are discernible in the bi- or even multilateral cartel treaties, which were used by the military powers to arrange the exchange of prisoners and payments of subsidies.[9] However, the lack of a codified law of war did not mean that there were no rules governing the conduct of war and the protection of the civilian population. These rules were largely derived from standards of Christian theology and ideas informed by natural law shared by most European nationalities, and as such were generally expressed in legal and theological treatises on just war, its conditions (*ius ad bellum*) and its conduct (*ius in bello*).[10] Furthermore, military discipline and the correct treatment of civilians – alongside military duties and pay – already figured in the contracts of service in the armies of mercenaries of the late fifteenth and sixteenth centuries, with which the mercenaries tied themselves to their masters, still in the main under private law. Compliance with these contracts of service, which increasingly assumed the character of public law, as well as the prosecution of general crime (such as theft and murder) was enforced in most armies by the regiment's own judicial system, which until well into the seventeenth century was linked to the regimental commander rather than the prince as commander-in-chief.[11] However, a trend towards a 'nationalisation' of military justice began to emerge in the late sixteenth century following the example of the Spanish Netherlands where the office of an *auditor general* was created in 1587. A royal high commissioner who supervised regimental justice became the norm among most of the larger warring powers (such as Sweden) from the beginning of the Thirty Years War and the formation of standing armies after 1648 (in Brandenburg-Prussia and other German territories).[12] Meanwhile, the soldiers' law of service came under the responsibility of the prince and thus became public law during the course of the seventeenth century.

In France, the situation regarding royal jurisdiction was somewhat different. The jurisdiction of the *Connétable*, the highest-ranking military commander, dated back to the thirteenth century, and the origins of the *maréchaussée*, the later military police, can be found at least by the beginning of the Hundred Years War.[13] The *prévôts des maréchaux*, who were initially responsible for the protection of the civilian population behind the lines to prevent plundering and such like, received the entire jurisdiction over the army in garrisons as well as the baggage train at the beginning of the sixteenth century.[14] In parallel, armed and

9 Corvisier, 'Renouveau', p. 368; Duchhardt, *Krieg und Frieden*, pp. 24–28.
10 McKeogh, *Innocent Civilians*, pp. 75–122; Haggenmacher, *Grotius*.
11 Möller, *Das Regiment der Landsknechte*.
12 Meumann, 'Generalauditeur'.
13 Bluche, 'Connétable'; Orgeval, *La justice militaire*; Larrieu, *Histoire de la maréchaussée*, p. 34.
14 Drilleau, *La maréchaussée*, pp. 12–13.

mounted permanent companies were formed, which were put under the authority of the *prévôts* and soon also assumed responsibility for the pursuit of civilian
vagrants (such as gangs and vagabonds).[15] However, alongside the *maréchaussée*
there were further offices, themselves mainly independently acting jurisdictions
for the military. Their responsibilities were only theoretically defined, for in
practice they overlapped. First among these was the *Tribunal de la connétablie
et maréchaussée de France*, which amalgamated the originally distinct jurisdictions of the *Connétable* and the marshals of France, and which was in principle
responsible for all offences committed by soldiers outside the *enceinte militaire*
(but de facto probably only for the aristocracy).[16] Dependent on the tribunal,
there was the *prévôt général de la connétablie* nominally the highest-ranking
military judge of France, who exercised military justice through his subordi-
nated *lieutenants*, the *prévôts généraux de l'armée*, who accompanied the armies
on campaign with their companies.[17] Alongside these, the individual units (for
example regiments) possessed their own *prévôts des bandes* (named after the
infantry units created under Francis I), who exercised jurisdiction within the
military in the name of the commander-in-chief of the respective branches of
the army, particularly representing the *Colonel général de l'infanterie française*.

In 1584 an ordinance of Henry III attempted to finally establish a clear
allocation of responsibilities. It stipulated that the *Colonel général de l'infanterie*
through his subordinate *prévôts* should judge all matters internal to the military, although with the involvement of the officers.[18] In parallel with these
attempts at the clarification of administrative and jurisdictional responsibilities, royal edicts and ordinances issued during the second half of the sixteenth
century repeatedly aimed at improving military discipline and the protection
of the civilian population.[19] These texts, foremost among them the *déclaration*
of Henry II of March 1550, known as the *ordonnances militaires*, set down
punishments for common criminal offences such as murder of, or an attack
on, a fellow soldier, blaspheming, slander and cheating at games, as well as
crimes committed within the army and violations of military discipline; they
also covered attacks against civilians, expressly the rape of women and girls and
the plunder of church property.[20]

However, in light of the weakening of royal authority during the Wars of
Religion from 1562 to 1598 and in recognition of the fact that this conflict was

---

15 Ibid., pp. 18–19; Lorgnier, *Maréchaussée*, p. 8.
16 Bluche, 'Connétablie'; Orgeval, *La justice militaire*.
17 Larrieu, *Histoire de la maréchaussée*, pp. 57–67.
18 Bodinier, 'Conseil de guerre'; Bonin, 'L'exercice', p. 212.
19 Cf. Wood, *King's Army*, pp. 226ff.
20 Bonin, 'L'exercice', pp. 204ff.; Wood, *King's Army*, pp. 227–28.

conducted not only by the royal army but by 'private armies' under the command of aristocratic generals and urban civil militias,[21] it seems likely that justice within the army was carried out mainly by the company captains, who claimed for themselves to be their soldiers' *juges naturels* until well into the seventeenth century.[22] The upshot of this system was that the civilian population probably could not count on being protected: 'Officers refused to hear the complaints of victims of mistreatment, operated under false names, tolerated the presence of unenrolled vagabonds and criminals, refused to discipline or supervise their men, and granted unauthorised permission to leave the army. Not even the army's provosts escaped accusations of extortionist practices.'[23]

After the Estates-General of 1614–15 had expressed their desire to end soldierly violence against civilians,[24] a series of royal edicts and ordinances threatening severe punishment for any disorder were issued during the first half of the seventeenth century with the aim of maintaining (or better, re-establishing) military discipline and preventing assaults by military personnel.[25] Thus, the responsibility of the *prévôts des bandes* for military jurisdiction was confirmed in principle. Additionally, steps were taken to reform the institutions charged with military justice. In 1627 the office of the *Connétable de France*, formally the highest-ranking holder of military justice, was abolished.[26] The *Grande ordonnance* of January 1629, commonly referred to as *Code Michau*, achieved a clear separation of responsibilities between the *prévôts des bandes*, who thereafter dealt with all conflicts and crimes within the army, and the *prévôts généraux d'armée*, the jurisdiction of which was restricted to military personnel outside their units (*hors leurs drapeaux et hors des fonctions militaires*) as well as members of the baggage train.[27] As the *Code Michau* never obtained

---

21 Trim, 'Huguenot Soldiering', pp. 12–16.

22 Chagniot, 'Justice militaire'; Lynn, *Giant of the Grand Siècle*, pp. 403–04; Bodinier, 'Conseil de guerre'.

23 Wood, *King's Army*, p. 228.

24 Corvisier, 'La paix nécessaire', p. 342.

25 'Reglement sur le restablissement de la discipline, forme et ordre du payement, tant de la cavalerie que de l'infanterie françoise' (1623), cited in Bonin, 'L'exercice', p. 213; 'Règlement fait par le roi pour establir un bon ordre en la discipline et police de toute sa cavallerie, 15 May 1638': BnF Châtre de Cangé vol. 7, fo. 143. See also Parrott, *Richelieu's Army*, p. 526.

26 Following a more traditional interpretation, the office of *Connétable* was suppressed because the Wars of Religion had revealed that the concentration of military power in the hands of a single person posed a threat to the king (cf. Bluche, 'Connétable'; Corvisier, 'La paix nécessaire', p. 342). By contrast, David Parrott argues that Cardinal Richelieu used this measure to hinder his opponent, the Duke of Montmorency, from becoming *Connétable* after Lesdiguières' death in 1626: Parrott, *Richelieu's Army*, pp. 469–70.

27 Poitrineau, 'Code Michau'. See also Lorgnier, *Juges bottés*, p. 6; Larrieu, *Histoire de la maréchaussée*, p. 179.

legal force, it is highly dubious that its stipulations concerning military justice were followed in practice. More likely, from the late 1630s onwards, judgement over crimes within the military was passed by the so-called *conseils de guerre* (i.e. courts martial), while the *prévôts des bandes* or regimental provosts gradually lost their judicial competence and became merely executive officers.

These developments saw the military judiciary, in line with the army's entire administration, subjected to supervision by royal commissioners specifically sent to the army for this purpose, the intendants of the army (*intendants aux armées*).[28] This rise in legislative activity can be viewed as part of a sustained effort by the Crown to enforce order within the army and protect the civilian population through a system of military justice. Increased legislative activity, however, can also suggest a repeated failure to achieve practical results. The latter interpretation, in this instance, is supported by the fact that the number of ordinances relating to military discipline increased during periods of political instability and civil war such as the Wars of Religion or, in the mid-seventeenth century, the *Fronde*. We thus need to examine more closely whether military discipline and the protection of civilians improved noticeably during this period when compared with the sixteenth century, as the French army was nearly permanently on campaign for about twenty-four years from 1635 onwards and royal authority was still weak, especially during the *Fronde*, from 1648 to 1653.

2. Military Discipline and the Conduct of the French Army towards Civilians during the Thirty Years War and the Franco-Spanish War, 1635–1659

Scholars vary significantly in their assessments of the French army's conduct and maintenance of discipline during the reign of Louis XIII and the minority of Louis XIV, when politics were dominated by Cardinal Richelieu and his successor Mazarin. According to Jean Meyer, who provides the most positive appraisal, the French army's discipline and its behaviour towards the civilian population during the Thirty Years War were remarkably better than those of other armies of the period. Thus, the French troops in Alsace were seen, according to Meyer, as less dreadful than other armies, and people preferred to place themselves under French protection on the grounds that they represented the lesser evil. To justify his assumption, Meyer then refers to the

---

28   Bodinier, 'Administration militaire', p. 44; Bluche, 'Connétablie'. On the intendants see Baxter, *Servants of the Sword*.

strict orders of the French army and the fact that 'victims could complain to the King's Council, the *Conseil du roi*'.[29]

Unfortunately, Meyer does not provide the documentary evidence to support his analysis. The *archives de la guerre* at the Service Historique de la Défense at Vincennes, to which he refers, are extremely extensive, which makes it difficult to verify his statements. The papers of the *série A¹* up to 1700, which include the correspondence of the *Secrétaire d'état à la guerre* (the Secretary of State for War) from 1630, are contained in about 1500 substantial volumes. This renders any systematic study covering a longer period extremely difficult, the more so as the volumes are ordered not by subject but strictly chronologically, with inadequate theme indexing. Any analysis is therefore dependent on single pieces of evidence and we not only need to accumulate but compare such material in order to create a more representative picture.

My own research using material from the same *série A¹*, which covers predominantly the southerly provinces of the Netherlands formerly held by Spain but successively conquered by France after 1635 and incorporated into France by the peace treaties of 1659 and 1668, in large part reveals a completely different picture for the late 1640s. With infrequent supplies and their pay in arrears, the French troops turned to assaulting the local population in Boulonnais, Picardy, Artois and the southern part of the county of Flanders in 1648, the year of the Peace of Westphalia.[30] Similar incidents occurred in Normandy and in the centre of France.[31] The locals for their part reacted by employing violence. The peasants around La Bassée in Artois took up arms, pursued and robbed smaller units of soldiers.[32] Elsewhere, individual soldiers were subject to attacks and assaults.[33] Taking into account similar reports from Catalonia, Italy and Lorraine, it becomes clear that this situation was repeated in other theatres of war, a fact confirmed by research on Lorraine and other territories in this period,[34] and that it continued in the following years.[35] Such a high level of civil–military violence resulted not only in revolts among the civilian population, but also in mutinies in the army: in Breisach in 1644, Turenne's German army in 1647, the cavalry in Flanders in 1650 and at Cateau-Cambrésis in 1651.[36]

---

29   Meyer, *La France moderne*, p. 266.
30   For example, SHDAT série A¹ no. 468, docs. 31 (Bourgbourg), 34 (Abbeville), 64, 67, 76–77 (Vesly), 81–82 (Ypres), 84 (near St Quentin), 85, 87 (Dreux and Longprès?).
31   SHDAT série A¹ no. 110, docs. 146, 147, 149.
32   SHDAT série A¹ no. 110, docs. 78, 87, 93, 96.
33   SHDAT série A¹ no. 468, docs. 68, 71, 78, 96.
34   SHDAT série A¹ no. 110; Gaber, *La Lorraine meurtrie*; Martin, *Une guerre de trente ans*.
35   SHDAT série A¹ no. 468, docs. 111–12, 124–25, 127, 134, 141, 155, 156, 181.
36   Lynn, *Giant of the Grand Siècle*, p. 399.

Of course, it is likely that military discipline was particularly poor during the years from 1648 onwards. Weakened royal authority caused by the *Fronde* led to a collapse in the supply of the army and the *étapes* (supply depots). It also brought about the spread of hostilities to regions that were far from France's external borders and that up until then had been spared any devastation, such as the Loire valley, which was ransacked by loyal troops under the command of Turenne.[37] The sieur de Pontis, who had served under Louis XIII as *maréchal de bataille* in the armies in Germany and the Netherlands, complained in 1649 that the discipline of the troops he commanded had been much better 'du temps du feu roi', that is before the death of Louis XIII in 1643.[38] Louis André drew on Pontis's remark when he concluded, in his study *Michel Le Tellier et l'organisation de l'armée monarchique* (1906), that 'discipline was better during 1643–45 than it was for the next period, 1646–53, when it was at its worst, and that things improved after the *Fronde*'.[39]

To test this idea, let us take a look at the first decade of the Franco-Spanish War from 1635 onwards and examine whether Jean Meyer's positive assessment does perhaps apply after all and whether there are further examples that might support such a conclusion. A glance at the progress of the war in the southern part of the Low Countries reveals a clearly different picture. The first year of the conflict, in 1635, saw violent assaults on, and massacres of, civilians, for example in Tirlemont in Brabant, as well as retaliatory violence by the local population against the soldiery, repaying the atrocities in kind.[40] After the fall of Arras in 1640 the army ravaged the surroundings. 'All of the towns were set on fire and bloodied; all of the country is ravaged, ruined, destroyed, so that nothing will grow there.'[41] Comparable atrocities committed against civilians continued during subsequent years, including, according to eyewitness reports, the burning of villages and even churches, which had served as refuges for the villagers. David Parrott, in his well-researched study *Richelieu's Army*, based on a comprehensive analysis of the *série A¹*, also describes similar attacks on civilians and their retaliation against the soldiers during the early years of the war.[42]

The most convincing argument against the assumption that military discipline had been better under Louis XIII and Richelieu is provided by a *mémoire sur le logement des troupes* written by the *Surintendant des finances*, Claude de

---

37 Kroener, *Les routes et les étapes*, pp. 123–54; Corvisier, 'Renouveau', pp. 380–82.

38 André, *Michel Le Tellier*, p. 579.

39 Cited in Lynn, *Giant of the Grand Siècle*, p. 398.

40 Bois, *Les guerres en Europe*, p. 81; Corvisier, 'Renouveau', p. 354. An eyewitness report can be found in Denys and Paresys, *Les anciens Pays-Bas*, p. 92.

41 Lottin and Guignet, *Histoire des provinces françaises du Nord*, p. 188.

42 Parrott, *Richelieu's Army*, pp. 523–25.

Bullion, in 1637. Complaining about the fact that regulations had not been executed until now, he explicitly refers to

> the robberies that are committed every day and the abuses committed by the captains who instead of paying the men who are at their charge [...] commit thousands upon thousands of excesses which cause the people not only to lose hope but reduce them to such a level of helplessness that the King His Majesty and the public will soon know the inconveniences resulting from such disorders

– that is to say 'that the people could begin to revolt'.[43] Other memoirs dating from the 1640s draw a similar picture of a lack of military discipline and in 1640 a letter by the king mentions 'an infinity of complaints of disorders' reported to him from Moulins.[44]

Here is clear evidence that the maintenance of military discipline was not only of immense importance to the civilian population, but was also of interest to the authorities. It seems beyond doubt that the royal government was clearly intending to prosecute offences against military law and to punish disorder severely.[45] Officers who permitted their troops to leave their assigned routes 'were, according to the *Code Michau*, to be punished in peacetime by confiscation of office, and by death in time of war'.[46] However, it remains uncertain whether and to what extent such threats of punishment were actually carried out.

It appears that the *conseils de guerre* at least, which were constituted of military officers, tended to be lenient to their own kind when it came to implementing military justice, and a lack of clarity continued in terms of responsibilities and overlapping jurisdictions.[47] This had an impact on conflicts within the military, but applied particularly to the so-called *délits mixtes* between the military and civil authorities, in which jurisdiction was claimed by military officers as well as by various civilian officials.[48] Additionally, civilians suspected, often with good reason, that the military courts disregarded the interests of civilian victims when set against any military concerns. As a consequence municipal authorities were given authority at the end of 1641 to arrest officers whose soldiers had been disorderly or committed assaults against civilians.[49]

---

43 BnF Châtre de Cangé, vol. 9, fos. 366–67.
44 BnF Châtre de Cangé, vol. 9, fos. 378–79: 'santimans d'un Zele françois sur les soufranses des armées et des peuples, par le manque de disipline aux ians de gueirre' (1644), and fos. 381–83: 'Lettre d'Avis donné a Monseigneur le Cardinal Mazarin, pour l'Entretement & Logement des Troupes (1649)'; Vol. 25, fo. 108: 'Lettre du Roy a M de Bussy-Rabutin' at Moulins, 19 December 1640.
45 Ibid. In this letter the king threatened the *mestre de Camp général* of the cavalry with making him personally responsible for any crime committed by his troops in the future.
46 Parrott, *Richelieu's Army*, p. 526.
47 Cf. André, *Michel Le Tellier*, pp. 582–88.
48 Parrott, *Richelieu's Army*, pp. 528–33.
49 Ibid., p. 531.

Nonetheless, David Parrott suspects that already before the *Fronde*, royal officials were unable, and military officers often not even willing, to prevent assaults by soldiers on civilians or to prosecute the perpetrators.[50] One particular problem was posed by 'foreign' troops in the service of the French king, that is to say the Swiss, Scottish, Irish, Italian, Polish and German regiments, which accounted for up to a third of the troop strength in the middle of the seventeenth century, and which exercised their own jurisdiction.[51] Parrott's observation that attacks were at their worst when the troops were foreigners in their area of operation is wholly corroborated by my own findings. Irish and Polish infantry, as well as German cavalry, took a lead in atrocities against the local population, and even officers joined in revenge attacks on civilians.[52] Furthermore, unauthorised assaults by individual troop units as well as by disbanded soldiers and marauders posed a particular threat to the local population.[53] For example, the *curé* of Lisbourg near Arras reported in 1645 that 'there are around four to five hundred cavalry detached from the main army who run wild, committing cruelties and abhorrent villainies, without regard for anyone'.[54]

There is little evidence to suggest that the conduct of the army had been markedly better before 1648. As Parrott remarks, the lack of discipline during the *Fronde* 'should not be seen as the consequence of a sudden breakdown of previously effective systems of control and discipline, but as the high-water mark in a process of deteriorating authority'.[55] It can be assumed that this situation applies equally to the years immediately following the *Fronde* until the Peace of the Pyrenees in 1659, even though there is not much information covering this period either in the sources or in any studies. For the year 1654 alone, however, there are repeated reports of pillaging and disorder from various border regions of France.[56] Near Bourg-en-Bresse, soldiers of the cavalry regiment d'Aligne set fire to several houses and even plundered the local church following an argument over the billeting of soldiers in the *curé*'s house.[57] While there is isolated evidence for the years 1656–57 that the royal authorities did take action against officers in the context of fundamental reforms to the

---

50 Ibid., pp. 543–46, 551.
51 Meyer, *La France moderne*, p. 265. On the jurisdiction regarding foreign troops see Parrott, *Richelieu's Army*, pp. 530–31; André, *Michel Le Tellier*, p. 590.
52 SHDAT série A¹ no. 468, docs. 34, 67, 71, 77, 84–85, 87, 111–12. Cf. Parrott, *Richelieu's Army*, pp. 518, 520; Lottin and Guignet, *Histoire des provinces françaises du Nord*, p. 188.
53 Parrott, *Richelieu's Army*, pp. 539–43.
54 Cited in Lottin and Guignet, *Histoire des provinces françaises du Nord*, p. 188.
55 Parrott, *Richelieu's Army*, p. 545.
56 Alsace, Foix, Bigorre, Guyenne. BnF Châtre de Cangé, vol. 28, fos. 315, 326.
57 SHDAT série A¹ no. 468, doc. 181.

billeting of troops,[58] the conduct of the army in their quarters in France as well as in hostile territory does not indicate that any substantial improvement in discipline had occurred.[59] Parrott also supposes that discipline still had not improved by the later years of the Franco-Spanish War, referring to the fact that fundamental administrative reforms in the army, although already planned by the Secretary of State for War, Michel Le Tellier, in the 1650s, did not come about until the 1660s.[60] However, did these reforms coincide with and/ or promote improved discipline and better effectiveness of military justice, as most historians have assumed?

3. DISCIPLINE, MILITARY LAW AND JURISDICTION UNDER THE PERSONAL REGIME OF LOUIS XIV

WHILE HISTORIANS have reached different conclusions when assessing the nature and impact of military discipline and justice in the royal army during the Franco-Spanish War, most scholars, including specialists such as Lynn and Corvisier, the doyen of French military history, nearly unanimously agree that the discipline of the French troops improved and military justice became more effective after Louis XIV personally took over government.[61] Indeed, without a doubt, Louis XIV made military discipline a principal task for his government.[62] A fundamental reorganisation of military jurisdiction followed directly after his assumption of personal control over government in spring 1661. First of all, the post of the *Colonel général de l'infanterie*, the highest-ranking commander of the troops *à pied*, who had, at least formally, exercised military justice since 1584, was not filled again after the death of the

---

58 BnF Châtre de Cangé, vol. 29, fo. 114: 'Ordonnance du Roy pour casser des Capitaines et Officiers des Cavalerie qui ont exigé de l'argent dans les Lieux de leur Logement pendant l'Hyver, malgré les deffenses portées par l'ord.ce du 20 9.bre dernier', March 1656 (five officers were dismissed for having demanded payment from civilians); fo. 218: 'Lettre du Roy a M. le Marquis de Nangis po. luy ordonner de remettre entre les mains de la Justice les Soldats du Reg.^t de Picardie qui seront accusés de Crimes ou les habitants des lieux de leurs garnisons ou aut. auront Interest, 5 Jan. 1657'.

59 BnF Châtre de Cangé, vol. 29, fo. 216; Lottin and Guignet, *Histoire des provinces françaises du Nord*, p. 188.

60 Cf. Parrott, *Richelieu's Army*, pp. 544–45, 554–56. Concerning the reforms of Le Tellier see Lynn, *Giant of the Grand Siècle*, pp. 401–02; for more detail, André, *Michel Le Tellier*.

61 Bluche, 'Connétablie', p. 389; Corvisier, 'Louis XIV', pp. 402–03; Lynn, *Giant of the Grand Siècle*, p. 398; Lottin and Guignet, *Histoire des provinces françaises du Nord*, p. 206; Denys and Paresys, *Les anciens Pays-Bas*, pp. 91–92. A more sceptical view is presented by Jean Chagniot: Chagniot, 'Justice militaire'; Chagniot, 'Autorité militaire et justice'.

62 Lynn even speaks of a 'fetish': Lynn, *Giant of the Grand Siècle*, p. 400.

last incumbent, the duc d'Épernon, in July 1661.[63] On 12 October in the same year the king issued an ordinance that placed all garrisoned troops under the command of the responsible governor or local commander. In matters of military jurisdiction, too, these officials were ranked above the regimental officers. They were allowed to arrest soldiers without the permission of their officers, and they alone decided on the soldier's release or the convening of courts martial, the already-mentioned *conseils de guerre*.[64]

This measure appears to have met with some resistance from officers.[65] Disputes over authority and rank caused by the ordinance of 1661 resulted in a further ordinance being issued on 25 July 1665, repeating the original provisions and expanding them at the expense of regimental autonomy.[66] The *prévôts* as well as the *capitaines* were no longer responsible for any offences within the military or violations of discipline, which now came exclusively under the jurisdiction of the *conseils de guerre*. The composition of the *conseils* were also strictly regulated. They had to be composed of seven officers, captains if possible, who, it was made clear a year later, should belong to a different branch of the army from that of the accused.[67] In the spirit of the two ordinances, the *conseils* were chaired by the garrison commander or his deputy, and the investigation was led by the *major de la place*, a high-ranking officer who was in charge of the garrison's administration. A conviction could only be passed by a majority of votes and had to be documented in writing. In addition the process was monitored by a single (civilian) *commissaire des guerres* who was able to suspend sentence

---

63 Bonin, 'L'exercice', p. 199; Corvisier, 'Louis XIV', p. 400. Most of the foreign troops also lost this post during the 1650s and 1660s; only the Swiss troops retained their colonel general until 1792: Bodinier, 'Colonel général'; André, *Michel Le Tellier*, pp. 155–58.

64 'REGLEMENT FAIT par le Roy, concernant le Commandement, l'Ordre, & la Discipline, que sa Majesté veut être dorénavant gardez par ses Troupes d'Infanterie, dans les Villes & Places où elles tiendront garnison. Du 12. Octobre 1661', in *Reglemens et ordonnances du roy pour les gens de guerre*, pp. 117–32; 'Ordonnance du Roy, portant que les Sergens Majors des Villes & Places donneront leurs conclusions és procés criminels des Soldats, à l'exclusion des Sergens Majors des Regimens. Du septiéme Aoust 1663', in *Reglemens et ordonnances du roy pour les gens de guerre*, pp. 204–06. Cf. Bodinier, 'Conseil de guerre'.

65 'Reglement fait pour lever plusieurs difficultez meuës entre les Officiers de ses Troupes, & entre eux et les Officiers Majors des Villes & Places où elles sont en garnison, depuis le Reglement du douziéme Octobre 1661. & en interprétation d'aucuns Articles d'icelui, Du 25 Juillet 1665', in *Reglemens et ordonnances du roy pour les gens de guerre*, pp. 266–304.

66 Ibid.

67 'Ordonnance du Roy, portant que les Officiers de Cavalerie aßisteront dans les Conseils de qui seront tenus pour le jugement des Soldats d'Infanterie, & les Officiers d'Infanterie pour le jugement de ceux de Cavalerie, lors qu'il n'y aura pas nombre suffisant d'Officiers, soit d'Infanterie ou de Cavalerie, pour rendre les dits jugemens. Du 22. Aoust 1666', in *Reglemens et ordonnances du roy pour les gens de guerre*, pp. 403–06.

and reported to the Secretary of State for War. The same rights extended to the provincial intendants.[68]

Did these procedural changes produce any visible effect on the army's discipline? Looking at the first major military venture after the start of Louis XIV's personal reign, the conquest of Flanders in 1667, there appear to be signs of the reforms being successful. Marshal d'Aumont, *Commandant de l'armée du Roy en Flandres du costé de la Mer*, reported on the good behaviour of the French troops from their camp near Bergues on 6 June of that year. 'The troops are living so discreetly that people were astonished about it everywhere we passed.'[69] It is noteworthy, though, that he was recording the amazement of the population at this fact. However, in the following years there were again lootings by French troops and a series of clashes between soldiers and civilians in the annexed *châtellenie* Lille-Douai-Orchies, which continued even after the signing of the peace on 2 May 1668.[70]

During the Dutch War (1672–78/79), the situation was even worse. In the part of Flanders already annexed in 1667, soldiers again assaulted civilians regularly over the whole length of the war.[71] In the course of the conquest of northern Hainault, the region of the county today belonging to Belgium, parts of the French army in 1678 were mistreating the rural population and killing townspeople during brawls, even behind their own lines.[72] Prosecutions for these offences tended to come to nothing as it was difficult to identify the soldiers responsible owing to troop movements and probably also due to the officers' lack of enthusiasm for the task. The troops' behaviour in enemy territory was even worse. Lacking effective protection against the assaults, the local population initiated their own resistance, resulting in a series of smaller and larger revolts, which peaked in the so-called *guerre de Thuin* in 1679, the repression of which required a significant military effort.[73]

The start of the Nine Years War (1688–97) in turn reveals a complex picture. The military courts did not hesitate to punish breaches of military discipline and to impose stiff penalties, which led to an obvious improvement in the

---

68 Bodinier, 'Conseil de guerre'. See also Bodinier, 'Administration militaire', p. 44; Chagniot, 'Commissaires des guerres'.

69 SHDAT série A¹ no. 209, doc. 28.

70 SHDAT série A¹ no. 251, doc. 69, Talon to Le Tellier, 20 April 1668 (Audenarde); ADN série VIII B nos. 17382, 17793.

71 ADN série VIII B nos. 16572, 17396; série C no. 1985. Lynn also states that 'the army's conduct in the early years of the Dutch War was hardly exemplary': Lynn, *Giant of the Grand Siècle*, p. 400.

72 ADN série C nos. 9737, 9740, 9742. For more detail, see my article 'Comment les conflits entre militaires et civils étaient-ils réglés au XVIIe siècle?'

73 SHDAT série A¹ nos. 630–31, 633, 667, passim.

soldiers' conduct. In 1690 the intendant of Flanders, Louis Dugué de Bagnols, reported to the Secretary of State, the marquis de Louvois, that '[g]ood order and discipline are clearly re-establishing themselves in the army. The two examples made by M de Luxembourg [i.e. the marshal] produced the best results one could desire.'[74] However, there were violent incidents later that year, and in 1692 Dugué de Bagnols was reporting a state of virtual chaos to Louvois' son and successor Barbezieux, which he blamed on the officers. 'The troops that move from one town to another of my department create much disorder in their travels and behave with increasing license and liberty; the soldiers rampage in the towns, pillaging and robbing the villagers and often mistreating them, the officers do not make much effort to keep their men marching in good order, from which stems this general disorder.'[75] German and Irish troops were again seen as particular offenders in this respect. It was said of the Irish in 1692 that 'they [the officers] have no authority over their soldiers, who are without any discipline, and who are more like bandits and brigands than soldiers. They leave not only their battalions but even their detachments to go marauding, I've already told the head officers to make examples of them, they promised to do so but as of yet have done nothing.' Apparently, the Irish officers even joined in the plunder and shared the loot with their soldiers.[76] Mutinies still occurred during the personal reign of Louis XIV, although to a lesser extent than before and, up to the mid-eighteenth century, famine and shortages in army supplies produced unrest in the garrisons of the northern provinces as well as in Alsace.[77]

In view of the examples cited above, one certainly cannot speak of a fundamental and ongoing improvement in military discipline during Louis XIV's reign. If the decade between the Dutch War and the Nine Years War really marked the apogee of French discipline, as Corvisier speculates, the events at the beginning of that war show definitely that it soon declined again.[78] It is easier to concur with Lynn, who also assumes that 'discipline improved over the course of the grand siècle', but who concedes that 'amelioration was not linear and even'.[79] Given the difficulties of directing systematic research on the subject and the lack of comparative studies it appears that, rather than making generalised assertions, statements are better confined to geographically or temporally restricted contexts. As Lynn observes, 'when conditions in the field

---

74   SHDAT série A¹ no. 948, doc. 54.

75   SHDAT série A¹ no. 1150, doc. 7 (16 January 1692).

76   SHDAT Série A¹ no. 1236, doc. 23 (11 October 1692). On the Irish troops of Louis XIV see Rowlands, 'Capitalisation of Foreign Mercenaries'.

77   Lynn, *Giant of the Grand Siècle*, p. 399; Chagniot, 'Les progrès de l'administration', p. 45.

78   Corvisier, 'Louis XIV', p. 402.

79   Lynn, *Giant of the Grand Siècle*, p. 398.

decayed in later wars, discipline again declined'.[80] Thus, any assessment of the discipline of the French army has to distinguish between time and place as well as between times of war and peace.

This leads to a related question: what did the reforms introduced under Louis XIV during the early 1660s mean for the civilians who came into contact with the French army, and did these reforms produce any positive effects? Military jurisdiction in principle was always obliged to punish offences committed against civilians in as much as the acts constituted breaches of the articles of war or royal ordinances. These provisions, for example, expressly banned the murder of civilians, particularly women, children and the old, rape, the violation of church property, or plunder without permission from officers. Even though the *conseils de guerre* passed down severe judgements, such examples are isolated.[81] In practice officers often still had little inclination to punish their soldiers harshly or, worse, condemn them to death. This was a widely known fact, explicitly mentioned in the ordinance of 1665 and probably the cause that led the king to withdraw jurisdiction from the regiments and grant his civilian administrators the right of supervision over court martial proceedings.[82]

Recognising the inadequacy of the existing system, the ordinance of 1665 went even further when it came to regulating conflict between the military and civilians within garrisons. As long as these cases occurred outside the narrowly military sphere, within France they were subject, on principle, to the jurisdiction of the *justice ordinaire* (i.e. the local courts): 'when the officers, or infantry soldiers commit a crime, or offence, in the neighbourhood of the garrison, the investigation into these crimes, or offences, belongs to the local judges, while it is prohibited for the officers of those troops to investigate in any manner at all'.[83] This inevitably led to harsher punishments being meted out to soldiers than those they received from the military courts, a consequence readily accepted by the Crown. Recognising this bias, Louvois granted jurisdiction to the intendants in cases of conflict between civilians and military personnel in Flanders and other *pays conquis*.[84] However, as examples from Flanders and Hainault show, the intendants, too, had a tendency to protect the civilian population from assaults by the military and to severely punish offences committed by soldiers.[85] This in turn was done with the approval of Louvois, who admonished an intendant for passing only sentence of hanging on two soldiers

---

80 Ibid.
81 See SHDAT série A¹ no. 468, passim.
82 *Reglemens et ordonnances du roy pour les gens de guerre*, p. 297. This problem continued throughout the eighteenth century: Chagniot, 'Les progrès de l'administration', p. 46.
83 *Reglemens et ordonnances du roy pour les gens de guerre*, pp. 293–94.
84 SHDAT série A¹ no. 1657, Dugué de Bagnols to Chamillart, 18 August 1703.
85 SHDAT série A¹ no. 667, doc. 11, Faultrier to Louvois, 9 January 1679.

who had attacked a citizen in Lille at night, rather than condemning them to death on the wheel.[86] Dugué de Bagnols obtained sanctions in some cases even against officers, who were in general able to count on leniency, or even acquittal, from the *conseils de guerre*.[87]

Thus, the fact that from 1665 onwards incidents between civilians and the military within garrisons were made subject to the civil jurisdiction of the *justice ordinaire* or the intendants doubtless improved civilians' chances of success in court in the long term and so probably increased the protection of civilians from military violence. Nevertheless, the state of military discipline during times of war, well into the 1690s and probably beyond, suggests that the prospect of support for civilians from the military courts was limited. The population was just as unprotected from assaults by the military as they had been during the middle of the seventeenth century. This was brought about not only by the decline in effectiveness of military justice during times of war, but also by the opportunistically changing or even contradictory intentions of royal policy. One cannot doubt the authorities' basic desire to protect the population from violence and their intention to take decisive measures, especially as government depended on the cooperation of the local population in annexed or occupied territories in the long term. However, the necessity of keeping the army together and, by implication, in good humour while *en campagne* became a higher imperative, against which strict prosecution and punishment of offences could prove counterproductive as it caused resentment among the troops. Thus it was that at the beginning of 1661 a comprehensive indemnity was issued concerning the crimes committed by members of the army during the previous war.[88] Similarly, attempts by civilians to seek justice for themselves were blocked by force if it appeared expedient for the military to do so.[89]

To conclude, it appears that earlier scholarly assessments of military discipline and the effectiveness of military justice in the French army probably reflect more a general inclination to overrate ordinances and declarations of intent by the authorities rather than the reality of the situation on the

---

86 Lottin and Guignet, *Histoire des provinces françaises du Nord*, p. 207.

87 Ibid., p. 216.

88 'Declaration du Roy Du mois de Nouembre 1660. Portant Pardon, et abolition, en faueur de ceux des Troupes, qui ont commis des excès & desordres durant la guerre, & des Habitans de la Frontiere, & des Prouinces du Royaume, où lesdits Gens de Guerre ont passé, logé, & seiourné. Registrée en Parlement le vingt-unième Ianuier 1661': ANF série M no. 638, 21 January 1661.

89 When peasants arrested a couple of French soldiers near Liège in 1678, the French governor of Maastricht, the marquis de Calvo, sent 400 *cavaliers* and 800 foot soldiers to free the last three French detainees from the city's prison: SHDAT série A[1] no. 584, fos. 185–285.

ground – even if discipline in the French army may well have improved over the course of this period and exceeded that of other armies, as both Corvisier and Lynn suspect.[90] Any realistic assessment of this question needs to distinguish more clearly than has been done so far between different regions and theatres of war, as well as between times of peace and war. Furthermore, even while irregular assaults by individual soldiers or regiments may have declined during the last decades of the seventeenth century, there was a parallel increase in organised violence against civilians to obtain forced contributions or for other military purposes; the best-known example of its kind is the devastation of the Palatinate at the beginning of the Nine Years War, which included plenty of incidents where the soldiery slipped the leash of their officers and the War Ministry officials.[91]

The idea that the latter part of the seventeenth century saw the beginnings of a 'taming' of warfare as a result of increasing constraints on its prosecution must be viewed equivocally. As the result of the intensification of armed conflicts, and the requirement for military discipline and prosecutions for offences against it, military law and military justice were already remarkably well-developed by the seventeenth century, and in this sense the proverbial 'taming of Bellona' emerged prior to the eighteenth century. Nevertheless, despite these efforts and the strengthening of military justice by the reforms of the 1660s, a 'taming' (in the sense of the development of 'humane' warfare that spared civilians) certainly did not occur during the seventeenth and early eighteenth centuries (apart from a few exceptions), owing to the lack of effectiveness of military justice while on campaign and the ambivalent intentions of the authorities. Certain improvements may have been achieved over the course of the eighteenth century, but these were offset by new burdens on the civilian population, such as conscription, as well as new forms of less regulated warfare such as *la petite guerre*.[92] Given the vast number of war crimes committed against civilians in the twentieth century, the 'taming of Bellona' appears to have been a fragile and transitory phenomenon that arguably may only have ever existed as an ideal.

---

90 Of course, this supposition is difficult to substantiate. Alongside contemporary testimonies from the seventeenth century, on which Corvisier's analysis appears to be based (Corvisier, 'Louis XIV', p. 404: 'La bonne tenue relative des troupes françaises stupéfia l'Europe'), any balanced analysis should take into consideration a structural comparison with other armies' discipline and systems of military justice, for example those examined by Maren Lorenz in the Swedish territories in Germany in the second half of the seventeenth century: Lorenz, *Rad der Gewalt*. Due to constraints of space I am unable to do so in this chapter.

91 Lynn, 'Brutal Necessity?'

92 Picaud-Monnerat, *La petite guerre*; Rink, *Vom "Partheygänger" zum Partisanen*.

8

Restricted Violence?
Military Occupation during the
Eighteenth Century

HORST CARL

1. A History of Occupation as a History of the Rationalisation of War

MILITARY OCCUPATION as a phenomenon plays a paradigmatic role in any analysis of the relationship between civilians and war as a situation where the military's interaction with the civilian population is at its most overwhelming. It also provides, through comparative examples of military occupation, a means by which we can identify lines of development in regulating civil–military relations. If the eighteenth century is particularly prominent in this chapter, it is because this period can be seen as a culmination of early modern developments, insofar as the various experimental approaches of the late sixteenth and, above all, seventeenth centuries appeared to now be systematised in practice – as well as being reflected in 'classical' European international law. For the most part, these standards still applied to the wars waged by nineteenth- and twentieth-century European states and, in this respect, can be viewed as something of an early modern achievement.

This chapter thus argues against the frequently expressed view that military occupation has been a transhistorical feature of war since ancient times. Those who advocate such a view rarely make a clear distinction between military occupation, conquest and domination by a foreign power.[1] By contrast, this chapter insists on the historically specific character of military occupation

---

1   For example, Carlton, *Occupation*.

in the context of continental European warfare. It had ancient and medieval precursors, but military occupation as a specific complex of practices only came to be realised in the early modern period, because that is when the decisive preconditions were available. Occupation requires an orderly administration of the extraction of resources, and this makes it at once an index and a component of the 'bureaucratisation' or rationalisation of war. This in turn requires that distinctions be drawn between combatants and non-combatants. Both preconditions were first realised in the early modern period, though always within limits.

In the eighteenth century international law developed a definition of military occupation that corresponds to later usage. Military occupation (*occupatio bellica*) of a territory exists when the occupying force establishes actual authority within a territory and the occupier is prepared to exercise this authority in a regulated form until a final decision about the future of the territory is reached.[2] This authority is defined as temporary, and temporally limited. Military occupation does not give the occupier a legitimate claim to possession of a territory, since the final fate of an occupied territory will be decided only after the occupation – usually on the basis of a peace treaty.[3]

The development of military occupation into a legally and customarily defined situation, which can be distinguished from the bare facts of military conquest, territorial annexation or regime change, was very closely linked to the fundamental process of early modern state-building.[4] In the case of military occupation, as well as in a number of other contexts, war and bureaucratic administration became interwoven as a signum of modern state power. Occupation can therefore serve as a particularly revealing indicator for the processes of the growth of state control and rationalisation of war.[5]

In view of the importance of the Hundred Years War between the French and English monarchies for the development of warfare and the consolidation of states, it is not surprising that both the phenomenon of occupation[6] and its corresponding terminology arose for the first time within this context. In the propagandistic *Traités contre les Anglais*, written between 1413 and 1417

---

2   Wolff, *Grundsätze*, § 1205; Vattel, *Droit*, Liv. III, §§ 201, 211, 862–70; Steiger, 'Occupatio Bellica', pp. 225–37; Carl, 'Militärische Okkupation im 18. Jahrhundert', pp. 351–53.

3   See Art. 42 and 43 of the Hague Convention (1907); Bothe, 'Occupation after Armistice', pp. 761–66; Strupp, *Wörterbuch des Völkerrechts*, pp. 154–71.

4   Steiger, 'Occupatio Bellica', pp. 220–24; Haggenmacher, 'L'occupation militaire', pp. 285–301; Carl, 'Französische Besatzungsherrschaft', pp. 42–44; Carl, *Okkupation und Regionalismus*, pp. 1–10.

5   Contamine, 'Growth of State Control', pp. 173–93. Contamine, 'Growth of State Control', pp. 173–93.

6   Bourassin, *France anglaise*, pp. 218–30.

by Jean de Montreuil, the English king is qualified as 'invaseur, occupeur et intruz' (invader, occupier and intruder); in the Latin version of the treatise, the verb *occupare* can also already be found with the sense of military occupation.[7] However, the problem of administrating a defeated country during periods of military occupation was not an object of late medieval reflection. Occupation was not yet a fully formed course of military practice, and it did not gain clear theoretical contours until the early modern period.[8]

In contrast with France, there developed within the Holy Roman Empire an awareness of the precarious legitimacy of conquest as the sole legal foundation of territorial gain and an understanding that military occupation represented a specific (because temporary) situation. This was due to the complicated territorial situation and, above all, to the general legal framework of the Holy Roman Empire. The idea that the occupier's status was merely provisional, with no legal right to permanent possession, found expression in the Empire in the imperial *ius sequestrationis*, to which the emperor or his allies had recourse in order to legitimise occupation and subject the occupied territory to a temporary forced administration, as in the case of the Duchy of Jülich-Berg in 1609, the Upper and Lower Palatinate after 1621, or in occupied Bavaria from 1704 to 1714.[9]

2. INTERNATIONAL LAW AND MILITARY PRACTICE

THE LITERATURE on international law from the seventeenth and eighteenth centuries reflects the development of military occupation into an independent legal phenomenon. The term *occupatio bellica* was used for the first time in the title of a juridical treatise of 1599 by Heinrich Bocer on different types of property acquisition.[10] Hugo Grotius may not have used the term explicitly in his *De jure belli ac pacis*, which appeared in 1625, but – as we have seen in Colm McKeogh's earlier chapter – he had already discussed in detail the problems for the laws of war resulting from an occupation, for example the status of the civilian population. The first relevant legal dissertations appeared on the subject of *occupatio bellica* while the Thirty Years War was still ongoing and in Samuel Pufendorf's influential law of nature and nations of 1672,

---

7   Montreuil, *Opera*, Vol. II, p. 197; Kintzinger, 'Auftrag der Jungfrau', pp. 84–85.

8   Rogge, 'Theorie, Praxis und Erfahrung', pp. 123–25.

9   Egler, *Spanier in der linksrheinischen Pfalz*, p. 90; Carl, *Okkupation und Regionalismus*, pp. 7–8.

10   Bocer, 'De Dominio', cited in Steiger, 'Occupatio Bellica', p. 215.

De jure naturae et gentium, the criteria of an *occupatio bellica* in the context of contemporary laws of war (*ius in bello*) were already largely formed.[11]

These reflections were in response to developments in military practice for which the Thirty Years War in particular offered a wide experimental field. Strategies that can already be observed during the eighty-year Dutch–Spanish war towards the end of the sixteenth century – such as an increasing bureaucratisation of war, the shift from selective to territory-wide war contributions, from mercenary to standing armies, and from seasonal military conflict to the accommodation of armies in winter quarters[12] – were systematised during the Thirty Years War. The result was an increasingly regulated exploitation of enemy territory in the form of long-term occupation. First in this respect was Spain, as the most advanced of the European powers, with the occupation of the Palatinate after 1622, followed by the extensive occupation of ecclesiastical territories by the Swedish army under Gustavus Adolphus and his allies after 1631 and of parts of Bohemia by the Swedish army after 1643.[13] The differentiation and systematisation of occupation praxis in the context of war between European states between 1648 and 1748 can be traced through the example of the southern (Spanish and Austrian) Netherlands. The southern Netherlands had been the main target of French military policy since Louis XIV, and thus became the preferred theatre of war for the late seventeenth- and early to mid-eighteenth-century conflicts motivated by concerns over the balance of power in Europe. It was the repeated object of foreign occupation, from the War of Devolution (1667–68), to the Nine Years War (1688–97), to the French occupation of large parts of the country during the War of the Austrian Succession – an occupation that lasted until 1749.[14] A comparison of these situations of occupation (which also include the occupation by the Dutch and British in the War of the Spanish Succession from 1708 to 1713)[15] shows that, as a rule, the occupying forces in the eighteenth century no longer linked occupation to an immediate change in sovereignty in order to exercise ruling authority. In the eighteenth century, an occupying force was no longer allowed to make long-term interventions into the laws and status of an occupied territory, such as the French had controversially undertaken between 1688 and 1697 under the guise of a hereditary claim with the re-Catholicisation of the occupied Palatinate territories (whose populations were Lutheran or Reformed).

---

11 Fisch, *Die europäische Expansion und das Völkerrecht*, p. 355.
12 Parker, *Army of Flanders*, pp. 127–57; Asch, 'Warfare', pp. 53–66; Glete, *War and the State*, pp. 42–66.
13 Egler, *Spanier*; Müller, *Schwedische staat in Mainz*; Meumann, 'Schwedische Herrschaft', pp. 245–52.
14 Houtte, *Occupations étrangères*; Bély, 'L'occupation française', pp. 337–50.
15 Denys, 'L'occupation hollandaise', pp. 313–28.

If military occupation finally became a fixed element of wars between eighteenth-century continental European states, the Seven Years War formed the pinnacle of this process. While Prussia occupied the formally neutral Saxony from 1756 to 1761, Prussia's military opponents, for their part, occupied Prussian outposts for many years. Russia occupied East Prussia from 1758 to 1762, while the French and Austrians occupied the Prussian province of the Lower Rhine for the entire duration of the war. While the French repeatedly occupied Hanover and Hessen as territories connected to Britain, Prussia's ally, the British and their allies compensated themselves with the ecclesiastical principalities of Westphalia.[16] From this point on, oscillating occupations became a fixed element of the entangled national histories of France and Germany. The Rhinelands were occupied from 1794 to 1801 by the revolutionary armies,[17] the Prussian Stein-Hardenberg reforms of 1807 were implemented in the occupied Prussian heartland,[18] while the Prussians remained in occupied Champagne after the defeat of Napoleon. Military occupation became a pattern of the very special relationship between Germany and France, which continued until after the Second World War.

3. The Restricted Right of Conquest versus Fiscal Efficiency

THE RELATIONSHIP between the military and the civilian population was initially defined by the fact that military occupation was a situation of force based on the right of conquest. In the proclamations regularly made in the eighteenth century by representatives of the occupying forces to civilians in an occupied territory, the regulated exercise of authority was declared to be a voluntary self-imposed restriction to the unconditional powers that the laws of war and conquest allowed. This carried with it the ever-present threat that the unlimited power of the conqueror would be brought to bear on the conquered subjects in the case of resistance or unwillingness to pay. However, it seldom came to this, even if it was not so much Christian or humanitarian considerations that motivated an occupying power to maintain peace and order in the occupied territory through a regulated administration and judiciary as the 'experience that with order, heavy demands are more easily borne', as the head of an Austrian occupation administration put it at the beginning of the Seven

---

16   Carl, *Okkupation und Regionalismus*, p. 17.
17   Blanning, *French Revolution in Germany*, pp. 83–134; Rowe, *From Reich to State*, pp. 48–85.
18   Münchow–Pohl, *Zwischen Reform und Krieg*, pp. 49–62.

Years War.[19] This logic, which implied the protection of conquered populations, was a prerequisite for the effective utilisation of resources.

In the eighteenth century, the actions of occupying forces were determined by their efforts to exploit the occupied territory more comprehensively. Arbitrary and short-term attacks were increasingly replaced by compulsory measures aimed at tapping into sources of revenue beyond those which were readily available, for example compulsory loans, whereby the occupying army compelled occupied provinces to take on debt (which the province in question had then to repay to its creditors after the war) in order to meet its financial demands. Such a strategy could only work effectively if demands were not unrealistic.[20]

Since an occupier could overrule the inherited participatory rights of the nobility, occupation also appeared attractive as a model for the expansion of the state administration in times of peace, so that in the eighteenth century occupation regimes, such as the French occupation of the southern Netherlands (1745–49) or the Austrian occupation of Bavaria (1743–45) served as models for administrative reform in the Habsburg monarchy.[21] The Prussian War Commissioners who acted as occupation administrators in Silesia in 1741–42 became the civil organs of administration following the annexation of Silesia in 1742.[22]

Nevertheless, every occupying power in the eighteenth century came up against structural limits. The many tempting opportunities for personal gain open to the military and civil functionaries of an occupying power were barely controllable. After all, the promise of plundering the enemy country was one of the most important factors in keeping together mercenary armies up until the seventeenth century, and this problem remained virulent in the standing armies of the cabinet wars, albeit in altered form.[23] However, the methods of plunder became more subtle and institutionalised, and therefore were limited to a smaller circle of officers and members of the military administration. The often chaotic circumstances surrounding invasion were critical here, since they constituted a more or less licensed freedom in which to exploit the uncoordinated demands made during the initial attack or in the immediate area of military operations for personal gain. More lucrative than extorting money from individuals were swindles that extorted large sums of money from occupied communes or provinces, under the pretext of raising funds for army

19 Carl, 'Militärische Okkupation im 18. Jahrhundert', p. 351.
20 Gutmann, *War and Rural Life*, pp. 54–71; Carl, *Okkupation und Regionalismus*, pp. 171–200.
21 Walter, *Geschichte der österreichischen Zentralverwaltung*, pp. 111–12.
22 Johnson, *Frederick the Great*, pp. 134–55.
23 Redlich, *De Praeda Militari*, pp. 59–67.

maintenance, of which a large portion then disappeared into the swindlers' own pockets. Both the civilian population and army provisioning bore the cost of these corrupt practices.[24] The French were especially notorious in this respect and their generals and war commissioners enriched themselves shamelessly during both the Seven Years War and the Revolutionary Wars in particular.[25] In this respect, the Prussian occupiers in Saxony from 1756 onwards were no saints either. However, it was in the interest of both the occupying power and the defeated population to channel the demands of the occupiers, usually via contractual regulations that stated the amount of contribution required, and that approximated the level of financial exploitation to peacetime conditions.[26]

Even if the level of contributions was agreed on, the possibility of physical force remained as an expression of the relationship between conqueror and conquered. Indeed, the occupying power sought to lend weight to its demands through compulsory measures. Through the strict regulation of these compulsory measures by all parties, international law sought to mitigate precisely this delicate area of confrontation between the military and civilian population. Beyond this legal discourse, pragmatic considerations saw to it that the civilian population was not treated 'with fire and sword'. Artists such as Jacques Callot (1592–1635) and novelists such as Hans Jakob Christoffel von Grimmelshausen (1622–75) had turned the harassed and tortured peasants of the Thirty Years War into a vivid topos of the suffering of the civilian population, even if the image of everyday life in wartime as a permanent battlefield of horror is overdrawn. With very few exceptions, such images of horror are without any basis in reality as far as the Seven Years War was concerned. Under the aim squeezing as much as possible out of the population, it was counterproductive to confront individuals with disproportionately severe levels of coercion in the course of compulsory measures and 'uncoordinated' looting. This simply turned the despairing population into martyrs, and then there was no getting anything out of them – as the French Brigadier Johann Christian Fischer, a specialist in compulsory measures, summed up his experiences in Germany in 1760.[27]

The most common means of exerting pressure were through incarceration or hostage-taking, as well as the compulsory billeting of soldiers or military impoundment. Above all, these processes had the advantage of being concentrated on specific individuals or groups of people. Preferred target groups were public officials and members of the nobility, since they were the primary addressees of any demands. However, measures such as compulsory billeting

---

24 Carl, *Okkupation and Regionalismus*, pp. 177–78, 213–21.
25 Kennett, *French Armies in the Seven Years' War*.
26 Carl, *Okkupation und Regionalismus*, pp. 188–201.
27 Ibid., p. 224.

lost some of their horror for those affected by them, since privileged groups were permitted to lodge the soldiers at their own cost in guesthouses and to recoup these costs later through public funds – as was the case for Prussian public officials during and after the Seven Years War.[28] In this way, coercive measures generally became more bearable for those affected. At the same time, representatives of the occupying power generally recognised that they could not afford to push repressive measures too far, since a modicum of cooperation from local elites, the nobility and, above all, public officials was needed in order to make the mobilisation of resources possible. An occupying power remained dependent on the knowledge of local functionaries in order to gain information about the occupied territory's resources.

4. LIMITS TO THE 'CONTAINMENT' OF WAR – KLEINER KRIEG AND PATRIOTISM

IN THE eighteenth century military occupation was viewed by contemporaries as an exemplary instance of 'civilised' interaction between the military and the civilian populations. This was because it had a particularly clear premise – the strict division of 'combatants' from 'non-combatants' (i.e. civilians) as a precondition for the rationally founded guarantees of protection provided by the laws of war for the civilian population.[29] Admittedly, however, there were two sensitive areas in which this division was or became fragile, even in the eighteenth century with its commitment to a rhetoric of rationality and humanity.

The first area affects the gap purposely left open by international law and the laws of war in order to defer to military necessities. Here I mean irregular warfare, the so-called *kleiner Krieg*, or rather its actors, the *leichte Truppen* or *Freikorps*. The *kleiner Krieg* offered an area of freedom within the 'contained'[30] cabinet war in which the laws of war with their protective mechanisms for the civilian population could be overruled.[31] In this type of war, looting as a necessity was more or less institutionalised since the *leichte Truppen* were not provided for by the commissariat officer, as were the regular troops, but largely had to take care of board and lodging for themselves. Moreover, the prospect of booty was one of the main incentives for recruitment to the corps. The indiscipline of the *Freikorps* ensured that they were seen by the defenders

---

28 Ibid.
29 Steiger, 'Occupatio bellica', pp. 229–33.
30 The characterisation of European wars since the seventeenth century as 'gehegte Kriege' ('contained wars') goes back to Schmitt, *Nomos*, p. 176.
31 Kunisch, *Kleiner Krieg*; Duffy, *Military Experience*, pp. 268–79; Pepper, 'Aspects of Operational Art', pp. 195–201.

of regular warfare as being reminiscent of an irregular 'Asiatic' form of war – embodied by the Russian Cossacks and Austrian Pandurs – and undermining the attainments of a 'civilised', European form of warfare.[32] Nevertheless, none of the belligerent powers wanted to do without these formations.

In the Seven Years War it was just such a *Freikorps* – the French so-called 'Fischer' *Freikorps* – whose actions in the theatre of war came closest to those horrific images usually connected to the wars of the seventeenth century. In 1761 the 'Fischer' *Freikorps* arrived in Eastern Friesland, far away from the main theatre of war, where, for the purposes of extorting an immense sum of money, they created a week-long climate of terror and violence among the civilian population through rape, slaughter and other acts of atrocity. As a result, the only organised armed resistance of conquered subjects against an enemy military power with the characteristics of a peasant uprising took place here.[33] The last time that something similar had occurred on German land was in 1705 with the Bavarian peasant uprising against the Austrian occupiers.

Significantly, unease was articulated on the French side at the excesses of the *leichte Truppen*, just as it was on the Prussian side regarding the spontaneous resistance of the conquered subjects. Both incidents broke with the model of war in which civilians were granted the role only of spectators, leaving armed conflict to the professional military. The regular French troops, brought in to restore order in the upstart province, behaved in accordance with this idea of 'contained' war. Although the insurrectionary peasants could not have done much to counter any punishment meted out by the regular military, the French commander Chrétien-Louis Baron de Wurmser did not order the feared reprisals; rather, his first act was to grant an amnesty. Thus the threat of enforcing the laws of war, which in such cases would grant soldiers the right to act 'by discretion' – 'worse than beasts' according to Johann Jakob Moser – remained rhetoric.[34] We might note, here, that Eastern Friesland was a territory with a tradition of armed resistance among the peasantry, which had manifested itself into the eighteenth century mainly through conflicts resembling civil war.[35] If, therefore, Eastern Friesland can be qualified as something of an exception, then the eighteenth century increasingly saw violent confrontation between the military and the civilian population becoming a second-hand experience that was chiefly conveyed through propaganda or tendentious contemporary historiography.[36]

---

32 Kunisch, *Kleine Krieg*, pp. 34–49.
33 Carl, *Okkupation und Regionalismus*, pp. 235–37, 373–74.
34 Moser, *Grund-Säze*, p. 45.
35 Kappelhoff, *Absolutistisches Regiment oder Ständeherrschaft?*
36 Michaelis, *Lebensbeschreibung*, pp. 51–52; Archenholtz, *Geschichte des Siebenjährigen Krieges*, pp. 14, 124.

However, the Seven Years War also represents a turning point in eighteenth-century understandings of the division between combatant and non-combatant, and the containment of war in situations of occupation. Extensive propaganda and the beginnings of a widespread discourse of patriotism during the Seven Years War aimed to awaken and inspire feelings of partisanship within civilians caught up in military conflict. Thus, the dividing line between armed and civilian partisanship could no longer be clearly drawn. The extent of this change should not be over-exaggerated. German sources during the Seven Years War were remarkably balanced, and even positive, in their judgements of the French occupiers. Xenophobic pronouncements, the accompanying music to a budding nationalism from the Revolutionary Wars onwards, were rare exceptions during this period. Goethe's favourable appraisals of the French in Frankfurt from 1759 to 1762 in his autobiography *Dichtung und Wahrheit* are well-known. Even in Hanover, where the French ran a hard regime in 1757–58, we find comments such as the following from the famous Göttingen Orientalist Johann David Michaelis, who stated that 'with all the misfortune one could not thank God enough that he had chastised us through the French, and not through others'.[37]

However, at precisely the time that these sentiments were being voiced, the premises for this kind of comparatively 'tension-free' coexistence under conditions of war were becoming uncertain. Love of the fatherland was demanded not only of the aristocracy, but propagated as the duty of every subject. This patriotism, which had emphatic expression in Thomas Abbt's *Vom Tode für das Vaterland* (1761), found resonance not only with officers and public officials, but with large sections of the population. Its impact can be particularly discerned where it took on a new quality in the form of patriotic merchandise, mass-produced during periods of foreign occupation, such as silk ribbons embroidered with appropriately patriotic slogans for women, or tobacco tins for men.[38]

During the Seven Years War, the altered geo-political constellation meant that confessional borders matched political antagonisms for the first time in a long while. Protestant Prussia and Britain were allies against Catholic France and Austria, and this may have played a contributing role in shaping this new type of patriotism, at least in Germany. Confessional factors could be used to mobilise the partisanship of wider sections of the population beyond what was usual for the cabinet wars. In the end, this kind of patriotism undermined efforts directed towards the 'containment' of war. The prerequisite for a 'clinical' campaign that harmonised the era's rationalising and humanitarian tendencies was the isolation of warfare to an inter-state occurrence that made

---

37 Carl, *Okkupation und Regionalismus*, pp. 366–67; Carl, 'Französische Besatzungsherr-schaft', pp. 61–63.

38 Clark, *Iron Kingdom*, pp. 220–25.

possible a clear division between the civilian population and the profession-alised military. The military occupations of the Seven Years War are marked by an ambivalent character. They are characterised by the achievements of the cabinet wars, such as the realisation of a systematic mobilisation of resources while, at the same time, restraining violence towards the civilian population. In this way, the Seven Years War was still a war of the *ancien régime*, even if the intensification of warfare pushed the model of the cabinet war, with its built-in restrictions, to its limits.

We need to be sensitive to occupation as a historically specific phenomenon. The early to mid-eighteenth century saw the consolidation of practices in the conduct of military occupation that built on developments of the late sixteenth and seventeenth centuries. By the second half of the eighteenth century, these developments were starting to come under strain with the spread of patriotic ideas and a burgeoning sense of national identities. Elements such as the birth of widespread patriotism already point towards the new kind of nationalised peoples' war that grew up during the Revolutionary and Napoleonic wars, and that made both the containment of war and the business of military occupation harder and more difficult to calculate and to control.[39]

---

39 Blanning, *French Revolution in Germany*, pp. 317–36.

9

British Soldiers at Home: The Civilian Experience in Wartime, 1740–1783

STEPHEN CONWAY

HISTORIANS OF previous generations tended to see eighteenth-century European wars before the French Revolution as tame or 'limited' affairs, their self-control a conscious reaction to the widespread destruction and brutality of the Thirty Years War (1618–48), which had left much of Germany depopulated and in ruins. To these historians, a key ingredient of the limited nature of eighteenth-century warfare was its minimal impact on civilians in the theatres of operation.[1] Contemporary works on the law of nations, such as the influential *Le droit des gens* (1758) of the Swiss jurist Emmerich de Vattel, certainly urged the military to show restraint in their dealings with those not in arms against them; a new spirit of proportionality and moderation, so characteristic of the Enlightenment, pervaded his and other writings on the laws of war.[2] Army commanders, older accounts imply, followed the lead of the jurists, and civilians, in return for their not becoming involved in the fighting, were spared the horrors of war. The French Revolution, the same accounts tell us, ended the era of limited war, sweeping away the restraint and decorousness

---

1 In the eighteenth century the term 'civilian' was not used; nor indeed was 'non-combatant'. The usual description was 'inhabitant'. The nearest usage to 'civilian' that I have come across is a letter of 1777, written by Charles Gould, the British army's judge advocate general, which explains that courts martial are usually for the trial of 'Military persons' only, and that 'Civil persons' are not normally to be brought before such courts. See TNA, War Office Papers, WO 72/8, Gould to Sir William Howe, 20 June 1777.

2 For Vattel and his reputation, see Best, *Humanity in Warfare*, p. 36.

associated with aristocratic control, and restored to armed conflict all its elemental fury.[3]

The idea that the French Revolutionary and Napoleonic wars marked a new beginning, the start of modern 'total' conflict, continues to be debated.[4] But the associated notion that earlier eighteenth-century struggles were limited in their impact on non-combatants is no longer fashionable. Modern scholarship has demonstrated beyond any doubt that European wars of that time were highly intrusive affairs and could be truly terrible for civilians unlucky enough to be in the vicinity of the competing armies.[5] Some historians argue that on the eastern fringes of Europe, in wars where the Turks were belligerents, non-combatants who found themselves caught up in military operations suffered particularly badly. The bloody fate of the inhabitants as well as the garrison of Ochakov, on the Black Sea coast, captured by the Russians from the Ottomans in 1788, seems to prove the point, as do other similar incidents in the same war.[6] But the experience forty years earlier of the people of Bergen-op-Zoom in the Dutch Republic is a reminder of the horrors to which civilians were exposed even in western Europe. The Dutch city was taken by storm by the French, and the subsequent orgy of murder, rape and destruction cast a long shadow.[7] As a leading military historian of our own day has put it, those townspeople who were about to die in Bergen-op-Zoom's streets would not 'have appreciated being told that they lived in an age of limited war'.[8]

The three other chapters in this section add to our understanding of the realities of warfare for peoples in the west of Europe. Their authors consider military–civilian relations through the prisms of military law and the problems of occupation in territories taken from an enemy and the treatment of captured enemy soldiers. They raise interesting issues, of importance beyond the places and times that they examine. To complement these studies, the current chapter looks at an army operating in its own country, where one might expect a quite different relationship to exist between soldiers and civilians. The chapter draws

---

3   For older surveys see, for example, Robson, 'Armed Forces and the Art of War'; Fuller, *Conduct of War*, ch. 1. Carl von Clausewitz, the nineteenth-century Prussian military theorist, famously welcomed the change introduced by the French revolutionary armies; indeed, his disapproval of the decorous timidity, as he saw it, of eighteenth-century warfare played a big part in influencing subsequent depictions of the so-called limited conflicts of *ancien régime* Europe: see Clausewitz's *On War*, esp. pp. 589–91.

4   See Bell, *First Total War*.

5   See, for example, Friedrichs, *Urban Society*; Gutmann, *War and Rural Life*; Childs, *Armies and Warfare*; Black, *European Warfare, 1660–1815*.

6   See, for example, Wilson, 'Warfare in the Old Regime, 1648–1789', p. 72.

7   See, for example, Anderson, *War and Society*, p. 194.

8   Black, *Military Revolution?*, p. 57.

on my research on the interactions between the British military and the British people during the War of the Austrian Succession (1740–48), the Seven Years War (1756–63) and the War of American Independence (1775–83).[9]

From a British point of view each of these wars was, of course, very different. The scale of mobilisation of domestic manpower varied considerably, for instance, from the relatively low levels of the Austrian Succession conflict to the much higher levels in the Seven Years War, and the still greater rate of military participation in the American struggle.[10] The political context was also different in each case. In the War of Austrian Succession there was much domestic discord, and a rising in Scotland in favour of the deposed Stuart dynasty that threatened briefly to topple the Hanoverian regime. In the Seven Years War, by contrast, a remarkable degree of political unity emerged, at least in the period of Pitt the Elder's ascendancy. The American war saw a revival of political fractiousness, with government and opposition, and their supporters in the country, divided over the merits of coercing the American colonies. These different political contexts almost certainly influenced the way in which civilians reacted to the military. In the Seven Years War, enlistment was actively encouraged and supported by local elites, whereas in the American war the army met with some resistance from local magistrates to its recruiting efforts, at least while the conflict was simply a struggle against the rebel colonists.[11] But, for all the differences, there was at least one essential similarity. In all of these conflicts, Britain was threatened with invasion, or at least attack – from the Spanish in 1740–41; the French in 1744–48, 1756–60 and 1778; the French and Spanish combined in 1779 and 1781; and the French, Spanish and Dutch in 1782.

To counter a feared enemy landing, the normal pace of military activity at home increased substantially. Even in peacetime the army had an impact on civilian life, but during these eighteenth-century wars that impact became much greater and much more widespread. Military recruitment intensified, encampments were established across southern and eastern England to concentrate and train troops, and large numbers of regular soldiers moved about the country and came into contact with non-combatants. In the Seven Years War and the American conflict, the British army at home was reinforced by the English and Welsh militia. As this militia was a uniformed force that

---

9 See Conway, *British Isles and the War of American Independence*; Conway, *War, State, and Society*.

10 See Conway, 'British Mobilization in the War of American Independence'; Conway, 'Mobilization of Manpower'.

11 For landowner influence in the Seven Years War see Middleton, 'Recruitment of the British Army'. For obstruction in the early stages of the American war see, for example, the situation in Nottingham, as reported in Barnes and Owen, ed., *Private Papers of John, Earl of Sandwich*, Vol. I, p. 340.

rapidly became an adjunct to the regular army, it will be considered here as an integral part of the British military deployed to resist an enemy descent.[12] On the other hand, for our current purposes the military will *not* include the assorted bodies of armed volunteers formed in many communities when invasion threatened, particularly in the American war. These volunteers retained the character of civilians. They were never incorporated into the army proper, and were run on quite different lines to the regular troops and the militia; indeed, many Britons saw them as a local antidote to the army and an increasingly centrally controlled militia.[13]

A more clearly military group is also off my agenda: the chapter will not look at the relationship between British civilians and the foreign troops imported to help put down the Jacobite rebellion in 1745–46, and to deter a French invasion in 1756–57. To include the Dutch, Swiss, Hessian and Hanoverian soldiers who came to Britain on one or other of these occasions might take us some way from a study of the interactions between local people and a 'friendly' military – not because the foreign troops behaved particularly badly, or should be seen as 'unfriendly', but because they were foreigners and therefore some Britons were predisposed to view them unfavourably (it was notable how speedily in 1745–46 the Dutch were blamed for the spread of disease in northern England).[14] Nor will this chapter discuss the situation in Ireland, where relations between the army and the local people were often complicated by religious differences and the sense, among the Catholic inhabitants at least, that the British troops constituted an alien occupying force.[15] Also omitted is any engagement with the wider impact of war; no attempt is made to consider the stimulus provided to certain sectors of industry, or the deleterious effect of increased wartime taxes, or the diversion of savings into government debt rather than other forms of investment.[16] The focus is on the ways in which civilians were affected by the presence of soldiers in, or near, their communities.

It seems reasonable to assume that the British military authorities would have been particularly keen to avoid causing distress, or even offence, to the people of their own country. Even when operating abroad, the army high command had a number of strong incentives to ensure that its soldiers behaved in an acceptable manner towards the civilian population. Ill conduct by the

---

12   See Gould, 'Strengthen the King's Hands', and, more generally, Western, *English Militia*.

13   See Conway, 'Like the Irish?'

14   See, for example, Cowper, *Letters of Spencer Cowper*, p. 71.

15   See, for example, Bagshawe, *Colonel Samuel Bagshawe and the Army of George I*, p. 110, for the view of Lt-Col. Matthew Sewell in 1752 that 'if Roman Catholics were permitted to be on Grand Juries, They would present the whole English army as a Nuisance'.

16   For consideration of these matters see Conway, *War, State, and Society*, ch. 3; Conway, *British Isles and the War of American Independence*, ch. 2.

military could lead to a lack of local cooperation over supplies of foodstuffs, transport and information, and might even, in the most extreme cases, provoke a violent response. A breakdown of discipline also threatened the effectiveness of military units; soldiers who were accustomed to disobey instructions against plundering might cease to be reliable tools of their commanders: as one military manual of the time explained, without discipline '[t]roops may become more dangerous than useful, more hurtful to ourselves, than to our enemies.'[17] But at home the army's senior officers had an added incentive to prevent outrages against the inhabitants. Undisciplined or even just burdensome British soldiers were likely to incur the wrath of powerful local interests – big landowners, borough corporations and even MPs – many of whom enjoyed some degree of access to political decision-makers at a national level. The views of such influential individuals and bodies mattered for the simple reason that the army in Britain, unlike some armies in other parts of Europe, was not a state within a state, but subject to the control of politicians at Whitehall and Westminster. The seventeenth-century experience of the rule of Cromwell's major-generals during the Interregnum, and then James II's building up of a strong army to support his allegedly absolutist intentions, led the English Parliament to impose significant limitations on the army's independence once William of Orange took the throne. The very existence of the army now required legislative sanction, as the ability of the army's officers to discipline their men relied from 1689 on the annual passage of a Mutiny Act. The army's pay was also dependent upon the Secretary at War presenting to the House of Commons estimates of the cost of the army, and accounts of extraordinary expenditures, which had to be approved by a majority of MPs.[18] Yet, as we will see, the contrast between the interactions of British soldiers and inhabitants of their own land and the relationship between European soldiers generally and enemy civilians was not as great as one might imagine.

We should, of course, acknowledge important differences. Courts martial, both general and regimental, while employed in Britain to punish certain offences committed by military personnel against civilians, were not the main courts at which such offences were tried. Military men were brought before the civil authorities, in the form of magistrates operating in petty or quarter sessions, or even assize court judges.[19] Other contrasts are more striking. Even though the War of the Austrian Succession saw a significant domestic rebellion (the Jacobite uprising of 1745–46), which caused much disruption and some loss

---

17   [Bever], *The Cadet*, p. 1. See also Saxe, *Reveries*, p. 79.

18   For the constitutional position see Clode, *Military Forces of the Crown*, esp. chs. 6–8.

19   See, for example, the case of soldiers tried before Essex magistrates in the spring of 1776: ERO, Quarter Sessions Book, Q/SMg 22, 16 April 1776.

of property, British non-combatants were spared the awful experience of indiscriminate blood-letting common after a besieged town, refusing a summons to surrender, eventually fell to enemy storm. Nowhere in Britain experienced the fate of Bergen-op-Zoom.

The inhabitants of parts of the Highlands certainly suffered at the hands of British troops after the final defeat of the Jacobites at Culloden, when the Duke of Cumberland and his senior officers seem to have adopted a concerted policy of severity;[20] on this occasion, British officers boasted of their involvement in widespread destruction of property and theft of livestock.[21] But in doing so they appear to have distinguished between the rebellious Highlanders and the civilian population of Britain in general. The army's officers saw the Highland rebels as beyond the pale, as much an alien 'other' as any menacing external enemy. In part this categorisation was based simply on the perceived sinfulness of rebellion, but it also owed much to the related assumption that the Highlanders were 'savages' who did not deserve to be treated as legitimate enemies.[22] But, the rebel clans aside, civilians in Britain were not exposed to harsh official treatment by the British army. 'Contributions', a euphemism for enforced exaction of money or supplies from a community, were imposed by the Jacobite forces in 1745,[23] but not by British troops.

The benefits of a military presence were also more obvious when the army was operating in friendly territory than when it was occupying enemy country. Increased local business opportunities, and the development of close personal relationships between soldiers and civilians, can be seen as positive aspects. But if some individuals or even communities in general were advantaged, in many cases the positive features were counterbalanced by the problems – sometimes very severe problems – caused by the army's activities. Even a supposedly friendly army was at best a mixed blessing for the inhabitants with whom it came into contact.

---

20 See Duffy, *The '45*, esp. ch. 21.

21 See, for example, WSRO, Goodwood MS 111, fo. 200, James Hamilton to [the Duke of Richmond], 20 May 1746. All citations from the Goodwood Collections are by courtesy of the Trustees of the Goodwood Collections and with acknowledgements to West Sussex Record Office.

22 See, for example, WSRO, Goodwood MS, 112, fo. 374, Thomas Thompson to [Richmond], 8 April 1746. For a depiction of the filthiness of the Highlanders, designed to portray them as outside civilised society, see 'A Plain, general, and authentic account of the Conduct and Proceedings of the Rebels, during their stay at Derby', printed in Derby in 1745, in Allardyce, ed., *Historical Papers relating to the Jacobite Period*, Vol. I, p. 292.

23 See, for example, Renwick, ed., *Extracts from the Records of the Burgh of Glasgow*, Vol. VI, pp. 217, 219.

1

B EFORE WE explore the negatives in some detail, something more should be said about the positives. The camps formed to concentrate troops and train them to counter an invasion often contained enough military personnel to be the equivalent of new towns.[24] In the summer and autumn of 1778, Warley Common, near Brentwood in Essex, was the temporary home to some 11,000 regular soldiers and militiamen, plus assorted camp followers. In other words, Brentwood – more a village than a town – found itself in close proximity to a military population as numerous as were the inhabitants of contemporary Hull or Coventry. Coxheath camp, established at the same time near Maidstone in Kent, was even larger; its 17,000 military occupants put it on a par with the Leeds of its day.[25] The demands created by such encampments were considerable. 'A General Estimate of the Quantities of Bread, Straw, Wood, and Forage, to be furnished [...] at the several Encampments of the Troops in South Britain 1778', probably drawn up by Treasury officials, reckoned on the need for 59,377½ lbs of bread a day, 31,668 lbs of straw every three weeks, and for the same period 2,493,855 lbs of wood and at least 215,670 rations of forage, each comprising eighteen pounds of hay and a peck of oats.[26] The opportunities were even greater than these figures suggested, as the encampments acted as an important public attraction, drawing vast crowds of sight-seers. Within a few weeks of its being formed, Warley camp was drawing large crowds; up to 20,000 on one Sunday, according to a press report, many probably coming from London.[27] In the early autumn of 1741 an officer based at the Colchester encampment reckoned that a review of the 'Whole line [...] together in Front of the Camp', drew an audience of '40 or fifty thousand spectators'.[28]

Although contractors, often based in London, agreed with government the provision of standard rations for the soldiers,[29] fresh food was sold to the

---

24 For the cultural impact of the camps, which falls outside the purview of the current chapter, see Russell, *Theatres of War*, pp. 33–46; Conway, *British Isles and the War of American Independence*, pp. 121–22.

25 Houlding, *Fit for Service*, p. 330; Conway, 'Locality, Metropolis, and Nation', p. 549.

26 TNA, Treasury Papers, T 1/543, fo. 12.

27 *Chelmsford Chronicle*, 17 July 1778.

28 Tyne and Wear Archives, Gateshead, Ellison Papers, A19/20, Cuthbert Ellison to his brother, 4 September 1741.

29 See, for example, Shaw, ed., *Calendar of Treasury Books and Papers, 1739–1741*, p. 566, for £1,318 paid to Abraham Cortissos for ammunition bread for the camps in southern England established in 1740; TNA, Treasury Papers, T 52/41, pp. 83, 139, 238, 243, 297, 378, for payments to George Wright for supplying hay, straw and wood to the camps in 1740–41. For a recent study see Bannerman, *Merchants and the Military in Eighteenth-Century Britain*.

military by local people, and vast quantities of beer were made available in stalls set up on the fringes of the camps. The military authorities tried to regulate the number of local people selling their men food and drink, but they had no wish to discourage them altogether, as supplements to the standard ration boosted the troops' morale, reduced desertion and took away one of the incentives for soldiers to steal. Nor, of course, was it simply the military that constituted a new market for local people. Inns in the vicinity of the camps did a roaring trade ('a fine Harvest', in the words of one commentator in 1756),[30] providing dinners for officers and sleeping space for sight-seers who had travelled too far to return home. In July 1778, an officer based at Coxheath reported that '[t]he accommodations immediately about the Camp are [...] always crowded', and that the inns in Maidstone, four miles away, were 'from the great resort of people to this camp [...] generally full'.[31] Indeed, another report suggests that Maidstone's inns could not cope with the increased demand, and beds were being hired in private homes.[32] Even the owners of roads near the camps were able to benefit from the increased traffic generated by so many visitors; turn-pike trusts might waive the tolls for officers travelling to and from the camps, but they were careful not to extend this patriotic dispensation to civilians.[33] As a visitor to Salisbury camp noted on 1 October 1778, 'It was [...] a glorious day for the Turnpike, as I believe the Cavalcade of Coaches, Chaises Waggons, Carts, Horses &c extended near 2 Miles.'[34]

It was not just the camps that brought financial benefits to the non-combatant population. The expanded British military, in camps or on the march, offered civilians opportunities for profit. Non-military labour was vital to enable the army to function – especially to carry its baggage, munitions and food supplies. The Board of Ordnance, responsible for the artillery, hired civilian drivers for each year's campaign to move its guns, powder and ammuni-tion.[35] Even infantry regiments and militia corps on the march needed wagons to carry their baggage, and accordingly hired civilian carts and drivers.[36] While the purchasing power of the army often put it in a strong position to secure a

---

30   Savile, *Secret Comment*, p. 319.
31   WiltSHC, Savernake Estate MSS, 9/34/138.
32   BL Hardwicke Papers, Add. MS 35,659, fo. 393.
33   Centre for Kentish Studies, Maidstone, U333 Z1, General Orders, Coxheath Camp, 18 July 1779.
34   Huntington Library, San Marino, California, Diaries of John Marsh, MS HM 54457/6.
35   See, for example, TNA, WO 55/2, fos. 25, 120.
36   See, for example, WSRO, Petworth Turnpike Trustees, Minute-book, 1757–1801, Add. MS 2212, p. 268, where there is a reference to George Elliott, a local farmer, 'employed in carrying Soldiers Baggage' in wagons.

good deal, and even reduce prices,[37] on occasion civilian contractors were able to take advantage of the army's desperate need. In 1745, to give an example, when regular troops were moving north to engage with the Jacobite forces, the government instructed the Earl of Cholmondeley, lord-lieutenant of Cheshire and governor of Chester Castle, to provide essential items for the soldiers who would pass through his area. Cholmondeley was worried that the local farmers would combine to push up prices, and soon found that his concerns were justified. Local shoemakers, sensing an opportunity, insisted on a higher rate per pair than they had originally agreed.[38]

The presence or proximity of the army also offered opportunities of a less obviously material kind. Social contact between soldiers and civilians seems sometimes to have been amicable. In 1781 Thomas Hawkins, a young officer in the Tenth Dragoons, recorded in his diary a breakfast given by his regiment to about a hundred inhabitants of York, the grandstand on the racecourse being used for the purpose. Hawkins was especially keen to note his social calls on the leading families of the area, making a careful list of the names of the eligible daughters.[39] Women's fascination with soldiers even appeared as a theme in contemporary literature; in John Dobson's *Robin: A Pastoral Elegy* (1746) the eponymous central character sees his beloved Susan fall for a soldier, recently returned from Flanders to combat the Jacobite invasion ('He came from Flanders with the red-coated crew,/ To fight with rebels, and he conquered you').[40] The disruptions and uncertainties of wartime probably had the effect, overall, of delaying marriage; this is certainly the impression conveyed by the records of Edinburgh for the middle years of the eighteenth century.[41] But where soldiers were concentrated, the pattern was somewhat different. In Exeter, for instance, the number of marriages seems to have risen sharply during the mid-century wars, especially in the Austrian Succession conflict. The proportion of marriages involving military personnel also increased, which suggests that local women benefited from a more favourable marriage market created by the availability of more men.[42] Perhaps such conjugal ties, as well as the economic advantages of a military presence, account in part for the

---

37 For an example from the Seven Years War see TNA, C 103/202, John Warrington's Account-book, 1760–1.

38 CRO, Cholmondeley of Cholmondeley Papers, DCH/X/9, 10. See also 17, 21, 42.

39 Cornwall Record Office, Truro, DD J 2245, Diary of Thomas Hawkins.

40 Lonsdale, ed., *New Oxford Book of Eighteenth-Century Verse*, p. 406.

41 Grant, ed., *Register of Marriages of the City of Edinburgh*, pp. 440–582 (a sample of those registered under 'M'), suggests a fall in the number of marriages during the Seven Years War, followed by a surge in 1763 and 1764.

42 These conclusions are based on a sampling exercise, extracting information from Tadley-Soper, ed., *Registers of Baptism, Marriages and Burials of the City of Exeter*, pp. 23–57.

enthusiasm of some communities for soldiers to remain in their midst. In March 1780 the mayor of Canterbury appealed to the War Office not to move the Thirteenth Regiment of Foot from his city, as 'the inhabitants [...] will be exceedingly happy for them to continue the remainder of [the] Winter'.[43]

2

NEGATIVE COMMENTS by civilians about the problems associated with the army are much more common. Indeed, if the mayor of Canterbury was eager for his military visitors to remain, it should be said that his apparent enthusiasm was more comparative than absolute. He wanted the particular troops in his city to stay because he was worried that if their regiment left 'it might be thought necessary to order another Corps in their room' – in other words, he was motivated by fear of something worse.[44] Rather more communities displayed unambiguous hostility to the prospect of soldiers arriving and staying in their area. In 1760 the corporation of Newbury decided to petition local dignitaries to use their influence to ensure that an encampment rumoured to be intended for the neighbourhood of Reading was *not* established near their town instead.[45] Memories of the last war, when there was a camp not far from Newbury, apparently persuaded the corporation to wish to avoid any repetition of the experience. We should not be surprised by the keenness of the good burghers of Newbury to be spared a military presence, for the difficulties such a presence could create were many and varied.

If the army generated business for civilians, local producers and retailers could rue the day that they sold goods or services to soldiers. Aggrieved innkeepers, merchants and manufacturers complained bitterly to the War Office of officers who had failed to honour debts incurred on their own account, or on behalf of their military units.[46] The wider community, meanwhile, might find itself paying more for necessaries as a result of the increased demand created by the military; a number of commentators noted the inflation common in garrison towns and the proximity of large encampments.[47] While the army was expected to pay for the transport it required, requisitioning of horses, carts and carriages could lead to local shortages and disrupt the movement of goods needed by the civilian population, and thereby add to inflationary pressures.

---

43 TNA, WO 1/1007, p. 393.
44 Ibid.
45 Berkshire Record Office, Reading, Newbury Borough Records, N/AC/1/1/2, council minutes, 19 May 1760.
46 See, for example, TNA, WO 4/110, p. 177.
47 See, for example, TNA, WO 1/1007, p. 789.

Valuable local labour could also be lost to army recruitment. In the Seven Years War, Isaac Fletcher, a Cumberland tradesman, was vexed to discover that one of his apprentices had apparently 'gone away with the souldiers'.[48] Other inhabitants complained of the illegitimate tactics used by recruiting parties to entice men to join the army. The ill feeling that dubious recruiting practices engendered sometimes spilled over into violence. In April 1780 residents in an Essex village physically attacked a corporal and private soldier who had just enlisted a local man in doubtful circumstances.[49]

But perhaps the most frequent causes of protest by local people were the problems associated with accommodating the military. Barracks were in short supply in England, not least because they were ideologically unacceptable reminders of the dangers of a standing army. The French had barracks, which meant that they were necessarily un-British, and building them was therefore shunned as a solution to the problem of finding somewhere to house troops on the march or in postings without established military buildings. As a result, soldiers on the move, or in winter quarters, had to be put up in local inns. The burdens of accommodating the soldiers were a regular cause of complaint. The sums paid to inn-keepers did not always cover their costs, and the military squeezed out the civilian customers who might have paid more. A report from a Canterbury brewer in 1756 reckoned that what the inn-keepers of the city were paid by the troops quartered on them would 'not amount to above a fourth part for such their Loss'. Many, he continued, had 'flung up their Licences' as a result of their inability to continue sustaining such burdens.[50] This report, we might note, came from the very same place – Canterbury – that in the next war was to ask for its military visitors to stay (or at least not be replaced by another regiment); a circumstance that sheds interesting light on the then mayor's comments. The mayor and principal inhabitants of Great Yarmouth, in Norfolk, wrote to the Secretary at War in the spring of 1782 to point out that the troop of cavalry quartered on the town's inns the previous summer had taken up all the available stables, making it impossible for the local taverns to put up travellers with horses, and so driving the inn-keepers 'to the brink of ruin'. Had the cavalry not been withdrawn, Great Yarmouth's worthies continued, the consequence for the inn-keepers would have been the 'shutting up their houses'.[51] Soldiers quartered in local taverns, furthermore, displayed an unfortunate tendency to help themselves to what they wanted;

---

48 Fletcher, *Diary of Isaac Fletcher*, p. 22.
49 ERO, Quarter Sessions Records, Q/SBb 300/23.
50 TNA, Chatham Papers, PRO 30/8/45, fo. 121, John Hubbard to William Pitt, 28 December 1756.
51 Norfolk Record Office, Norwich, Great Yarmouth Borough Records, Y/TC 36/20/15.

in February 1760, for instance, the inn-keeper of the Castle, in Marlborough, lost fowls stolen from his stables by three members of the Wiltshire militia.[52]

Indiscipline, a word that could cover a multitude of sins, was not confined to soldiers quartered in local taverns. Military men were prone to take what they wanted wherever they were. In some instances, this regrettable propensity seems to have owed something to the presence (or influence) of soldiers who had served abroad, and become used to living at the expense of the local inhabitants. An officer who had been on campaign in North America during the War of Independence noted that on his regiment's return home to recruit, a great many offences were committed by his non-commissioned officers, who 'had been so long accustomed to kill their own mutton in America, that they thought they might do the same in England'.[53] Here, perhaps, we can see a manifestation of what might be described as a 'plunder culture' – a sense of entitlement among soldiers who felt that access to the good things around them was only their due, a just recompense for the hardships and dangers to which they were exposed. We should also note that soldiers were often short of money; as General John Wentworth explained in October 1745, as the forces under his command prepared to block the Jacobite advance into northern England, 'if the Troops are not regularly paid, they will of course plunder the Country'.[54] When the supply system failed to deliver the rations required, soldiers might be hungry too. In such circumstances, officers might overlook, if not approve, their men's acquiring foodstuffs without paying for them; in the words of a military manual for officers, 'everyone is unwilling to occasion the death of a poor wretch, for only having been seeking perhaps to gratify his hunger'.[55] Troops far from home might also be encouraged by their anonymity to do things that they would hesitate to do in their own neighbourhoods. They might equally be emboldened by a sense of soldierly solidarity – a feeling that their colleagues were unlikely to denounce them to the authorities. Sometimes contemporaries claimed that not enough officers were present to keep the soldiers in order – a problem no doubt magnified by home service, which facilitated officers' visits to family and friends.[56]

Whatever the reasons, the frequency of offences committed by soldiers on the civilian population is striking. A few examples will suffice to establish the nature and variety of such outrages. At the minor end of the scale was

52   WiltSHC, Savernake Estate MSS, 9/34/124.
53   Hunter, *Journal of Gen. Sir Martin Hunter*, p. 45.
54   Nottingham University Library, Nottingham, Newcastle of Clumber MSS, NeC 1691.
55   Simes, *Military Guide for Young Officers*, p. 2.
56   For a complaint that 'these soldiers are generally without any Commissioned Officers to Controul them' see TNA, WO 1/1008, p. 893, petition of John Luther of Ongar, Essex, 8 May 1780.

the pilfering of fruit from orchards or fish from ponds.[57] More serious was the systematic and wholesale plundering undertaken by detachments of the army. In the spring of 1779 William Jolliffe, MP for Petersfield in Hampshire, complained that his town had been exposed to the 'excessive depredations' of a party of the Foot Guards. 'They have stolen more than twenty Sheep and Lambs a great number of Hogs, and poultry without number, within a fortnight,' an enraged Jolliffe wrote to the War Office, adding ominously that 'they threaten to break Houses'.[58] The following year Francis Buller, a Cornish squire, similarly protested at the impositions of the Fiftieth Foot, quartered in his vicinity. 'Hardly a night passes,' Buller fumed, 'that some Felony is not committed by them, they have broken open several Houses, committed Highway Robberies, stolen four sheep from one man & three from another, stripped a third of all his Poultry, & robbed Orchards & Gardens without End & to a considerable Value.' He went on to explain that '[t]hey are so daring that they go in large Gangs, & generally arrived with their side arms'.[59]

Soldiers might pose a threat to local people as well as to their property. To some extent the danger was unavoidable, or at least not the result of deliberate acts of indiscipline. Despite strenuous efforts to make camps sanitary, they were breeding grounds of disease and distemper. In all camps a high proportion of soldiers tended to be ill at one time or another. Both Warley and Coxheath were reported to be 'very sickly' in November 1779, just before they were broken up and the troops moved into winter quarters.[60] As a result of local trading activities and the vast numbers of visitors that the camps attracted, ailments generated in the tented military towns readily spread to neighbouring communities. During the American war, the sharp rise in the number of burials at St Mary the Virgin, Great Warley, in 1779 is surely attributable to the presence nearby of Warley camp.[61]

In civilian minds, one particular disorder tended to be associated with the military – venereal disease. Soldiers at Warley were known to use prostitutes who operated on the fringes of the camp, and several were upbraided by their officers for catching 'the Foul Disease'.[62] The military was widely believed to be morally as well as biologically contaminating, and its presence in a community to be a recipe for an increase in the number of illegitimate

---

57 See, for example, NLS, Wade Papers, MS 3076, fos. 34, 45 (orders relating to Newbury camp, 1740).
58 TNA, WO 1/1004, p. 395.
59 TNA, WO 1/1007, p. 259.
60 TNA, Chatham Papers, PRO 30/8/25, fo. 206.
61 Conway, *British Isles and the War of American Independence*, p. 293 (fig. 8.1).
62 East Sussex Record Office, Lewes, ABE/D 560/17, Monmouth Militia Order-book, 30 April 1779.

children.[63] Assumption and reality were not always one and the same; but on at least a few occasions soldiers lived up to their reputations. In October 1745, to give an example, Andrew Anderson, a corporal in Bragge's Regiment of Foot, was summoned to appear before Leicester's magistrates to answer charges relating to 'the bastard child of Sarah Hickling, widow'.[64] It hardly needs to be added that sexual relations between soldiers and local women were not always consensual. In March 1761 a trooper in a cavalry regiment that had just come from Ireland was confined to Chester Castle for raping a local woman.[65] In the next war a dragoon was committed at Salisbury for assault and attempted rape in the spring of 1779. It was perhaps noteworthy that he was rescued from gaol by fellow soldiers.[66]

3

WHAT GENERAL points can be drawn from this brief investigation of civilian–military interactions in Britain? The first is surely that there were positive as well as negative aspects to the presence of the army in or near a community. But the negatives were often considerable and, in general terms, predominant. For civilians in Britain the ill effects of their own army's activities may not have been as great as for civilians confronted with enemy troops, but they were bad enough. The extent to which non-military Britons regarded the British army as their own is perhaps worthy of further consideration. On the one hand, the army was clearly seen as offering protection against enemy attack – an important factor in civilian responses to the behaviour of the military. An officer in the Duke of Cumberland's army, writing to his father from Macclesfield in December 1745, commented on how the local people were delighted that the Jacobite forces had retreated and that the regular troops had arrived, and that 'the Women all declare in this Country that they will never marry for the future but in the Army, for they are the only People that have shew'd their Heads & offer'd to Protect them in this time of distress'.[67] On the other hand, anti-standing army sentiments were particularly strong at the beginning of the period examined in this chapter, and were only muted by the success of the army abroad in the Seven Years War. In the highly charged political atmosphere of the American war, when government and opposition were

---

63 See, for example, Greene, *Correspondence of the Reverend Joseph Greene*, p. 44.
64 Chinnery, ed., *Records of the Borough of Leicester*, p. 91.
65 *Adams's Weekly Courant*, 3 March 1761.
66 TNA, WO 1/1006, pp. 521–24.
67 BL Hardwicke Papers, Add. MS 35,354, fo. 150.

bitterly divided over the legitimacy of conflict with the rebellious colonists, the standing army again came in for criticism as a tool of ministers, and there was a revival of enthusiasm for military alternatives, notably locally controlled bodies of volunteers.[68]

The importance of the local perspective – throughout the period considered in this chapter – is indeed striking. What emerges from many of the examples cited is the ways in which the army was conceptualised as an outside, alien body, causing many different difficulties for communities. When contemporaries complained about the ill conduct of the troops, they were usually looking not so much for an improvement in their behaviour as for their removal. Only by moving the problem elsewhere, the complainants seemed to think, would relief be secured. If, as some of the chapters in this collection suggest, foreign armies campaigning in one's own country might, in a reactive way, increase identification with the nation, by the same token the activities of one's own army serving at home might heighten a sense of local loyalty.

---

68   See Conway, 'Politics of British Military and Naval Mobilization'.

PART III

Who is a Civilian? Who is a Soldier?

10

Conflicted Identities:
Soldiers, Civilians and the
Representation of War

PHILIP SHAW

J OSEPH WRIGHT'S *The Dead Soldier* (frontispiece) highlights the issues addressed by the chapters in this section. First exhibited at the Royal Academy in May 1789, a few weeks before the dramatic inception of the French Revolution, Wright's painting depicts the corpse of a British soldier, his grieving widow and their newly orphaned child. Most likely a recollection of the recent war against the American colonies, the legal, political and social distinctions between civilians and combatants are blurred in this image. As the circle of suffering extends beyond the immediate scene of devastation, the message of the painting appears insistent to the point of banality: it is one thing for a soldier to lay down his life in defence of his country, but what of the effects of war on ordinary men, women and children?[1]

The question prompts some further reflections on the relations between war, critical debate and the nature of citizenship. Writing in 1767 in *An Essay on the History of Civil Society*, the social philosopher Adam Ferguson announced that 'he who has not learned to resign his personal freedom in the field [with] the same magnanimity with which he maintains it in the political deliberations of his country, has yet to learn the most important lesson of civil society, and is

---

1   The intellectual background to this discussion of the effects of 'distant wars' on ordinary civilians has been explored by the literary critic Mary A. Favret, initially in her frequently cited essay 'Coming Home: The Public Space of Romantic War' and, most recently, in her book-length study *War at a Distance: Romanticism and the Making of Modern Wartime*.

only fit to occupy a place in a rude, or in a corrupted state'.[2] Not only the soldier but the citizen too must learn to renounce his personal liberty so that the nation, considered as a whole, may be free. Some years later, Immanuel Kant argues along related lines that only one who is 'enlightened [...] and at the same time has at hand a large, well-disciplined army as a guarantee of public peace [...] can say what a republic cannot dare: *argue as much as you want and about whatever you want, only obey!*', the point being that freedom of expression, or enlightenment, is dependent on the recognition of necessity. Thus, as Kant goes on to argue,

> it would be very destructive, if an officer on duty should argue aloud about the suitability or the utility of a command given to him by his superior; he must obey. But he cannot fairly be forbidden as a scholar to make remarks on failings in the military service and to lay them before the public for judgement.[3]

Free thinking depends, then, on the maintenance of a rigid distinction between the public and private spheres. The realm of the private, Kant suggests, emerges only when individuals accede to the primacy of the public, but once this realm is manifested it cannot be allowed to undermine the authority of the public sphere from which it is derived. As Marx goes on to argue, critical debate must therefore be seen as a key element in the ideological superstructure of society, providing a semblance of intellectual freedom while sanctioning the social inequalities that are an effect of the economic base.

In light of the above, how should we understand the ideological significance of *The Dead Soldier*? The painter, Joseph Wright of Derby, has been regarded for many years as a politically progressive, even radical figure in late eighteenth-century British culture. But as the art historian Matthew Craske has recently argued, this idea of Wright has little, if any, grounding in reality.[4] While it is true that the artist associated with a number of prominent industrial, scientific, religious and political figures of the day, many of whom were undoubtedly of the Old Whig, Foxite or radical persuasion, the sense of Wright as a left-wing painter is an image fostered in large measure by Marxist historiography. Craske has in sight here Francis Klingender's highly influential 1947 study *Art and the Industrial Revolution*, but he might also have mentioned the work of Benedict Nicolson, Judy Egerton and Albert Boime, all of whom lay stress on the artist's connections with leading social reformers, natural philosophers and rational

---

2   Ferguson, *Essay*, p. 148.
3   Kant, 'An Answer to the Question: What is Enlightenment', pp. 60, 63.
4   Matthew Craske presented his revisionist account of Wright scholarship at the Wright of Derby Symposium held in Liverpool in November 2007.

theologians.[5] Thus Wright is placed in the same light as the free-thinking, English Rousseauean Sir Brooke Boothby; he is perceived to share the liberal, enlightened values of the Derby Philosophical Society; and, as result of his friendship with Erasmus Darwin, he becomes linked with the anti-slavery campaign, with scientific materialism and with the radical fringes of the Lunar Society. Yet not a single document written by Wright can be found to support this image. As Craske provocatively concludes, radical or left-wing Wright is a fabrication born out of a reductive, neglectful reading of the past.

In what sense, therefore, should we regard *The Dead Soldier* as an anti-war painting? As the historian Martin Ceadel has argued, the British peace movement was restricted in the late eighteenth century to the radical margins of society.[6] Only limited numbers of Quakers and a handful of Unitarians would have defined themselves as fundamentally opposed to war. Those movements that arose in the 1790s to protest against Britain's involvement in the war against revolutionary France were prompted not by underlying philosophical objections to state-sanctioned violence but rather by pragmatic considerations about the object of the war and its costs – both economic and human – to the nation. Wright's painting predates Britain's involvement in the Allied campaign against French radicalism. Therefore, so that we may get a sense of its precise ideological significance, we must consider its connections with the political and social milieu of the post-war period in the 1780s.

At the Royal Academy in May 1789 Wright's close friend, the Whig poet William Hayley, could be observed crying in front of *The Dead Soldier*.[7] Hayley was clearly moved by the painting's unstinting portrayal of misery on the field of battle. Unlike, say, Benjamin West's *The Death of General Wolfe* (1770) or John Singleton Copley's *The Death of Major Peirson, 6 January 1781* (1783), the victims in the painting are unnamed and the depiction of the soldier's corpse, with its detailed attention to decaying flesh, the unalloyed grief of the widow and the unbearable gaze of the orphaned child results in an overwhelming affective charge. One could argue that Hayley's tears were prompted by political objections. As an opponent of the war against America, Hayley would most likely have connected the individual suffering shown in the composition with the larger political, social and economic deprivations that followed in the wake of Britain's defeat. Hayley's view is therefore sentimental, in the particular

5   Klingender, *Art and the Industrial Revolution*; Nicolson, *Joseph Wright of Derby*; Egerton, *Wright of Derby*. Boime, in *Art in the Age of Revolution*, goes so far as to claim that 'Wright would do for the Industrial Revolution what David did for the French Revolution': Boime, *Art in the Age of Revolution*, p. 234.

6   Ceadel, *Origins of War Prevention*, pp. 1–3, 166–221.

7   For further details and discussion of this painting see Shaw, 'Dead Soldiers'.

sense in which this word circulated in the late eighteenth century, but it is also, importantly, ideologically conservative and ought not to be confused with out-and-out pacifism. As Ceadel has suggested, such a response ought more properly to be regarded as 'pacificist', that is, as a restricted, pragmatic objection to a particular war and not to war per se.[8] Such a reading takes on further validity when we consider Hayley's earlier endorsement of military art in his 1781 *An Essay on Painting*:

> [N]or do [military paintings] only administer to the benefit of the artist, and the pleasure of the public: they have a still more exalted tendency; and when national subjects are painted with dignity and force, our exhibitions may justly be regarded as schools of public virtue. Perhaps the young soldier can never be more warmly animated to the service of his country, than by gazing, with the delighted public, on a sublime picture of the expiring hero, who died with glory in her defence.[9]

Here, then, is a portrayal of the painter's idealised viewer: a national subject 'animated to the service of his country' by a 'sublime picture' of a dying hero. Wright, for his part, was not averse to painting scenes that conformed to this pattern. His *A View of Gibraltar during the Destruction of the Spanish Floating Batteries, 13 September 1782* (1785) was an attempt to celebrate the British victory over the combined French and Spanish blockade of Gibraltar on the night of 13 and 14 September 1782. Coming hot on the heels of the humiliating outcome, from the British point of view, of the recent war with America, the successful defence of the British garrison against Bourbon oppression was hailed widely as a great national triumph, uniting figures of all parties in expressions of popular acclaim.[10] For Hayley, who as a Rockingham Whig had supported the rights of the colonies in their struggle for independence, Gibraltar had a long and august association with the cause of liberty. It is certainly possible that Wright shared Hayley's enthusiasm and was drawn to Gibraltar as a symbol of the Old Whig cause. The point I wish to make here is that Wright, on the strength of the visual evidence presented by *The Dead Soldier*, cannot be simply categorised as a pacifist. Such a designation is crude for a number of reasons, historical inaccuracy being chief among them.

A further point of fact that must be taken into account when considering *The Dead Soldier* is Wright's relationship with the man who purchased the painting: the Manchester cotton and silk manufacturer, volunteer soldier, amateur

---

8 Ceadel, *Origins of War Prevention*, pp. 35–44.
9 Hayley, 'Essay', pp. 98–99.
10 For detailed discussion of Wright's painting and other representations of this event see Bonehill, 'Laying Siege'.

botanist, antiquarian and art collector John Leigh Philips.[11] Clearly, Wright's work was much prized by its owner. But what, precisely, was the nature of the relationship between painter and patron and what significance did a painting such as *The Dead Soldier* have for a man like Philips? In his study of British responses to the threat of French invasion, Mark Philp pays close attention to Philips's involvement as commander of the Manchester and Salford Volunteers. The historian notes Philips's membership of the Manchester Pitt Club and the appearance of his signature on numerous loyalist addresses and petitions. The picture of Wright's patron that emerges here is thus of a committed opponent of reform and an ardent supporter of the ministry.[12] Philips's political allegiances, together with his military interests, make him an unusual friend for the liberal-minded Wright – but unusual only if we accept the prevailing view of the 'Wright circle' as a group bound by a shared commitment to enlightened, republican virtues. We cannot know with any precision what Philips would have seen in *The Dead Soldier*, and how his response may or may not have differed from that of his ideological opponent William Hayley, but his interest in Wright's work places pressure on any reading of the painting that would regard it as an unequivocal expression of anti-bellicist sentiment. Perhaps as a civilian Philips allowed himself to give vent to that side of his mind that could regard war as a hideous imposition on the lives of ordinary men, women and children even while, as a soldier, he could regard it as a necessary evil – necessary, that is, for the preservation of the Crown and for the promotion of British trade. In making this distinction we should recall the arguments advanced by Ferguson and Kant in support of the conceptual separation of the public and private spheres.

There is, however, a sense in which Hayley's tears, and indeed Philips's, assuming he cried, may be read as the body's solution to a vexed ideological problem: how to give vent to the pity of war while maintaining a sense of the necessity of war's role in the founding and maintenance of civil society. Like many prints and poems created in the aftermath of the American war, and then again in the wake of Britain's entry into the campaign against Revolutionary and Napoleonic France, anxieties about the effects of war on the domestic sphere are centred in *The Dead Soldier* on the image of the destitute wife, mother and child. If, as Mary Favret has claimed, one of the fictions motivating public support for war is that it keeps violence from coming home, then we can

---

11   From correspondence exchanged between Wright and Philips in the spring of 1789 it is evident that Philips eventually purchased *The Dead Soldier*, framed, for the sum of 100 guineas. In 1814 the painting was listed along with eight other Wright paintings in *A Catalogue of the Valuable Collection of Paintings and Drawings, Prints and Etchings [...] of the Late John Leigh Philips* (MSS held in Derby Local Studies Library, LSL 8962).

12   Philp, *Resisting Napoleon*, pp. 62–66.

see how the painting seeks to expose this fiction.[13] The loosely draped canvas shelter that frames the family group is, in all senses, a temporary shelter – a home that is literally vulnerable to attack. Within this shelter the public warrior becomes, once more, the private man of feminine longing: no longer the inviolable man at arms, but a suffering human being, subject to the effects of death and wounding. The viewer's concentration on the distraught demeanour of the widow and the innocent appeal of her baby brings to light the impact of the soldier's death on ordinary civilians. The boundaries erected by states to protect individuals from the knowledge of the proximity of violence are shown in this painting to be frail indeed. To cry, therefore, is to relieve oneself of an unwelcome insight into the labile relations between war and society.

But it is not only tears that enable human beings to bear such knowledge. Humour, as Matthew McCormack points out in his essay on Georgian satirical prints, also has an important part to play. In Charles Williams's satirical print 'After the Invasion' (1803), three civilian soldiers are shown triumphing over the defeat of the French invaders. A militiaman and a farmer congratulate themselves while a volunteer brandishes the head of Napoleon on the end of a pitchfork. As McCormack observes, the civilian soldiers are shown to be motivated by love of 'family, property and country. As Linda Colley has noted, however, prints such as this retain an ambivalence about arming plebeians.' In this case, ambivalence emerges in the contrast between the portly, ragged appearance and unrefined speech of the farmer and the militiaman and the classical elegance of the upper-class volunteer. As McCormack goes on to state, if 'the militia meant arming the lower orders – men who were not citizens in a political sense – then that was a matter for concern rather than celebration'. Just as war transgresses the boundaries between public and private, so war has a dynamic effect on class distinctions, presenting, as Dror Wahrman argues, an acute 'problem of identity'.[14] In *The Making of the Modern Self* Wahrman suggests that Britain's war against America brought about a cultural crisis that resulted in a shift away from the relatively mobile subject positions of the *ancien régime* towards fixed, recognisably modern categories of race, gender and class. As McCormack notes, within this context the militiaman emerges as a potentially dangerous figure. Since his identity, in class terms, is 'uncertain and unfixed' the militiaman threatens to undo the work of modernity, returning society to a state in which the distinctions between citizens and soldiers, gentlemen and plebeians are no longer secure.

With the internal violence of the English Civil War a not too distant memory, graphic satire in the wake of the 1757 Militia Act thus takes on a dual

---

13   Favret, 'Coming Home: The Public Space of Romantic War'.
14   Wahrman, *Making of the Modern Self*, pp. 221–27.

function: on the hand it gives vent to public concern about the arming of the lower classes; on the other it suggests ways of managing these concerns. The dominant image of the militiaman as an ill-disciplined 'hapless amateur' serves, that is, to alleviate fears about the spread of militarisation – for this raggle-taggle army, the prints suggest, will never become a threat to the state – while testifying, at the same time, to the militiaman's capacity for decisive action come the hour of need. The image of the stout-hearted yeoman, with rifle or pitchfork in hand, rising up to defend his liberty from foreign invasion thus becomes a complex symbol of British identity. This militiaman is brave, the prints assure us, but he is also ridiculous and, as such, ought not to be feared.

In Alan Forrest's study of insurgency and counter-insurgency in continental Europe from the 1790s to 1815 a related picture emerges of the ability of war to provoke unsettling inversions in the relations between men and women, soldiers and civilians. Like the English militiaman, insurgents and guerrillas occupy an 'ambiguous place [...] between military and civil society', often blurring the lines between legal and illegal acts of violence. As Forrest notes, the danger of civil defence is that participants are not bound by the laws of conventional warfare. Indeed, many irregulars in France, Spain and Italy also made a living as bandits or smugglers, using their knowledge of local customs and terrain to gain an advantage over their oppressors. Such men who had 'no right to bear arms, no legal claim to be soldiers, men who, living on the margins of civil society, were endangering the lives of others and were in breach of the criminal law' could claim no immunity, as soldiers in uniform could, 'that would protect them from the consequences of their actions'. Insurgents and guerrillas were thus usually tried and executed as common criminals.

In war, distinctions matter. When soldiers refuse to wear uniforms to identify themselves as soldiers, and when fighting is no longer confined to the field, it becomes difficult to distinguish between legitimate and illegitimate targets. Rules must be in place if battle is to be prevented from deteriorating into carnage and mere barbarism. During the Revolutionary and Napoleonic wars, hostilities between soldiers and partisans often descended into atrocities. Forrest pays close attention to the massacre at Machecoul in 1793 in which civilians plotted to exterminate all the republican supporters in the area, an act that resulted in the deaths of hundreds of men, women and children. Republican troops, for their part, retaliated against the rebels with extreme acts of cruelty, 'slaughtering even babies-in-arms in a bid to destroy the base from which a new generation of insurgents could grow'.

During the Napoleonic invasion of Spain, relations between the occupying army and the populace descended rapidly, resulting in sickening acts of inhumanity, with French troops responding in kind to partisan outrages. While the French were portrayed as brutal oppressors, the guerrillas, by contrast, were celebrated as nationalist heroes. In England the successes of the guerrillas were commemorated in a series of sonnets by the former republican William Wordsworth. In one of these poems the 'power of Armies' is described as 'a visible thing, / Formal, and circumscribed in time and place'. By contrast, the 'power' of a 'brave People' is limitless; it can be brought 'into light' or hidden 'at will' and no military 'craft this subtle element can bind'. Like 'water from the soil', the liberty of the people is rooted in natural law, whereas the power of the invader is an artificial imposition and is therefore destined to fail.[15]

Wordsworth's romanticised account of Spanish insurgency should be set alongside Goya's rather more shocking portrayal in his series of etchings, *Los Desastres de la guerra*. The art historian Juliet Wilson-Bareau has written that *Los Desastres* provides an illustration of 'the cruelty within all human nature, the desire for dignity and the betrayal of a people's sense of its own humanity'.[16] The etchings, with their vivid portrayals of rape, genocide, torture and genital muti-lation, in which distinctions between soldiers and civilians, foreign invaders and partisan defenders, are difficult to sustain, compel us to adopt a moral stance against war. But as anyone who has looked closely at *Los Desastres* will know, the sense in which war collapses the distinctions between right and wrong makes it very difficult for viewers to maintain a coherent position.[17]

In addition to Goya's visual conflations, the ironic verbal 'play' of the cap-tions further adds to an overall sense of moral indeterminacy. In *Los Desastres* 16, for instance, the text runs 'They equip themselves', though the Spanish is ambiguous: *Se aprovechan* could mean 'they're of use to each other', 'they help themselves', 'they're learning' or even 'good eating'.[18] This latter connotation echoes Ronald Paulson's Freudian stress on the oral and anal eroticism in Goya's prints. According to Paulson, the ingestion of the dead is the means by which a threatened totality, be it a nation or an individual, endeavours to re-integrate itself.[19]

In his own account of the atrocities committed by civilians and soldiers during the Spanish occupation, Forrest argues that acts of sexual violation were prompted by a desire to 'subvert the masculinity' of the enemy. 'These attacks reflected,' he concludes, 'stored-up hatred [...] with the victims being ritually feminised, deprived of their masculinity in a charade that concentrated the whole community's rejection of the invader, symbolically aborting the product of his rapes and violations by destroying his sexual organs before his

---

15 Wordsworth, *Shorter Poems*, p. 74.
16 Wilson-Bareau, 'Goya', p. 37.
17 Aspects of this discussion of Goya first appeared in Shaw, 'Abjection Sustained'.
18 Williams, *Goya*, p. 8.
19 Paulson, *Representations*, pp. 336–37.

eyes.' Goya's treatment of these atrocities is acutely disturbing. In plate 39, for example, *Grande hazaña! Con muertos!*, or 'What a feat! With dead men!', the inhumanity of war is depicted at its most unsettling: there is something wilfully excessive, even contrived about Goya's composition, which qualifies the integrity of its moral stance. What we see are three castrated corpses, suspended from a tree, their absurdly suggestive poses at odds with the solemnity of death. The notion is underscored when we meditate on the ironic contrast between the leaf-laden tree, symbolic of the cyclical economy of nature, and the unregenerate mortality draped and skewered on its branches. There is an allusion here as well to the crucifixion of Christ, but instead of differentiating the abject and the sacred, Goya succeeds in a kind of violent yoking, suffusing the abject with sacrificial meaning while subjecting the sacred to sadomasochistic defilement.

In war, as these chapters suggest, the boundaries between genders, classes and nations are frequently transgressed, resulting in new configurations of identity. But as Forrest's discussion of the untrammelled violence of guerrilla warfare implies, the transgressive reach of war extends even to the category of the human. Through Goya's fascination with the horrifying spectacle of retributive justice we gain an insight into a people's capacity for violence that no amount of sublimation can ever wholly efface. When, moreover, *Los Desastres* is located on a continuum with Jacques Callot's *Les misères et malheurs de la guerre* (1633) and with Otto Dix's *Der Krieg* (1924), the effect is particularly acute: at what point does the representation of war find relief in a certain kind of libidinal pleasure? An aspect of Joseph Wright's *The Dead Soldier* that remains unexamined, in this respect, is the disturbing eroticism of the painting. As war severs the connection between husband and wife, parent and child, it also makes the widow available as an object of sexual exchange. David A. Bell has observed that during the Seven Years War 'as many as a quarter of the persons' in British army encampments 'were women (who had, by definition, no military status). In addition to wives, servants, and the inevitable prostitutes, women served as sutlers, nurses, clerks, wagoners and laborers.' Bell goes on to note that some critics blamed General Burgoyne's defeat at Saratoga, in the American Revolution, 'on the 2,000 women who accompanied his 4,700-man army. As late as 1812, the Duke of Wellington allegedly complained of his army in Spain: "We are a marching brothel."'[20] In his discussion of satirical prints of militia camps McCormack argues that images of 'bold', 'sexually dominant' women in 'military costume' and of 'hunched and effeminate' men gave expression to anxieties about the fluidity of 'social and gender distinctions' in times of war. Although *The Dead Soldier*, with its concentration on the raw,

---

20 Bell, *First Total War*, p. 25.

unaffected grief of the widow, presents a respectable image of military femininity, the focus on the woman's bare breast and the languid, even fey modelling of the soldier's hand raise similar concerns about the effects of war on sexual behaviour and gender identity. For Wright, the figure of the semi-naked, bereft young widow serves, I would suggest, as a dialectical image: a solicitation of desire as well as pity, and of enjoyment as well as pain.

11

'Turning Out for Twenty-Days Amusement': The Militia in Georgian Satirical Prints[1]

MATTHEW McCORMACK

JAMES GILLRAY's 'Supplementary Militia, turning out for Twenty-Days Amusement' of 1796 (fig. 1) is the quintessential image of part-time soldiering.[2] On the face of it, Gillray pokes fun in predictable ways, using several visual techniques to suggest that the militiamen are hapless amateurs rather than professionals. First, each man bears the tools of his civilian trade: from left to right we have a cobbler, a plasterer, a painter, a tailor, a hairdresser and a suitably rotund butcher. Secondly, the print underlines their lack of uniformity and discipline by sharply characterising them as individuals: the men are of various heights and builds, with ill-matching and dilapidated uniforms. Their bodies are either extremely thin or fat, with short legs and narrow shoulders – in pointed contrast to the ideal military body of the age. With such a rag-tag assortment, their effort to march in step is in vain. Gillray literally has a field day with the comic possibilities of the civilian soldier, a liminal figure whose uncertain position between the military and civilian worlds is ripe for visual mockery. This was as true of the militia in the eighteenth century as it was to be of the Yeomanry in the nineteenth and the Home Guard in the twentieth: Gillray's print has pride of place in a long tradition within British graphic satire.

---

1   I would like to thank the editors and Glenn Steppler for help with this chapter; and the Lewis Walpole Library for the Fellowship that enabled me to carry out this research.
2   BM 8840 (25 November 1796). Where possible, images used in this article will be identified by their British Museum (BM) catalogue number in Stephens and George, eds., *Catalogue of Political and Personal Satires.*

FIGURE 1. James Gillray, 'Supplementary Militia, turning out for Twenty-Days Amusement' (1796), © The Trustees of the British Museum.

This chapter, however, will argue that there is a lot more going on in the print than cheap jokes about the militia's ineptitude or failure to be true soldiers. Historians recognise that the militia was a key political issue in eighteenth-century Britain, since it went to the heart of constitutional debates about executive power, national strength and the rights and responsibilities of the ordinary citizen. In contrast with continental Europe, in the Anglo-American tradition the 'citizen soldier' was a citizen first and a soldier second: its 'amateur military tradition' celebrated the power of the individual rather than that of the state.[3] Indeed, the militia had pride of place in the political theory of the opposition, which condemned the state militarism associated with the English Civil War and Interregnum, absolute monarchs abroad and German influences at home (personified by the Duke of Cumberland, the leading general of the day and the son of George II). The militia was held up as a safer and more constitutional alternative to a 'standing army', since it provided a counterweight to the executive rather than a means to oppress the people. The militiaman also epitomised the classical virtues that critics of government held so dear, namely patriotism, vigilance, propertied independence and martial masculinity. In the wake of the sluggish response to the '45

---

3   The phrase is Ian Beckett's: Beckett, *Amateur Military Tradition*.

Rebellion and growing apprehension about a French invasion in the 1750s, the militia cause gained ground and became a rallying cry against the sitting government. At the beginning of the Seven Years War it was presented as a patriotic alternative to the government's policy of bringing over 'mercenaries' from Hanover and Hesse to defend the coasts.[4]

The Militia Act was passed in 1757. After this date, the militia was more than just an abstract issue, since most adult males were liable to serve in the county forces: at any one time, 32,000 men were supposed to be enrolled.[5] In an era when as many as one in four men had direct experience of wartime service, this was a society that was richly literate about military life.[6] We should therefore expect representations of the militia to be complex affairs. Diana Donald has noted that 'militias were a traditional butt of humour and [...] often featured in Georgian satirical prints'.[7] Although images of soldiers and sailors in this period have received systematic study,[8] no such survey has been carried out for the militia.

This chapter will largely focus on the period from the mid-1750s to 1796, the date of Gillray's print. Whereas there were virtually no prints on the militia in the first half of the century, many appeared during the campaign to reform the institution at the onset of the Seven Years War; and the militia-man remained a stock figure until changes to civilian defences during the wars against Revolutionary France make them difficult to distinguish visually from other types of soldier. Telling militiamen and regulars apart is a confusing business throughout the period: Cecil Lawson merely notes that their uniforms were 'very similar' and that those of militia officers were 'more richly laced'.[9] Colours are of little help since both militia and regulars wore red coats with regimental facings, and prints were either uncoloured or inconsistently coloured. We therefore have to rely on other textual, contextual and curatorial information. I have so far identified around a hundred prints that depict militiamen or comment on the institution.[10] As well as being a popular topic for satirical prints, I will argue that the militia was a significant one. These representations shed light on both the ideological nature of the institution and

---

4   On this tradition see McCormack, 'New Militia'.

5   Western, *English Militia*, p. 245.

6   Conway, *British Isles*, p. 28.

7   Donald, *Age of Caricature*, p. 191.

8   George studied 'sailors and soldiers' as one of her five recognisable social groups in George, *Hogarth to Cruikshank*, chs. 4, 11, 20; McCreery, 'True Blue'.

9   Lawson, *History of the Uniforms*, Vol. II, pp. 213–14.

10   Regarding 'militiamen', I have included prints of London's City Militia and Trained Bands, which were technically distinct from the 'New Militia' but were depicted in the same way.

the political function of graphic art, since the relationship between satirical prints and the militia was a close and reciprocal one. The classic 'caricature' and the Militia Bill were effectively born together, from the pen of the same man; prints played a key role in the campaign to bring the institution into being; they shared a golden age during the American war; and arguably the ongoing debate about the militia was informed in important ways by the medium that had originally been called to its aid.

Satirical prints are much studied by historians of eighteenth-century Britain. There is a tendency to use them in an illustrative way, since conventional wisdom has it that they 'reflect public opinion'.[11] More recently, there has been a growing recognition that prints are complex cultural artefacts with specific patterns of production and reception. One commentator has warned that it is too easy to make assumptions about the 'popular' audience for prints and that, far from extending politics to the illiterate, they were (and are) very difficult to 'read'.[12] Historians of art have shown that satirical prints were a sophisticated genre with a complex and highly allusive symbolic language.[13] We will see that prints on the militia employed an emblematic vocabulary that assumed a wide frame of reference on the part of the viewer. Besides an understanding of military terminology and materiel, consumers of these prints would have required a working knowledge of contemporary theatre, fashion, politics, high society and – indeed – other prints in order to pick up on all of the messages and in-jokes. To say that prints reflected contemporary opinion on the militia would therefore do them a disservice: rather, we will see that they actively participated in an ongoing debate, and that the genre served in many ways to constitute the institution in the Georgian visual imagination.

1

ONE IMPORTANT respect in which satirical prints did not reflect 'public opinion' was the fact that leading politicians acted as patrons to print artists and distributors, commissioning prints to support their careers and causes. What is remarkable about the campaign to re-establish the militia in the 1750s is that the artist and the politician were one and the same. George Townshend was the eldest son of a prominent Norfolk dynasty, and would become 4th Viscount and 1st Marquess Townshend. He had an impressive military career in the 1740s, serving under the Duke of Cumberland and rising

---

11 George, *English Political Caricature*, Vol. I, p. 1. Tamara Hunt has recently argued that prints 'reflected and comment upon public attitudes': Hunt, *Defining John Bull*, p. 2.

12 Nicholson, 'Consumers and Spectators'.

13 Hallett, *Spectacle of Difference*, p. 1.

to the rank of lieutenant colonel. Townshend was openly critical of the duke's military competence and considered him a bar to his further advancement, so he retired from the army and entered politics as an opposition Whig. It was natural that Townshend would be drawn to the militia issue: besides his own military experience, the militia had long been an article of faith among the opposition. Privately, Townshend doubtless also wished to create a parallel military establishment within which his own career could prosper, free from Cumberland's patronage.[14]

Besides being a soldier and a politician, Townshend was a talented artist. His forte was comic caricature, and Horace Walpole testifies to his 'talent for buffoonery in black lead'.[15] Townshend was an inveterate doodler, and while the Militia Bill was being debated he adorned 'the shutters, walls and napkins of every tavern in Pall Mall' with caricatures of his political enemies.[16] Townshend sought to ridicule his subjects by pinpointing aspects of their appearance that were suggestive of their personality. In an age when public men were expected to be outwardly 'polite' but inwardly 'sincere', physiognomy was a guide to innate moral character: caricature was therefore a useful weapon for those seeking to test the patriotism of their governors.[17] Donald notes that Townshend was influenced by the Italian style of *caricatura*, wherein 'the degree of caricature exaggeration was never so great as to overwhelm the element of recognisable portraiture'.[18] For example, a knowing audience would not have required any captions to appreciate his famous take on the Duke of Cumberland (fig. 2), a corpulent figure in bombastic pose, haughtily twirling away from the viewer.[19]

As well as lampooning great men of the day, Townshend's surviving sketches show that he caricatured a range of other subjects. The album of his sketches from the 1750s now held in the National Portrait Gallery shows that he had a particular fondness for sketching soldiers.[20] Some of these were heavily caricatured, such as the 'Hanoverian Grenadier' who appears next to Cumberland in a tableau of German militarism.[21] Like other contemporary representations of

---

14 Fordham, 'Organizing the Avant-Garde', p. 63.
15 Walpole to Henry Seymour Conway, 19 September 1758: Walpole, *Correspondence*, p. 573.
16 Horace Walpole, cited in Donald, 'Calumny and Caricatura', p. 48.
17 Amelia Rauser describes caricature as 'a kind of personality x-ray machine […] to look deep beneath the surface of a man and avoid the unspecified dangers of entrapment by a deceptive, artificial character': Rauser, 'Hair', p. 107.
18 Donald, 'Calumny and Caricatura', p. 47.
19 Townshend made numerous sketches of the duke, for example, NPG 4855(37–39); NPG 4885a.
20 The sketchbook is reproduced in full in Harris, ed., *Townshend Album*.
21 NPG 4855(40); NPG 4855(38). See also NPG 4855(42).

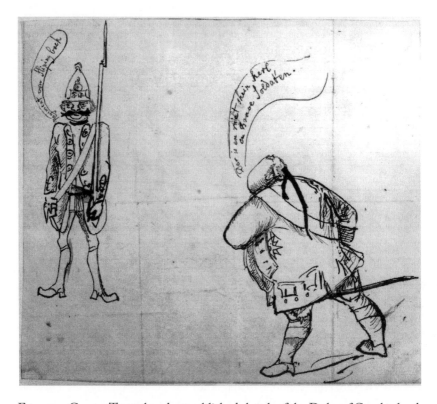

FIGURE 2. George Townshend, unpublished sketch of the Duke of Cumberland (1750s), © National Portrait Gallery, London.

German soldiers,[22] the grenadier has the build of a marionette to suggest that the inhumanity of Teutonic military discipline has reduced him to the status of an automaton. These images dwell on the visual signifiers of national character: a sketch of an unknown French gentleman pointedly contrasts his degenerate appearance with that of the erect British grenadier officer standing next to him, scowling with distaste.[23] The five sketches of militiamen in the album are by far the most sympathetic caricatures of the set, and suggest a desire to celebrate the solid martial qualities of the English civilian male.[24] Given that these doodles date from the period of his Militia Bills, when Townshend was

---

22 Duffy, *Englishman and the Foreigner*, p. 15.
23 NPG 4855(20).
24 NPG 4855(61–5).

codifying detailed plans for a new military force, it is likely that they give us an insight into the thought processes of a man with a vivid visual imagination.

That an educated gentleman should have enjoyed sketching is unremarkable: it was a fashionable accomplishment and caricatura became a favourite pastime among the elite.[25] What was remarkable was that Townshend published them, and so blatantly in support of his own political causes. His opponents protested that bringing a private medium and private quarrels into the public domain ill befitted a 'Man of Honour': 'He boldly paints his Lyes [...] in his Rage of Scandal.'[26] Townshend's most famous caricature was 'Recruiting Sergeant or Britannia's Happy Prospect' of April 1757. Like all of Townshend's caricatures it was published anonymously, although pamphlets and diaries of the time suggest that its authorship was widely known. The print satirises Fox's attempt to create a ministry: he is cast as a recruiting sergeant, marching reluctant or venal recruits past a statue of Cumberland (*à la* Townshend). It features six caricatured figures that he had rehearsed in his sketchbooks.[27] It is possible that the printseller Darly assembled the tableau, but this only adds to the incongruity of the group: these are not well-drilled soldiers.[28] Besides the print's military theme, this was a pointed intervention in the campaign in support of the passage of the Militia Bill, which was receiving its third reading in the Commons. Fox and Cumberland were its key opponents, and militia reform was part of the opposition platform against a government that was mismanaging the war.

Bringing private caricatura into the public domain also involved a stylistic change. Townshend's prints from 1756–57 represent a watershed in British graphic art, away from an emblematic tradition that relied heavily on explanatory text and symbolism, and towards genuine 'caricature' that presented less cluttered images with more emphasis upon physiognomic character definition. These simpler images could be distributed on small 'cards' measuring only 10 cm across, which proved hugely popular in 1756.[29] Walpole attributes this 'new species' of satires to Townshend, and credits them with making the Militia Bill's opponents 'the general topic of ridicule'.[30] Several of these cards employed idealised images of militiamen in campaigning for the Bill. 'The 2 H. H.'s' has

---

25 Atherton, 'George Townshend, Caricaturist', p. 448.

26 *Essay on Political Lying*, p. 6. This pamphlet was written in support of – and doubtless was commissioned by – Fox. Its reply defends the artist, 'a truly honourable gentleman [...] *innocently* amusing himself with drawing certain likenesses in *caricatura*': *Seasonable Reply*, p. 7.

27 BM 3581 (April 1757); Atherton, 'George Townshend Revisited'.

28 Donald, 'Calumny and Caricatura', p. 50.

29 These prints were collected in a series of annual books entitled *Political and Satyrical History*.

30 Walpole, *Memoirs and Portraits*, p. 60.

Figure 3. 'The 2 H. H.'s' (March 1756), © The Trustees of the British Museum.

been attributed to Townshend himself (fig. 3).[31] It contrasts two mercenaries with a huge moneybag with two chained militiamen: through the medium of bodily caricature it suggests that British citizen soldiers are more manly and virile than their German counterparts – as we have seen, Townshend was pre-occupied with this theme in his sketches. The title of the similar 'In Neat Silver Coin, 500,000 L.' refers to the sum paid to the Hanoverians and Hessians. Its simple caption rams the 'patriot' message home: 'Let English Men Guard English Land / Divided power can never Stand.'[32]

It was precisely because the militia was an *opposition* cause that it was so amenable to the genre of the satirical print. To satirise is to expose vice or folly, to disrupt the status quo in a radical way through ridicule. Mark Hallett notes that in the eighteenth century the term had more aggressive connotations than it does today: 'anything sharp or severe is called a Satyr'.[33] Satire was an appropriate medium for an issue that emphasised the martial power of the ordinary citizen – the presumed reader – in order to combat a range of caricatured 'others'. It is therefore comprehensible that when the militia was an opposition *cause célèbre* there were so many prints published in its favour and virtually none against. The only print artist who remained ambivalent on the issue was William Hogarth. His 'Invasion' series from 1756 depicts two countries mobilising for war. The English scene is bucolic in comparison with the stock images of French poverty and oppression, but there are still coded references to the dangers of militarism: the soldiers drilling in the background; the 'Duke of Cumberland' pub sign; the recruit being measured against a halberd that resembles a gallows.[34] In a likely dig at the soldier-artist Townshend, a grenadier paints a caricature of Louis XV on a wall while onlookers laugh with approval. Hogarth suggests that the public, captivated by Townshend's cartooning, are blithely unaware that he seeks to militarise society by means of his New Militia.

---

31 BM 3342 (March 1756). Atherton claims that the image is 'probably Townshend's': Atherton, 'George Townshend, Caricaturist', p. 439. For a detailed reading of its gendered imagery see McCormack, 'New Militia', pp. 487–88.

32 BM 3502 (16 September 1756).

33 The definition from *Croker's English Dictionary* (1704), cited in Hallett, *Spectacle of Difference*, p. 5.

34 'France', BM 3446 (March 1756); 'England', BM 3454 (March 1756). For a reading of the prints see Fordham, 'Organizing the Avant-Garde', p. 65.

2

Townshend's Militia Bill passed into law in 1757, and quickly switched from being an opposition issue that was popular in theory to an establishment issue that was unpopular in practice. If some country gentlemen remained committed to the ideal and put themselves forward as officers, others regarded the militia as an unwelcome obligation imposed from the centre. It was not popular among the lower ranks either, who often greeted attempts to draw up lists of recruits with rioting.[35] The backlash had begun.

The militia was embodied again during the American war, as fears of a French invasion returned. Being a permanent, highly visible and sometimes controversial fixture on the scene, the militia once again became a popular subject for graphic satire. The militia prints of the 1770s and 1780s were very different to those of the 1750s. This is partly because the medium had changed. Prints in the age of H. W. Bunbury and John Collett were conceptually simpler, visually more striking (often available coloured) and less reliant on text, employing short captions if at all.[36] They were also intended to amuse with social comment rather than to pursue a specific political cause. No longer an opposition shibboleth, the militia was ripe for satire: whereas militiamen in the Seven Years War prints had been idealised, abstract figures of propaganda, prints from the American war engaged humorously with the realities of service. One consequence of this was that representations of militiamen became more socially specific, clustering around four main 'types': corpulent old gentlemen, foppish young officers, social climbers from the middling sorts and ragged lower ranks.

The reluctance of propertied gentlemen to join the militia, and the uninterestedness and incompetence of those who did, was evidently a prominent concern at the time of the American war. The rotund, elderly officer became a stock figure in the prints. 'The Church Militant' (fig. 4) depicts a chaplain delivering a sermon at the drum head: the young officers with rosy cheeks and immaculate uniforms look bored and one yawns, but the senior officer is contentedly snoring in a chair, his hands folded over his belly. John Cardwell suggests that the print is a comment on the perceived apathy of country gentlemen regarding the defence of British religion and liberty.[37] Several prints played on the caption 'light infantry' to depict officers of a

---

35 Conway, *War, State, and Society*, p. 158.
36 George, *English Political Caricature*, vol. 1, p. 111.
37 'The Church Militant', BM 3752 (September 1779); Cardwell, *Arts and Arms*, p. 220.

The CHURCH MILITANT.

From the Original Picture by John Collett, in the possession of Carington Bowles.

Printed for & Sold by Carington Bowles, *at his Map & Print Warehouse, N°69 in S.t Pauls Church Yard, London.   Published as the Act directs.*

Figure 4. 'The Church Militant' (September 1779), © The Trustees of the British Museum.

decidedly heavy build,[38] and 'A Gross Adjutant' depicted Captain Grose of the Surrey militia, who apparently lived up to his name.[39]

If senior officers were portrayed as fat and somnolent, their younger counterparts were depicted in the mould of the 'macaroni'. The macaroni was a prominent figure in social commentary in the 1770s, named after the pasta dish that Grand Tourists brought back from Italy.[40] Prints of macaronis were hugely popular and spurred the revival of Italian-style caricature: this stock figure is instantly recognisable by his skinny build, elaborate tight costume and poses suggestive of effeminacy and vanity. The macaroni was not necessarily a homosexual figure: rather, he served to highlight the pitfalls of polite masculinity in a social sense, the result of an excessive attachment to (foreign) mores in opposition to solid, sincere (indigenous) ones. The macaroni was therefore bound up with a political critique of the ruling class and their hangers-on as being culturally distant from the people.[41] This political context is of course relevant to the militia: casting militia officers in the mould of macaronis serves to insinuate that the institution had fallen from its original 'patriot' design, as well as suggesting that its officers were sartorially, corporeally and morally unsuited to the business of war. The 'military macaroni' struck home because army officers were vulnerable to accusations of foppery, in an age when they were associated with ornate uniforms, polite sociability and mannered formality. A critic of the militia in 1785 protested that militiamen are distracted from their purpose by dressing them in 'fancy caps and feathers, and other ornaments of parade'.[42]

The 1772 print 'The Chymical Macaroni' explores several of these themes (fig. 5). It depicts an officer in the city militia, who was an apothecary in civilian life, in the mould of a macaroni. His militia uniform is rendered ridiculous, with huge frilly cuffs and wig with an extended queue bearing the inscription 'Family Medicine Chests neatly fitted up'. He affectedly grinds a pestle and mortar to produce an aphrodisiac.[43] During the American war, Carrington Bowles published a whole series of coloured mezzotints featuring military macaronis – given that the prints reference the large camps that were dominated by militia regiments, it is likely that the soldiers they depict are militia officers (fig. 6). These militiamen all wear fine, tightly fitting uniforms with fashionable wigs and slender shoes, and two wear gorgets to signify that

---

38 BM 4562, 'An Officer in the Light Infantry, driven by his Lady to Cox-Heath' (1778); BM 5525, 'The Warley Heroes or the Light Infantry on Full March' (November 1779).

39 BM 5511, 'A Gross Adjutant, Saddle White SURRE for the Field to morrow' (10 November 1778).

40 Rauser, 'Hair', pp. 101–02.

41 McCormack, *Independent Man*, ch. 3.

42 *Some Observations on the Militia*, p. 23.

43 BM 5069, 'The Chymical Macaroni, Capt Ludgate' (November 1772).

FIGURE 5. 'The Chymical Macaroni, Capt Ludgate' (November 1772), © The Trustees of the British Museum.

FIGURE 6. 'Capt Jessamy learning the Proper Discipline of the Couch' (1782), © The Trustees of the British Museum.

they are officers on duty. The artist suggests that they are too obsessed with their appearance and amorous adventures to be of any public service to their country.[44] The macaroni figure dwelt in particular upon the theme of artifice. Given that militiamen were not fully soldiers, and yet claimed the gentility that traditionally accompanied the uniform, these prints articulate an acute contemporary concern that militiamen used their appearance to claim that they were something they were not.

This concern also manifests itself in the third 'type' of militiaman depicted in the prints, the man from the middling sorts with ideas above his station. The militia struggled to recruit the propertied gentleman whom its designers regarded as its natural officer class, and so commissions were frequently taken by those lower down the social scale.[45] The comic incongruity of this situation was exploited by printmakers who, from the 1770s, cruelly attacked the pretensions of the social climber:[46]

> Can we Invasions dread, when Volunteers
> Like these, propose to Fight the Gay Monsieurs?
> Certainly No! Such Taylors, Cobblers, Bakers,
> Always must Conquer; led by Engine Makers.[47]

As in Gillray's 'Supplementary Militia', caricatures could reference the civilian statuses of militiamen with visual symbols of their trades. In the case of officers, this served to highlight the distance between their humble origins and their professed gentility, especially when they were well known in civilian life. A caricature of a portly officer of the City Militia (fig. 7) makes some notable additions to his fine uniform: his shoulder-belt bears a pastry brush, his cockade is replaced with a tart and his cartridge pouch resembles a pork pie. George identifies him as Thomas Vanhagen, 'a famous fat pastry cook' who had a shop opposite St Paul's.[48] A pair of prints featuring another London militia officer exposed the contrast even more starkly. In the first he struts proudly in uniform, sniffing a nosegay; in the second he is in his workplace manufacturing buttons, an apron covering his uniform, his arms and accoutrements on the

---

44 BM 5950, 'Master Lavender qualifying himself for the Army' (1781); LWL 782.6.0.2 'Ensign Rosebud reposing himself after the Fatigues of the Parade' (1782); BM 6156, 'Capt Jessamy learning the Proper Discipline of the Couch' (1782); BM 6157, 'Narcissus and the Nymph Echo' (1782).

45 Conway, *British Isles*, p. 40.

46 Donald, *Age of Caricature*, p. 80.

47 BM 5552, 'The Terror of France, or the Westminster Volunteers' (1779).

48 BM 5785, 'He Leads the Van Again' (26 August 1780): Stephens and George, eds., *Catalogue of Political and Personal Satires*, Vol. V, pp. 476–77.

HE LEADS THE—VAN—AGAIN.

Pub by MDarly Aug!26 1780/39 Strand

FIGURE 7. 'He Leads the Van Again' (26 August 1780), © The Trustees of the British Museum.

floor. Tellingly, he stares glumly at a copy of the first caricature, as if militiamen needed to be told that their pretensions were the object of public mockery.[49]

The final group of militiamen depicted in the prints was the rank and file. Here too the prints comment upon the institution's social composition: all men were liable to be balloted, but those who could afford it bought themselves out, so service fell overwhelmingly on the poor.[50] The militia in practice was never the force of propertied citizens that its promoters in the 1750s had envisaged, so ragged portrayals of the lower ranks had a political edge. Images of new recruits poked fun at the unpromising human material with which the militia had to work. 'A Militia Meeting' depicts two newly drawn civilians arguing with two portly officers: their faces and postures are comically grotesque, and their insubordination at the recruiting stage does not bode well for their future service. One officer consults a copy of the Militia Bill, highlighting the difficulties facing those who were tasked to implement it.[51] There are numerous prints of militiamen being marched or drilled that present scenes of comic disorder. Militiamen march out of step in ill-matching tatty uniforms, and come in all shapes and sizes, all ages and physical conditions.[52] 'Advance Three Steps Backwards, Or the Militia Heroes' (fig. 8) presents two frustrated officers trying to drill six hopeless recruits: a peg-leg, a tall thin man facing the wrong way, two short bumpkins, a fop and a Scot.[53] Human disorder is a favourite theme in graphic satire, but these prints also make a serious military point, since eighteenth-century infantry tactics demanded uniformity. Muskets were too inaccurate to be of any use on their own, so battlefield tactics sought to concentrate fire by assembling men of a similar height in a straight line, and hours of drill accultured the men to perform complex motions in unison with their comrades. The prints' chaotic drill scenes therefore questioned the militia's readiness for war.

On the other hand, the scenes of disorder and folly in prints of all four militia 'types' could also be said to celebrate the institution. If the military ideal of the age strove for homogeneity and obedience, the sharply individuated militiamen depicted in the prints were far closer to the cherished civilian ideal

49   BM 5783, 'He wou'd be a Soldier' (August 1780); BM 5784, 'The Soldier tired of Wars Alarms' (September 1780).
50   Beckett, *Amateur Military Tradition*, pp. 66–67.
51   BM 4579, 'A Militia Meeting' (n. d. 1770?). See also BM 4766 'Recruits' (1780).
52   See also BM 4578, 'The Victorious Return of the City Militia' (May 1772); BM 4791, 'The Chelsea Guard' (December 1771); 'A March of the Train Bands' (April 1777); BM 7612, 'City Militia' (1789); BM 7613, 'City Trained Bands' (1789).
53   Scotland was not included in the Militia Act, largely due to doubts about its loyalty in the wake of the '45 Rebellion. 'Advance Three Steps Backwards, Or the Militia Heroes' (n. d. 1779?).

FIGURE 8. 'Advance Three Steps Backwards, Or the Militia Heroes' (c. 1779), © The Trustees of the British Museum.

of individualism and liberty. As Hogarth's 'Invasion' prints suggest, the excesses of military discipline were a foreign anathema to the British self-identity, a key reason why the regular army was held in such opprobrium. The militiaman of the satirical prints may be ridiculous, but that in itself is a sign of his humanity: with oak-leaves in his hat and love of country in his heart, he will deal with French invaders in his own way.[54] We should not therefore assume that these representations were wholly negative: indeed, as we will now see, the contexts in which militiamen are placed in these prints often give them a further layer of ambiguity.

3

As a citizen soldier, the militiaman moved between the civilian and military worlds. Strikingly, the prints from the American war sought to empha-sise this by repeatedly placing the militiamen in contexts that were domestic, familial or heterosocial. This was undoubtedly intended to mock the militia's

---

54 BM 5774, 'Recruiting Serjeant and Contented Mates' (January 1780).

soldierly credentials, but in doing so the prints were also participating in a wider debate about the state of the nation. Many historians have argued that Georgian Britain underwent cultural panics during times of war: indeed, the political and cultural crisis during the Seven Years War helped to bring the militia into being.[55] Dror Wahrman has argued that the war with America was particularly important in this respect, as this essentially civil war entailed a comprehensive 'problem of identity' for Britons. He argues that the effect of this cultural crisis was to close down the fluid identity categories of the *ancien régime*, and to shift towards fixed modern notions of class, gender and race.[56] This helps us to understand why, in this specific cultural moment, the militia-man was such a transgressive figure, as his identity is uncertain and unfixed. Caricatures of militia macaronis or officer tradesmen were pointed in their attempts to expose the social reality behind the artifice: visually marking them out as 'apothecaries' or 'button makers' was an effort to brand militiamen with their actual class identity. This section will suggest that Wahrman's argument also helps to explain why the militia prints emphasise the incongruity of male effeminacy, female boldness and the blurring of the public and private spheres.

As concern about a French invasion grew and the militia was embodied full-time, large military camps were established in the southern counties from 1778. The two most famous were Coxheath near Maidstone and Warley near Brentwood. Partly because of their proximity to London, they attracted large numbers of visitors and became an object of fascination among fashionable society. In the slightly surreal atmosphere of preparing for an invasion that might never come, these 'holidays camps' acquired a reputation for hedonism and sexual intrigue. As a song of the time put it:

Ye beaux and ye belles pray attend to my song
'Tis new, I assure you, and will not be long
From the Camp I'm arriv'd, that scene of delight
Where they romp, sing, and dance, all the day and the night.[57]

The camps came to be portrayed as a dangerous melting pot of ranks and sexes that threatened to corrupt public morals. Ironically, the militia camps became the very opposite of what they were supposed to be: instead of a homosocial environment of republican virtue, where citizens would prepare to defend their community, camps threatened to weaken the nation by spreading 'effeminacy' at the hour of its greatest danger.

---

55 On the cultural panic of the Seven Years War see Cardwell, *Arts and Arms*; Carter, 'An "Effeminate" or "Efficient" Nation?'; Conway, *War, State, and Society*; McCormack, 'New Militia'; Wilson, *Sense of the People*.
56 Wahrman, *Making of the Modern Self*, p. 221.
57 'Coxheath Camp', in *The Billington*, p. 288.

The camp craze was fuelled by its many cultural products, including two stage plays, a fashionable novel, pamphlets, songs, endless newspaper report-age and numerous satirical prints. Camp scenes were one of the most popular subjects for caricature during the American war. These ranged from affection-ate observations of camp life – many by Bunbury, who was himself a veteran of the West Suffolk militia – to the downright scatological.[58] It is striking how many prints of militia camps feature women. Women were of course an accepted fixture at military camps as tradeswomen, washerwomen and prostitutes.[59] Soldiers' wives could become camp followers, and the wives of militia officers sometimes stayed in their elaborate, quasi-domestic tents or in lodgings nearby.[60]

These unremarkable camp women feature much less often in the prints than the society ladies who made the camp a locale of fashionable leisure. Prints abound of ladies visiting the camp, ladies who are often portrayed as being more formidable than their menfolk. In 'A Visit to the Camp' three such cou-ples tour the camp while a soldier points the way, complicit in their tourism.[61] Famously, the Duchess of Devonshire followed her husband to Coxheath, and set about trying to rehabilitate the Whigs' reputation for patriotism by organis-ing the ladies into an auxiliary corps.[62] The prints depict her in military-style riding habits, since elite women deliberately aped regimental styles to express support for their menfolk. This decidedly masculine style became all the rage in the era of the camps: 'Female delicacy is changed into masculine courage, and as much of the garb assumed as at first view almost leaves the difference of sex indistinguishable.'[63] The many prints of militiamen alongside bold women in military costume did not just undermine their credentials as men and soldiers, but raised wider questions about the gender order.

The satirical prints fostered the militia camps' reputation for dangerous sexual mixing. 'Public Ordinary' of January 1780 depicts a group dining in the open air, while in the background men and women dance in a circle outside the rows of tents; a serving maid spills a drink as she is accosted by John Wilkes, the notorious rake and former officer in the Bucks militia. They ignore the two aggressive cockerels in the foreground, suggesting that the denizens of the

---

58 George, *Hogarth to Cruikshank*, p. 104.
59 Hendrix, 'In the Army'.
60 Western, *English Militia*, p. 387.
61 BM 5602 'A Visit to the Camp' (November 1779). See also BM 4765, William Bunbury, 'A Visit to the Camp' (December 1779).
62 Foreman, 'A Politician's Politician', p. 182; BM 5600, 'The Three Graces of Cox-Heath' (November 1778); BM 5601, 'The Coxheath Race for £100, no Crossing nor Jostling' (October 1779).
63 Pennant, 'To the Editor', p. 99.

FIGURE 9. 'A Trip to Cocks Heath' (28 October 1778), © The Trustees of the British Museum.

camps are complacent about the threat of France.[64] The most obviously obscene camp print is attributed to Gillray, entitled 'A Trip to Cocks Heath' (fig. 9): even the name of the foremost camp invited sexual puns.[65] A motley band of officers, invalids, lecherous gentlemen and courtesans descend on the camp, where three fine ladies (probably the Duchesses of Devonshire, Grafton and Gordon) admire the most erect of the many phallic cannons. The scene is one of confusion and overt sexuality: men appear hunched and effeminate whereas women are sexually dominant and don masculine garb. The camp prints there-fore support Wahrman's thesis that the American war witnessed a panic about the fluidity of social and gender distinctions. As Robert Jones has argued, 'the uncertain environment of the camp site [...] revealed the unsettling mutability of identity which was thought to characterize contemporary culture'.[66]

As well as the camp scenes, prints also located militiamen in domestic and familial settings. The Bowles series of military macaronis present them in richly

---

64 BM 5776, 'Public Ordinary' (January 1780).
65 BM 5523, 'A Trip to Cocks Heath' (28 October 1778).
66 Jones, 'Notes on *The Camp*', p. 464.

furnished drawing rooms, reclining on couches while women in regimental riding habits lord over them, a window showing the outside world where soldiers should in theory be conducting their trade. The most sexualised of the set, 'Captain Jessamy learning the Proper Discipline of the Couch' (fig. 6), possibly depicts the Lady Worsley affair. Sir Richard Worsley commanded the Isle of Wight militia, and accused his wife of conducting 'criminal conversation' with one of his officers: this was the biggest sex scandal of the day and inspired numerous lewd cartoons where the male protagonists are referenced by their militia uniforms.[67] Note the woman's unbuttoned military jacket and the decidedly phallic chandelier dangling above them. The presence of women in militia prints therefore departed from the emblematic roles that eighteenth-century audiences would have come to expect: rather than being passive objects for militiamen to defend – a means to reaffirm their martial masculinity – women instead served to dominate, corrupt or distract men. The militiaman of the American war prints was therefore a victim of the pervasive sense of 'gender panic' but, by the uncertainty of his masculine identity, also served to contribute to it.

4

DOROTHY GEORGE terms the period after 1783 'the classic age of English caricature'. Prints by artists such as Thomas Rowlandson, Isaac Cruikshank and the later Gillray exhibited 'a lighter touch, both in conception and draughtsmanship', and the medium also came into its own politically.[68] Prints became a potent weapon in the party-political controversies of the 1780s, and in the response to the French Revolution and the rise of Napoleon. The militia was important in both contexts and prints featuring militiamen continued to appear. In this third and final period under consideration, however, the prints departed from the amusing social comment of the American war and the figure of the militiaman became politicised in important ways.

When ragged militiamen appear in prints after 1783, this was not just a comment on the militia's actual social composition but was often intended to make a political point. Sometimes militiamen appeared ragged because a corrupt system had reduced them to this condition. 'Dedicated to the Newly Created Earl of Lonsdale' of 1784 depicts a coat of arms flanked by two scrawny but noble militiamen. They are dressed in tatty uniforms – one lacks breeches, the other shoes – and their shoulder-belts identify them as 'WM', or Westmorland

---

67   McCreery, 'Breaking All the Rules'.
68   George, *English Political Caricature*, Vol. I, pp. 171, 180.

militia. The Earl of Lonsdale was a Lord Lieutenant and thus responsible for equipping the militia, but a petition to parliament had accused him of enriching himself at the expense of the men: the coat of arms bears legends such as 'fake returns', 'false musters' and 'retention of cloathing'.[69]

The onset of war with Revolutionary France made Britain's civilian defences a matter of crucial public concern, and the 'long embodiment' of the militia began in 1792. The citizen soldier was a favourite topic for prints during the French wars, particularly after 1796 with the beginning of the invasion scares and new initiatives to get civilian men under arms. After this period it is more difficult to distinguish militiamen from other types of citizen soldier: indeed, the patriotic volunteer receives much more interest and more sympathetic portrayals from print artists than the militia, perhaps suggesting that the militia had long since lost sight of its founding ideal of propertied independent citizens defending their own. In the 1790s the culture of patriotism itself shifts from the opposition to the establishment, taking the same journey as the militia had done over the previous half century. Whereas John Bull was a wary or unreliable militiaman in the early 1790s,[70] later loyalist images of soldier citizens appropriated the symbolic repertoire of radical patriotism to these defenders of Britain's historic liberties.

Charles Williams's 'After the Invasion' (fig. 10) portrays three civilian soldiers who have prevailed with ease over the French invaders: from left to right, they probably represent a militiaman, a farmer and a volunteer. The farmer has just killed Napoleon whose head is impaled on his pitchfork: he declares, 'I never liked Soldiering afore, but some how or other when I though[t] of our Sal, the bearns, the poor pigs, the Cows and the Geese, why I could have killed the whole Army my own Self.'[71] As is proper for a civilian soldier, he is motivated by his love for his family, property and country. As Linda Colley has noted, however, prints such as this retain an ambivalence about arming plebeians. The militiaman and the farmer are decidedly unsoldierly: their round shoulders, fat ruddy faces and rural dialect mark them out as bumpkins, in contrast to the classical proportions of the bourgeois volunteer (and indeed those of Napoleon, whose head has the statuesque nobility of the professional

---

69 BM 6579, [T. Rowlandson], 'Dedicated to the Newly Created Earl of Lonsdale' (May 1784). See Stephens and George, eds., *Catalogue of Political and Personal Satires*, Vol. VI, pp. 127–28.

70 BM 8141, James Gillray, 'John Bull bother'd: or, The Geese alarming the Capital' (December 1792); BM 8503, Thomas Rowlandson, 'Village Cavalry Practising in a Farm Yard' (1794).

71 BM 10052, 'After the Invasion - the Levée en Masse - or Britons Strike Home' (August 1803).

FIGURE 10. Charles Williams, 'After the Invasion – the Levée en Masse – or Britons Strike Home' (August 1803), © The Trustees of the British Museum.

officer and gentleman).[72] If the militia meant arming the lower orders – men who were not citizens in a political sense – then that was a matter for concern rather than celebration.

In conclusion, let us return to Gillray's 'Supplementary Militia, turning out for Twenty-Days Amusement'. As we have seen, this image comes at the end of a long and complex tradition of militia prints: it is doing a lot more than mocking militiamen for being unsoldierly. Their grotesque, sallow faces are symbolically closer to Gillray's famous depictions of Jacobins than John-Bullish Englishmen. The print was a response to Pitt's proposal for a 'Supplementary Militia' of 60,000 men: Fox denounced it as a form of impressment and Gillray here insinuates that this was a despotic measure more redolent of French Revolutionaries. The obese, bossy officer is a particular target in this respect: Gillray's father had been a soldier and his prints commonly side with the rank and file against their superiors.[73] As with many of these militia prints, Gillray's

---

72 Colley, *Britons*, pp. 282–85.
73 George, *Hogarth to Cruikshank*, p. 104.

print is therefore an intervention in a highly politicised debate about the nature of national defence.

By 1800 the image of the militiaman had come a long way since he started to appear in prints in the 1750s. What had been an abstract idealised figure during the Seven Years War had become the subject of anxious social commentary during the American war, and an intensely politicised figure in the period of the French wars. Caricature seeks to expose the reality behind the artifice. By the time of Gillray's print, it had helped to puncture once and for all the convenient myth that the militia was a constitutional and effective alternative to a standing army. The militia was permanently embodied during the French wars and became virtually indistinguishable from the regular army, to which it became an adjunct and recruiter: as Williams's print suggests, the ideal of the citizen soldier instead lived on in the form of the volunteers. Satirical prints therefore allow us to chart the British public's changing expectations of the militia, as a political idea and as an institution.

As this chapter has suggested, however, we should not regard changes in the visual representation of the militia as a straightforward reflection of its changing reputation. The birth and evolution of the satirical print was itself a significant development in mid-Georgian epistemologies, since it presented novel ways of articulating social, political and cultural concerns, to the extent that it had a formative influence upon them. The creation of the modern caricature was bound up with the campaign to establish a militia; the militia's creators had a very 'visual' conception of what the citizen soldier was to be; and thereafter the uncertain identity of the civilian soldier placed him at the centre of caricature's ongoing debate about Britain's national strength. We should not therefore assume, as historians often do, that the cultural history of warfare is secondary to the real business of military life. In the case of these militia prints, 'representation' has important implications for military 'reality', as well as the reverse.

12

Insurgents and Counter-Insurgents between Military and Civil Society from the 1790s to 1815

ALAN FORREST

Tнe ambiguous place that insurgents and guerrillas occupied between military and civil society helps to explain the fear that they aroused in others and the threat that they posed to the Revolutionary and Imperial state. They were not without precedent in European warfare: indeed, until the seventeenth century the sovereigns of invaded countries would routinely order their subjects to attack approaching armies, while in China as early as the fourth century BC governments and their advisors were already studying the techniques of counter-insurgency warfare.[1] In moments of danger partisan warfare was a natural form of defence, especially in those regions where mountain ranges and coastal marshes provided natural protection, from the sand dunes of Dunkirk to the rocky passes of the Alps, the Dolomites and the Apennines; all offered cover for local men who knew the terrain and were not constrained by the laws of conventional warfare. Insurgency and lawlessness were natural bedfellows in frontier regions, and those to whom local people turned for protection in wartime had often served their apprenticeship as bandits or smugglers, terrorising passing traders, slipping unseen across national frontiers or tax boundaries, and learning the essential survival kit for any outlaw – a sense of place in a poorly mapped landscape, a knowledge of the goatherds' tracks that were unpatrolled at night, a feel for those in the local community who might denounce or betray them. They continued to behave in very much the same way once war was declared, associating with the bandits who infested

---

1 Corvisier, 'Guerrilla Warfare', pp. 337–39.

the highways of Europe, especially southern Europe with its traditions of autonomy and factionalism, family honour and vengeance. Indeed, they saw little contradiction between the two careers, smugglers and bandits turning effortlessly into local freedom fighters. They often basked in the approval of their fellow villagers, whose liberties they defended; they also relished a freedom of their own, including the freedom to live on their own terms, outside the law.[2] Under a variety of identities – as partisans and guerrillas, *barbetti*, *miquelets* and *Schützen* – they were a recognised part of the landscape right across the Mediterranean. All eighteenth-century armies, including the French, were prepared to use their services when circumstances demanded it.[3]

The attitude of traditional armies to partisans had always been hostile: in their eyes irregulars made poor soldiers, were undisciplined, at times sadistic, and did not live by agreed rules of war. Above all they did not understand the notions of honour and justice that army officers saw as central to their professional identity, even to their identity as men.[4] But if these were long-standing views across Europe, they gained a new potency in the Revolutionary and Napoleonic wars, when insurgents played a larger role in the fighting and contributed very significantly to the outcome. In part this reflected the scale and outreach of these wars, fought by large, young armies, often in the name of ideals or nation states. From the 1790s the French recruited citizen soldiers, men of all social classes plucked by ballot from their communities to fight in their name, while in the face of defeat at the hands of Napoleon, others, not least Prussia, turned to some form of conscription. These were circumstances that demanded a clear distinction between soldiers and civilians, an understanding of rights and obligations, who had and had not the right to kill, who was and was not subject to military discipline. Yet all over Europe armies found themselves facing armed bands of irregulars – in the civil war in the Vendée and in Brittany, in the valleys of Piedmont and northern Italy, in the Wars of Liberation in Germany, in Russia during the Moscow campaign and, unremittingly, in the Peninsular War in Spain. It was in Spain, indeed, that the word guerrilla first entered common usage. It was not simply that they harried the French and impeded their advance, goading them into the sort of retaliation and atrocity that the Spanish artist Goya immortalised in his *Disasters of War*. Often their leaders claimed to be acting out of principle, against a foreign invader and in the name of the Spanish people; after all, much of Spain was in a state of rebellion, and even before Joseph Bonaparte had placed his foot on the soil of the land he was to inherit, 17 insurrectional juntas had sprung up to

---

2   Broers, *Napoleon's Other War*, pp. 1–18.
3   Forrest, 'Ubiquitous Brigand', pp. 25–43.
4   Dudink and Hagemann, 'Masculinity in Politics and War', pp. 3–21.

oppose him.[5] That is how the guerrillas would be remembered in nineteenth-century Spain, when their struggle, like partisan risings elsewhere against the Emperor, would be integrated into a new grand narrative of national liberation. Whereas to the French they were bandits and outlaws, to nineteenth-century Spanish nationalists they were patriots and freedom fighters. Already we see the tension that remains to this day a critical element in the discussion of guerrilla warfare and terrorism.

Bandits and insurgents had much in common, defying the agents of the state in whatever form they presented themselves – mayors or gendarmes, tax men or customs officers – and inhabiting a marginal world where they were in constant fear of capture and denunciation. The majority were country-dwellers, united by a hatred of taxation and policing and by a distrust of any intrusion by the state into the affairs of their community. They were defending their families and their valleys, their autonomy and their tradition, and they often did so with a violence that shocked the young troops who were sent against them. They generally did not wear uniform and belonged to no recognised military arm, preferring to shelter amid the villagers from whom they had sprung and to whom they could at any moment return.[6] The French army refused to recognise their status as combatants when they captured them, and regarded them as 'brigands', men who had no right to bear arms, no legal claim to be soldiers, men who, living on the margins of civil society, were endangering the lives of others and were in breach of the criminal law. When they killed and maimed others they could claim no immunity, as soldiers in uniform could, that would protect them from the consequences of their actions. Soldiers, indeed, figured prominently among their victims, including French troops trudging between Provence and the Army of Italy.[7] In the eyes of the authorities they had no special status and they were hunted down as common criminals, thieves and murderers. Their position between military and civil society could leave them terribly exposed, especially as they had opposed a polity that identified itself with ideas of truth, liberty and constitutional government. They were neither fish nor fowl and were condemned to be regarded as both morally flawed and steeped in reaction, a combination that could expect neither mercy nor leniency from the courts. Under the Directory and the Consulate, especially, they would be subject to special laws and military jurisdictions.[8]

The discourse of the French Revolution, the language of pamphlets and editorials in the press, of decrees and speeches in the Convention, had at its

---

5   Roux, *Napoléon et le guêpier espagnol*, p. 75.
6   A full-length study of bandits and insurgents in this period is Broers, *Napoleon's Other War*.
7   Clay, 'Le brigandage en Provence du Directoire au Consulat', p. 70.
8   Brown, *Ending the French Revolution*, pp. 214–33.

core the ideal of civil society and the rights and obligations that it implied. By emphasising the importance of citizenship, and by making citizenship the defining identity of Frenchmen, the Revolution had sought not only to define the relationship of private individuals to the state, but also to reform the most basic relationships in society, the relations between individuals, which were now to be grounded in human rights, civic equality and mutual respect.[9] The army was not to be exempted from this code: it was composed of citizens, plucked from the bosom of a civil society to which they would one day return as heroes, and the young men who filled the regiments were not allowed to forget that they, too, were of the people, a part of the body politic. An army of citizens, as it was defined in republican theory and evoked in nineteenth-century mythology, saw civilians as their brothers, men and women with whom they were united in a shared ideological purpose. They were fellow toilers in the national endeavour, producing food for the army, mothering and raising children for the nation, maintaining the administrative and judicial functions of the state. Moreover, once his work was done the *soldat-laboureur* would return to civil society to resume his place on the farm or in the workshop. Military and civil society coexisted in the interests of the French people: soldiers and civilians in the Revolutionary nation were as one.[10]

Of course it was never quite as straightforward as that, and even during the most ideologically charged months of 1794 there are signs that this ideal was coming to be regarded with a certain cynicism as an army of volunteers gave way to battalions filled with those forced into service by balloting or by conscription. By the end of the decade the French army had acquired a more clearly professional identity. Its soldiers were increasingly housed in barracks while they were on French soil, to keep them away from the distractions of civilian life; while beyond the frontiers they were condemned to long, exhausting campaigns across Europe, during which their commanders had every interest in discouraging too much fraternisation with local people. Relations with civilians were, predictably, often tense and strained. Increasingly they were judged by their value to the war effort – their ability to grow crops, to provide requisitions, to supply the carts and horses and donkeys the army needed to pursue its objectives. Or else they were seen as producers and repairers of weapons, forgers of pikes and bayonets, collectors of night soil for gunpowder, tailors and cobblers and blacksmiths and surgeons whose services could be useful to an army in the field.[11] Above all, they were a source of manpower. Under the Consulate and Empire military conscription became the litmus test of

---

9 Rétat, 'Evolution of the Citizen', pp. 3–15.
10 Puymège, *Chauvin, le soldat-laboureur*, pp. 126–45.
11 Ruggiero, 'La présence de l'armée', pp. 155–66.

patriotism and obedience, the central plank of loyalty, and this was something that a number of prefects in the more recalcitrant areas of the west and south would discover to their cost.[12] Civil society might be protected from military violence and abuse, but it was still expected to be loyal, and it constituted a fundamental part of the body politic.

The high incidence of draft-dodging during the Revolutionary and Napoleonic period led to a deterioration in relations between the army and civil society. It was almost unavoidable that soldiers' reactions to those who evaded their military obligations should reflect in some degree the official disdain in which the draft-dodgers were held, even if in the soldiers' case that disdain was often fertilised by a tinge of envy. A war that had been sold to them as involving the mobilisation of the whole of society in shared sacrifice could appear as something decidedly less egalitarian, a war where some still escaped the draft by working in reserved occupations (most particularly in the state administration), and where many others avoided personal service by a welter of ruses, deceits, bribes and corruption. The sight of young men like themselves living freely in the communities through which they passed, or eking out an existence in hiding in the woods and on the pasture lands that stretched beyond their village, could strain any feelings of fraternity or sympathy they might have had. War on this scale could so easily turn young men against one another, those in uniform against those spared personal service. In the process it could question the legitimacy of the status of civilians, associating them with privilege, favouritism or even cowardice. The man of military age who was not in the army was easily suspected of avoiding service and personal risk.[13] He risked being reviled for being an *égoïste*, self-interested and self-consumed, or, in the language of 1914, an *embusqué*, a shirker, someone to be despised.[14]

And what of the rest of civil society, the farmers and tradesmen they encountered on their marches, or the women and old folk who, as the war years dragged on, formed an ever-increasing majority in village society? How did French troops behave towards them, or react to the deprivations that the war imposed on them? In principle, since the first tentative efforts to establish some theory of the just war, an attempt had been made to distinguish between combatants and non-combatants, the strong and the weak; but it was not always clear who were and who were not to be treated as combatants. Civilians, even in the eighteenth century, lacked any clear definition in law, while collective memories of former wars produced many damaging stereotypes of civilian behaviour that eighteenth-century humanism had done little to erase. Were

---

12 Forrest, *Conscripts and Deserters*, pp. 219–26.
13 Ibid., p. 64.
14 Ridel, *Les embusqués*, pp. 24–33.

they to be viewed as objects of suspicion, as *égoïstes* sheltering in the safety of their homes, or *accapareurs* hoarding foodstuffs and exploiting their monopoly position to overcharge any conscripts unwise enough to cross their paths? There is plenty of casual evidence in soldiers' own accounts that this was often an immediate suspicion among the troops, especially when they talked of grain merchants, rich farmers and Jews.[15] Military orders were usually clear enough, at least when soldiers were at home on French soil: civilians must be treated with respect, and they must do nothing that could jeopardise the army's relations with those on whom it was ultimately dependent for food and protection. Stealing from peasants' barns or cottages or taking chickens from farmyards was widely condemned, and might be severely punished, resulting even in death sentences. Much depended on the military fortunes of the moment: morale, military discipline and public support were all at stake.[16]

The further the armies travelled from the French frontier, the more cavalier many of the troops became in their treatment of local people, and the less the concept of a distinct civilian status seemed to matter. Foreign peoples, like their armies, risked being seen as part of the same, imperfectly distinguished enemy against whom they were ranged, and could be threatened and despoiled as circumstances dictated. French soldiers developed an unwanted reputation for pillage and looting in these wars, and there was little their generals could do to stop it. The attitude of successive governments to occupation, combined with the armies' lack of adequate food supplies and their need to live off the land everywhere they went, meant that they survived by forced requisitions – which were often not paid for – and by what many saw as a form of legitimised looting.[17] Cattle and horses were seized and driven away, and their owners would be lucky to receive more than a derisory level of compensation. Corn, bread and valuables of all kinds were seized by the state as a contribution to the costs of the war. Extraordinary taxes had to be paid to maintain the 'protector' armies with which conquered nations were blessed; by 1798 these constituted as much as a quarter of the Directory's income.[18] To their victims this was looting by another name, and it led to widespread anti-French sentiment in the lands that France occupied. But it proved hard to restrict such pillage to official channels alone. French soldiers learned by example that there were circumstances where the theft of property was not only tolerated, but actively sanctioned. Any sense of shame was quickly dissipated in an army that was close to starvation.

---

15 Demay, 'Les volontaires auxerrois de 1792', p. 542.
16 Lévy, 'La vertu aux armées pendant la Révolution française', p. 359.
17 Rowe, *From Reich to State*, pp. 55–56.
18 Woolf, *Napoleon's Integration of Europe*, p. 17.

Of course there was nothing new in such behaviour, nothing that was exclusive to the Revolutionary or Napoleonic forces. Throughout history relations between soldiers and civilians in wartime have been the subject of dispute and recrimination, as societies have tried, whether by laws, threats or moral treatises, to define what is and is not permissible, what is justified by contingency and what should be prosecuted as common criminality.[19] The question is never an easy one, and the same commander might adopt very difficult policies depending on the position his army found itself in, its level of deprivation or the attitude of local people to legal requisition, its levels of discipline and frustration in the face of the enemy. What was acceptable was determined by a delicate balance between feelings of shame and decency on the one hand, necessity and survival on the other. For without clear laws to back them up, these judgements were necessarily subjective and dependent on a mixture of whim and realism. How, before the emergence of an agreed international law on the subject, was improper treatment of civilians to be defined?[20] And with mass armies such as Napoleon's, inadequately supplied and forced to forage for food and fodder, we might legitimately ask whether the treatment reserved for civilians was ever likely to take account of legal and moral considerations. Yet this varied widely across the continent, which raises the question of why different peoples incurred such different treatment. Did it depend on the reception that the French received when they invaded? Did the civil population itself not bear some responsibility for its relations with the French, and for the levels of abuse and violence that followed?

In some parts of Europe, relations were conspicuously friendly. There was always something immediately interesting, even mildly exotic, about other cultures, and first impressions were often drawn from stereotypes culled from the travel literature of the eighteenth century. For soldiers were first and foremost travellers, encountering faraway places and unknown cultures, and the natural curiosity that these evoked is reflected in their diaries and memoirs. Their response to the civil population also varied immensely, according to the warmth and generosity they encountered. Sometimes local people were depicted as glowering and threatening, defensive of food stocks and ready to denounce or to cheat any young soldier who fell foul of them. Language barriers did not help, of course; nor did rumours that swept the armies, such as the belief that those unfortunate enough to fall into the hands of Cossack soldiers would be sold on to Russian villagers who would torture and brutalise them. It was better by far to be taken prisoner by the Russian army; then, at least, you stood the chance of being treated with a modicum of decency. But

---

19   Walzer, *Just and Unjust Wars*, esp. pp. 138–59.
20   For a comprehensive overview see Best, *Humanity in Warfare*.

language differences did not exclude a degree of communication, and in many places French soldiers were pleasantly surprised by the kindness and humanity they were met with. Their travelogues also provided opportunities to praise local customs, to take note of the urbanity of foreign cities, or the inhabitants' gallantry towards women (always a symptom in French eyes of a polite and advanced civic culture). They also bear witness to heart-warming moments when they were fed and sheltered by local families, when they were taken in by local people while they recovered from their wounds, or when they forgot all political differences and admitted to feelings of friendship or had love affairs with local girls. This was a Europe-wide war, one that scattered young Frenchmen across an entire continent, and for much of the war large parts of that continent were friendly territory, its people allies, its soldiers integrated into Napoleon's legions. Here civilians could be appreciated for their culture, praised for their politeness and hospitality, and even, on occasion, compared favourably to people they had encountered in regions of France they had passed through on their march, where some troops had felt they were strangers in their own country. War could bring Europeans together as well as wrench them apart. When civilians behaved like civilians, levels of conflict were limited.[21]

In many of the soldiers' accounts it is clear that their perceptions of civilian life were a kind of barometer of civilised values as they, in France, understood them. But their vision of what constituted civilisation was, it may be thought, a rather particular one, the product of their youth, their upbringing, their generation. For the French, in particular, that last element is important, and not just because the army introduced them to a largely youthful and masculine world with discrete values of its own. They were the sons of Revolutionary fathers, born in an age of dramatic self-questioning and the rejection of so much that was traditional to European culture. As Stuart Woolf acutely observed, they were always prone to show a northern European contempt for those who lay on the periphery of the Enlightenment.[22] This was especially true of those Napoleonic soldiers who had passed their boyhood during the Revolutionary years, who had been raised to believe that they had rights and a rightful place in the sovereign nation. There was a religious side to this too, which may well have affected their perception of others. For theirs was a generation that had not attended church on Sundays, that had been raised to despise piety as superstition, and that had little awareness of Christian culture or biblical imagery. Like young Frenchmen in the twentieth century, brought up in secular schools and communist homes, these were things they would have little knowledge of, and little use for. If they heard Bible stories in later

---

21 Forrest, *Napoleon's Men*, pp. 142–46.
22 Woolf, 'French Civilization and Ethnicity', pp. 96–120.

life they might find they had a certain charm – but they were always just that, stories, the sorts of simple moral tales one might tell to one's children. They had no reason to doubt that their secular, rational ideology reflected a more advanced, humanist consciousness, or that the ostentatious piety of peasant communities in countries such as Spain or Poland was a sign of ignorance and backwardness. Not all, of course, adhered to this philosophy – some may even have regretted a more traditional rural world they had lost – but many, clearly, did. It was easy for them to deride religious practices and a religious faith that civilised France had renounced, and to imagine that they came bringing the benefits of a superior civilisation. Theirs was, of course, the culture of a historical moment and a particular generation that had lived through two decades of Revolutionary ideals and institutional renewal.[23]

This sense of superiority becomes apparent during those campaigns when the soldiers felt alienated by the countries they passed through, and when the very sight of civilians became tinged with a sense of threat. This was true of much of Eastern Europe during the Moscow campaign, when a Napoleonic army that stole and looted its supplies could hardly expect local people to welcome them as friends or liberators. And it was even more true when those they took for civilians might at any moment turn into an overt enemy, ambushing and torturing the soldiers who came too close. Irregular and guerrilla fighters almost invariably aroused anger and contempt as well as fear, since, as soldiers, they judged others by the manner in which they made war. Did they fight honourably, openly, on the field of battle, with an acceptance of proper distinctions between soldiers and civilians, distinctions akin to those of the French army? Did they wear uniforms to distinguish themselves as soldiers, uniforms that indicated that they were subject, like the French, to a clear system of military discipline? Was it evident who was a fighting man – whom it was legitimate, under the laws of war, to attack and kill – and who was not? All soldiers appreciated such clarity, since it lay at the heart of their military existence. Their very survival depended on it. In the same way, they expected a certain minimum level of humanity if they were taken prisoner by the enemy, in return for which they undertook to treat their own prisoners of war with a degree of care. In the centuries before the Geneva Convention, when generals looked to ideas of reciprocity and notions of a just war to determine their treatment of the enemy, armies depended on such distinctions if they were to prevent battle deteriorating into uncontrolled slaughter and war from descending into barbarism.[24] If there were laws of war across Europe, however loose their legal

---

23 The idea of French history being characterised by precise generations, each with its own coherence and social network, is discussed by Spitzer, *French Generation of 1820*, pp. 3–34.

24 See, for instance, Keen, *Laws of War in the Late Middle Ages*.

underpinnings and however imprecise their implementation, they existed for very good reasons.

Soldiers hated *la petite guerre*, that indeterminate state where they did not know for sure who the enemy was, and where at any moment civilians could turn into soldiers and village women into spies and torturers. Whether guerrilla fighters in Spain, bandits in Illyria or *ordinantes* in Portugal, soldiers without uniform continued to torment Napoleon's armies, pinning them down and luring them into traps before fading into the landscape. They seldom won outright military victories, but they harassed the troops and made civil administration well-nigh impossible, while turning every villager and every peasant into a potential terrorist. They also forced the French into counter-insurgency measures of their own.[25] Fighting against guerrillas was never a soldier's war. Even the language they used betrayed their fear and contempt. Generals and administrators sought to belittle the enemy, just as they had done earlier, during the revolt in the Vendée in the 1790s, to deny them any vestige of honour or military sensibility; they were simple brigands, outlaws, common criminals whose only goal was to pillage and murder. Of course, the conflict in the Vendée was a civil war, and it was their fellow citizens who were diverting regular units back from the defence of the frontiers to deal with a peasant insurrection fought in the name of Christ and King. For the regular troops this served to make the war doubly unsavoury; in their eyes the Vendeans were criminals before they were soldiers, criminals whose actions weakened the nation and whose tactics were unworthy of professional soldiers. Their vocabulary reflected this as they systematically dehumanised the enemy – depicting them not as men but as wild beasts, who, like the wolves of the fields and upland prairies, hid behind bushes and leapt out at their prey before dragging themselves back to their lairs in the *bocage*, to lick their wounds and prepare their next crime. And there was, as every French peasant knew well, only one way to deal with wolves.[26]

There was little honour to be gleaned from eradicating brigands, whom soldiers did not see as a worthy enemy, and little in the manner of the campaign to suggest the ideals of a just war. French soldiers went into the Vendée with preconceptions that were difficult to eradicate, despising the Vendeans as rebels, counter-revolutionaries and traitors. What they found when they got there further entrenched these prejudices: insurgents who rarely fought in the open, preferring to snipe from behind hedgerows and ambush stragglers who could be isolated from their columns and picked off individually; peasant fighters blending into the landscape; women and children guiding guerrillas

---

25 Alexander, *Rod of Iron*, p. xix.
26 Tyson, 'Role of Republican and *Patriote* Discourse', pp. 96–97.

to safe-houses and hiding them in their homes. Their lingering image of the war was of gratuitous and callous cruelty in which the whole rural community was complicit. In Turreau's words, 'the leaders of the rebels kidnap our soldiers and make then die in the most indescribable manner'.[27] No one was innocent: guerrillas and their families, terrorists and the communities that sheltered them, all became indistinguishable in the soldiers' perception of the war. For the republican soldiers, indeed, the template for depicting the rebels' behaviour was the massacre at Machecoul in 1793, of which most had heard and which some had experienced. André Amblard, a junior officer from Lussas in the Ardèche, was not there himself, but he heard graphic accounts of the massacre from a friend and fellow officer, Captain Fayolle from Largentière. He did not doubt his account, since Fayolle had married the widow of one of the massacre's victims. Ordinary villagers, he believed, had plotted to 'exterminate all the patriots' in the area. 'They set out, ten or twelve thousand of them, seized Machecoul, and pitilessly massacred all those they found who had taken part in the Revolution.' Then – and here he turns to their gratuitous cruelty – 'tired of slaughter, or as a refinement to their cruelty, they took five or six hundred of their victims, roped them together, and led them to high ground where there was a windmill; and there, on the grass, they beat them to death with iron bars. Women and children, all beat the prisoners.'[28] Civilians, he particularly noted, had stopped behaving like civilians; they became callous killers who deserved neither respect nor sympathy. All were equally guilty and deserved the punishment that would follow.

The republican troops in the Vendée did not disguise the hatred they felt for the enemy, nor their own savagery in putting whole villages to the sword. Nor, really, did they try to excuse it, other than with reference to the character of the war itself. On returning from dinner after a carnival, for instance, Joliclerc's battalion stumbled upon over fifty of their own, left for dead on the road with their heads smashed in or their chests lacerated by bayonet thrusts. He had lost friends, young men from his own village, who had been executed in cold blood by the guerrillas. It was hardly surprising, he felt, if the French, too, abandoned all moral qualms. They were formed into columns to raze all trace of their opponents in hamlets and villages across two departments, the Vendée and Deux-Sèvres, and, in his own words, 'We went in with steel and flame, a musket in one hand and a torch in the other. Men and women, all will be put to the sword. All must perish, all except little children. For these departments must serve as an example to others that might be tempted to revolt.'[29] Some

---

27 Chatry, ed., *Turreau en Vendée*, p. 270.
28 Boulle, ed., 'Le journal du capitaine Amblard', p. 66.
29 Jolicler, ed., *Joliclerc, volontaire aux armées de la Révolution*, p. 155.

units went further, slaughtering even babes-in-arms in a bid to destroy the base from which a new generation of insurgents could grow. 'What was saddest of all,' wrote a sergeant from the First Battalion of the Gironde, 'was the sight of those poor little children', a vision which, he admitted, would remain with him for the rest of his life.[30] It is unsurprising that they should have made so many comparisons between the Vendée and Spain, or that the Spanish society that produced this dirty war should be scorned by the French as impoverished and backward, even as barbarous and degenerate.

Thanks to the war paintings of Goya and the writings of nineteenth-century nationalist historians it is the outrages committed by the French against Spanish civilians that are most vividly remembered among the many acts of inhumanity that marked the war in Spain. Their desecration of churches in deeply Catholic regions only added to the deep-seated xenophobia that many in southern Spain already nurtured towards foreigners, in particular foreigners from the north such as the French and the British. The guerrillas, by contrast, were turned into nationalist heroes.[31] Unquestionably French troops did abuse civilians to a quite unparalleled degree in the Peninsula, as the many stories of murder, rape and summary execution make plain. But atrocities were not one-sided, for if the French were guilty of a massive loss of military discipline in the revenge they wrought on the civilian population, that population, in its turn, was guilty of sickening acts of cruelty towards the invader and those in their own community who were adjudged to have collaborated with Napoleon. Often the clergy became involved, sometimes to the extent of using Church funds to finance guerrilla bands. If the French troops behaved brutally, they were sorely provoked by terrorist tactics and public collusion.[32]

Of course the more educated French officers crossed the Pyrenees with a very different preconception of a civilised Spain, a country that once stood at the heart of a great empire and whose towns were blessed with some of the most sumptuous buildings in Europe. When they passed through cities such as Madrid and Valencia, they remarked with undisguised admiration on the glories of the urban architecture, the magnificence of the palaces and cathedrals. But for the greater part of their time in the Peninsula, it was not the cities that the French saw but the countryside of Spain, which they regarded as an impoverished rural backwater where the peasants were forced by their poverty to subsist on a miserable diet and to live in filthy, cramped hovels. Inevitably this impacted on their view of the Spanish people. They were seen as subservient to the nobility and in the thrall of priests, factors

---

30 Pages, 'Lettres de requis et volontaires de Coutras en Vendée et en Bretagne', p. 158.
31 Esdaile, *Fighting Napoleon*, pp. 1–26.
32 Lafon, *L'Andalousie et Napoléon*, pp. 10–11.

that, in French eyes, accentuated their social backwardness and lack of civilisation. In turn these attributes were reflected in their lack of compassion and
human empathy – qualities that were increasingly acknowledged in men in
the later eighteenth century – and their desire to subvert the masculinity of
their enemies. In the sexually defined, self-consciously masculine world of the
legions, these atrocities, among them castration and rituals of sexual inversion,
caused a particular disgust that almost invited retaliation. The violence that
Jean-Marc Laffon describes in Andalusia left an indelible imprint on all who
witnessed it, and for good reason. Victims were stripped and sexually humili-
ated by their captors, were impaled on stakes, thrown live into vats of boiling
water, buried alive in the sand, hung upside-down by their feet. Many were
ritualistically castrated before being left hanging from gibbets, their genitals
stuffed ostentatiously in their mouths as a final sign of contempt, theatric-
ally staged in the centre of the village. And, what might seem worse, whole
communities joined in: it was often reported that men and women alike took
part in these outrages, mocking and humiliating the French in front of their
neighbours, their patrons, their children. These attacks reflected stored-up
hatred, expressed through sexual inversion as in the traditional charivari, with
the victims being ritually feminised, deprived of their masculinity in a charade
that concentrated the whole community's rejection of the invader, symbolically
aborting the product of his rapes and violations by destroying his sexual organs
before his eyes.[33] Once again, the clear delineation between soldiers and civilians was cast aside, and civilians threw away any claim to understanding and
special treatment that they might otherwise have sought.

This was terrorism by any other name, a terrorism marked by a thirst for
revenge and by acts of extreme savagery. In Spain it achieved what acts of terror
so frequently do – one need look no further than the calculated attacks by the
FLN on French military personnel and their families during the Algerian War
in the early 1960s – producing a flurry of parallel outrages from the French
soldiers directed against the guerrillas and their civilian allies.[34] In turn this
served to give entire Spanish communities a sense of acute grievance and
further reason for unity. This is why, for the French army in the Peninsula,
Spain was unlike any of the other countries where they operated. It was a land
of savagery and treachery and constant danger: every civilian was a potential
threat, an enemy, a murderer. That is why the normal decencies towards the
civilian population, those that pertained across the bulk of mainland Europe,
were not applicable in Spain, why there could be no question of offering

33   Ibid., p. 104.
34   An excellent account of the Algerian experience is Aït-el-Djoudi, *La guerre d'Algérie vue
     par l'ALN*, pp. 161–89.

protection to civilians or sparing them the rigours and the brutality of war. The vocabulary they used was not innocent; it betrayed a mindset that was increasingly suspicious of difference and that made it easier for the French to forget the distinction between men of arms and non-combatants and to justify harsh repressive measures against them – even, in extreme cases, killing them. In Spain, unlike most other parts of Napoleonic Europe, the sight of civilians did not remind the young soldiers of the mothers and the families they had left behind in France. They remained foreigners and enemies of the new polity, men and women who posed a constant, if unspoken, threat to the troops and who offered them little comfort or reassurance. They remained loyal to their king even if some were critical of the House of Bourbon, which had alienated the more liberal elements by laying claims to absolute rule;[35] and they were ready – or so the French immediately assumed – to defend Catholicism against an invader many identified with Antichrist. Under the constitution promulgated in 1812 in Cadiz, 'in every village of the Monarchy primary schools will be established to teach children reading, writing and arithmetic, as well as the catechism of the Catholic religion, which will also include a brief account of civic obligations'.[36] Civilians, as much as Spanish soldiers, were at war with the French, and they were educating the next generation to reject all traces of French influence.

Spain, with its long tradition of adulation for the supposedly nationalist crusade led by the guerrillas, has pleaded for them to be recognised as freedom fighters and patriots, though the evidence for this is thin, and their true character was closer to that of the traditional bandits of southern Europe, those analysed so graphically by Eric Hobsbawm.[37] They were largely local men, peasants, rural craftsmen and farm labourers attracted by money and the chance of notoriety to exchange the humdrum reality of their daily existence for a moment of glory and the adrenalin of danger. A few were men from more privileged backgrounds, idealistic, bored with life and seeking, like young men of every generation, solace and excitement in war. Matias Calvo, for one, was a doctor's son from Aragon who had read philosophy at university and who, as a student, allowed himself to be recruited by a member of his own family to support the nationalist cause. After his father died in 1811 Matias would find himself the eldest son in a large family, educated and cultured but without a clear sense of vocation, and in these circumstances he elected to take up arms. Matias takes up the story.

---

35 Kamen, *Imagining Spain*, p. 68.
36 Aymes, 'Catéchismes français de la Révolution', passim.
37 Hobsbawm, *Bandits*, pp. 17–29.

> Almost immediately one of Mina's officers asked me to accompany him, in fact
> offering me a horse and arms [...] That very afternoon I was part of his group of
> twenty horse and fifty soldiers in the sierra of Llanaja whose task was solely to
> recruit people and send them to Navarra for training.[38]

He was, of course, somewhat exceptional within the guerrilla movement. A son
of the bourgeoisie had thrown in his lot with ploughboys and farm servants,
army deserters and professional bandits, in a shared desire to push the French
out of Spain. In this capacity he killed and looted with the others, and harried
and ambushed French troops. The French feared him and the disruption he
caused. And though Napoleon had little respect for the fighting skills of the
guerrillas, or the contribution they could make on the battlefield, his courts
could afford to offer them little leniency. Feeling under attack themselves, the
French promised little other than repression in return.

> Assassins, thieves, those rising in armed rebellion, the seditious, rumour-mon-
> gers, spies, recruiters for the insurgents, those caught communicating with them,
> or those who are found with daggers or sharp-edged weapons on their person
> will, if convicted, be hanged irremissibly within twenty-four hours without any
> right of appeal.[39]

In the repression that followed they were indeed hanged, and shot, and gar-
rotted on public squares. It was a harsh measure that drove yet another spike
into the already-strained relations between local people and the occupying
army, and that helped to increase public sympathy for the guerrilla fighters
and their cause.

Spain was the most flagrant example, in French eyes, of a society where
civilians had transgressed established conventions, blurring all the recognised
distinctions between themselves and the army. But it was not the only theatre
of the Napoleonic campaigns where French forces found themselves hounded,
ambushed and tortured by irregular troops, or ill-treated by local people. They
encountered the same, and worse, during the Moscow campaign. Here, too,
the French were met with stubborn resistance from the general population,
from peasants who made common cause with partisan units to harass them.
Conditions in Russia were as bad as any the French had encountered, with
whole cities burned and their army left without food or fodder – 'a hundred
leagues of smoking ruins', in the words of Lamy, a young French supply officer,
in a letter home to Paris.[40] Increasingly, it was not the Russian army the soldiers feared but the treatment they would receive if they fell into the hands

---

38 Fraser, *Napoleon's Cursed War*, p. 40.
39 Decree of 16 February 1809, establishing the Extraordinary Criminal Tribunal in Madrid,
     cited in Fraser, *Napoleon's Cursed War*, p. 427.
40 Hennet and Martin, *Lettres interceptées par les Russes*, p. 171.

of villagers, who were known to strip and torture their captives, mutilate their bodies and even bury them alive, inflicting the greatest possible pain or passing them over to the Cossacks and a certain death. It was in Russia that Napoleon's soldiers learned to expect no humanity from local people, who worked hand-in-glove with partisan units to thwart the French advance. Together they defended their homes and villages; and in the classic style of guerrilla war, as Dominic Lieven reminds us, they helped one another out in times of danger:

> The partisan commanders often distributed arms to the peasantry and came to their assistance when large enemy parties were spotted. The peasants in turn provided the intelligence, the local guides and extra manpower which enabled the cavalry to track down and ambush enemy detachments and to evade capture by superior forces.[41]

In partisan war of this kind irregulars and villagers made common cause to the point where their roles became interchangeable, and any real distinction between soldier and civilian had ceased to exist. It was a context that turned soldiering into an experience from hell. 'They will hardly believe it in Paris,' concluded Lamy rather poignantly, 'but all those who had fought in the war in Spain regretted leaving that country when they found themselves in this.'[42]

Nothing in their experience of guerrilla warfare during the previous twenty years would alter the prejudices of the military to men who were not answerable to military rules, who did not wear a distinguishing uniform, and who, if caught, would be granted none of the honours of war. The Napoleonic Wars had, if anything, increased the gulf between the civilian and the military experience in war, as armies had become more professional and officers more aware of the value of training, tactical deployment and issues of grand strategy. They contributed to success and helped develop morale, as did the development of a distinct military culture that revolved around questions of honour and justice, a culture that showed itself in regimental pride, promotions and medals, ceremonial and symbolism, or in the French case, Napoleonic eagles and elevation to the Legion of Honour. It was a culture that was understood by all European armies, French and Austrian, Prussian and Russian, whose officers showed one another respect and who exercised reciprocity in such matters as the treatment of prisoners of war and prisoner exchange. And where their officers led, the soldiers followed. Their status, but also their survival, depended on it, and they had no interest in being confused with irregulars. That does not mean, of course, that when irregulars fought well, when they displayed bravery or other soldierly qualities, real soldiers did not grant them a grudging respect. Or that in 1814, when France lay open to invasion from the

---

41   Lieven, *Russia against Napoleon*, pp. 245–46.
42   Hennet and Martin, *Lettres interceptées par les Russes*, p. 171.

east after Leipzig, peasants in Lorraine and the Ardennes did not unearth their shotguns and, with wide popular support, turn to partisan warfare against the invading army. Suddenly the tables were turned, and it was the Prussians who were denouncing Frenchmen as brigands, executing them as outlaws when they fell into their hands.

Throughout much of Europe, indeed, the dividing line between showing respect for civilians and abusing them mercilessly was thin and porous. In many theatres of war the French faced sullen opposition from local people that could at any moment turn into open aggression, and in these circumstances it was not difficult to justify the use of force, or to claim that acts of brutality were forms of self-defence. The harsh policing of civilian society was justified as a means of maintaining law and order, of avoiding a return to the unrest and turbulence that, to Napoleon's eyes, had been the unhappy hallmark of the Revolutionary years. Gendarmes were not asked to treat civilians with gentle decorum; they were expected to be as rough as the people they were policing, especially in areas of the Empire that were difficult to subdue and that threatened to slip out of the control of the state.[43] Piedmont, Dalmatia, Saxony – almost anywhere that dared to oppose the imposition of the Imperial regime, or that baulked at paying taxes or providing conscripts for the Emperor's campaigns, risked crossing the line into disorder and facing the wrath of the Imperial army. The habit of disorder was difficult to break: it followed the armies into the Balkans, to North Africa, to the Caribbean and Spanish America. War had a pernicious effect on civilian populations, turning them into outlaws and bandits, guerrillas and collaborators – a habit that would outlive the Napoleonic Wars and continue to dog regular armies across the nineteenth century. From Mexico in 1818 the Spanish viceroy reported to the Minister of War back in Madrid that his army now faced the same problem that had confronted Napoleon's forces in Spain.

> When the King's troops pass through they see them in the fields, with their ploughs and their hoes, busily tilling their land, and then they inform the rebel leaders of the district, abandon their pretence of working, get their weapons, mount their horses, and form a band capable of attacking a superior number of His Majesty's troops, or surprise a convoy, or rob and attack them.[44]

The troops knew what they had to do to see them off, and so the whole cycle of violence, by and against civilians, was resumed.

---

43   Broers, *Napoleon's Other War*, p. 86.
44   Cited in ibid., p. 151.

PART IV

Contradictions of the French Revolutionary and Napoleonic Wars

13

The Limits of Conflict in Napoleonic Europe – And Their Transgression

DAVID A. BELL

L IKE ALL wars, the Napoleonic Wars were anything but a uniform experience. Their character varied over time, and from place to place. Some elements of the conflicts looked back to the past, while others seemed to foreshadow the practices of later years. The opposing powers operated in different ways and even articulated different sets of rules for themselves. And of course all these differences subsequently informed a wide range of writing about the wars. The challenge for historians, then, is twofold: first, to give as complete a description as possible of the range of experiences, highlighting their differences, nuances and complexities; but secondly, to venture the best possible generalisations about the experiences as a whole, trying to discern overall patterns and tendencies.

The task of generalisation can be difficult, particularly when it comes to the relationship between civilians and war. In the Napoleonic period, at one extreme, we have the horrors of the Peninsular War: whole villages torched in retribution for guerrilla attacks; civilian hostages taken and killed by brutal occupation authorities; soldiers seized and tortured to death by non-uniformed fighters. But at the other extreme, there was the rather idyllic treatment meted out to the imprisoned French officers studied by Mark Towsey, where the only instruments of torture in sight seem to have been grilled sheep's head, haggis and hodge-podge, their administration eased by the copious helpings of whiskey that generous Scottish hosts pressed upon their continental visitors. In the first instance, we see the stirrings of modern total war; in the second, the apparent continuation of older 'cabinet wars' conducted by armies whose cultured officer classes had more in common with each other than with their own rank and file.

Still, we should not shrink from the task of generalisation. Even in the Second World War, not all relationships between civilians and war fit the horrific model elaborated by the Germans on the Eastern Front. In occupied France, especially between 1940 and 1942, a good many German officers – university-educated, speaking good French – tried to maintain a veneer of 'civilised' relations with the populations under their control, and met with a warm reception from local collaborators when they did so.[1] Later in the war, German officers imprisoned in Mississippi lived in private houses within POW camps, while Afrika Korps commandant Colonel-General Hans-Jürgen von Arnim was given a car and driver, and even allowed to attend the local movie theatre.[2] Yet clearly such examples, if not precisely 'atypical' (what was the 'typical' Second World War experience?) were contrary to the overall tendencies of the war, in which the contending parties were driven to ever-greater degrees of mobilisation and engagement, and defined victory as the total subjugation of their adversaries.

With the Napoleonic Wars as well, what matters is not so much to identify a 'typical' wartime experience as to discern general trends. To take one obvious example: before 1790 very few European battles had involved more than 100,000 soldiers. In 1809 the battle of Wagram (the largest yet seen in the gunpowder age) involved 300,000. And in 1813 the battle of Leipzig had 500,000, of whom 150,000 were killed or wounded. The frequency of major battles increased as well, so that of all the major battles fought on the continent between 1490 and 1815, more than a fifth took place between 1790 and 1815 alone. Of course, some campaigns had relatively few battles, and some involved mostly small ones. But the overall trend matters more than these exceptions, and the overall trend was – exponentially – towards more battles, and bigger ones.[3]

Similarly, in my recent work *The First Total War*, I argued that the Napoleonic Wars saw increasingly difficult, violent relations between the military and civilians. I placed particular emphasis on the brutal repression, by the French army, of insurrections in Calabria, the Tyrol and Iberia. In these areas, the conflict between an overstretched French army attempting to impose radical reforms on the one hand, and local populations trying to defend their property and customs (especially religious ones) on the other, frequently degenerated into a vicious, no-holds-barred guerrilla conflict that deserved the label of 'absolute enmity'. They also fit into a pattern of steadily increasing ideological hostility

---

1   See, for instance, Gildea, *Marianne in Chains*.
2   Skates, 'German Prisoners of War in Mississippi, 1943–1946'.
3   Bell, *First Total War*, p. 7.

between France and its adversaries, in which each side could see no end to the wars other than the overthrow of the other's regime.[4]

It is important to note that even at the worst moments of the Iberian struggle, the French and Spanish never found themselves in a situation where every person desired and worked towards nothing but the destruction of the other side. Just as in the Second World War not every battle was Stalingrad, and not every insurrection the Warsaw Ghetto, so in the Napoleonic Wars Europe was not divided into groups of people supposedly programmed to desire the complete annihilation of one another. I would argue that in total war, states do indeed push their populations *towards* an attitude of utter hatred towards and demonisation of the enemy, as well as towards complete mobilisation in the service of that enemy's destruction. But their attempts are always, necessarily, partial and incomplete. What marks 'total war' is not the specific levels of hatred, mobilisation and destruction, as if 'totality' had a quantitative threshold, but the political dynamic that relentlessly pushes states *towards* ever higher levels of these things, in an inexorable spiral of escalation that ultimately ends with the collapse of one side or another from sheer exhaustion and exsanguinations.[5]

Therefore, if the 'first total war' of the Revolutionary and Napoleonic period had a lasting effect on the relationship between civilians and war in Europe, it was not simply because of the experience of conflict at new levels of intensity, as in Napoleon's Russian campaign, or the hideous siege of Saragossa. It was also because of more subtle transformations in the broad culture of war. As I pointed out in my book, the modern distinction between 'civilian' and 'military' itself only appeared in this period. Before the 1790s, in Western Europe, the very word 'civilian' (or 'civil') in French had lacked the modern meaning of 'non-military' (in English, a 'civilian' meant an expert in civil law). The distinction did not yet exist, because the ruling elites of Old Regime societies refused to draw sharp lines between their professional role as military officers and their social identity as aristocrats.[6]

Paradoxically, the coming of total war in 1792–93 at first seemed to collapse the distinction. France's *levée en masse* of 1793 famously proclaimed every French citizen a soldier.[7] But this call for universal mobilisation, and the ones that followed it in Iberia, Austria, Prussia and other parts of Europe, did not demand the *permanent* militarisation of all civilians. Rather, they stated that individuals should stand ready to give up 'civilian' life in times of national emergency, and embrace a military role for its duration. In this sense, the events

---

4   Ibid., pp. 223–62.
5   See the discussion in ibid., pp. 7–13.
6   Ibid., pp. 11, 322–23.
7   See Moran and Waldron, eds., *People in Arms*.

of the period actually reinforced the civilian–military distinction. It came to be thought that in normal times, society would stand divided into separate 'military' and 'civilian' spheres. But times of war would require individuals to pass from the latter to the former. And by extension, times of total war would require the complete but temporary absorption of the latter into the former – the 'militarisation' (to cite another neologism that significantly dates from this period) of an entire society. During the period from 1792 to 1815, most combatant powers did not experience militarisation to this degree for any but relatively short periods. But over the course of the wars, they experienced it more and more, in keeping with the escalation of the overall conflict. And these experiences, in turn, left a cultural legacy that endured well beyond the coming of peace in 1815. The copious memoir literature that Leighton S. James highlights in his essay – which had equivalents throughout Europe, but virtually no precedent in previous European history – was crucial in transmitting this legacy, as Europeans of all social classes looked back in wonder at the transformations of their own lives that the wars had brought about. The legacy has helped to shape military–civilian relations ever since.

The chapters by Mark Towsey, Leighton S. James and Gavin Daly each add fascinating dimensions to the story of the Napoleonic Wars, while reinforcing our understanding of the sheer variability of experience throughout Europe during these years. To my mind, they strongly underline the point that if this period did indeed see 'total war', that phrase should not be taken as implying any grim uniformity of behaviour on the parts of governments, military forces or civilian populations.

To be sure, each author acknowledges the massive changes that Napoleonic warfare brought to Europe. For example, as Towsey notes, the sheer number of wartime prisoners dwarfed anything seen in Europe before 1789, reflecting the vastly increased scale of warfare after that date, and making possible far more, and more varied, interactions between prisoners of war and their host societies. Yet at least in the case of these French officers, he writes: 'their engagement with the local civilian population [...] recalls the bonds of polite civility that tied together the European officer class in earlier generations, rather than the all-out belligerence that is said to differentiate the Napoleonic conflict'.

Leighton S. James's contribution, meanwhile, discusses what he calls the 'mixed impact' of the Napoleonic occupations on German central Europe in terms that recall Hubert van Houtte's classic study of foreign occupations of the early modern southern Netherlands.[8] While James does not play down the terrible consequences that the war often had for civilians – the indiscriminate violence that followed assaults on fortified communities, frequent plunder and

---

8   Houtte, *Les occupations étrangères en Belgique.*

rape – one can point to countless examples of similar outrages from before 1789. And James particularly stresses the benefits that civilians could reap unexpectedly from occupation: selling goods and services to the occupying forces; not paying taxes or rent; violating laws governing hunting and wood-gathering on manorial estates, and so forth. Van Houtte pointed to precisely these sorts of benefits in his account of the southern Netherlands in the eighteenth century (Adam Smith, similarly, quipped that Dutch peasants positively looked forward to military occupation because they could stop paying rent and could sell provisions to the occupiers at hugely inflated prices).[9] The principal novelty James identifies is that the Germans of the Napoleonic period found a way of profiting even from the horrors, by selling sensational memoirs describing their mistreatment at the hands of the French.

Finally, Gavin Daly's meticulous account of plunder by British forces in the Peninsular Wars would not seem misplaced as an account of British troops in the War of the Spanish Succession. True, Daly is ready to endorse the Duke of Wellington's assertion that Revolutionary and Napoleonic France produced 'a new [...] system of war' that systematically plundered occupied countries while dehumanising its opponents. He shows that plunder, even by the British, 'became normalised and routinised amongst both rankers and junior officers', as part of 'a barbarisation of warfare on a scale, duration and intensity that was unique in the Revolutionary and Napoleonic wars'. Still, he also notes that 'British plunder was never on the scale of the French.' It was more sporadic and circumstantial, driven by the failure of the British army adequately to pay and feed its soldiers, as well as by simple opportunistic greed, and could later be defended in a Romantic vein as 'roguish' or 'harmless fun'.

So how to fit these three fascinating case studies into the larger patterns and trends? Most obviously, the experiences of the French officers imprisoned in Scotland, which Towsey has studied in remarkable detail, must stand as possibly the most pleasant episode of captivity in the history of warfare, occupying the opposite end of the bell curve from the far more common experiences of slaughter and starvation exemplified (for instance) by the fate of Soviet prisoners during the Second World War. Yet, as Towsey himself writes, the experience of these officers was not even representative of French prisoners in Britain during the Napoleonic Wars: '122,440 combatants were confined in Britain, many under horrific conditions'. We do not yet have a full survey of wartime captivity in the early nineteenth century, but Gavin Daly, in earlier work, suggests that the broad trend was clearly away from the relatively humane arrangements that had prevailed before the French Revolutionary Wars, where captives (especially officers) had multiple opportunities to mix with local populations,

---

9   Anderson, *War of the Austrian Succession*, p. 53.

and perhaps to return home before the end of hostilities.[10] In its place was arising the regime of captivity that has become familiar to us today: confinement
in prison-like conditions for the duration of hostilities. Furthermore, as Daly
notes, French figures suggest that by the war's end 33 per cent of all French
prisoners in Britain were housed in 'hulks' – decommissioned naval vessels
where the deplorable conditions ensured a mortality rate above 3 per cent,
leading one French officer to call them 'floating tombs'. Other prisoners ended
up in notorious British prisons such as Dartmoor.[11]

The British record of plundering during the Peninsular War examined in
Gavin Daly's chapter does not, of course, come close to matching the systematic campaigns of exploitation, complete with punitive taxation and forced
'contributions', that the French inflicted upon many of the countries that they
occupied during the course of the Napoleonic Wars. Rather than encouraging
and managing the plunder, as French commanders did, British commanders
tried as best they could to suppress it. After all, Spain and Portugal were their
nominal allies. Furthermore, the most important British force of the war was
led by its most aristocratic commander, Wellington, who, as Daly notes, deliberately distinguished his own methods from the 'new French system of war'.
And as Daly also argues, 'The British army did not emerge out of an earlier era
of revolution and total war.'

Under these circumstances, the fact that British plundering took place on
the scale Daly has discovered is itself significant, and supports his conclusion
that the Peninsular War was in fact 'a crucible of "total war"'. But it was not just
in the scale of plundering that even the very non-revolutionary British army
ended up adopting very different methods of dealing with civilian populations
in the first decade of the nineteenth century. British forces never exercised any
serious degree of political domination in Spain, where they cooperated with
the authorities loyal to the exiled monarch Ferdinand VII and with guerrilla bands. Portugal, however, was a very different matter. There, after 1808,
British general William Carr Beresford for a time acted as a virtual dictator,
reshaping Portuguese institutions so as to impose effective conscription and
ordering the evacuation of any territory in danger of French occupation. By
January 1812, thanks to his efforts, there were some 110,000 Portuguese serving
in the army and militia – a far greater proportion of the population than even
Revolutionary France had ever managed to call up.[12] No territory under British
rule had been treated in this manner before, suggesting that it was not only the

10 Daly, 'Napoleon's Lost Legions', pp. 361–80. Renaud Morieux is currently engaged in a
    large-scale study of wartime captivity in the Napoleonic Wars.
11 Daly, 'Napoleon's Lost Legions', pp. 364, 374. See also Masson, *Les sépulcres flottants*.
12 See Bell, *First Total War*, p. 254. In general on the conflict in the Peninsula see Esdaile,
    Peninsular War.

general barbarisation of warfare that influenced Britain during the Napoleonic Wars, but also the generalisation of new, radical means of mobilising populations and resources.

The experience of German central Europe, studied by Leighton S. James, seemingly offers a striking counterpoint to the situation in Iberia. The German lands saw few violent civilian uprisings against French authorities and relatively little violent repression of civilians. The largest exception came in the Tyrol, where a popular revolt against the French client state of Bavaria in 1809 quickly raged out of control, and direct French intervention became necessary to crush it. But elsewhere in Germany, violence between French soldiers and German civilians remained at the level described by James. Occupying armies initially indulged in plunder, rape and general mayhem. The successful storming of a fortified town could bring large-scale bloodshed. But these atrocities, which did not differ significantly in kind from the sort routinely practised in pre-1789 warfare, did not lead to a systematic looting of the country, still less to absolute enmity between occupiers and the civilian population. And once the initial violence had died down, the two sides soon reached a modus vivendi in which many civilians found ways, not just to survive, but to enrich themselves. French soldiers who had served in both Germany and Spain, and survived to write memoirs of their experiences, could rarely resist contrasting the supposedly docile, cooperative Germans to the obstreperous, dangerous Spaniards. The French officer Albert-Jean Rocca later wrote that unlike in Spain, 'in Germany we dealt with a submissive people [...] whose national character, the sole invincible barrier that nations can oppose to foreign invasions, was weakened by their sovereigns, who had accustomed them to precise and painstaking obedience'.[13]

It is worth remarking, though, that if Germany escaped the fate of Iberia, it may have been due more to the vagaries of military fortune than to 'national character'. During the year 1813, following his disastrous retreat from Russia, Napoleon fought a brave, occasionally brilliant but ultimately futile series of campaigns to preserve his position in central Europe, and within twelve months found himself forced back towards the French homeland.[14] During this period he never established effective occupation authorities in northern Germany. Yet in Prussia, which had remained his ally until March, the potential for an Iberian-style conflict certainly existed. As German literary elites participated in what would become known as the 'War of Liberation', they produced an unprecedented wave of anti-French propaganda, which matched anything seen in Spain in its virulence. 'I want hatred against the French', wrote the most vocal of these German patriots, Ernst Moritz Arndt. 'Not just for

---

13   Rocca, *Mémoires*, p. 2.
14   See Leggiere, *Napoleon and Berlin*.

this war, but for a long time, forever [...] This hatred glows as the religion of the German people, as a holy mania in every heart.'[15] Furthermore, Prussia's rulers began to take steps to translate this rhetoric into action. In March King Frederick William created a national *Landwehr* (Home Army), with compulsory service for all men aged eighteen to forty from the middle classes and landed peasantry. Then, on 21 April, he issued an edict supplementing it with a *Landsturm* (Home Guard) that in theory would include all adult males under sixty. The edict also contained the following orders for the entire population: 'Every citizen is required to resist the advancing enemy with weapons of all sorts, not to obey his verbal or written orders, and if the enemy attempts to enforce these with violence, to harm him using all available means.' The text explicitly invoked earlier Spanish proclamations that had justified guerrilla war against the Bonapartist regime there.[16] So it is entirely conceivable that, had Napoleon done better in the 1813 campaign, he might have then faced a massive German popular uprising, leading to a German version of the Peninsular War. Significantly, apart from the Tyrol, the only other major German uprising against the French army took place in Hamburg in 1813, during which Marshal Davout expelled some 25,000 civilians from the fortified city.[17]

Luckily for Germany, this nightmare scenario never came to pass. Napoleon fell back towards France, and a year later his regime collapsed entirely. Nonetheless, it is arguable that the broad trend of the wars was towards the generalisation of Iberian-style conflicts to other parts of Europe (given the attempts by hussar officer Denis Davidov to create a partisan force to fight Napoleon in Russia, one wonders might have happened there as well if Napoleon had not been forced to retreat from Moscow).[18] Had Napoleon's empire survived for longer, many more regions would likely have found themselves torn apart by Iberian-style total war. The fact that Napoleon could not sustain this degree of mobilisation and engagement points to the physical limitations on warfare's destructive capacity in this pre-industrial era.[19] But on the other hand, the fact that the politics and culture of war were now driving both sides towards complete mobilisation, in an inexorable process of acceleration that could only end with one side's collapse, reminds us just how much these wars differed from the limited, cabinet wars of the Old Regime, and how much they anticipated the total wars of the twentieth century.

---

15   Cited in Jeismann, *Das Vaterland der Feinde*, p. 93. In general on this phenomenon see Jeismann, *Das Vaterland der Feinde*; Bell, *First Total War*, pp. 293–301.

16   Huber, ed., 'Verordnung über den Landsturm', pp. 50–53.

17   See Esdaile, 'Patriots, Partisans and Land Pirates in Retrospect', p. 16.

18   See Zamoyski, *Moscow, 1812*, pp. 327–29.

19   See Broers, 'Concept of "Total War"', pp. 247–68.

14

Plunder on the Peninsula: British Soldiers and Local Civilians during the Peninsular War, 1808–1813

GAVIN DALY

ON 17 July 1815 the Prince Regent signed a Royal Warrant granting the British army that served under the Duke of Wellington in Portugal, Spain and France from 1809 to 1814 the sum of £800,000 'for the ordinance, arms, stores, magazines, shipping and other booty captured by it from the enemy'.[1] This was the only prize the British soldiers of the Peninsular War were ever formally granted by the Crown. Yet behind this 'official prize' were thousands of other stories of British plunder, including objects taken from Spanish and Portuguese civilians.

All regular armies in the Peninsular War – French, Spanish, Portuguese and British – plundered the local inhabitants. The plunder practised by the French invasion and occupation forces has always, and justifiably so, overshadowed the behaviour of the British army. When Napoleon's Imperial troops crossed the Pyrenees, in the words of Charles Esdaile, they 'fell upon the Peninsula like wolves'.[2] Public merchandise and estates were confiscated, crippling war contributions were levied on the provinces, harvests requisitioned, and church property and valuables seized. In the face of popular resistance, guerrilla warfare and spiralling cycles of insurgency and counter-insurgency, French troops committed atrocities against civilians and razed villages, towns, churches and monasteries to the ground, looting as they did. The most outrageous looting, however, came from the top. Napoleon demanded nothing less than fifty

---

1 Wellington, *General Orders*, ed. Gurwood, General Order, 10 August 1815, p. 434.
2 Esdaile, *Peninsular War*, p. 242.

paintings for the Louvre, while marshals and generals in the provinces acted with impunity, lining their own pockets and stealing national treasures.[3]

Looking on with horror at the conduct of the French army during the Peninsular War, the Duke of Wellington claimed this 'new French system of war is the greatest evil that ever fell on the civilised world'.[4] Wellington, like many historians since, saw French behaviour as new relative to the 'limited' warfare and practices of armies in eighteenth-century Europe, and traced its genesis to the French Revolution, particularly the *levée en masse* of 1793.[5] Certainly, some of the characteristics of the French Revolutionary and Napoleonic wars – for example, ideology as a motivational force, and the blurring of the traditional distinctions between combatants and non-combatants – had existed in various forms and degrees in earlier eighteenth-century conflicts involving European armies.[6] Nevertheless, the French Revolution had a transformative impact on many of the ideals and practices of war. States and societies mobilised for war on an unprecedented scale, especially France, which experienced 'total war' under the Jacobins in 1793–94. Through French Republican eyes, the Revolutionary Wars were conceived as a 'people's war', with war as both national defence and a means to export revolutionary ideology and enlightened 'civilising' models. Moreover, the sheer size of France's new national conscript armies presented practical problems of supply, the solution being to live off the land of occupied territories. All these changes had consequences for the relationship between war and society, and for military attitudes and practices towards civilians. Civilians found their lives increasingly affected by war, whether it be through mobilisation, fighting or military occupation. This was never more the case than in the Peninsular War.

Wellington recognised that French armies in the Peninsula survived 'by authorised and regulated plunder of the country and its inhabitants'.[7] This was certainly not the British way in the Peninsula. British plunder was never on the scale of the French, and for good reason. The British army did not emerge out of an earlier era of revolution and total war; it was not an invading army intent on revolutionising local state and society; it was not involved in a barbarous war against irregulars; it was far smaller and did not have to live off the land; and

---

3   For an overview of French plundering practices in the Peninsula see Esdaile, *Peninsular War*, pp. 242–45.

4   Wellington, *Dispatches*, Vol. V, Wellington to Baron Constant, 31 January 1812, pp. 494–95.

5   See especially, Bell, *First Total War*.

6   For questions of change and continuity see, for example, Black, 'Military Revolution II'; Forrest, 'Nation in Arms I'.

7   Wellington, *Dispatches*, Vol. IV, Wellington to Marquis Wellesley, 26 January 1811, pp. 555–56.

its commanders-in-chief did not set the example of systematic looting. Last but not least, it was among supposed friends and allies.

Yet, for all this, at times the British plunder of civilians in the Iberian Peninsula was the equal of the French. If the French were professional robber barons, the British were at least amateur bandits. Plunder, drunkenness and violence accompanied the 1809 retreat to Corunna, and the 1812 retreats from Burgos and Madrid.[8] Worst of all was the British sacking of the three siege cities – Ciudad Rodrigo, Badajoz and San Sebastian – with the plunder of homes, shops and churches, and atrocities against Spanish civilians.[9] These notorious and extreme cases, as significant as they are, nevertheless tend to obscure the extent and diverse nature of the British plunder of civilians over five years of campaigning. This chapter is not concerned with the exceptional plunder of the sieges or with physical violence to civilians. Rather, it explores the general British plunder of local property and objects. First, it considers British soldiers' perceptions of their plundering of Portuguese and Spanish civilians. Secondly, it illuminates the diverse practices and cultures of everyday British plunder, whereby forms of plunder became normalised and routinised among both rankers and junior officers. Finally, it seeks to understand British plunder within both old and relatively new practices, mentalities and cultural contexts. In common with traditional military plunder, British soldiers were motivated by necessity and opportunism, yet there was also an invigorated 'spirit of collecting', especially among officers. Moreover, British plunder was also a product of condescending cultural attitudes towards the Iberian peoples. Old and new historical forces shaped these prejudices, including the anti-Catholic traditions of the Black Legend and contemporary enlightenment critiques of civilisations and peoples. Finally, the very destructiveness and intensity of the Peninsular War itself informed British behaviour towards local civilians and property.

To begin with, British military codes and regulations, in keeping with most Continental customs, distinguished between lawful and unlawful plunder.[10] Distinctions were drawn between combatants and non-combatants, and between collective and individual plunder. The property of the enemy state and its army was considered lawful plunder and was officially regulated and

---

8 Esdaile, *Peninsular War*, pp. 151–52, 416–18; Oman, *History of the Peninsular War*, Vol. I, pp. 565–78, Vol. VI, pp. 143–54.

9 Esdaile, *Peninsular War*, pp. 379–80, 383–87, 467–71; Oman, *History of the Peninsular War*, Vol. V, pp. 183–85, pp. 256–64.

10 For military plunder in early modern Europe see Redlich's classic study *De Praeda Militari*. For the rules of war, including the rights of non-combatants, in the Age of the Enlightenment see Best, *Humanity in Warfare*. For English rules of war and military pillage and plunder in conflicts of the seventeenth and eighteenth centuries see Donagan, *War in England*, pp. 134–95; Conway, "'Great Mischeif Complain'd Of'".

known as 'prize'. Following Roman practice, enemy plunder was to be collected and divided up among the troops present according to rank, reinforcing both the hierarchical and collective values of the army. The question of plundering the civilian population, however, as opposed to the enemy state and army was another matter entirely. With few exceptions – such as paid requisitioning and the circumstances of a siege – seizing the property of civilians was deemed criminal, punishable under military law. This was a point Wellington stressed even before the army set foot in Portugal. As the British Expeditionary Force rode the tide in Mondego Bay on 31 July 1808, Wellington issued a General Order addressing how the troops should behave with respect to local persons and property:

> The troops are to understand that Portugal is a country friendly to His Majesty, that it is essentially necessary to their own success that the most strict obedience should be preserved, that properties and persons should be respected, and that no injury should be done which it is possible to avoid. The Lieut. General declares his determination to punish in the most exemplary manner all who may be convicted of acts of outrage and of plunder against the persons or property of any of the people of the country.[11]

Wellington was empowered to do this under the British Articles of War, which allowed for regimental and general courts martial to be set up overseas to hear cases of British soldiers 'accused of wilful Murder, Theft, Robbery, Rape [...] or of having used Violence or committed any Offence against the Persons or Property of any of Our Subjects, or of any others entitled to Our Protection'.[12] The most serious offences, including all capital offences, were heard by general courts martial presided over by a Judge-Advocate or his delegate. Soldiers found guilty, depending upon the severity of the crime, faced the prospect of death, transportation or the lash.

For over five years British soldiers lived among the Portuguese and Spanish peoples, often billeted on local families. Not surprisingly, there was a wide gulf between, on the one hand, British military regulations and official expressions of military–civil goodwill, and on the other, the day-to-day practices of redcoats living among their hosts in the crucible of war. A range of sources – from Wellington's correspondence and General Orders, to general courts martial records, to the letters, diaries and memoirs of officers and rankers – reveal that the British army's plunder of local inhabitants was common and widespread.

---

11   Wellington, *Dispatches*, Vol. III, General Order, 31 July 1808, p. 42.
12   *Rules and Articles* (1804), Section XXIV, Art. IV, 81–82. For the historical evolution of the Articles of War and the Mutiny Act see Clode, *Administration of Justice*, pp. 1–38. For eighteenth-century British military law and courts martial see Gilbert, 'Law and Honour'; Steppler, 'British Military Law'.

In the case of official records, of 174 cases brought before general courts martial in the Peninsula between 1810 and 1812, the majority were for desertion, but 31 cases involved the plunder of locals, with 28 separate incidents.[13] Of these 28, the majority involved breaking into and robbing houses, and ten involved physical violence against civilians, including murder. Significantly, these incidents were not confined to a handful of regiments but were widely dispersed throughout the army, involving members of 24 different regiments and departments. At times Wellington grew exasperated by the number of cases brought before him, Judge-Advocate Larpent recording in his journal in March 1813: 'He [Wellington] swore, and said his whole table was covered with details of robbery and mutiny, and complaints from all quarters, in all languages and that he should be nothing but a General of Courts-Martial.'[14]

Of course, courts martial heard only the most serious cases, and only those that came to light and where there was a will to investigate and to punish. Soldiers' own narratives illuminate the fuller range of plunder. Redcoats plundered as they marched; they plundered from civilians they met on the road; they plundered from their billets, from occupied and unoccupied homes, and from local churches and monasteries; they stole wine, fruit, pigs, sheep, cattle, horses, mules, carts and, famously, honey from roadside beehives;[15] they stole money, personal valuables, clothing, crucifixes, church silver and candles; to build fires they stripped wood from houses, barns, doors and even coffins; they plundered from the rich and the poor, and from the living and the dead. Writing to his brother from northern Spain in late 1813, the officer George Hennell lamented: 'We are like locusts.'[16] And this was all at the expense of allies and civilians whom the British had come to liberate.

From Wellington's perspective, of course, this plunder was inexcusable and criminal, reflecting poorly on the discipline and honour of the British army. It also risked alienating the local population, thereby undermining the British war effort. Reflecting contemporary class prejudices, Wellington notoriously characterised the plunder as the product of an army composed of the 'scum of the earth'.[17] Moreover, his infamous circular letter of 28 November 1812 ensured that British plunder, and the army's reputation, became a public matter. Issued in the heat of the moment following the disastrous retreat from Burgos, Wellington's

---

13 Compiled from Wellington, *General Orders: Spain and Portugal*.

14 Larpent, *Private Journal of Judge-Advocate Larpent*, p. 63.

15 So incensed was Wellington with the plundering of beehives around Badajoz in September 1809 that he issued three General Orders and had three privates tried by a court martial, their taste for honey being rewarded with 500 lashes each: Wellington, *General Orders*, ed. Gurwood, pp. 30–32, 150.

16 Hennell, *Gentleman Volunteer*, p. 133.

17 Wellington, *Dispatches*, Vol. VI, Wellington to Bathurst, 2 July 1813, p. 575.

circular letter to his commanding officers claimed that the discipline of the army had fallen away to a 'greater degree than any army with which I ever served, or of which I have ever read'.[18] Wellington's rebuke then found its way back home into the newspapers. From that time on, soldiers writing about plunder did so in the broader context of Wellington's circular and its legacy.

Yet what were the attitudes of soldiers and junior officers to the issue of plunder? Contemporary writings and memoirs reveal at least three broad responses. First, there were many soldiers who justified plunder by appealing to the law of 'necessity' – itself a long-standing military tradition – and the idea of the 'suffering soldier'. Necessity and suffering were born of hunger and starvation. To feed their armies in the Peninsula, the French and British adopted very different approaches, shaped by different traditions, the legacy of the French Revolution and campaign circumstances. Over the course of the eighteenth century, the feeding of European armies in occupied territories had been increasingly regulated by a 'contribution' system, whereby the local population paid the occupying army in cash or kind.[19] This was nothing short of 'blackmail', but allowed the local population to buy off the worst excesses of military violence and looting.[20] Napoleon's troops in the Peninsula, however, following the custom of French Revolutionary armies, lived off the land, with the idea that 'war could feed off war'.[21] In short, the huge French armies simply took what they wanted from the civilian population, often by recourse to terror. The British army in the Peninsula faced different circumstances, being much smaller in size and having the advantage of access to the sea. In contrast to the French, British troops were provisioned by a depot system supplied by sea and road, supplemented with paid requisitioning from local resources organised by the Army's Commissariat department in conjunction with local magistrates.[22] However, despite Wellington's great vigilance and minute attention to the details of provisioning his men – he once remarked that it was necessary to know how 'to trace a biscuit from Lisbon into a man's mouth on the frontier'[23] – the British army was not always adequately supplied with daily rations, nor regularly paid. Wellington, himself, on occasion, stressed to the government that failure to provide the troops with adequate supplies would naturally, and justifiably, lead to plunder:

---

18 Wellington, *General Orders*, ed. Gurwood, Circular Letter, 28 November 1812, pp. 63–66.
19 Redlich, *De Praeda Militari*, pp. 62–70.
20 Duffy, *Military Experience in the Age of Reason*, p. 166.
21 Chapman, ed., *Diaries and Letters of G. T. W. B. Boyes*, Vol. I, p. 50. For French Revolutionary practices see Best, *Humanity in Warfare*, pp. 94–95.
22 See Oman, *Wellington's Army*, pp. 307–19.
23 Cited in Brett-James, *Life in Wellington's Army*, p. 111.

It is impossible to punish soldiers, who are left to starve, for outrages committed in order to procure food; and, at all events, no punishment, however severe, will have the desired effect of preventing the troops from seizing what they can to satisfy their appetite, when neglected by those whose duty it is to supply their wants.[24]

On four noted occasions – the retreat to Corunna in the winter of 1808–09, the Talavera campaign in 1809, the British advance through Portugal in early 1811 and the 1812 retreat from Burgos – the provisioning system completely broke down, with soldiers receiving neither their daily bread nor alcohol ration.[25] Faced with such chronic shortages, starving soldiers plundered farms, cellars, villages and towns. In soldiers' writings, deprivation and hardship are the most common defences used to excuse British plundering. The officer Moyle Sherer claimed it was completely understandable that soldiers turned to plunder when they were neither 'fed, clothed, or paid with regularity';[26] similarly, the ranker Douglas accused those of criticising the British army's conduct of failing to appreciate the 'hunger, the hardships, the cold and nakedness, which we endured'.[27] He summed up plundering in such circumstances with simply: 'necessity has no law'.[28] Soldiers appealed to necessity in order to defend individual, regimental and army honour. In response to Wellington's claim that the army on its retreat from Burgos had 'suffered no privations' nor 'suffered any hardships' save that of inclement weather, Guards Officer John Aitchison wrote home to his father: 'Is it no privation to be without food – absolutely for 24 to 36 hours? Yet this was the case on the retreat [...] Is it no hardship to march fourteen hours without food, on the worst of roads in bad weather?'[29]

Plunder was therefore rationalised as an unfortunate product of the harsh circumstances of the war. It was not uncommon for soldiers to draw a distinction between those who stole food from necessity and the few who went further, Douglas accusing the latter of having failed in their duty as soldiers. In some accounts too there is also a romanticisation of soldiers' suffering and a comic bravado. John Cooper wrote that upon enlisting a man 'should have parted with half his stomach';[30] and Leach recommended to any of his 'corpulent' readers a weight-loss programme at Almaraz.[31] Deprivation here served

---

24 Wellington, *Dispatches*, Vol. IV, Wellington to Charles Stuart, 3 March 1811, p. 648.
25 Anthony Brett-James highlights the latter three occasions: Brett-James, *Life in Wellington's Army*, p. 111.
26 Sherer, *Recollections of the Peninsula*, p. 131.
27 Douglas, *Douglas's Tale of the Peninsula*, p. 60.
28 Ibid., p. 56.
29 Aitchison, *Ensign in the Peninsular War*, p. 228.
30 Cited in Haythornthwaite, *Armies of Wellington*, p. 62.
31 Leach, *Rough Sketches*, pp. 95–96.

as a badge of honour that authenticated the soldier's experience of war, feeding into ideals of romantic suffering and setting the Peninsular veteran apart from both the reading public and Waterloo veterans.[32] Fireside critics were assured that they were in no position to judge the behaviour of such military men.

A second group of soldiers, however, with a higher representation of officers, were more critical of British plunder. Their focus was less on the claims of 'suffering soldiers' than on the 'suffering civilian'. They were uncomfortable with the principle of necessity and were troubled and ashamed by official British requisitioning, in a sense plunder by another name, let alone widespread unauthorised plunder. August Schaumann, a deputy assistant-commissariat general attached to the King's German Legion, remembered cutting down corn amid 'lamenting, howling, crying' locals, and admitted that 'often, when I am thus engaged my eyes are streaming with tears'.[33] The artillery officer William Swabey wrote in his diary: 'Marched to Villa Franca once more, I felt ashamed of showing my face there. We now have no bread, but such as we can press, which is hard on the inhabitants [...] war and charity are two things truly incompatible with each other.'[34] Travelling through Portugal in May 1813 the hussar officer George Woodberry felt similarly: 'We are daily approach'd by the women and children with tears & moans, begging us to leave them a little to subsist on.'[35] The behaviour of the hussars made matters only worse, Woodberry lamenting in his diary: 'Our men have commenc'd rompag'ing every place they stay in; at Cortizes they broke open a cellar & robbed it of oil [...] Last night they got into a poor man's house & stole two shorts [...] this last vexed me, the whole village having shown us so much respect.'[36] Such men were sensitive to the sufferings of civilians in war. They self-identified as soldiers of sensibility and emotion, in tune with the pain and trauma of their fellow humanity.[37] Furthermore, some soldiers took issue with the claim that the army was often deprived of rations. Private Wheeler, for instance, wrote that, with a couple of exceptions, the British army was well supplied and 'I know many have plundered when there has been no excuse.'[38]

Wheeler's comments point to another attitude to plunder. While identifying the relationship between deprivation and plunder, some soldiers nevertheless

---

32   For romantic suffering and travel see Thompson, *Suffering Traveller*.

33   Schaumann, *On the Road with Wellington*, p. 169.

34   Swabey, *Diary of Campaigns in the Peninsula*, p. 101.

35   Cited in Hunt, ed., *Charging Against Napoleon*, p. 80.

36   Ibid., p. 78.

37   On soldier-writers sentimentalising war in the late eighteenth and early nineteenth centuries see Harari, *Ultimate Experience*, pp. 199–213.

38   Wheeler, *Letters of Private Wheeler*, p. 196.

made light of plunder and felt relatively comfortable writing about it and acknowledging their own participation. This was especially true of memoirs, with soldiers arguably feeling more at ease writing about plunder with the passage of time. For some, plunder was less a source of shame than a source of pride, adventure and entertainment, demonstrating, among other things, the resourcefulness, daring and camaraderie of British soldiers. The historian Geoffrey Best has been critical of this particular tradition of writing about the plunder of civilians in this era:

> The grim facts of the matter have been obscured for subsequent generations by the sentimental folklore of popular militarism in which the depredations of patriotically uniformed men become as innocent and engaging as schoolboy's apple scrumping, and it is implied that the terrified civilian cannot mind having his geese and pigs and seed-potatoes eaten, and his doors and window-frames burnt for firewood, by such jolly chaps.[39]

Within this tradition are the memoir-writers of the 95th Rifles, such as Kincaid, Leach and Costello.[40] As part of Robert Craufurd's celebrated Light Division, the Rifles were a rather special case when it came to plunder because they were often the army's advance or rear-guard, distant from supply lines and in devastated landscapes and towns. The Rifles' reputation had suffered because of Craufurd himself, on one notorious occasion, claiming they had 'committed more crimes than the entire British army'.[41] In their memoirs, many Riflemen played up to this reputation, but presented their behaviour as light-hearted and relatively benign, the work of romantic rogues rather than criminals. The 95th ranker, Costello, recounted tales of derring-do, for example the lengths to which soldiers went to plunder local wine supplies: laden with empty canteens, men risked drowning by lowering themselves with ropes into deep and dark subterranean wine vaults.[42] At the same time, Costello was at pains to inform his readers that such 'foragers', far from being 'indifferent soldiers', were indeed the 'very men whose bravery and daring in the field far exceeded the merits of their more quiet comrades in quarters'.[43] Some soldiers also took a carnivalesque delight in destroying the abandoned property of the wealthy, Costello recalling how in the Portuguese town of Arruda – 'a country resort for the rich citizens of Lisbon' – the men used beautiful furniture and a carriage for firewood.[44]

---

39   Best, *Humanity in Warfare*, p. 93.
40   For the 95th Rifles see Urban, *Wellington's Rifles*.
41   Cited in Urban, *Wellington's Rifles*, p. 136.
42   Costello, *Rifleman Costello*, pp. 145–47.
43   Ibid., p. 167.
44   Ibid., pp. 61–62.

In William Lawrence's memoir of life in the 40ᵗʰ regiment, it is almost de rigueur for the men to steal livestock, food, valuables and money from their host families no matter what the circumstances. This was naked opportunism and theft with no attempt to disguise the fact. At times Lawrence expresses shame and regret, but he revels in the telling of the tale. One plundering incident after another follows. One time the men stole 7,000 dollars hidden in the floor of their Portuguese host's cellar; on another occasion they stole a pig from a farm because 'pork was a thing which the company had not tasted for some time, so we made up our minds to treat ourselves'. When living with a Spanish family in Guinaldo they stole 30 pounds of sausages hidden or preserved in a large jar of olive oil. Even when staying with a 'kind old lady' who used to give them chestnuts, the men did not hesitate to steal her pig. The plunder is always at the expense of unsuspecting locals with soldiers getting the better of 'Spanish wiles', but it is all presented as a bit of harmless fun.[45]

We therefore have a range of attitudes among British soldiers on the nature and impact of plunder with respect to civilians. This in some senses reflected the contradictions of the time: on the one hand, the escalating warfare of the Revolutionary-Napoleonic Age and its impact on civilian life; and on the other, the pressing questions of natural rights, the humanitarian concerns of the Enlightenment and the epoch's cultural sensitivity to sentiment and sensibility. British soldiers sometimes display mixed and contradictory attitudes to the plunder of civilians, and differ over what could be acceptably taken and in what circumstances. There was consensus, though, on two counts: first, necessity could justify certain types of plunder; and secondly, plunder procured through violence to civilians was unacceptable.

The weight of evidence from soldiers' accounts, however, whether defensive, critical or boastful, indicates that plunder for many became normalised and routinised. Writing of Portugal in 1809, Cooper remembered 'no sooner was the day's march ended, than the men turned out to steal pigs, poultry, wine etc'.[46] Both rankers and junior officers developed their own distinct, but overlapping, plundering practices, rituals and language. Common soldiers perfected their plundering techniques: they searched for buried food and valuables with bayonets and ramrods, and watered floors to reveal hidden treasure spots, a practice they borrowed from the French.[47] Rankers had codes of collective silence against inquisitorial locals and commanding officers,[48] and in keeping with the distribution practices of official prize, they evenly divided up the spoils, helping

---

45 Lawrence, *Dorset Soldier*, pp. 45–51, 59, 73.
46 Cooper, *Rough Notes of Seven Campaigns*, p. 12.
47 Browne, *Napoleonic War Journal*, pp. 139, 181.
48 Lawrence, *Dorset Soldier*, pp. 45–48.

to foster group solidarity and collective responsibility. The officer Grattan was condescending of the practice, amused 'to see the scrupulous observation of *etiquette* practised by our men, when any fall, such as a chest or bread or bacon, happened to fall to the lot of a group of individuals in their foraging excursions'.[49] Once soldiers had first breached official regulations on plunder, overcoming their initial pangs of guilt, the easier plunder became. There was group initiation. Grattan recalled soldiers plundering abandoned Portuguese houses for the first time: those whose 'consciences at first felt anything like a qualm, in a little time became more at ease, so that by the time the houses had been half-sacked, there was no one who [...] could not have considered himself much to blame had he pursued a different line of conduct'.[50]

Soldiers used the term plunder but they also had a richer lexicon to describe their practices. 'Foraging' and 'poaching' described the theft of local food, wine and wood; the phrase 'searching the ground' meant looking for hidden food and treasures.[51] One particular Irishman in Lawrence's group even developed a nickname based on his prowess at finding food – 'Pig Harding'.[52] As evident in this relatively innocuous language, soldiers wrote about their own everyday plunder within prescribed limits, carefully distinguishing between what they saw as acceptable and unacceptable practices. Terms such as 'foraging' and 'searching the ground' implied non-violent behaviour towards civilians. Lawrence assured his readers, 'I am sorry to say that we committed depredations too but not to the extent of bloodshed.'[53] There was a degree of self-regulation. Theft and violence to property were acceptable; violence to civilians was not. Personal and group values aside, soldiers knew that armed and violent robbery was much more likely to alert locals and to test the tolerance threshold of commanding officers, landing them before a general court martial. Nonetheless, others of course crossed the boundary of violence to civilians, appearing, as they do, in the courts martial records and in soldiers' accounts. At the same time, there may well be a degree of self-censorship on the part of soldier-writers, making their own involvement palatable and sanitised for a reading audience.

Church property was a common target. Fresh off the boat, when George Woodberry's 18th Hussars reached the Spanish village of Villalba in May 1813 some of the men had no qualms about robbing the local church.[54] In soldiers' accounts, there is often a strong anti-Catholic and iconoclastic dimension

---

49   Grattan, *Adventures with the Connaught Rangers*, pp. 71–72.
50   Ibid., p. 44.
51   *Vicissitudes in the Life of a Scottish Soldier*, p. 144.
52   Lawrence, *Dorset Soldier*, p. 59.
53   Ibid., p. 59.
54   Hunt, ed., *Charging Against Napoleon*, p. 90.

to the plunder of church property. Private Wheeler and others, for example, recounted stories of soldiers removing interred friars and smashing the coffins for firewood;[55] in the convent of Almastairs a ranker from the 71st regiment allegedly threw the wooden image of a saint into a fire, yelling out 'Down with Popery!';[56] and the soldier George Booth, incensed by the false accusation of a local priest, stole a gold cross with an image of the infant Jesus.[57]

What Booth had in his hand was also a souvenir. Soldiers collected trophies and mementoes, whose value was shaped not only by their utility or monetary worth but by the status and cultural meanings the objects conveyed. Soldiers have always taken mementoes but there was a new 'spirit of collecting' in eighteenth- and early nineteenth-century Britain. This was shaped in part by the Grand Tour, by the Enlightenment, by British imperialism and by romantic attachments to fragments and relics.[58] This was a time when the British Museum and India House displayed classical antiquities and Indian treasures and curiosities. In respect of British officers in India purchasing objects at auction after the sacking of Seringapatam in 1799, Maya Jasanoff writes that this kind of 'self-conscious collecting by soldiers was unusual in itself'.[59] Yet soldiers were indeed conscious collectors, and recent scholarly interest in the 'history of collecting', which has all but ignored soldiers, nevertheless provides a valuable framework for understanding some of the daily plundering practices of British soldiers, especially those of officers.[60]

British plunder in the Peninsula is always associated with ordinary soldiers, but officers were keen participants when it came to collecting. John Kincaid's first material encounter with the Peninsular War came not when he landed in Portugal, but rather when he first entered his fellow officers' barracks at Hythe in 1809: 'I could have worshipped the different relics that adorned their barrack-rooms – the pistol or the dagger of some gaunt Spanish robber – a string of beads from the Virgin Mary of some village chapel – or the brazen helmet of some French dragoon.'[61] On display here was a particular romantic representation of war in the Peninsula – bandits, Catholicism and French soldiers – captured and signified in material objects. Sensitive to the individual and regimental empowerment that came with the display, Kincaid longed 'for

---

55 Wheeler, *Letters of Private Wheeler*, p. 84.

56 *Vicissitudes in the Life of a Scottish Soldier*, p. 130.

57 Pearson, *Soldier Who Walked Away*, pp. 111–12.

58 Jasanoff, *Edge of Empire*; Pascoe, *Hummingbird Cabinet*; Semmel, 'Reading the Tangible Past'.

59 Jasanoff, *Edge of Empire*, p. 183.

60 On collecting see especially Pearce, *On Collecting*; Pearce, ed., *Interpreting Objects and Collections*.

61 Kincaid, *Rifle Brigade*, p. 183.

the time when I should be able to make such relics and such tales mine own'.[62] For British soldiers in the Peninsular War, like all soldiers since the time of Homer, the most prized relics were those taken from the enemy.[63] But as Kincaid's story reveals, soldiers valued souvenirs not only from the fallen enemy but also from foreign countries, highlighting the importance that soldiers attached to capturing not only their combat experience in objects, but also their broader cultural experience of travelling through exotic lands. The collector's box set of the Peninsular War was not complete without some local object.

Religious objects were common mementoes, taken from a variety of sources: churches and monasteries, French soldiers and civilians, living or dead. In the deserted Portuguese village of Melo in 1811, Wilkie of the 95th Rifles took a 'set of beads with a gold cross at the end' from the neck of the dead body of an elderly woman he found in the street.[64] Crucifixes and crosses were coveted for their gold and silver, but like the rosary beads in Kincaid's barracks or George Booth's cross, they also, for a largely Protestant army, captured in miniature the 'confessional Other' and conveyed a sense of place: Catholic Spain and Portugal.

The journal of Thomas Browne of the 23rd Royal Welsh Fusiliers, who was attached to the General Staff between 1812 and 1814, provides a rare insight into the plundering practices of officers. Browne openly professed that by 1812 more and more officers in the army had developed their own unique culture of souvenir-taking called 'making'. This was the officers' euphemism for stealing items from households and tourist sites. This was a practice rich in meaning, with its own gentlemanly codes and values. Just as gentlemen on the Grand Tour collected items to remember and authenticate their experiences, and to help fashion their post-travel identities,[65] so too did the officers of Wellington in Spain and Portugal. They took, in Browne's words, 'little memorials of the houses' in which they stayed. This was the war's itinerary captured in material fragments, the officers consciously collecting an 'object autobiography'.[66] Browne wrote that it was a 'pity to leave a King's palace without carrying off some proof positive of my having lodged in it'. For his part, Browne first appropriated a 'blue silk counterpane' from the royal palace at San Ildefonso in August 1812. 'Making' was also secretive and transgressive, with Browne acknowledging that 'this rising art had not yet found its way to the General Officers or Heads of Department'. An officer caught stealing from his host risked the charge of conduct unbecoming an officer and a gentleman. So officers did it by proxy, with their servants stealing for them. According to

62 Ibid.
63 For enemy trophy-taking in modern war see Bourke, *Intimate History of Killing*, pp. 37–43.
64 Costello, *Rifleman Costello*, p. 87.
65 Jasanoff, *Edge of Empire*, pp. 36–37.
66 Pearce, *On Collecting*, p. 32.

Browne, a glance and a wink between the officer and the servant was enough
to secure the desired prize. This was discreet and refined plunder, gentlemen
style. It was also competitive, with the secret group display of objects. Browne
ultimately lost his collection on the retreat from Burgos, and with space at a
premium, he shifted to taking items of practical use. After the war the trophies
of 'making' were displayed back home. As Browne wrote: 'From displays which
I saw on my return to England [...] others had managed much better than
myself in this respect.'[67]

Necessity, opportunism and collecting all played their part in motivating
British plunder. Yet plunder also needs to be understood in the cultural context
of British soldiers' mentalities regarding the Spanish and Portuguese people,
which went beyond traditional military–civil enmity. Given the widespread
plundering practices of many British soldiers it is all too easy to forget that the
Portuguese and Spanish were the allies of the British and not their enemy. Yet
the British, like the French, generally thought themselves to be in a backward
Peninsular world, largely removed from what they considered civilisation.[68]
Many British prejudices against the Portuguese and Spanish were born out
of the anti-Catholic traditions of the Black Legend, which stretched back
to late sixteenth-century Protestant England.[69] Yet, especially among officers,
the contemporary Enlightenment informed new critical responses to Portugal
and Spain. In an age when Scottish and French enlightened thinkers established civilising hierarchies, stadial models of human progress that moved from
the primitive to the modern, contemporary British soldiers in the Peninsula
thought they were in a cultural backwater. Just as eighteenth-century European
travellers were increasingly interested in empirically observing, recording and
classifying foreign environments and cultures, so too did British soldier-writers
in the Peninsula describe and comparatively evaluate local manners, customs,
religious beliefs, politics and economic practices.[70] Through British soldiers'
eyes Portugal and Spain were found wanting with respect to these markers of
civilisation and progress. In a letter home William Bragge summed up Portugal:
'This Nation in all the Arts, Sciences and comforts of this Life is many hundred
Years behind the rest of the world.'[71] Spain did not fare much better. After
landing in Corunna in 1808 the Welsh hussar officer Edwin Griffiths wrote:
'I can only say that it appears some centuries behind England in everything.'[72]

---

67 Browne, *Napoleonic War Journal*, pp. 175–76, 181.
68 Daly, 'Dirty, Indolent, Priest-Ridden City'; Montroussier, 'Français et Britanniques dans
    la Péninsule'.
69 Gibson, *Black Legend*.
70 Daly, 'Dirty, Indolent, Priest-Ridden City'.
71 Bragge, *Peninsular Portrait*, p. 21.
72 Cited in Hunt, ed., *Charging Against Napoleon*, p. 53.

Having officially come to liberate the Portuguese and Spanish from French tyranny, many British soldiers found the enemy was just as much the local people and culture as it was the French. Indeed, enemies on the battlefield, British and French soldiers nevertheless often saw themselves as having much in common when compared to the local people. Often billeted with local families, British soldiers felt little connection or affinity with the inhabitants, only difference. They perceived many of the people as primitive, vulgar, filthy, indolent, ignorant, treacherous and cruel. For the majority of the British soldiers, with the exception of the Irish Catholics among their ranks, they were also in a Popish land of superstitious, idol-worshipping Catholics. Soldiers were especially scathing of the Portuguese, Private Wheeler writing: 'What an ignorant, superstitious, priest-ridden, dirty, lousy set of poor Devils are the Portuguese. Without seeing them it is impossible to conceive there exists a people in Europe so debased.'[73] British soldiers often felt a sense of cultural superiority, arrogance, condescension and self-entitlement towards their local hosts. These feelings were only compounded by the British belief that their exploits and personal sacrifices were not fully appreciated or supported by an indifferent population. This lack of respect, indeed at times utter contempt and loathing, for the local people, customs and religion helped break down military and cultural restraints on plundering the local civilians of their property and possessions.

Finally, British plunder must also be understood in the context of the nature of the war itself. The Peninsular War was, in many respects, a crucible of 'total war', with a breakdown in traditional military and civilian distinctions, dehumanisation of the enemy and the clash of ideological values between Old Regime Portugal and Spain and Revolutionary-Napoleonic France.[74] Relative to enlightened models of 'civilised warfare', there was a barbarisation of warfare on a scale, duration and intensity that was unique in the Revolutionary and Napoleonic wars, let alone in Europe over the long eighteenth century. The British, for their part, were shocked by the brutality and destructiveness of the French occupying forces, but they were particularly disturbed by the atrocities that local soldiers and civilians committed against French soldiers. This further convinced British soldiers they were in a barbaric land. As William Swabey wrote of Spanish soldiers executing French prisoners by the roadside, this was 'barbarity more suited to savages than a Christian people claiming to rank in the order of civilisation'.[75]

Yet the British were not simply passive observers of this ferocious war between the French and the Spanish and Portuguese; they became an inextricable part

---

73 Wheeler, *Letters of Private Wheeler*, p. 49.
74 See Bell, *First Total War*, pp. 280–93.
75 Swabey, *Diary of Campaigns in the Peninsula*, p. 153.

of it. In the scale and long duration of the war; in the various armies competing for ever-diminishing local resources; in the extraordinary brutalisation and violence; in the blurring of distinctions between soldiers and civilians; in the guerrilla war and spiralling cycles of reprisals and counter-reprisals; in the French example of wholesale plunder; and in the desolate agricultural landscapes, ruined monasteries and abandoned villages and towns – in all of this British soldiers found further opportunities and impulse to plunder the local civilians. As Costello wrote of the British plunder of the abandoned Portuguese town of Arruda, 'if we had not, the French would have done it for us'.[76]

In the end plunder, in its many guises, was carried out by a broad cross-section of the British army in the Peninsula, cutting across class, regimental and ethnic identities. Without wishing to make light of the extraordinary hardships that British soldiers, especially rankers, sometimes encountered, necessity goes only so far in illuminating the extent and diverse nature of British plunder in the Peninsular War. A whole range of shifting factors – legal, military, customary, cultural and environmental – restrained and facilitated British plunder. The drivers of plunder included hunger, cold, alcohol, desertion, opportunism, personal enrichment, souvenir-taking, military traditions of looting and military–civil tensions. All these factors were common to war in the eighteenth century. However, British soldiers also found themselves in a war where the French Revolution cast a shadow over French military practices and mentalities; where old and new belief systems and cultural values collided; and where distinct military and civilian spheres and identities often collapsed. The convergence of all these elements in the Peninsula transformed some British soldiers into *banditti* in red coats.

---

76 Costello, *Rifleman Costello*, p. 61.

15

Invasion and Occupation: Civilian–Military Relations in Central Europe during the Revolutionary and Napoleonic Wars[1]

LEIGHTON S. JAMES

In May 1809 French forces swept into Kahlenberg, an Austrian village that lies between Vienna and the town of Klosterneuburg. The arrival of the French and the subsequent chaotic events in the village were chronicled by the local priest, Blakora. Even before their arrival, grim rumours of the violence and ill-treatment that the villagers could expect at French hands had reached the unfortunate community as those in the path of the army fled, 'some into the woods, some onto the Kahlenberg [mountain]'. The first French soldiers appeared in Kahlenberg on the afternoon of 11 May and their actions appeared to confirm the worst stories of French excesses. Blakora wrote:

> They went from one house to another, ripped open all the chests and cupboards and took everything out [...] Scarcely had they made off with their booty, when others as barbaric as the first came, disturbed everything again and took away what they found. In the rectory all the doors, which were locked and all the windows smashed in, the furniture partially destroyed and what was useful and transportable stolen. Even the church was not spared. They demanded I give them the church plate.[2]

Unwilling to wait for him to open the door, Blakora claims that the marauders beat it down and divested him of all his clothes before stripping the church of all its fabrics, including the altar cloths. Unfortunately, Blakora's ordeal was

---

1   I would like to thank the editors for their comments on an earlier draft of this chapter.
2   Stift Klosterneuberg, Klosterneuberg, Handschrift 60, Chronik der Pfarrkirche auf dem Kahlenberg.

not yet over. 'After these came others and they robbed and mistreated us. So it went until it was evening.' Finally, Blakora and his fellow priests were driven from the house and forced to flee into the woods.

Here Blakora's chronicle of events took an even darker turn. Among the other refugees hiding in the woods, Blakora found the local tailor. The man was distraught over the fate of his wife who, he explained, had been seized by the French soldiers as they had fled the village. He feared that 'they would mistreat her and torture [*martern*] her to death'. In order to set his mind at rest, Blakora agreed to accompany the tailor when he returned to the village in search of his wife. When they arrived at the tailor's house they were confronted by three soldiers, 'robbers and marauders', who merely mocked their plight. Angry words soon led to violence. The tailor was bayoneted in the thigh and when Blakora failed to find the soldiers some lamp light he was beaten and '[they] set a musket against my breast with the threat to shoot me if I did not provide them with light'. Fortunately, Blakora managed to give his tormentors the slip and escaped back into the woods.[3]

Blakora's tale may stand as an exemplar of thousands of other interactions between civilians and the armies of France in German central Europe between 1792 and 1814. Indeed, the most common experience of Austrian and German civilians during this period seems to be that of robbery and looting. That a large audience existed for such tales in the nineteenth and twentieth centuries is evident from the vast number of diaries, letters and memoirs published after the climax of the war. Surprisingly, however, there has been little scholarly interest in the everyday civilian experience of warfare in that region until relatively recently. Some earlier works, such as those by Bernd von Münchow-Pohl and Werner Blessing, have examined the impact of the wars on civilian society. More recently, however, this dimension of the conflict has commanded more attention. In particular, works by Ute Planert, Karen Hagemann and Katherine Aaslestad have exposed the complexities of military–civilian relationships in southern Germany, Prussia and Hamburg, respectively.[4] This chapter suggests that the grim portrayal provided by Blakora does not encompass the entirety of soldier–civilian interaction in the German states during the French wars. The conflict undoubtedly brought hardship to many and the details of individuals' suffering at the hands of the French were assiduously recorded in various forms. In recognition of this, the first section of this chapter will briefly deal with the hardships, which can be summed up as looting, violence, requisitioning and

---

3   Ibid.
4   See Planert, *Mythos vom Befreiungskrieg*; Hagemann, 'Occupation, Mobilization and Politics', pp. 580–610; Hagemann, 'Unimaginable Horror and Misery'; Aaslestad, *Place and Politics*.

disease. However, behind these desperate stories, these 'horrors of war', there is also evidence of civilians enjoying what might be termed the 'pleasures of war'. I will argue that some civilians were able to profit from the episodic campaigns to enrich themselves, even to the extent of packaging their negative experiences for public consumption.

1. Encounters with the French 'Marauder'

MANY OF the scenes depicted in Blakora's account are repeated in the diaries, letters and memoirs of both German civilians and soldiers. These eyewitness accounts often minutely record the French propensity for plundering and mistreating the local inhabitants and suggest that wherever the French armies went they brought fear, anarchy and desolation. This seems particularly the case during the 1790s when the Revolutionary armies appeared to enthusiastically embrace the challenge of living off the land. In the eyes of several witnesses the ragged ranks of the Revolutionary armies appeared to be little more than thieves.[5] Indeed, such was the extent of the havoc unleashed by the arrival of French troops in a given community that several accounts evocatively refer to it being as if 'hell had opened'.[6]

As Blakora's account illustrates, however, looting and violence were not the sole preserve of the French citizen soldier of the Revolutionary armies. Widespread plundering continued throughout the Napoleonic period. Areas of northern Germany, particularly Prussia, were devastated during the 1806 and 1807 campaign.[7] Throughout the various campaigns the extent of the violence was uneven and much depended on local circumstances. Unsurprisingly, the levels of violence perpetrated by French soldiers against German civilians were particularly high during the initial phases of an invasion, when officers often appear to have had difficulty in controlling their men. Anarchic and opportunistic looting was often accompanied by violence, or the threat of it, towards civilians. This was especially the case when looters suspected civilians of concealing valuables or when villagers and townspeople attempted to physically resist demands for goods or food. Blakora's chronicle suggests that nothing of any value was safe from the avarice of the soldiers and several accounts accuse the French of the wanton destruction of anything that could not be readily transported.[8]

5   Schüller, ed., 'Eine Bopparder Chronik aus der Franzosenzeit', pp. 33–49.
6   See Planert, *Mythos vom Befreiungskrieg*, p. 134; Arand, *Im Vorderösterreichs Amt*, p. 191.
7   Münchow-Pohl, *Zwischen Reform und Krieg*, pp. 49–63.
8   See Heintz, *Kriegstagebuch aus dem französischen Revolutionskrieg*.

Unfortunately for those living in occupied territory, this anarchic phase of looting was replaced by the scarcely less onerous and seemingly endless requisitions of supplies and foodstuffs. Reluctant communities and individuals could easily be forced to comply. A common coercive tactic employed by the occupying forces was to threaten resentful communities with *Execution*, the billeting of troops on the inhabitants.[9] Apart from the unwelcome presence of foreign and potentially unruly troops, the cost for a community or individual family of supporting the soldiers could be exorbitant. The chronicle for the parish church of Hietzing outside Vienna revealed that hungry French soldiers had exhausted food supplies that were meant to last for several months in just eight days.[10] The consequent shortages stoked inflation, compounding the difficulties that civilians faced.

Civilians also faced other dangers from foreign troops. The fate of the tailor's wife in Blakora's account hints at the potential for sexual violence between soldiers and civilians. Few eyewitnesses were ready to openly record such assaults for fear of stigmatising the victims as 'soldiers' whores' or undermining the masculinity of the men who failed to protect them. Instead, diarists and memoirists hid the reality behind oblique phrases such as 'no woman was safe' or claims that women were 'bestially treated' by the French.[11]

These direct hardships were compounded by the much more insidious threat of disease. As in other early modern conflicts, diseases such as typhus (*Nervenfieber*) and dysentery accounted for the lives of many more combatants and non-combatants than did enemy action. The citizens of Leipzig, which became the focus of the famous Battle of Nations from 16 to 18 October 1813, suffered the trinity of hardships: looting, requisitioning and disease. Its citizens weakened by food shortages, it was estimated that some 700 to 800 individuals fell ill per week. Between 5 and 10 per cent of all those who fell sick died. By the end of 1813 2,700 had died, while in the following year a further 1,000 died as a result of typhus.[12] Even this level of suffering pales in comparison to those communities, such as Hamburg, that endured prolonged sieges.

The dangers and hardships that attended invasion and occupation by the French are common to many civilian narratives of the period. Regions invaded and occupied by the French often took years to recover fully, particularly if they had been unfortunate enough to provide the main site of battle. Even after the

---

9   On the military exploitation in the Rhineland see Blanning, *French Revolution in Germany*, pp. 102–23.

10 Stift Klosterneuburg, Pfarrchronik Heitzing, Karton 532, Nr. 3.

11 Planert, *Mythos vom Befreiungskrieg*, pp. 175–91. On the stigmatisation of women who became pregnant by soldiers, whether as the result of consensual or forced sexual relations, see Rublack, *Crimes of Women*, pp. 183–85.

12 Hagemann, 'Unimaginable Horror and Misery', p. 170.

fighting was over, occupied communities found that the uncontrolled looting was often replaced by the less dangerous, but no less burdensome, imposition of requisitions. However, these experiences were also to some extent defined by factors of status, wealth and gender. Wealthier people often sought to protect their own property and, in the case of sexual relations, their physical bodies and personal honour by deflecting the predatory attentions of French soldiers on to the poorer, more vulnerable sections of society. Richer farmers, for example, might purchase livestock from poorer neighbours rather than give up their own prized herds to requisition. Similarly, the wealthier *Bürger* might buy commonly requisitioned goods from the poorer members of their communities.[13]

Despite these variations, the overwhelming impression from the personal narratives is one of disaster and distress. Wealth and status might temper hardship but few, it seems, were able to escape its effects entirely. Certainly, in its often gruesome detail, it is the negative interaction with the French that usually arrests the reader's attention. However, although these narratives illustrate a very real aspect of civilian experience, they also typically occlude more positive interactions between the French and German-speaking civilians that are evident in the sources. Indeed, some civilians were even able to benefit, at least initially, from the conflict.

2. The Profits and Pleasures of War

THE MOST obvious beneficiaries from the wars were those areas that were, temporarily at least, free from the fighting. Hamburg provides a particularly good example of how German civilians were able to benefit from the war. Following the conclusion of the Treaty of Basel between France and Prussia in 1795, a large swathe of northern German territory was turned into a neutral zone under Prussian dominance. The great merchant city-state of Hamburg lay within this neutral zone, but its patricians had already declared the city neutral in 1792. Throughout the 1790s and the early 1800s, the city leaders attempted to avoid becoming entangled in international rivalries. Their neutrality policy ultimately failed and the city was occupied in 1806 and incorporated into the French Empire in 1810. Although these events entailed many of the hardships outlined above, Aaslestad points out that in the 1790s the city experienced an economic boom. The economic dislocation and disruption of trade caused by the Revolutionary Wars elsewhere led many firms to relocate to Hamburg. Meanwhile, the native merchant houses benefited from supplying

---

13 See Planert, 'From Collaboration to Resistance', pp. 676–705.

the combatants and from the effective elimination of their Dutch rivals following the occupation of Holland in 1795.

In this febrile economic atmosphere vast fortunes were made and by 1800 the city boasted more than forty millionaires. There were losers too as wild speculation led to the failure of a number of firms, particularly in 1799. However, Hamburg's economy quickly recovered from these setbacks. Indeed, Aaslestad argues that so great was the influx of wealth into the city that it posed a serious challenge to the existing urban political culture, which emphasised a sober, thrifty republicanism. Contemporary critics attacked the unseemly new materialistic concern with luxury and fashion, with *Luxus und Mode*, as a corrupting influence on traditional morals and lifestyles. Critics pointed to the enervating effects of French culture, something supposedly promoted by the many French émigrés who had found refuge in the city. The popularity of French theatres, cafés, food, style and music suggests that such criticism largely fell on deaf ears. Instead, it took the experience of occupation to reduce the appeal of French tastes and fashion.[14]

It was not only Hamburg that was able to profit from the conflict. Other trading cities, such as Lübeck, also benefited. The economic prosperity, however, was unevenly distributed and inflation sometimes adversely impacted on the lives of those lower down the social scale. The teacher Carl Friedrich Christian von Großheim, for example, found that house prices in Lübeck had risen because of the booming trade with England. Nevertheless, Großheim was able to purchase a house in 1806 due to his successful establishment of a teaching institute and his income from the provision of private lessons.[15]

Großheim's account also reveals the extent to which the conflict could be very distant from the everyday lives of civilians. He had served in the Revolutionary Wars and witnessed many battles in France and Holland, before he finally secured his release from the army in 1795. His memoirs suggest that he intensely disliked his military service. He quickly sold everything that reminded him of the army before beginning his new career. More significant, however, is the absence of any reference to the war until 1806, something that suggests that he did not regard the conflict as impinging directly upon his life. Unfortunately for Großheim, the war arrived on his doorstep in the form of looting French soldiers in 1806 just after he took possession of his new property.[16] Other civilian narratives also pay little attention to the war until it directly impacts upon their everyday experience.[17]

---

14 On events in Hamburg see Aaslestad, *Place and Politics*, pp. 145–202.

15 Großheim, 'Meine Lebensbeschreibung', pp. 225–56.

16 Ibid., p. 241.

17 See, for example, the diary of the Austrian student and future government official Karl Kübeck, *Tagebücher des Graf Friedrich Freiherrn Kübeck von Kübau*.

Even when civilians did find themselves caught up in the war there were ways in which enterprising individuals could profit. The civilians who benefited most directly from the conflict were the sutlers. Most eighteenth- and early nineteenth-century militaries attempted to regulate the number of sutlers, camp followers and soldiers' wives that accompanied the army when on campaign. Indeed, some armies, such as that of Prussia, tried to exclude women altogether from the late 1800s. But the sheer mass of humanity on the move between 1792 and 1815 must have made strict enforcement difficult. Moreover, although the French armies were accompanied by their own sutlers, it appears that locals often temporarily attached themselves to passing forces. For example, German soldiers' accounts of the Russian campaign frequently refer to Polish villagers trailing after the army in search of a sale.[18] It is likely that similar scenes occurred in German central Europe. These individuals are frustratingly elusive in the sources and few left their own personal narratives behind. However, their fleeting appearance in soldiers' accounts suggests that they could often do well from the campaigns. Apart from the sale of food and drink, sutlers also provided a useful, mobile market for looted valuables and goods. In Vienna in 1809 the area around St Stephen's was transformed into a great market as French soldiers and sutlers sold off booty captured during the march on the capital.

Civilians other than sutlers could also profit from the sale of goods and services to the armed forces. More research on the social history of the period is required, but it does seem that it was not only those businesses and individuals in Germanic states and regions untouched by war that could benefit from the conflict. In the 1790s some German civilians profited from supplying the Coalition forces en route to the French border, and one Rhenish farmer noted that the war actually increased the economic prosperity of the region. The ability to enrich oneself through the war often depended, however, on one's status and circumstances. Landowning farmers and peasants, for example, were particularly well placed to profit from increased prices for wheat and other staple foodstuffs. However, those without direct access to agricultural produce could not capitalise on higher prices. The same writer who noted that farmers benefited from the war also recognised that landless labourers and the urban poor felt the worst effects of inflation.[19]

This mixed impact of the war continued following the French invasion. Although the arrival of the French was often accompanied by the kind of pillaging described above, civilians were also able to trade with the French armies.

---

18 HStaS, J 56, Nr. 1, Christian von Martens, *Allgemeine Tagebuch* (1793) bis 1836, 23 July 1812.

19 See Delhoven, *Die rheinische Dorfchronik des Johann Peter Delhoven*, p. 83.

The farmer Joseph Magdeburg, for example, complained more about the effects of inclement weather on his prosperity between 1806 and 1812 than he did of ravening French soldiers. In fact, his son, Ephraim, drove a wagon for the French and was able to earn enough money to fund the construction of a new barn on the farm. Unfortunately for Magdeburg, much of this good fortune was undone in 1813 by requisitions imposed, not by the French, but by the Prussians. Much worse was the death of his eight-year-old daughter from illness, a personal tragedy for which he blamed the war. Nevertheless, he admitted that the war, although testing, had by no means ruined him and his family.[20]

Civilians could also benefit from the conflict directly by the simple expedient of looting the bodies of the dead after battle. Unsurprisingly, few civilian authors confess to such behaviour. However, the image of the local peasantry stripping the dead of their valuables and clothing or the sight of the naked bodies on the battlefield is a common theme in many soldiers' memoirs. The memoirs of Ignaz Berndt provide an illustrative example. Recalling the Coalition advance through German central Europe in 1813, the Austrian officer claimed that the bodies of soldiers stripped by the peasants, but left unburied, had a demoralising influence upon his young recruits.[21] Such pickings might represent poor recompense for loss of property, a burnt-out home or an abused loved one, but we can only speculate as to how many soldiers' coats were recycled as peasants' clothing both during and after the war.

Other autobiographical evidence suggests that peasants also used invasion as a pretext to violate existing laws, such as restrictions on hunting or the gathering of wood on manorial estates. Meanwhile others sought to avoid labour obligations. This was especially the case during the Revolutionary Wars, and in the eyes of several authors the freedom promised by the French Revolutionary armies appeared to mean the dissolution of the existing order.[22] However, not all were sorry to see that older order end. As Tim Blanning has pointed out, in the confessionally mixed Rhineland, occupation by the French was welcomed by some religious minorities as it seemed to promise an end to discrimination. It was not only the Jewish population who benefited from religious toleration, but also minority Christian denominations, such as the Calvinist community in Speyer.[23]

---

20   DTA, Emmendingen, Sig. 1400/II, [Joseph Magdeburg], *Ora et Labora. Familenchronik des Joseph Magdeburg.*

21   ÖKA, Vienna, B 683, Ignaz Berndt, Bemerkungen aus dem Leben eines Pensionierten Stabsoffiziers der österreichischen Armee, p. 256.

22   Arand, *In Vorderösterreichs Amt*, pp. 174–75.

23   Blanning, *French Revolution in Germany*, p. 246.

Farmers, peasants and minority religious groups were not the only civilians who could potentially profit from the armed struggle. Although more research is required on the fate of prisoners of war during this period, anecdotal evidence suggests that some artisans were able to employ French prisoners as cheap labour in the 1790s, a phenomenon that appears to have occurred elsewhere.[24] Moreover, some French soldiers and prisoners appear to have married local women.[25] This suggests that not all sexual relations between the French and German civilians involved force or prostitution.

Other enterprising individuals sought to turn their linguistic skills to their pecuniary advantage. Recent research on the Kingdom of Westphalia has highlighted the publication of *Dolmetscher*, or phrase books. These books, whose quality ranged from cheap publications to expensively bound volumes, contained not only short dictionaries but also French phrases alongside their German equivalents. The authors and publishers of these volumes claimed that their products would help ease communication between the locals and the foreign invaders. The owners could thereby avoid unpleasant situations arising from linguistic misunderstandings, while also protecting their property. Later in the Napoleonic Wars publishers began to produce German–Russian phrase books that aimed to prepare the owners for the arrival of the feared Cossacks and Russian army. From 1812 onwards the ownership of such books increasingly became seen as an indication of political loyalties and drew attention from the police authorities.[26]

Members of the *Bürgertum* and the nobility sought service in the new regimes established by Napoleon, both in the bureaucracy and in the military. This was often a matter of necessity rather than choice. The reduction or outright extinction of many German states meant that officials and officers often had to find new employers. The Napoleonic satellite states of Westphalia and Berg offered an opportunity to continue a career and, if few appear to have developed a deep-seated loyalty to the new order, some at least could recognise the advantages that it held over the old.[27] In fact, such was the attachment of the Rhinelanders to the Code Napoleon that they resisted the imposition of Prussian law after 1814. Prussia's western provinces were only brought fully in line with the rest of the kingdom in 1900.[28]

---

24 Pflug, *Aus der Räuber- und Franzosenzeit Schwabens*, p. 31. Several accounts penned by German soldiers captured in Russia refer to their employment by locals, for example the Nürnberger Joseph Schrafel's account of his employment by an apothecary: Schrafel, *Des Nürnberger Feldwebels merkwürdige Schicksale*, p. 99.

25 Giebel, *Die Franzosen in Berlin*, p. 60.

26 Paye, "der französischen Sprache mächtig…", pp. 81–191.

27 For a comparison of French and Hessian military service see Conrady, *Aus stürmischer Zeit*, p. 170.

28 Rowe, 'Between Empire and Home Town', pp. 643–74.

As the example of Hamburg and the Hanseatic city-states demonstrated, the Continental System and blockade generally had a deleterious impact upon the economy of German central Europe. The reduction in seaborne trade, the scarcity of colonial wares and the customs duties imposed by the French Empire often served to hamper economic development. However, in some areas, such as those Rhineland territories directly annexed to the French Empire, early industrialists and merchants were able to prosper from the reduced competition. Political and legal reform also meant that members of the professional and merchant classes, already adept at negotiating the baroque administrative structure of the Old Regime, could now play a greater role in municipal affairs than had hitherto been the case. Elites in the Rhineland and elsewhere in central Europe were often able to turn the reforms to their own advantage, or at the very least mitigate their worst effects, to preserve their influence. Moreover, the experience, wealth and connections they accumulated through their involvement in the governance of the Rhenish departments placed them in a prime position to capitalise on the transition of power after 1814.[29]

Civilians could therefore turn the armed conflict to their advantage in myriad ways. At one end of the scale were those who took advantage of the chaotic situation that inevitably accompanied an invasion. Such individuals could loot the dead or purchase booty from passing troops at low prices. They could also seize the chance offered by the dissolution of older structures of authority to poach or collect wood on their landlord's estates. At the other end were the *Bildungsbürgertum* and nobility. They could involve themselves in the administration of occupied and reorganised territories. For others the arrival of the French heralded greater religious and intellectual freedom. Meanwhile, farmers and artisans could profit by trading with both friendly and hostile forces or employing prisoners of war in their workshops.

None of the above should, however, obscure the essentially precarious position of Austrian and German civilians in their relations with the French military. For every French soldier who was content to pay for goods, there were many more prepared to use force, particularly during the early phases of an invasion. Much depended on the attitudes of commanding officers and their ability to exercise control over their men. Other factors such as drunkenness, the ferocity of the fighting and the scale of logistical problems faced by the army also played a role. Perhaps most crucial was the ability to communicate, since simple linguistic misunderstandings could quickly turn violent. Even here, however, there was money to be made. The publishers

---

29 See Diefendorf, *Businessmen and Politics in the Rhineland*; Rowe, 'Between Empire and Home Town'.

of phrase books capitalised on civilians' well-founded fears over pillaging by arguing that their books would prepare their owners for the arrival of foreign forces. Later these works promised to prepare civilians for the arrival of the Russians. In fact, many civilians were disappointed to find that their self-proclaimed liberators, be they Austrian, German or Russian, were equally prone to looting, theft and violence.[30]

There was, however, a way in which civilians could turn even these negative experiences to their benefit. One of the most distinctive features of the conflict between 1792 and 1815 was the number of individuals who felt impelled to record their experiences in the form of diaries and memoirs. Undoubtedly, this was partially due to increased literacy, but it also reflected the impact of literary and philosophical developments in the eighteenth century. Yuval N. Harari has argued that literary developments, such as the rise of sensibility and Romanticism, not only encouraged soldiers to reflect on their emotions but also led them to view warfare differently.[31] Civilians were subject to the same processes. The decades after the Congress of Vienna saw a veritable flood of published personal narratives. Indeed, such was the scale and number of these works that it is perhaps not too extreme to speak of the 'commodification' of the war experience. As we shall see, some authors certainly expected to profit from their narratives. More systematic work is required on the publication and dissemination of autobiographical works in the nineteenth century. However, even the most basic search in the British Library catalogue reveals a far greater number of such works dealing with the French wars than with the previous large-scale European conflict, the Seven Years War. Over a hundred works offer personal narratives of the Napoleonic Wars, compared with fewer than a dozen for the Seven Years War,[32] and a website dedicated to collecting personal narratives of soldiers lists several hundred individual works.[33] Unsurprisingly, the majority of these narratives were written by soldiers or veterans, rather than civilians, something that reflects the increased interest in the story of the common soldier.[34] This is particularly the case for Britain, where accounts of the Iberian campaign loom large. Unlike Britain, the German states experienced repeated invasions, military campaigns and extended occupation. Moreover, many German regions and states, particularly in the Rhineland, also had a

---

30   Janke, ed., *Feldbriefe eines Kriegsfreiwilligen*, p. 39.

31   Harari, *Ultimate Experience*. See also Bell, *First Total War*, p. 312.

32   A search for personal narratives of the Napoleonic Wars throws up 131 works, although these include anthologies and works of history dealing specifically with autobiographical material.

33   See www.napoleonzeit.de (accessed 29 September 2011).

34   See Fritzsche, *Stranded in the Present*, p. 172.

relatively high level of literacy.[35] Many German civilians, therefore, not only had the ability to express themselves in writing, but also something worth recording.

Some works were intended for publication and began to appear during the wars themselves. The 'reading revolution' and the expansion of the public sphere in the eighteenth century created the market for these works, a market that continued to grow as literacy increased in the nineteenth century.[36] Soldiers' accounts predominated. Perhaps the best-known example is the work of Christian Laukhard. His experiences of the Revolutionary War were published anonymously in a number of journals.[37] The polymath Johann Rühle von Lilienstern also published eyewitness accounts of the 1806 and 1809 campaigns. During the former campaign he had served as a Prussian officer, but he lost his position following the Treaty of Tilsit. His account of the 1806 campaign was meant to ease his precarious finances. Later he witnessed the 1809 campaign in a civilian capacity, as mentor and tutor to Prince Bernhard of Saxony-Eisenach-Weimar. His account, written in letter form to a fictional sister, was published just one year later in 1810.[38]

As the example of Lilienstern suggests, the division between military and civilian accounts is not always clear cut. For example, the novelist Georg Wilhelm Heinrich Häring participated in the Wars of Liberation as a volunteer. He published an account of his military experiences under his pseudonym, Willibald Alexis. He later parlayed his experience of the period as both a civilian and a volunteer into his historical fiction in his novel *Isegrimm*.[39] Drawing upon past experience of conflict to inform works of historical fiction, or 'novels of the recent past' as they are sometimes termed, was not new.[40] In the seventeenth century Grimmelshausen had drawn on his war experiences for his novels dealing with the Thirty Years War. However, the sheer scale of historical fiction and novels of the recent past published in the nineteenth and early twentieth century was unprecedented and suggests a voracious appetite among the book-reading public for war stories.[41]

---

35   François, 'Die Volksbildung am Mittelrhein in ausgehenden 18. Jahrhundert', pp. 277–304.

36   Melton, *Rise of the Public*, pp. 81–86.

37   Schneider, 'Revolutionserlebnis und Frankreichbild', pp. 289, 283.

38   See Lilienstern, *Reise mit der Armee im Jahre 1809*, particularly pp. 245–47; Lilienstern, *Bericht eines Augenzeugen*.

39   Alexis, *Als Kriegsfreiwilliger nach Frankreich*; Alexis, *Isegrimm*.

40   'Novels of the recent past' refer to those novels that refer to events within living memory. See Fleishman, *English Historical Novel*.

41   The recent research project 'The Memories of the Revolutionary and Napoleonic Wars in Europe (1815–1945)' directed Karen Hagemann and Etienne François has identified over 560 works set during the French wars that were published in German central Europe alone. I would like to thank Maria Schultz for sharing this information.

The extent to which civilians profited from the packaging and sale of their personal experiences is unclear. However, some at least believed they could make money while the conflict still raged. Johann Maaß provides one such example. Maaß was a bookseller based in the town of Wittenberg. His business had already been badly disrupted by the wars, but the invasion of Prussia by Napoleon completely stopped trade. As French soldiers advanced upon the town following their victory at the double battle of Jena and Auerstedt, Maaß decided to flee east into Lausitz. He spent several months travelling around Lower and Upper Lausitz before finally returning to Wittenberg in May 1807. His return was not a happy one. He found his business all but destroyed and trade sluggish. His answer to his financial difficulties was to publish an account of his temporary exile, in the hope that the profits would support his business and allow him to continue his studies.[42]

Maaß's work, which was presented in a diary form, represents a curious mixture of travelogue, war narrative and history, a popular blend of genres.[43] The book opens with rumours of the Prussian defeat at the battle of Jena. The worst is confirmed by the appearance of fleeing Prussian troops. In a similar manner to Blakora, he describes the desperate situation of the refugees and widespread fears over French outrages against the civilian population.[44] In the later entries, however, the war fades into the background somewhat as Maaß indulges in topographical and ethnographic observations. For example, he admires the romantic landscape around Zittau and describes the customs and morals of the Slavic Wends.[45] Yet war remains a constant underlying theme, often resurfacing as part of his travelogue. This is particularly the case when he describes social and economic conditions. He examines in detail the Berlin Decrees of 1806 and provides a brief history of the struggle between England and France since the 1790s. He links this to the rising price of food, which was hitting the artisans particularly hard and causing discontent among their apprentices.[46]

Other works were less personal in nature than Maaß's account. Johann Krais's diary of events in the Imperial town of Biberach is more akin to a chronicle than a personal narrative in that the author rarely refers to himself. Published in 1801, the work records the events of the Revolutionary Wars as they affected the town. These included the movement of troops of various states through the town, the transport of prisoners of war and the eventual conquest of the town by the French. Many of the horrors of war mentioned

---

42 Maaß, *Bemerkungen auf einer Reise von Wittenberg*, p. xxvi.
43 Hentschel, 'Krieg als Unterhaltung', pp. 335–52.
44 Maaß, *Bemerkungen auf einer Reise von Wittenberg*, pp. 10–25.
45 Ibid., pp, 130–43, 178–80.
46 Ibid., pp. 168–94, 258–65.

above are recounted here. Looting, violence, drunkenness, demands for money or supplies and euphemistic references to sexual assault all appear in the chronicle. The work was paid for by a large number of subscribers whose names are listed at the end of book, along with the costs to the town of the French occupation.[47] Many of these individuals may have been eyewitnesses to the same events described by Krais, yet they still felt the desire to memorialise what the town had suffered in writing. Despite the hardships and the suffering, the emphasis was on the preservation rather than the suppression of memory.

This desire to memorialise points to another reason why many civilians and soldiers wrote. Krais declares in his introduction that the diary was originally intended for him alone. It was only at the urging of his friends that he decided to publish the account. Many memoirs and autobiographies were indeed not meant for publication, but only to be read by an intimate circle of friends and family. There was no obvious pecuniary gain to be made from these works, although many were subsequently published by relatives, friends or academics. However, these narratives might be deemed to have provided another, less tangible benefit than hard cash. Autobiographies and memoirs are often designed to justify an individual's actions and to criticise others. Many of those written after the Napoleonic period are no different.[48] Another reason to write was that, as Peter Fritzsche has recently argued, the events between 1780 and 1815 were perceived as so momentous and epoch-defining that perceptions of time and history themselves were altered.[49] Narration was a crucial component in this transformation, for while other European conflicts had caused major upheaval, none were narrated as a period of fundamental change.[50] Even unpublished works, therefore, located the individual within this wider narrative of revolution and warfare. For this reason memories, and memoirs, of the French time were preserved and cultivated among families.[51] The demand of young Tom and Tony Buddenbrook to hear again the story of the thieving French sergeant Lenoir was not merely a fictional invention of Thomas Mann. Instead, the scene represented a real desire of later generations to hear the war stories of their elders.

---

47   Krais, *Tagebuch über diejenigen Begebenheiten*.

48   See, for example, the memoirs of the irascible *Junker* Friedrich August Ludwig von der Marwitz, who was briefly imprisoned because of his opposition to the Prussian Reform Movement: Marwitz, *Nachrichten aus meinem Leben*.

49   Fritzsche, *Stranded in the Present*, p. 8.

50   Ibid., pp. 16–17.

51   Ibid., p. 79.

There was a final reason why civilians felt impelled to write of their war experiences. In the course of the nineteenth century the memory of the conflict was increasingly forged into national and patriotic myths. Here the Wars of Liberation played a particularly important role, as they could be interpreted as a reawakening of German nationalism under the guiding hand of Prussia. The patriotic propaganda produced in 1813 and 1814 provided a ready-made basis for this process of myth-making, while the commemoration of the battle of Leipzig in 1913 provided a particularly useful outlet for the mobilisation of nationalistic sentiment directed at national enemies.[52] Individual stories, particularly those produced by the volunteers of 1813, could easily be folded into this process.[53] Alexis's work stands as an example. But so too could the narratives of civilians. Stories of hardship under the French could be juxtaposed with joyful liberation by German forces and their allies. Eyewitnesses could take their place in the heroic struggle against the French enemy, even if they did not fight. Descendants could situate their family members within that conflict. No doubt, astute authors and publishers also recognised an opportunity to cash in on periods of national commemoration.

However, it would be wrong to assume that civilian narratives, or those of soldiers for that matter, simply parroted the nationalist sentiments of propagandists. As Ute Planert has shown, there was no war of liberation in southern Germany. This did not prevent the southern German states from later writing themselves and their subjects into the patriotic narrative.[54] But the narratives of individuals often deviated from the official line. Soldiers' accounts reveal the tensions that existed between the soldiers of different states. Civilian narratives reveal similar tensions. On the left bank of the Rhine, for example, disillusionment with Prussian rule soon emerged. The art dealer Sulpiz Boisseré wrote in his diaries 'one hears only too often the sinful words: better French than Prussian'.[55] The memory of the wars was undoubtedly shaped by later interpretations, but those interpretations were equally filtered through the memories of individual writers. In this two-way process, those who purported to be the defenders and liberators of Germany did not always appear in the light they would have wished. Nor were the French always portrayed in the bestial, yet strangely effeminate, role assigned them by propagandists.

---

52 Jeismann, *Das Vaterland der Feinde*.
53 See Hagemann, *Männlicher Muth*.
54 Planert, *Mythos vom Befreiungskrieg*.
55 Cited in Herres, 'Und nenne Euch Preußen'. Herres also notes tensions between Prussian volunteers and those from the Rhineland, pp. 119, 129.

3. Conclusion

THE Revolutionary and Napoleonic wars undoubtedly caused civilians across the German states a great deal of financial, physical and emotional hardship. Invasion was often accompanied by looting as French soldiers plundered conquered cities. Misunderstandings could easily lead to violence, particularly where alcohol was involved. Although conditions improved as invasion became occupation, civilians were still burdened by contributions, increased taxation and conscription. Diseases, such as typhus, left a tragic legacy even after the troops had moved on, while devastated communities could take years to fully recover.

Two further factors, however, are equally clear. First, the hardships caused by the conflict, what might be termed the 'horrors of war', were differentiated by a variety of factors. Geography, social status, occupation, linguistic skills, the vicissitudes of the fighting itself – all these played a role in determining when and how heavily the burdens described above were felt by individuals and families across German central Europe. Civilians also developed many techniques to protect their lives, their families and their property. Secondly, as well as hardships, the fighting also offered opportunities. For some this was as meagre as acquiring a new coat or pair of boots from a dead soldier. Others, such as the Hamburg merchants, were able to make vast fortunes, making the most of the city's neutrality. These fortunes might be temporary and the war did eventually catch up with Hamburg. The profits made one year could be swallowed up by looting, inflation and requisitions. However, some, like the mercantile elite in the Rhineland, were able to make lasting gains that survived the collapse of French hegemony.

Finally, civilians could and did benefit from recording their own war experience. Some pioneers began this process before the conflict had even reached its conclusion at Waterloo. The episodic periods of peace allowed time for the writing and publication of works such as those by Maaß and Krais. In the later nineteenth century there developed a ready market for tales of the war that encompassed both the hardships and the glories. This market was fed by both works of fiction and autobiography. Sometimes, as in Alexis's case, the two were intertwined. Both genres tapped into the sense that the wars represented an epochal moment. These works could also be folded into the growing nationalist sentiment, although more research is required into the dissemination and reception of personal narratives. Nevertheless, the strength of demand for war stories, fictional or otherwise, seems beyond doubt. Here the 'war experience', including its hardship and suffering, was packaged and sold to be vicariously consumed by contemporaries and later generations. Here, it seems, the 'horrors of war' became indistinguishable from its pleasures.

16

Imprisoned Reading: French Prisoners of War at the Selkirk Subscription Library, 1811–1814[1]

MARK TOWSEY

We were too truly French to allow of our feelings being so utterly depressed by our captivity and the uncertainty of our relief as to make us pine away in useless sorrow or lamentations [...] [We] procured from Edinburgh a billiard table, and all the requisites for establishing a very good coffee-house, to which no admittance was granted, except to our nationality. Soon after, ascertaining that some of us had received musical instruction, we rented instruments from the Capital, and mustered twenty-two efficient performers, who, under the leadership of a very superior violinist constituted an orchestra superior to any that had ever resounded among the echoes of our Scottish residence. We invited to our concerts, gratuitously, of course, some of the inhabitants with whom we had become acquainted.[2]

---

1   The research on which this chapter is based was supported by the Bibliographical Society, the Past and Present Society and the Leverhulme Trust. The author thanks David Allan, Erica Charters, Gillian Dow, Eve Rosenhaft, Siobhan Talbott and fellow participants in the 'Civilians and War' conference for their helpful comments and suggestions on earlier versions of this chapter, as well as the staff of the Hawick Heritage Hub for their assistance and hospitality in accessing the surviving archives of the Selkirk subscription library.
2   Doisy, *Reminiscences*, pp. 77–78. Doisy was a *sous-lieutenant* in the 26th Regiment of Line Infantry. He fought in the battles of Essling, Ciudad Rodrigo and Buçaco, before being captured in an ambush close to Almeida in 1811. After returning home disillusioned in 1814, Doisy emigrated to the United States of America where he wrote up his memoirs at the grand age of 84.

IN MARCH 1811 nearly 150 Napoleonic prisoners of war arrived on parole in Selkirk, a county town in the Scottish borders whose relative proximity to Edinburgh, rural situation and compact population made it ideally suited to take on this vital role in the British war effort.[3] Some were naval officers and surgeons detained in British hands years earlier, including privateer Antoine Bertrand, seized on board the *Amis Reunis* in the Persian Gulf in 1805, and Ensign Philippe Jatriel, who survived the destruction of the frigate *Amphitrite* in Martinique in 1809. Many more had been complicit in Dupont's capitulation at Bailén in 1808, having suffered almost unimaginable hardships en route to the Scottish borders via the notorious prison hulks off Andalucía, the barren Balearic islet of Cabrera and the mass holding prisons in Portsmouth and Edinburgh Castle.[4] According to *sous-lieutenant* Adelbert Doisy, whose memoirs provide a detailed narrative of their stay in Selkirk, the prisoners responded to the unfamiliarity of their new surroundings by cocooning themselves within social structures imported from their lives back in France. But at the same time, they gradually developed cultural relationships with members of the local civilian community (including those graciously invited to attend their symphony concerts), facilitating close encounters between two 'nations' united only by bonds of implacable hatred. In Linda Colley's controversial account of British identity-formation in the long eighteenth century:

> Great Britain [...] was an invention forged above all by war. Time and time again, war with France brought Britons, whether they hailed from Wales or Scotland or England, into confrontation with an obviously hostile Other and encouraged them to define themselves collectively against it. They defined themselves as Protestants struggling for survival against the world's foremost Catholic power. They defined themselves against the French as they imagined them to be, superstitious, militarist, decadent and unfree.[5]

---

3   For a summary historiography and introduction, see Daly, 'Napoleon's Lost Legions', pp. 361–80. Relying on earlier county histories, Francis Abell claimed that 93 prisoners were stationed in Selkirk, but the Board of Transport's own records in the National Archives at Kew identify at least 140 prisoners: Abell, *Prisoners of War*, p. 324. All paroled officers were identified from TNA, ADM103, Registers of Prisoners of War 1755–1831.

4   For eyewitness accounts of the 'Calvary of the prisoners of Bailén', see Esdaile, *Peninsular Eyewitnesses*, pp. 17, 26, 129, 281. Another group of prisoners captured at Bailén were eventually transferred to Peebles, having been moved from Cabrera to the Valleyfield prison depot in Penicuik, via Portsmouth and Edinburgh; see MacDougall, *Prisoners at Penicuik*, p. 13.

5   Colley, *Britons*, p. 5. This chapter focuses on the encounter between British and French identities during the Napoleonic Wars, largely because it is not known whether the French prisoners detained in Selkirk consciously differentiated between Scots and Britons. This is not to deny that there remained very strong social, economic, cultural and even political links between France and Scotland in the eighteenth century, links

One intriguing venue for such encounters proved to be the Selkirk sub-scription library, whose members offered the prisoners of war access to the library's book collection for the duration of their stay. Remarkably, a full record of the prisoners' use of the library survives, providing a unique window into their reading habits and, by extension, their daily lives and preoccupations while on parole in Selkirk.[6] By detailing the reading habits of Doisy's 'colony' alongside the broader dynamics of their interaction with the local community, this chapter assesses the cultural encounters that resulted when Napoleonic prisoners of war arrived on parole in small, provincial British communities, highlighting the imagined voyage of discovery experienced by both parties as they gradually recognised mutual interests that transcended national or ethnic 'otherness'. With both communities discovering that their counterparts were not quite as different as they imagined them to be, this chapter also considers the viability of Napoleonic rhetoric 'to destroy and annihilate all who attack us, or to be destroyed ourselves' in the light of the common cultural identities that bound European elites together in the age of Enlightenment – including a love of reading, self-improving libraries, the theatre, amateur orchestras, coffee houses, freemasonry, polite associationalism and clubs and societies of all kinds. At the same time, this chapter reflects more broadly on the role of books in mediating warfare, framing soldiers' perceptions of the conflicts in which they participated and refashioning their memories (and memoirs) once they had left the front line.

1

THE NAPOLEONIC Wars have been described as 'the first total war', resulting in the displacement of millions of people on a global scale unprecedented in the history of warfare.[7] This process had profound cultural implications, facilitating personal encounters between soldiers, sailors and civilians that would rarely have happened otherwise and exposing participants to new places,

---

founded on an emotional attachment to the medieval Auld Alliance with which mem-bers of both civilian and military communities in Selkirk may have been familiar. See Dawson and Morère, eds., *Scotland and France in the Enlightenment*, especially the essays by Andrew Hook, Pierre Carboni and Harvey Chisick; Laidlaw, ed., *Auld Alliance: France and Scotland*; Mackenzie-Stuart, *French King at Holyrood*; Brumfitt, 'Scotland and the French Enlightenment'.

6   All subsequent references to the reading habits of the Selkirk prisoners of war derive from SBA S/PL/7 Selkirk Subscription Library Registers, 1799–1814.

7   Bell, *First Total War*; for recent discussion see Forrest, Hagemann and Rendall, eds., *Soldiers, Citizens and Civilians*.

languages, experiences and ideas. For prisoners of war, the Napoleonic Wars heralded a particularly revolutionary departure from the military history of the early modern period. The *ancien régime* systems of prisoner exchange and officer parole governed by common codes of honour and gentility were largely abandoned following the breakdown of the Peace of Amiens, with thousands of prisoners – both combatants and non-combatants – sitting out the duration of the conflict in enforced internment abroad.[8] Between 1803 and 1814 122,440 combatants were confined in Britain, many under horrific conditions in prison hulks moored in the Medway or off Portsmouth that one historian writing before the outbreak of the First World War insisted would 'remain a stain upon our national record'.[9] Thousands more were detained in over-populated prison 'depots', including Norman Cross, near Peterborough (considered the world's first purpose-built prisoner-of-war camp) and Dartmoor, which was notorious for 'its isolation, poor climate, reputed diseases, and brutality'.[10] The vast majority of these prisoners therefore had little opportunity to experience the foreign land in which they were detained – Francis Abell suggests that their daily existence 'was largely a sealed book to the outside public'[11] – but around 6,000 prisoners were embedded directly in British society, with parole granted on limited terms to commissioned officers of Napoleon's army and navy, and to the captains and officers of French privateers.

Fifty small towns were selected to host the paroled officers across England, Wales and Scotland, with local agents charged with ensuring that they did not break the terms of their parole – to behave respectably at all times, to observe a strict curfew morning and night, to maintain regular contact with their parole agent and to remain within a one-mile radius of their parole town.[12] The prisoners consequently provided towns such as Selkirk with their most immediate exposure to the consequences of 'total war', making a profound impression on the economic, social and cultural life of many parts of the

---

8   For the traditional systems of exchange and the reasons for their abandonment after the Peace of Amiens see Daly, 'Napoleon's Lost Legions', pp. 363–73; Forrest, *Napoleon's Men*, p. 159; Crimmin, 'Prisoners of War', pp. 17–18. Very occasional prisoner exchanges did take place but only on extremely limited terms, including the exchange of 24 seamen from the French frigate *Piedmontaise* held at Valleyfield for the same number from HM schooner *Laura* which took place in November 1812: MacDougall, *Prisoners at Penicuik*, p. 72.

9   Abell, *Prisoners of War*, pp. 1, 43.

10 Daly, 'Napoleon's Lost Legions', p. 374. For an account of three of the largest depots in Scotland see MacDougall, *Prisoners at Penicuik*.

11 Abell, *Prisoners of War*, p. 284.

12 Ibid., pp. 286–87; Daly, 'Napoleon's Lost Legions', p. 376. A parole pledge signed by *sous-lieutenant* Nicholas Mouton and witnessed by the parole officer at Kelso, John Smith, dated 21 May 1812, survives at SBA183, Collection 5, French Prisoners of War.

country that is still recalled in popular memory to this day.[13] Initially, however, there was a real fear that the prisoners might pose a threat to regional security and social cohesion. The sheriff-depute of Selkirkshire, none other than Sir Walter Scott, worried about the 'the multitude of French prisoners who are scattered through the small towns in this country [...] very improvidently', warning of the ease with which prisoners at Kelso, Selkirk and Jedburgh might coordinate to seize the arms of the local militia which 'were kept without any guard in a warehouse in Kelso'.[14] On occasion, Doisy and his comrades did indeed act out the bellicose roles expected of them, especially when news reached Selkirk from the front line. When the townsfolk 'had the bad taste, if not the indelicacy [...] to ring all the bells in the town, and to display an extravagant and insulting joy' in celebrating Wellington's Spanish victory, the prisoners retaliated some days later by ringing the town bells at midnight. The feast held by the prisoners to celebrate Napoleon's birthday in 1813 nearly provoked a riot, after leftovers were offered to the poor of the town on the proviso that 'each applicant for our bounty should, previous to his receiving it, take off his hat and shout, "Vive l'Empereur Napoleon!"':

> The people being unarmed, thought it best not to test our weapons [the officers had armed themselves with knives, forks and a few broken chairs], but at once deserted the square. A little later, however, the agent, Mr. Robert Henderson, came hurriedly to give us notice that a new mob was organizing with arms, and that the matter might become very serious; that, moreover, we were in one respect in the wrong, as it was now ten o'clock, whereas by the regulations which we had engaged implicitly to obey, we should have been in our respective lodgings by nine o'clock.[15]

Only very rarely did the prisoners' presence threaten civil unrest of this kind; on this occasion, the prisoners backed down and 'both parties shortly resumed better feelings towards each other'. Instead, paroled officers quickly made an impact on local economies, with many local traders making a healthy profit from their interned guests. Major Meinhard, a German prisoner of war captured by Nelson at the battle of the Nile and paroled in Sanquhar, reportedly paid out three shillings more than he received per week on vegetables, bread,

---

13 Cameron, *Prisons and Punishment*, p. 73. On hearing what I was working on, my neighbour at the Hawick Heritage Hub (where the Scottish Border Archives are now held) happily informed me about the survival of French surnames in the area down to the present day (inherited, it seems, from particularly amorous prisoners of war), and described some of the hand-made souvenirs that borderers continue to treasure as heirlooms of the prisoners' internment.
14 Cited in Abell, *Prisoners of War*, p. 316.
15 Doisy, *Reminiscences*, pp. 88–92.

coal, laundry and tobacco, with accommodation his most significant expense.[16] The French officers at Selkirk initially struggled to find lodgings, but 'matters soon altered in this respect; the people of the town found presently that we were each customers, and they vied with each other in obtaining among us occupants for such of their apartments as they could dispose of'.[17] The paroled officers received a government allowance of ten shillings and sixpence per week for captains and their superiors, and eight shillings and sixpence for lower ranks, although this was frequently bolstered by cash sent from home – £50 annually in the case of Adelbert Doisy, the relatively lowly son of a retired army officer, but as much as £1,000 per annum for more wealthy prisoners.[18] Altogether, Doisy calculated that the prisoners at Selkirk spent around £150 per week, implying that their thirty-month internment yielded no less than £19,500 for the local economy – and roughly the same amount was spent by the community of German prisoners on parole at Hawick.[19] If this was, in Doisy's opinion, 'quite a consideration in such a small town, without trade or manufactures',[20] many enterprising prisoners entered the market in their own right, selling clothing accessories (hats, gloves and bonnets), tea caddies, work boxes, pipes, jewellery, hair watch-chains, wooden toys and other trinkets to supplement their allowance.[21] The prisoners interned in the three prisoner-of-war camps at Penicuik (who numbered around 10,000 in total) reportedly made £2,000 a week on such goods, while at the Perth depot 'vast multitudes went daily to view the market, and buy from the prisoners their toys […] They had stands set out all round the railing of the yards, on which their wares were placed, and a great number of purchases was made every day by the numerous visitors, for which they paid high prices.'[22] Officers on parole usually lacked such prodigious infrastructure, but still astonished curious townsfolk and travellers with the novelty value of their homespun trinkets, fashioned from

---

16 Robison, 'Impressions of a German Prisoner of War', p. 21. For the economic impact made by the prison depot at Perth, where the need to feed the prisoners led to the culti-vation of an extensive crop of potatoes that was later to supply the London market, see Penny, *Traditions of Perth*, pp. 92–93.

17 Doisy, *Reminiscences*, pp. 75–76.

18 Daly, 'Napoleon's Lost Legions', p. 376; Doisy, *Reminiscences*, pp. 76–77.

19 Doisy, *Reminiscences*, p. 77; Forbes, 'French Prisoners of War', p. 3.

20 Doisy, *Reminiscences*, p. 77. Doisy's account was not quite accurate: although a small town largely dependent on pastoral farming, Selkirk did apparently have 'a considerable incle manufactory' (inkle being a kind of braided linen tape), as well as a stocking factory; see the account of the parish in Sinclair, *Statistical Account*, Vol. II, p. 438.

21 Daly, 'Napoleon's Lost Legions', pp. 376–77; MacDougall, *Prisoners at Penicuik*, pp. 58–59.

22 MacDougall, *Prisoners at Penicuik*, pp. 27, 58; Penny, *Traditions of Perth*, p. 93.

virtually any material that came to hand. Elizabeth Grant of Rothiemurchus, who passed through Jedburgh as a teenager in 1812, recalled that

> the ingenuity of these French prisoners of all ranks was amazing, really only to be equalled by their industry. Those of them unskilled in higher arts earned for themselves most comfortable additions to their allowance by turning bits of wood, and bones, straw, almost any thing in fact, into neat toys of many sorts, eagerly bought up by all who met with them.[23]

The paroled officers also engaged extensively in cultural transactions with local civilian populations. One 'handsome young painter' encountered by Miss Grant churned out a sequence of battlefield scenes commissioned by local worthies, while the Scottish border towns of Jedburgh, Hawick and Lauder were all portrayed on canvas for the first time by French prisoners in the early 1810s.[24] Officers on parole offered instruction in stereotypically effete accomplishments such as dancing, music, drawing or languages, with 'Mr Brement, Professor of Belles Lettres and French prisoner of war' advertising in the *Kelso Mail* that he taught 'the French and Latin Languages'.[25] In keeping with the immense popularity of theatres in Revolutionary and Napoleonic France (associated, of course, with disseminating revolutionary values and patriotic fervour),[26] the officers established ad hoc theatre companies, with barns converted to the purpose in conservative Scottish border towns such as Kelso, Peebles and Dumfries, as well as at Selkirk.[27] Although Selkirk's respected clergyman George Lawson reflected traditional Presbyterian antipathy to such institutions by politely refusing the officers' invitation to attend, lay members of the community were evidently far less reticent to endorse the prisoners' thespian aspirations.[28] A red carpet was rolled out for the Duchess of Roxburghe's arrival at the theatre in Kelso, while the bookseller, printer and memoirist Robert Chambers recalled

---

23 Grant, *Memoirs of a Highland Lady*, Vol. I, pp. 205–6.

24 Ibid., p. 205; Forbes, 'French Prisoners of War', pp. 4, 9, 15; a negative print of J. Bazin de Ste. Malo's *View of Jedburgh Abbey* (1812) held at NAS, GD1/405/6 depicts a group of the artist's fellow prisoners in the foreground.

25 Forbes, 'French Prisoners of War', p. 13; on French stereotypes see Cohen, *Fashioning Masculinity*.

26 Hesse, *Publishing and Cultural Politics*, pp. 195–97; Lough, *Introduction to Eighteenth Century France*, pp. 246, 272; Kennedy, *Cultural History*, pp. 168–85.

27 A programme for a performance of Beaumarchais's *The Barber of Seville* acted by the French officers on parole at Kelso in June 1811 survives among the papers of the Scott family of Harden, Lords Polwarth, Berwickshire; see NAS, GD157/2004.

28 Macfarlane, *Life and Times of George Lawson*, p. 116. The theatre had been one of the main battlegrounds between moderates and evangelicals in the Church of Scotland in the eighteenth century; see Sher, *Church and University*, pp. 74–93.

that admission to the theatre at Peebles 'was gained by complimentary billets distributed chiefly among persons with whom the actors had established an intimacy', including his own father, who was ultimately undone financially by the overly generous credit facilities he offered the French community.[29]

Although the prisoners at Selkirk apparently reserved their billiard room purely for those of their own nationality, French officers often set up cafés, billiard rooms and other clubs and societies that were open to the wider community, including a newspaper room founded by prisoners of war in Hawick.[30] Indeed, paroled prisoners of war usually participated fully in the refined entertainments that characterised provincial polite society, regularly enjoying local hospitality in civilian homes. One gentleman farmer living on the outskirts of Cupar, in Fife, recalled

> there was no thought of war and its fierce passions among the youth of the company in the simple dinners, suppers and carpet-dances in private houses. There were congratulations on the abundance of pleasant partners, and the assurance that no girl need now sit out a dance or lack an escort [...] Love and marriage ensued between the youngsters, the vanquished and the victors.[31]

Chaperoned interactions inevitably gave way to more intense flirtatious engagements, with a rash of marriages recorded across the country. General d'Henin settled down with a wealthy Scots lady he had met on parole in Chesterfield, Captain Levasseur married an aunt of Sir George Harrison (MP and former Provost of Edinburgh) at Kelso, while two of the Selkirk prisoners fought a bloodless duel over a local girl.[32] At the same time, paroled officers were often invited to participate in the formal associational life of civilian communities, with 23 being enrolled by their fellow freemasons as Honorary Members of St John's Lodge No. 32 in Selkirk.[33]

2

FREEMASONRY WAS, of course, a fundamental component of associational conduct on either side of the English Channel, providing an instant point of contact between the two communities.[34] The same could be said of privately managed book clubs and subscription libraries, which had become an

---

29 Abell, *Prisoners of War*, pp. 320, 336.
30 Robison, 'Impressions of a German Prisoner', p. 24.
31 Cited in Abell, *Prisoners of War*, p. 317.
32 Abell, *Prisoners of War*, pp. 305, 320, 323; MacDougall, *Prisoners at Penicuik*, pp. 59–60.
33 Thorp, *French Prisoners' Lodges*, pp. 265–66.
34 Kennedy, *Cultural History*, pp. 17–20, 365–68; Clark, *British Clubs and Societies*, ch. 9; Harland-Jacobs, *Builders of Empire*.

increasingly common feature of the urban landscape in provincial France and across the English-speaking world.[35] One of the earliest subscription libraries in Scotland had been founded in Selkirk in 1772, patronised by a healthy mix of local gentry (including the parole agent's brother, Andrew Henderson of Midgehope), lawyers, medical men, bankers, clergymen, tradesmen and tenant farmers drawn from a wide rural hinterland.[36] The decision to allow the prisoners use of the self-governing Selkirk library – which must have been endorsed by its civilian members and has no parallel in the surviving archives of any other subscription library in Britain – is not recorded. Since France was still at this time considered the most cultivated society in Europe (witness on the one hand the cultural creep that embraced French exiles in Britain during the Revolutionary period, or conversely the disdain with which many French aristocrats regarded British urban life),[37] we may imagine that provincial Scots hoped to profit culturally from entertaining the French officers in this way, but the invitation to use the library may also have been more simply a function of their other cultural activities in the town. To showcase the talents of their orchestra, they had rented a barn on the outskirts of Selkirk and constructed a rustic theatre there with space 'sufficient for the accommodation of two hundred spectators'. Although Doisy reports that 'the costumes, especially those for female characters, puzzled our ingenuity not a little' since none of them had ever been an 'upholster, tailor, or apprentice to a dress-maker',[38] the library itself provided a ready supply of plays to perform. Indeed, the very first book borrowed by one of their number from the library was an unspecified volume of plays taken out by Jules Le Gendre (an army captain captured at Bailén) a little more than a month after the prisoners' arrival in Selkirk. Play books were a consistent feature of their borrowing habits thereafter (recalling Napoleon's interminable play readings on Saint Helena), with indigenous

---

35 Allan, *Nation of Readers*; Raven, 'Libraries for Sociability'; Towsey, 'All Partners may be Enlightened and Improved'; Towsey, 'First Steps in Associational Reading'. For the European perspective see Munck, *Enlightenment*, pp. 98–99; Melton, *Rise of the Public*, pp. 104–10.

36 Towsey, *Reading the Scottish Enlightenment*, ch. 2. Since the death of Walter Scott's uncle, Colonel William Russell of Ashestiel, in 1804, there had been no active involvement of retired military officers in the Selkirk library who might otherwise have afforded an introduction for the interned French officers. Military and naval officers were a heavy presence in most English subscription libraries of the period: Allan, *Nation of Readers*, pp. 64–84.

37 The Comte d'Artois found Edinburgh 'tiresome and odd' during his enforced sojourn at Holyrood in the 1790s: Mackenzie-Stuart, *French King at Holyrood*, p. 70.

38 Doisy, *Reminiscences*, pp. 78–79. The Kelso prisoners proudly announced that 'the Dresses and Decorations' for their performance of *The Barber of Seville* in June 1811 had been 'made entirely by themselves': NAS, GD157/2004.

French playwrights such as Molière, Mercier and Marivaux complemented by highlights from Bell's canonical collection of *British Theatre* including plays by Shakespeare, Farquhar, Foote and Joanna Baille.[39]

Between April 1811 and May 1814 the prisoners registered 3,971 loans overall, borrowing books considerably more regularly than civilian library subscribers in the same period. Their interest in the library was initially quite hesitant, with prisoners collectively borrowing fewer than thirty books in each of the first five months they used the library. It was only during the prisoners' first winter in Selkirk that they approached the overall mean for monthly borrowing (107 loans), but once their appetite for English books was established they proved exceptionally rapacious readers – 192 loans were shared between the prisoners in April 1812 and 246 in May 1813. Purely on this basis, it is clear that the books provided by the library became an indispensable means of alleviating the boredom that was an inevitable by-product of parole conditions. Nevertheless, some officers were always more interested in the library's books than others: around a third never seem to have borrowed books at all, while less than a dozen – most of whom had been captured together at Bailén – registered over 100 loans.

The officers' uneven interest in the library and their apparently hesitant start to borrowing books might both be explained by simple, though culturally interesting factors. One of these, it seems certain, was education. Post-Revolutionary France was a highly literate society and the vast majority of officers in Napoleon's armies were able to read well. Even so, some prisoners of war are known to have used their time in detention to improve their reading skills, since literacy was a passport both to self-advancement and to promotion through the ranks.[40] Reading was also the means by which soldiers and sailors could pursue a more general education, especially for a generation whose formal schooling had commonly been cut short by war. Thus Lieutenant Gicquel des Touches, captured at Trafalgar and subsequently granted parole in Tiverton, 'took advantage of my leisure hours to overhaul and complete my education', relying on 'some of my comrades of more literary bringing-up' to administer 'lessons in literature and history'.[41]

More importantly, perhaps, the Selkirk library boasted an overwhelmingly English-language book collection, and even the French texts it possessed were

---

39 Molière's popularity with the French officers would seem to reflect his status as the third most regularly performed playwright of the Revolution: Kennedy, *Cultural History*, p. 394. For Napoleon's endless play readings on Saint Helena see Bell, *First Total War*, p. 306. For the reception of English theatre in eighteenth-century France see Hopes, 'Staging National Identities'.

40 Schama, *Citizens*, p. 180; Forrest, *Napoleon's Men*, p. 49; Bell, *First Total War*, p. 245.

41 Cited in Abell, *Prisoners of War*, p. 299.

held in translated editions. The Selkirk loan registers might therefore trace the hesitant and ongoing attempts of officers to improve their grasp of the English language in the first weeks and months of their internment. Prisoners elsewhere certainly made it their priority to learn English, including the Baron de Bonnefoux (paroled at Thame in Oxfordshire) and the Marquis d'Hautpol (at Bridgnorth, Shropshire).[42] Although his functional literacy was such that he acted as letter-writing (and reading) amanuensis for less literate comrades on the front line, Adelbert Doisy seems to have arrived in Selkirk with only a smattering of English vocabulary. He boasted that before abandoning his formal education to sign up for military service at the tender age of fifteen he had won a school prize for an extemporaneous translation of one page of Goldsmith's *Vicar of Wakefield*, but this seems to have been the full extent of his linguistic training.[43] No wonder, then, that the familiar *Vicar of Wakefield* duly became one of the first books he borrowed from the Selkirk library, before he later graduated to more complex books such as Robertson's *Charles V.*

Although typical of the vast majority of his comrades, Doisy's relatively modest library record of 47 loans bears little comparison to that of Lieutenant Tarnier of the 4th Legion, 'a young man of great talent, excellent education, and of remarkable gayety of disposition' who signed for 112 loans during his stay in Selkirk.[44] Only six officers borrowed more books than Tarnier, and he was a truly omnivorous reader, accounting for books ranging from Charlotte Turner Smith's novels to Shakespeare's plays, the poetry of Rabbie Burns, Chateaubriand's *Travels in Greece*, Smith's *Wealth of Nations*, Montesquieu's *Spirit of the Laws* and, indeed, Robertson's *Charles V.* The biographical context here is plainly vital in helping to understand the library records of both Tarnier and Doisy, and further biographical research will – it is hoped – eventually unlock the private lives and abilities of their fellow prisoners of war. It is not inconceivable, for instance, that some of the imprisoned officers who never used the library did so simply because they were actually unable to read English with sufficient proficiency. Even so, they may still have counted among the library's users, for their more capable comrades may easily have read aloud to them, perhaps translating as they went along – just as Lieutenant Gicquel des Touches received his historical and literary instruction orally from fellow prisoners at Tiverton.

---

42 Abell, *Prisoners of War*, pp. 300, 312. Abell relates the adventures of Captain Pequendaire, of *L'Espoir* privateer, who managed to escape Lauder successfully precisely because he had so well hidden his fluency in English: Abell, *Prisoners of War*, p. 355.

43 Doisy, *Reminiscences*, pp. 6–7. For English-language teaching in eighteenth-century France see Saunderson, 'English and the French Enlightenment' (I am extremely grateful to Michèle Cohen for bringing this essay to my attention).

44 Doisy, *Reminiscences*, p. 82.

As will be clear, we can learn a great deal about the interests, beliefs and daily lives of the officers imprisoned in Selkirk from the books that they borrowed. Inevitably, French authors loom particularly large, with well-known books such as Bossuet's *History of France*, Anquetil's *Memoirs of the Court of France during the Reign of Louis XIV*, Fenelon's *Telemachus*, Marmontel's *Incas*, Madame de Staël's *Corinna*, Abbé Prévost's *Life of Cleveland*, Mercier's *Nightcap* and Saint-Pierre's *Studies of Nature* (all in English translation) providing tangible links with their homeland for readers detained abroad for the duration of the war. This reflects anecdotal evidence relating to officers imprisoned elsewhere. Mrs Admiral Dunlop remembered that the naval officer François Espinasse (paroled at Jedburgh) 'always carried with him Montaigne, De Bruyere, Molière and Montesquieu, which he read in his spare half hours, and were his companions in his bedroom in the early morning'. Significantly for the kind of cultural exchanges that I suggest occurred between prisoners and their hosts, Espinasse apparently taught Mrs Dunlop 'to know and to love France; he explained to me the charms of her social life; and to him I owe the never ending enjoyment of her literature'.[45] German prisoners paroled at Sanquhar and Hawick also gravitated towards their own national literature, Major Meinhard securing a steady supply of German books from the widow of a Glasgow merchant who had once traded in Hamburg.[46]

The paroled officers at Selkirk also proved particularly keen readers of recent history such as Bertrand de Moleville's royalist *Annals of the French Revolution* and *Memoirs of Louis XVI*, the *Reminiscences* of the flamboyant 'Prince of Diplomats' Talleyrand, Wilson's *British Expedition to Egypt* (with its notorious accusations of cruelty against Napoleon) and, most appropriately for those who had served in the Peninsula, James Carrick Moore's *Narrative of the Campaign of the British Army in Spain* – largely a vindication of his brother's conduct in leading the defence of Corunna. As Alan Forrest suggests, 'soldiers were consistently and quite deliberately kept in the dark about what was happening around them – the progress of battles, the extent of casualties, the news from other fronts'.[47] For this reason, their need to read history autobiographically would certainly have been even more urgent than that of many other contemporary readers, such as John Dawson, an excise officer from London whose reading in the first half of the century has recently been analysed by Stephen Colclough: 'when Dawson read contemporary history he tended to

---

45   Forbes, 'French Prisoners of War', p. 11. Other forms of 'cultural exchange' between Britain and France are explored in Ogée, ed., *'Better in France?'*, although shared reading tastes do not figure.

46   Robison, 'Impressions of a German Prisoner of War', p. 24.

47   Forrest, *Napoleon's Men*, p. 26.

take it personally, searching out evidence of proceedings in which he had been involved and reconstructing the accounts of these'.[48] By reading both Moore and Wilson, Lieutenants Bellier, Graffan, Guyot and Josse (who all fought at Bailén) and Jean Baptiste Passement (erstwhile captain of the *Intrépide* privateer) could position themselves more firmly within the wider global conflict of which they were a part, allowing them retrospectively to clarify the fog of war – even if the accounts available to them were not entirely sympathetic to the Napoleonic cause. In the longer perspective such books inevitably helped participants to decipher the unprecedented constitutional upheavals of the entire Revolutionary and Napoleonic period. This process was evidently begun by readers such as Charles Bonzanigo and Vincent Simonet in the pastoral backwaters of the Scottish borders before Napoleon's *grande armée* had even set foot in Russia: Bonzanigo, a captain in the 4th Legion at Bailén, read both of Moleville's books consecutively in the summer of 1812, and Simonet, a surgeon on the *Cupidon* privateer seized two days out of Bayonne in 1811, borrowed the *Reminiscences of Talleyrand* in December 1812.[49]

Not only were the paroled officers attracted to books of contemporary history, they also proved avid readers of military biography, with classic accounts of French military legends such as Marshall Turenne borrowed alongside books on military heroes of the eighteenth century such as Frederick the Great and Prince Eugene. In one sense, this may convey the soldiers' continuing loyalty to Napoleon, since he carried accounts of campaigns conducted by the ablest military commanders of all time in his travelling library, exhorting those under his command to read and learn from them.[50] It most certainly reflected the cult of militarism that flourished in France under Napoleon, culminating in Turenne's remains being reinterred in an elaborate ritual at the *Temple de Mars* – an historic occasion enshrining the *maréchal-général*'s status 'as a moral paradigm for Enlightenment and Revolutionary France'.[51] At the very least, the names of famous generals from days gone by must have leapt off the pages of the Selkirk catalogue when paroled officers were first granted access to the library – with the *Military Memoirs and Maxims of Marshall Turenne* borrowed twice by Lieutenant Charles Frossard (an artilleryman captured at Bailén) and on no less than four occasions by the unfortunate Frederic Bablot, who had skippered the 14-gun privateer *Creole* to ignominy on its first voyage out of Bordeaux. They were familiar legends whose life stories might help this new generation of military and naval veterans renegotiate their own experiences

---

48 Colclough, *Consuming Texts*, p. 86.
49 Esdaile, *Peninsular Eyewitnesses*, p. x.
50 Henderson, *Prince Eugen of Savoy*, p. xi.
51 Lindsay, 'Mummies and Tombs', p. 482; Bell, *First Total War*, p. 246.

of conflict, constructing – or reinforcing – the sense of martial valour that comes through clearly in the 'conceit and literary flourish' of 'carefully scripted' Napoleonic memoirs such as those compiled by Adelbert Doisy.[52]

At the same time, the paroled officers' taste for contemporary travel writing probably satisfied some of the adventurous wanderlust that their captivity denied them. Napoleon himself had been inspired by the 'alluring fantasy' of travellers' adventures in Africa and the Orient, tempted to disaster in Egypt by accounts of 'a place where the daring, superior self might express itself more fully than amid the restraints of "civilized" Europe'.[53] Witness to their own share of adrenalin-filled adventures in far-flung exotic locations, it is no wonder that the bestselling fictitious *Travels of Anarchasis the Younger in Greece* or *Travels of Antenor in Greece and Asia* proved so popular with paroled officers at Selkirk, as did tales of the celebrated British adventurers Captain Cook, Abyssinian Bruce and Mungo Park (a local boy whose brothers continued to subscribe to the Selkirk library long after his tragic disappearance in western Africa). Although inherently escapist for the vast majority of European civilians who had no prospect of travelling abroad,[54] the experience of reading travel writing must have been rather different for Napoleonic prisoners of war – grounded instead in the painful memories of campaigning across the globe, 'moving inexorably from snow-capped Alpine passes to the hot plains of Castile, from the vineyards of Italy and the Rhineland to the deserts of Egypt and North Africa'.[55] Travel writing enabled them to retrace their steps at more leisure in the pages of books, just as the much-travelled British officer John Henry Slessor negotiated his own post-war peregrinations in the pages of Laurence Sterne's fictional *Sentimental Journey*.[56] Thus Jean Besancele, a lieutenant in the 3rd Legion captured at Bailén, borrowed Bourgoing's *Travels in Spain* in July 1812 and Swinburne's more dated *Travels through Spain* in August 1813, and Lieutenant Bertrand, the privateer seized in the Persian Gulf in 1805, borrowed *Travels in Upper and Lower Egypt* by Napoleon's archaeologist, the Baron de Denon, no fewer than seven times between 1811 and 1813.

More broadly, the Selkirk library undoubtedly enabled Napoleonic prisoners of war to become more familiar with the country in which they were detained. Although there is no evidence that Doisy was familiar with Scotland's

52 Forrest, *Napoleon's Men*, pp. 22–27 (citation is on p. 23).
53 Bell, *First Total War*, p. 211.
54 Although we still await a dedicated study of readers' uses of travel literature in the eighteenth century, James Buzard acknowledges that 'precious few actually could [...] travel': Buzard, 'Grand Tour', p. 37. For the gendered implications of reading travel literature see Goodman, *Becoming a Woman*, esp. pp. 260, 267–68.
55 Forrest, *Napoleon's Men*, p. xi; compare MacDougall, *Prisoners at Penicuik*, pp. 28–29.
56 Hayter, ed., *Backbone*, pp. 322–23.

traditionally close relationship with France, some of his colleagues did take the opportunity to read up on Scottish history and literature. More than a dozen read one of the standard histories of Scotland by William Robertson and Malcolm Laing, although only a handful opted to read the poetry of Burns or Ossian – despite the latter's prodigious impact on Napoleonic France.[57] The *Annual Register* – borrowed more frequently than any other title by both civilian and interned users of the Selkirk library – not only allowed prisoners to follow the progress of the war on the continent, but also provided them with a narrative account of British parliamentary politics and a guide to the latest releases in all forms of literature. British history was also popular, with David Hume's *History of England* and Robert Henry's voluminous *History of Great Britain on a New Plan* attracting a dozen readers each, and three officers sharing 26 loans of the more dated 15-volume *History of England* by the Huguenot historian Rapin. Two prisoners distinguished themselves by working their way through all three massive histories, namely Captain Chauvin, another veteran of Bailén, and Henri Tourat, a mate on the frigate *Los Dolore* seized in 1806. Hume's *History* was, of course, hugely influential in France in the 1780s and 1790s.[58] The Marquis de Sade had taken it to the Bastille with him in 1784, while Louis XVI is known to have discussed Hume's assessment of the fall of Charles I with his advisors as early as 1788 – hoping Hume's celebrated account of seventeenth-century regicide would help him to avoid suffering the same grisly fate.[59] Napoleon himself is said to have been 'fascinated by England, studying it at considerable length and displaying knowledge and understanding of its historical and constitutional development',[60] so it was perhaps inevitable that some of the prisoners would take advantage of the Selkirk library to further their understanding of the much-vaunted concept of English 'liberty'. Indeed, the celebrated 'ancient constitution' supposedly inherited by eighteenth-century Britain (and so thoroughly demolished by Hume)[61] demonstrably played on prisoners' minds elsewhere. Major Meinhard, the Rhinelander detained on parole in Sanquhar, was impressed by the historical consciousness displayed by local civilians, commenting that 'every family was usually in possession of a small library, chiefly on religious topics and historical topics. The ordinary man was better acquainted with the history of

57 Dawson and Morère, eds., *Scotland and France in the Enlightenment*, pp. 74, 96–97; Tieghem, *Ossian en France*; Gaskill, ed., *Reception of Ossian in Europe*.

58 The classic account of the reception of the *History of England* in France remains Bongie, *David Hume*.

59 Schama, *Citizens*, pp. 391, 659.

60 Schom, *Napoleon Bonaparte*, p. 9.

61 For Hume's revisionist approach to 'English liberty' and the 'ancient constitution' see Pocock, *Barbarism and Religion II*, pp. 163–68; Wexler, *David Hume*.

his country than learned people often were with that of theirs.'[62] More apocryphal, perhaps, is the anecdote concerning a conversation between a French officer on parole in Hawick and a local trader:

> you have de grand constitution, and de manners and equality dat we did fight for
> for so long; I see in your street the priest and de shoemaker, de banker and de
> baker, de merchant and de hosier, all meet togeder, be compagnons and be happy.
> Dis is de equality dat we French fight for and never get.[63]

Political considerations may even have impinged on the French officers' penchant for English novels, although it is noteworthy that avowedly anti-Jacobin novels by Robert Dallas and Robert Bisset were often borrowed indiscriminately alongside James White's *Adventures of John of Gaunt*, which reflected much more sympathetically on the revolutionary legacy.[64] Novels were perfectly suited to help the officers while away the long hours of confinement, to distract them from pangs of homesickness, or simply to improve their grasp of the English language. Doisy's library record was littered with such material, his early exposure to Goldsmith's *Vicar of Wakefield* presumably instilling a long-lasting predilection for books such as Agnes Maria Bennett's *Beggar Girl*, Maria Edgeworth's *Fashionable Tales*, Anne Radcliffe's *Mysteries of Udolpho*, Richardson's *Sir Charles Grandison*, Thomas Skinner Surr's *Winter in London*, Charlotte Turner Smith's *Emmeline*, White's *John of Gaunt* and the complete novels of Dr John Moore. Yet he clearly did not consider such reading unusual enough to earn the Selkirk library a place in his *Reminiscences*, even though his account of his detention dwells so fondly on the prisoners' cultural interaction with the civilian community of the Scottish borders. Rather, Doisy's demonstrable immersion in eighteenth-century novels manifests itself subconsciously in the narrative form of his *Reminiscences*, in the same way that they gave Napoleon himself 'a way of understanding his own unique and extraordinary life story'.[65] Doisy becomes the novelised hero of his own life, swashbuckling his way from the Spanish peninsula to the Scottish borders, his memoirs illuminated by his bravery, wit, magnanimity and derring-do.

Much more important to cultural historians is the fact that the paroled officers borrowed novels at all – and with such apparent enthusiasm, since novels accounted for over 40 per cent of the books they borrowed from the

---

62 Robison, 'Impressions of a German Prisoner of War', p. 23.
63 Forbes, 'French Prisoners of War', p. 5. Forbes's research notes survive at NAS, GD1/405, but even here he does not tend to identify his sources.
64 *ODNB*. For the impact of the French Revolution on British imaginative literature see Grenby, *Anti-Jacobin Novel*; Wallace, *Revolutionary Subjects*.
65 Bell, *First Total War*, p. 203.

Selkirk library. Although we might readily put this down to the stereotypi-
cal femininity that characterised French readers depicted in wartime British
propaganda, civilian readers borrowed a very similar proportion of novels from
the Selkirk subscription library. This has important ramifications, for there is
considerable debate about who actually read the novels that were becoming
an increasingly significant feature of associational library collections in Britain
and North America.[66] As James Raven points out, 'certain borrowing appears
to have been on behalf of other family members, especially for a wife or
daughter, but there is no way of determining this from borrowing registers'. It
is equally likely, he suggests, that 'the new orders for novels [...] also reflected
a broadened, more relaxed attitude by many of the gentlemen members themselves towards the sorts of books the library might properly stock'.[67] In this
case, we can at least offer a more concrete insight into this most intractable
problem in the history of reading, since there is no evidence to suggest that
any of the paroled prisoners of war were accompanied to Selkirk by female
relatives – although it is tempting to think that the French officers themselves
might have encouraged civilian readers to embrace their more imaginative
selves by reading novels, still more so to imagine them enticing local lovers
with romantic fiction.[68]

3

WHATEVER THE correlation may have been between the taste for novels
among military and civilian readers at the Selkirk subscription library, it
is clear that the library encouraged a degree of cultural interaction between the
prisoners of war and their hosts. Indeed, their engagement with the local civilian population – at the library as well as at the freemasons' hall, the assembly
rooms and civilian homes – recalls the bonds of polite civility that tied together
the European officer class in earlier generations, rather than the all-out belligerence that is said to differentiate the Napoleonic conflict.[69] As we have

---

66 St Clair, *Reading Nation*, p. 254.
67 Raven, *London Booksellers*, pp. 200, 220.
68 Jan Fergus argues that men and boys were significant consumers of imaginative literature
    in the English Midlands; see Fergus, *Provincial Readers*. A number of officers held at
    the prison depots at Penicuik and Perth were accompanied by their wives, some of them
    acquired since the prisoners' arrival in Britain, but this was exceptionally rare and there is
    no evidence in the Board of Transport records for Selkirk that women accompanied the
    prisoners there; MacDougall, *Prisoners at Penicuik*, pp. 34–36; Penny, *Traditions of Perth*,
    p. 92.
69 Comparative scholarship on the treatment of prisoners of war in the Napoleonic Wars

seen, officers on parole in other British towns enjoyed the genteel hospitality of local communities, and Doisy's *Reminiscences* certainly imply that relations were generally quite affable in Selkirk too:

> Few of us will have forgotten the kind attentions which we received from Mr Anderson, a gentleman farmer, who never seemed more pleased than when he could […] entertain in his home those of us who were enjoying the sport of fishing in the river on the banks of which stood his residence. Another friend of ours was a wealthy, retired lawyer […] whose only fault, in our estimation, was his manifest chagrin when we did not keep pace with himself in the copious libations with which he regaled us. A third kind friend was a Mr. Thorburn, also a gentleman farmer, a most cordial host, who seemed bent on making his French guests acquainted with such Scottish delicacies as a grilled sheep's head, haggis, hodge-podge, and a splendid kind of cheese, of his own manufacture.[70]

Obviously the borderers' generosity towards their enforced guests extended far beyond the literary, but there is no doubt that the library offered prisoners the opportunity to interact with their hosts in a more formal setting on a near daily basis. It is striking, for instance, that Messrs Thorburn and Anderson visited the library on the very day that French officers were first recorded borrowing its books. From that day onwards, the loan registers provide documentary evidence of French prisoners fraternising with civilian readers nearly every day as they stood in front of the library shelves deciding which books to borrow. This was an inevitable function of the library's restricted opening hours, with the managerial committee eventually implementing a ballot system in 1820 to alleviate the 'kind of warfare' that had long prevailed 'at the Library door' as readers scrambled to secure their first choice of books.[71] Although the minute books do not now survive, it is possible that the prisoners participated in the associational structure of the library, attending its self-governing annual meetings, suggesting books to be added to the collection and enjoying the 'distinctive sociability of the after-meeting dinner' inherent in such clubbable institutions.[72]

Doisy remembered certain convivial events with particular pride. On occasion, the paroled officers risked the wrath of the government agent charged with policing their curfew by riding out to dine at the house of an eminent local lawyer near Melrose, 'the honor of whose acquaintance I did not then appreciate as I should have done in later years':

---

and earlier conflicts is still at a formative stage but see Van Buskirk, *Generous Enemies*, esp. ch. 3.

70   Doisy, *Reminiscences*, pp. 80–81.

71   The original minute books do not survive, but a report on them was published in the *Southern Register*, 23 May 1901, from which these quotations are taken.

72   Raven, *London Booksellers*, pp. 57–58; Towsey, 'First Steps in Associational Reading'.

Anecdotes respecting Napoleon seemed to have an absorbing interest for our host, who, as we remarked, incessantly contrived to lead back the conversation to the subject [...] Little did we suspect that our host was then preparing a work, published ten years later, under the title of 'A Life of Napoleon Bonaparte'. In this unfair production, which is a stain on the name of its otherwise illustrious author, Sir Walter Scott relates anecdotes and circumstances connected with the emperor, many of which were communicated to him by us, but taking care to accompany each recital with sarcastic innuendoes, and self-invented motives of action, derogatory to the honor of Napoleon.[73]

Of course, since his host on these occasions was later revealed as the author of the *Waverley* novels, Doisy probably dined out on this story for the rest of his life,[74] but intellectual exchange clearly occurred on a less exalted level with other members of the civilian community. Evangelical clergyman George Lawson – singled out as a 'venerable, excellent man' in Doisy's *Reminiscences* – seems to have made a special effort to engage with French prisoners detained in both Selkirk and Melrose.[75] The officers paroled at Melrose – once again flouting the terms of their parole by venturing so far beyond the bounds of the burgh – visited Lawson for the express purpose of borrowing devotional and French-language books from his personal collection, with some continuing to correspond with him on doctrinal and philosophical topics well after their return to France. On one occasion, Lawson 'entertained them by reading [...] some old French authors',[76] while the *Southern Register* reported a local legend still current in 1901 that

> moved by a desire to bring these benighted foreigners to belief in the true faith, Dr Lawson added French to the more ancient languages he was already proficient in. But the aliens were nearly all men of education and knew their Voltaire, with the result that the Professor made poor progress with his well-meant efforts at proselytism, if he did not even receive a shock to his own convictions![77]

Besides possessing an impressive library of specialist material in his own right, Lawson actually borrowed more books from the subscription library than any other local reader (including books by the *philosophes* Marmontel, Montesquieu, Raynal, Rousseau and Voltaire), so would have had ample opportunity to discuss the more controversial strains of sceptical Enlightenment

---

73 Doisy, *Reminiscences*, pp. 81, 84–85.
74 Hook argues that Scott's popularity in France meant that 'in the decade 1820–30 Scotland and France were linked culturally in an embrace stronger than anything the politics of the "Auld Alliance" had ever achieved': Hook, 'French Taste for Scottish Literary Romanticism', p. 98.
75 Doisy, *Reminiscences*, p. 76.
76 Macfarlane, *Life and Times of George Lawson*, pp. 220–21.
77 *Southern Reporter*, 23 May 1901.

when encountering the Selkirk prisoners in front of the library shelves. Indeed, we can occasionally follow the broad contours of this engagement in the pages of the library's borrowing registers. Lawson borrowed William Robertson's *History of America*, for instance, on the very same day that Doisy borrowed another of Robertson's influential histories, the *History of Scotland* (4 April 1812), and Doisy later borrowed the *History of America* itself, perhaps on Lawson's advice.

Since the same books proved popular with readers from both communities, we can safely assume that the same processes of mutual self-improvement were at work among other borrowers from the library. Understandably, the *Annual Register* was the title borrowed most regularly by both the paroled officers and their civilian hosts, but Henry's *History of Great Britain*, Smith's *Emmeline*, the *Travels of Anacharsis*, Radcliffe's *Mysteries of Udolpho* and Moore's *Mordaunt* were all among the ten books borrowed most frequently by members of each community. Whether introducing one another to their own personal favourites, negotiating the implications of the recent upheavals, arguing over the implications of English 'liberty' and the Revolutionary 'rights of man', or revelling together in fictional narratives of adventure, mystery, love and romance, the two communities were seemingly brought together by their mutual interest in reading and their familiarity with the same literary, historical and philosophical canons. With military and civilian readers visiting the library on the same days to borrow the same kinds of books, the inevitable outcome of such encounters must have been a growing appreciation of the commonality of their cultural outlook – together with the discovery that they were not the incomprehensible 'aliens' depicted in contemporary propaganda on either side of the English channel.

4

'RATHER THAN providing a source of captive and escape narratives,' Gavin Daly insists, 'the history of French prisoners of war can illuminate [...] the political and social meanings of the French Revolution.'[78] This may be so, but close attention to the experiences of Napoleonic officers paroled in small British towns after 1803 has significant implications for our characterisation of the period in other ways. The multilayered cultural interactions that emerged between French prisoners of war and their civilian hosts – not least at the Selkirk subscription library – had profound ramifications for the way in which the two parties perceived each other, breaking down the politically constructed

---

78   Daly, 'Napoleon's Lost Legions', p. 363.

'otherness' that is said to have underpinned the 'total war' waged between Napoleon and the British Empire. Such encounters therefore challenge the likely success (and, hence, the social impact) of 'concerted political attempts to harness entire societies [...] to a single, military purpose'.[79] For in discovering the fundamental similarity of their everyday lives – their mutual enjoyment of plays, dancing, socialising, flirting and reading – two groups of people whose countries were engaged in a bitter and ideologically charged war with each other realised that they shared a common cultural identity. Although their relationship was inevitably fractious on occasion, Doisy and his comrades could thus take leave of their civilian hosts 'without entertaining, on either side, any remnant of grudge that might previously have existed between us'.[80]

---

79 Bell, *First Total War*, p. 9.
80 Doisy, *Reminiscences*, p. 96.

Bibliography

Published Primary Sources

Aitchison, John, *An Ensign in the Peninsular War: The Letters of John Aitchison*, ed. W. F. K. Thompson (London: Michael Joseph, 1981).

Alexis, Willibald, *Als Kriegsfreiwilliger nach Frankreich 1815* (Berlin: Reclam, 1915).

Alexis, Willibald, *Isegrimm* (Berlin: Janke, 1854).

Allardyce, James, ed., *Historical Papers Relating to the Jacobite Period, 1699–1750*, 2 vols. (Aberdeen: New Spalding Club, 1895–96).

'An Act of Free and Generall Pardon Indemnity and Oblivion', in *The Statutes of the Realm*, Vol. V, ed. John Raithby (London: Records Commission, 1819), pp. 226–34.

Arand, Johann Baptist Martin von, *In Vorderösterreichs Amt und Wurden: Die Selbstbiographie des Johann Baptist Martin von Arand (1743–1821)*, ed. Hellmut Waller (Stuttgart: Kohl-hammer, 1999).

Archenholtz, Johann Wilhelm von, *Geschichte des Siebenjährigen Krieges in Deutschland*, Vol. II (Berlin: Spener, 5th edn, 1840).

Augustine, *The Political Writings of St. Augustine*, ed. Henry Paolucci (Chicago: Gateway Publications, 1962).

Bagshawe, Samuel, *Colonel Samuel Bagshawe and the Army of George II, 1731–1762*, ed. Alan J. Guy (London: Army Records Society, 1990).

Bamford, Francis, ed., *A Royalist's Notebook: The Commonplace Book of Sir John Oglander Kt of Nunwell* (London: Constable & Co. Ltd, 1936).

Barich, Fritz, 'Nachrichten aus dem Kirchenbuch der Mariengemeinde, namentlich aus der Zeit des Dreißigjährigen Krieges', *Beiträge zur Geschichte Dortmunds und der Grafschaft Mark* 23 (1914), pp. 33–74.

Barnes, G. R., and Owen, J. H., eds., *The Private Papers of John, Earl of Sandwich*, 4 vols. (London: Navy Records Society, 1932–38).

Bernard, Richard, *The Bible–Battells. Or the Sacred Art Military* (London: E. Blackmore, 1629).

[Bever, Samuel], *The Cadet: A Military Treatise* (London: W. Johnston, 1762).

The Billington: Or, Town and Country Songster (London: E. Wenman, 1790).

Bocer, Heinrich, *De dominio proprietatis et acquirendi modis tum in specie de occupatione ac praedatione bellica* (Tübingen: Gruppenbach, 1599).

Boulle, Maurice, ed., 'Le journal du capitaine Amblard, de Lussas (Ardèche): les guerres de Vendée vues par un ardéchois républicain, 1793–1799', *Revue de la Société des Enfants et Amis de Villeneuve-de-Berg* 41 (1981), pp. 61–71.

Bragge, William, *Peninsular Portrait, 1811–1814: The Letters of Captain William Bragge*, ed. S. A. C. Cassels (London: Oxford University Press, 1963).

Browne, Thomas Henry, *The Napoleonic War Journal of Captain Thomas Henry Browne, 1807–1816*, ed. R. N. Buckley (London: Army Records Society, 1987).

Bulstrode, Sir Richard, *Memoirs and Reflections upon the Reign and Government of King Charles the 1ˢᵗ and K. Charles the IId* (London: N. Mist for Charles Rivington, 1721).

Burnet, Gilbert, *Burnet's History of My Own Time: Part I*, Vol. I, ed. Osmund Airy (Oxford: Clarendon Press, 1897).

Calendar of the Proceedings of the Committee for the Advance of Money, 1642–1656, 3 vols. (London: HMSO, 1888).

Calendar of the Proceedings of the Committee for Compounding, &c., 1643–1660, 5 vols. (London: HMSO, 1889–92).

Chandler, David, ed., *Robert Parker and Comte de Mérode-Westerloo: The Marlborough Wars* (London: Longmans, Green and Co., 1968).

Chapman, Peter, ed., *The Diaries and Letters of G. T. W. B. Boyes: Vol. 1* (Melbourne: Oxford University Press, 1985).

Chatry, Michel, ed., *Turreau en Vendée: mémoires et correspondance* (Cholet: Editions du Choletais, 1992).

Chinnery, G. A., *Records of the Borough of Leicester: Vol. VII: Judicial and Allied Records, 1689–1835* (Leicester: Leicester University Press, 1974).

Clausewitz, Carl von, *On War*, ed. and trans. Michael Howard and Peter Paret (Princeton, NJ: Princeton University Press, 1976).

Conrady, Wilhelm von, *Aus stürmischer Zeit. Ein Soldatenleben vor hundert Jahren* (Berlin: C. A. Schwetschke & Sohn, 1907).

Cooper, John Spencer, *Rough Notes of Seven Campaigns in Portugal, Spain, France and America during the Years 1809–1815*, introd. Ian Fletcher (Staplehurst: Spellmount, 1996).

Corbet, John, *An Historicall Relation of the Military Government of Gloucester* (1645), reprinted in [John Washbourn, ed.], *Bibliotheca Gloucestrensis: A Collection of Scarce and Curious Tracts, Relating to the County and City of Gloucester; Illustrative of, and Published During the Civil War* (Gloucester: John Washbourn, 1825), pp. 1–152.

Costello, Edward, *Rifleman Costello: The Adventures of a Soldier of the 95th (Rifles) in the Peninsular & Waterloo Campaigns of the Napoleonic Wars* (Driffield: Leonaur, 2005).

Cowper, Spencer, *Letters of Spencer Cowper*, ed. Edward Hughes (Durham: Surtees Society, 1956).

Delhoven, Johann Peter, *Die rheinische Dorfchronik des Johann Peter Delhoven aus Dormagen (1783–1823)*, ed. Hermann Cardauns and Reiner Müller (Dormagen: Amtsverwaltung, 1966).

Doisy, Adelbert J. de Villargennes, *Reminiscences of Army Life under Napoleon Bonaparte* (Cincinnati, OH: Robert Clarke and Co., 1884).

Douglas, John, *Douglas's Tale of the Peninsula and Waterloo*, ed. Stanley Monick (London: Leo Cooper, 1997).

Dugdale, Sir William, *Antient Usage in Bearing of Such Ensigns of Honour as are Commonly Called Arms* (London, 1811).

Esdaile, Charles, *Peninsular Eyewitnesses: The Experience of War in Spain and Portugal, 1808–1813* (Barnsley: Pen and Sword, 2008).

An Essay on Political Lying (London: S. Hooper, 1757).

Evelyn, John, *The Diary of John Evelyn*, ed. E. S. De Beer (London: Oxford University Press, 1959).

Ferguson, Adam, *An Essay on the History of Civil Society* (New Brunswick, NJ, and London: Transaction Books, 1980).

Fletcher, Isaac, *The Diary of Isaac Fletcher of Underwood, Cumberland, 1756–1781*, ed. Angus J. Winchester (Kendal: Cumberland & Westmorland Antiquarian and Archaeological Society, 1994).

Frederick V, *Unser Friderichs von Gottes Gnaden Königs in Böheim ... offen Außschreiben warum Wir die Cron Böheim und der incorporirten Länder Regierung auff Uns genommen* (Prague: Jonathan Bohutsky von Hranitz, 1619).

Friesenegger, Maurus, *Tagebuch aus dem 30 jährigen Krieg*, ed. W. Mathäser (Munich: Allitera, 2007).

Grant, Elizabeth of Rothiemurchus, *Memoirs of a Highland Lady*, ed. Andrew Tod (Edinburgh: Canongate, 1998).

Grant, Francis, J., ed., *Register of Marriages of the City of Edinburgh, 1751–1800* (Edinburgh: Scottish Record Society, 1922).

Grattan, William, *Adventures with the Connaught Rangers, 1809–1814*, ed. Charles Oman (London: Greenhill Books, 2003).

Greene, Joseph, *Correspondence of the Reverend Joseph Greene*, ed. Levi Fox (London: Dugdale Society, 1965).

Grose, Francis, *The Antiquities of England and Wales*, 8 vols. (London: S. Hooper, new edn, 1783–87).

Grose, Francis, *Military Antiquities Respecting a History of the English Army, from the Conquest to the Present Time*, 2 vols. (London: S. Hooper, 1786–88).

Großheim, Carl Friedrich Christian von, 'Meine Lebensbeschreibung', *Mitteilungen des Vereins für Lübeckische Geschichte und Altertumskunde* 14 (1928), pp. 225–56.

Grotius, Hugo, *The Law of War and Peace (De Jure Belli ac Pacis)*, trans. L. R. Loomis with an introduction by P. E. Corbett (Roslyn, NY: Walter J. Black Inc., 1949).

Grotius, Hugo, 'Letter from Hugo de Groot to Lancelot Andrewes, Bishop of Winchester', *Transactions of the Grotius Society* 22 (1936), pp. 133–36.

Grotius, Hugo, *A Literal Translation of the Latin Text of Hugo Grotius, On the Truth of the Christian Religion*, trans. Thomas Sedger (Charleston, SC: Bibliobazaar, 2008).

Hayley, William, 'Notes to the First Epistle of "An Essay on Painting"', in *Poems and Plays*, Vol. I (London: T. Cadell, 1785), pp. 4–106.

Hayter, Alethea, ed., *The Backbone: Diaries of a Military Family in the Napoleonic Wars* (Durham: Pentland Press, 1993).

Heintz, Philipp Casimir, *Kriegstagebuch aus dem französischen Revolutionskrieg* (Pirmasens: Deil, 1928).

Hennell, George, *A Gentleman Volunteer: The Letters of George Hennell from the Peninsular War 1812–1813*, ed. Michael Glover (London: Heinemann, 1979).

Hennet, Léon, and Martin, Emmanuel–César, *Lettres interceptées par les Russes durant la campagne de 1812* (Paris: La Sabretache, 1913).

'His Maiesties Speech at Shrewsbury on Michaelmas Eve Last, to the Gentry and Commons of the Countie of Salop There Assembled', in *The True Copie of a Letter Written by Captain Wingate, Now a Prisoner in Ludlow* (London: William Ley, 1642), [p. 6].

Hodgson, John, 'Memoirs of Captain John Hodgson', in *Original Memoirs, Written During the Great Civil War; Being the Life of Sir Henry Slingsby and Memoirs of Capt. Hodgson* (Edinburgh: A. Constable, 1806), pp. 89–198.

Huber, Ernst Rudolf, ed., 'Verordnung über den Landsturm', 21 April 1813, in *Dokumente zur deutschen Verfassungsgeschichte*, Vol. I (Stuttgart: Kohlhammer, 1961), pp. 50–53.

Hunt, Eric, ed., *Charging against Napoleon: Diaries and Letters of Three Hussars 1808–1815* (Barnsley: Pen and Sword, 2001).

Hunter, Martin, *Journal of Gen. Sir Martin Hunter*, ed. Ann Hunter and Elizabeth Bell (Edinburgh: Edinburgh Press, 1894).

Ironside, Gilbert, *A Sermon Preached at Dorchester in the County of Dorcet, at the Proclaiming of His Sacred Majesty Charles the II. May 15. 1660* (London: Robert Clavell, 1660).

Janke, Erich, ed., *Feldbriefe eines Kriegsfreiwilligen von 1813* (Berlin: Janke, 1901).

Jolicler, Étienne, ed., *Joliclerc, volontaire aux armées de la Révolution: ses lettres, 1793–96* (Paris: Perrin, 1905).

Journal of the House of Lords: Volume 11: 1660–1666, pp. 6–9, 107–109. http://www.british-history.ac.uk

Junius, Maria Anna, 'Bamberg im Schweden-Kriege', *Bericht des Historischen Vereins zu Bamberg* 52 (1890), pp. 1–168; 53 (1891), pp. 169–230.

Kant, Immanuel, 'An Answer to the Question: What is Enlightenment', in *What Is Enlightenment? Eighteenth-Century Answers and Twentieth-Century Questions*, ed. James Schmidt (Berkeley, CA: University of California Press, 1996), pp. 58–64.

Kincaid, John, *The Rifle Brigade Including Adventures in the Rifle Brigade and Random Shots from a Rifleman (Abridged)* (London: Pen & Sword Military, 2005).

Krais, Johann, *Tagebuch über diejenigen Begebenheiten, welche die Reichsstadt Biberach während des Französischen Kriegs vom Jahr 1790 an bis zum Jahr 1801 erfahren hat* (Biberach, 1801).

Kübeck, Karl, *Tagebücher des Graf Friederich Freiherrn Kübeck von Kübau*, Vol. I, ed. Max Freiherrn von Kübeck (Vienna: Gerold, 1909).

Larpent, Francis Seymour, *The Private Journal of Judge-Advocate Larpent, Attached to the Head–Quarters of Lord Wellington during the Peninsular War, from 1812 to its Close*, introd. Ian C. Robertson (Staplehurst: Spellmount, 2000).

Lawes and Ordinances of Warre, Established for the Better Conduct of the Army (London: John Wright, 1643).

Lawrence, William, *A Dorset Soldier: The Autobiography of Sergeant William Lawrence, 1790–1869*, ed. Eileen Hathaway (Staplehurst: Spellmount, 1995).

Leach, J., *Rough Sketches of the Life of an Old Soldier* (Cambridge: Ken Trotman, 1986).

Lilienstern, Johann Rühle von, *Bericht eines Augenzeugen von dem Feldzuge der während den Monaten September und October 1806 unter dem Kommando des Fürsten zu Hohenlohe-Ingelfingen gestandenen Königl. preußischen und Kurfürstl. sächsischen Truppen* (Tübingen: Cotta, 1809).

Lilienstern, Johann Rühle von, *Reise mit der Armee im Jahre 1809*, ed. Jean-Jacques Langendorf (Vienna: Karolinger Verlag, 1986).

Lister, Joseph, *The Autobiography of Joseph Lister*, ed. Thomas Wright (London: J. R. Smith, 1842).

Lithgow, William, *The Siege of Newcastle* (Newcastle: S. Hodgson, 1820).

The London Chronicle, or, Universal Evening Post, 29 January 1760; 26–29 September 1761.

Lonsdale, Roger, ed., *The New Oxford Book of Eighteenth-Century Verse* (Oxford: Oxford University Press, 1987).

Ludendorff, Erich, *Der totale Krieg* (Munich: Ludendorff, 1935).

Maaß, Johann, *Bemerkungen auf einer Reise von Wittenberg* (Wittenberg: Friedrich Bruder, 1808).

Macfarlane, John, *The Life and Times of George Lawson, D. D., Selkirk, Professor of Theology to the Associate Synod* (Edinburgh: William Oliphant and Co., 1862).

'Mandate of Charles, Earl of Derby for the Trial of William Christian, September 12, 1662', in *Illiam Dhône and the Manx Rebellion, 1651: Records and Proceedings Relating to the Case of William Christian of Ronaldsway: With an Introductory Notice Relating to the Time of the Rebellion, 1643–1663*, ed. William Harrison (Douglas, Isle of Man: Manx Society, 1877), pp. 1–2.

Marsden, R. G., ed., *Documents Relating to Law and Custom of the Sea: Vol. II 1649–1767* (London: The Navy Records Society, 1916).

Martindale, Adam, *The Life of Adam Martindale, Written by Himself*, ed. Richard Parkinson, Chetham Society 4 (Manchester: Chetham Society, 1845).

Marwitz, Friedrich August Ludwig von der, *Nachrichten aus meinem Leben, 1777–1808*, ed. Günter de Bruyn (Berlin: Buchverlag der Morgen, 1989).

Mercurius Rusticus: or, The Countries Complaint of the Barbarous Out-rages Committed by the Sectaries of this Late Flourishing Kingdome (Oxford: n.p., 1646).

Michaelis, Johann David, *Lebensbeschreibung von ihm selbst abgefaßt* (Rinteln: Exped. d. Theol. Annalen, Rinteln, 1793).

Military Orders and Articles Established by His Maiesty, For the Better Ordering and Government of His Majesties Army (Oxford: Leonard Lichfield, 1643).

Montreuil, Jean de, *Opera: Vol. 2*, ed. Nicole Gervy-Pons, Ezio Ormato and Gilbert Ouy (Turin: Giappichelli, 1975).

Moser, Johann Jacob, *Grund-Säze des Europäischen Völcker-Rechts in Kriegs-Zeiten* (Tübingen: Cotta, 1752).

A Most True Relation of Divers Notable Passages of Divine Providence in the Great Deliverance and Wonderful Victory … in the County of Devon (London: Laurence Blaikelocke, 1643).

Pages, G., 'Lettres de requis et volontaires de Coutras en Vendée et en Bretagne', *Revue historique et archéologique du Libournais* 190 (1983), pp. 153–62.

Pearson, Andrew, *The Soldier Who Walked Away*, ed. Arthur H. Haley (Liverpool: Bullfinch Publications, [1987]).

Pennant, Thomas, 'To the Editor of the General Evening Post' (February 1781), in *The Literary Life of Thomas Pennant, Esq.* (London: B. and J. White, 1793), pp. 97–99.

Penny, George, *Traditions of Perth: Containing Sketches of the Manners and Customs of the Inhabitants, and Notices of Public Occurrences, During the Last Century* (Perth: J. Taylor, 1836).

Pepys, Samuel, *The Diary of Samuel Pepys*, Vol. VI, ed. Robert Latham and William Matthews (London: G. Bell and Sons Ltd, 1972).

Pflug, Johann Baptist, *Aus der Räuber- und Franzosenzeit Schwabens: Die Erinnerungen des schwäbischen Malers aus den Jahren 1780–1840*, ed. Max Zengerle (Wießenhorn: Konrad, 1975).

Priestley, Jonathan, 'Some Memoirs Concerning the Family of the Priestleys … by Jonathan Priestley', in *Yorkshire Diaries and Autobiographies in the Seventeenth and Eighteenth Centuries: Vol. 2*, Surtees Society 77 (Durham: Andrews and Co., 1883), pp. 1–41.

Proceedings of the Committee Appointed to Manage the Contributions Begun at London Dec. XVIII MDCCLVIIII for Cloathing French Prisoners of War (London: Printed by Order of the Committee, 1760).

[R., J.], *A Letter Sent To the Honble William Lenthal Esq. ... Concerning Sir Tho: Fairfax's Gallant Proceedings in Cornwal* (London: Edward Husband, 1645 [1646]).

Reglemens et ordonnances du Roy pour les gens de guerre, Vol. 1 (Paris: Chez Frederic Leonard, seul Imprimeur du Roy pour le fait de la Guerre, 1675).

Renwick, Robert, ed., *Extracts from the Records of the Burgh of Glasgow*, Vol. VI (Glasgow: Scottish Burgh Record Society, 1911).

Robison, John, 'Impressions of a German Prisoner of War in Scotland, 1812–14', *Transactions of the Hawick Archaeological Society* (1916), pp. 21–25.

Rocca, Albert-Jean de, *Mémoires sur la guerre des Français en Espagne* (Paris: Gide fils, 2nd edn, 1814).

Rules and Articles for the Better Government of All His Majesty's Forces (London: Printed by Authority, George Eyre and Andrew Strahan, 1804).

Savile, Gertrude, *Secret Comment: The Diaries of Gertrude Savile, 1721–1757*, ed. Alan Saville (Nottingham: Thoroton Society, 1997).

Saxe, Moritz de, *Reveries, or Memoirs upon the Art of War* (London: J. Nourse, 1757).

Schaumann, August, *On the Road with Wellington: The Diary of a War Commissary in the Peninsular Campaigns*, ed. Anthony M. Ludovici (London: William Heinemann, 1924).

Schrafel, Joseph, *Des Nürnberger Feldwebels merkwürdige Schicksale* (Cologne: Amon, 2nd edn, 2005).

Schüller, A., ed., 'Eine Bopparder Chronik aus der Franzosenzeit', *Trierische Chronik: Zeitschrift der Gesellschaft für Trierische Geschichte und Denkmalspflege* 13:3/4 (1916–17), pp. 33–49.

A Seasonable Reply to a Scurrilous Pamphlet, Called an Essay on Political Lying (London: J. Cooke, 1757).

Shaw, John, 'The Life of Master John Shaw', in *Yorkshire Diaries and Autobiographies in the Seventeenth and Eighteenth Centuries: Vol. 1*, Surtees Society 65 (Durham: Andrews and Co., 1875), pp. 121–63.

Shaw, William A., ed., *Calendar of Treasury Books and Papers, 1739–1741* (London: Stationery Office, 1901).

Sherer, Moyle, *Recollections of the Peninsula*, introd. Philip Haythornthwaite (Staplehurst: Spellmount, 1996).

Simes, Thomas, *The Military Guide for Young Officers* (London: J. Humphreys, R. Bell & R. Aitkin, 1776).

Sinclair, Sir John, *The Statistical Account of Scotland*, 21 vols. (Edinburgh: William Creech, 1791–99).

Snyder, Henry L., ed., *The Marlborough–Godolphin Correspondence: Vol. 1* (Oxford: Clarendon Press, 1975).

Some Observations on the Militia, With the Sketch of a Plan for the Reform of It (London: T. and J. Egerton, 1785).

Statutes and Ordynances for the Warre (London: Thomas Barthelet, 1544).

Swabey, William, *Diary of Campaigns in the Peninsula*, ed. F. A. Whinyates (London: Ken Trotman, 1984).

Tadley–Soper, H., ed., *The Registers of Baptisms, Marriages and Burials of the City of Exeter*, ii. *The Parishes of Allhallows, Goldsmith Street, St. Pancras, St. Paul* (Exeter: Devon and Cornwall Record Society, 1933).

Vattel, Emmerich de, *Le droit de gens ou Principes de la loi naturelle, appliqués à la conduite et aux affaires des nations et des souverains*, 2 vols. (London, 1758).

[Venables, Elizabeth], *Some Account of General Robert Venables, ... Together with the ... Diary of his Widow, Elizabeth Venables*, Chetham Society 83 (Manchester: Chetham Society, 1872).

[Venables, Robert], *The Narrative of General Venables*, ed. C. H. Firth, Camden Society, n.s. 60 (London: Longmans Green, 1900).

Vicissitudes in the Life of a Scottish Soldier (London: Henry Colburn, 1827).

Walpole, Horace, *Horace Walpole's Correspondence*, Vol. XXXVII, ed. W. S. Lewis (New Haven, CT: Yale University Press, 1974).

Walpole, Horace, *Memoirs and Portraits*, ed. Matthew Hodgart (London: Batsford, 1963).

Wellington, Arthur Wellesley, Duke of, *The Dispatches of Field Marshal the Duke of Wellington during His Various Campaigns in India, Denmark, Portugal, Spain, the Low Countries and France from 1789 to 1815*, Vols. III–VI, ed. John Gurwood (London: John Murray, 1852).

Wellington, Arthur Wellesley, Duke of, *The General Orders of Field Marshal the Duke of Wellington in Portugal, Spain and France from 1809 to 1814; in the Low Countries and France in 1815; and in France, Army of Occupation, from 1816 to 1818*, ed. John Gurwood (London: W. Clowes and Sons, 1837).

Wellington, Arthur Wellesley, Duke of, *General Orders: Spain and Portugal, 1810–1812*, Vols. II–IV (London: T. Egerton, 1811–13).

Wesley, John, *An Extract of the Rev. Mr John Wesley's Journal from June 17, 1758 to May 5 1760* (Bristol: William Pine, 1764).

Wheeler, William, *The Letters of Private Wheeler 1809–1828*, ed. B. H. Liddell Hart (Moreton-in-Marsh: Windrush Press, 1999).

Wogan, Edward, 'The Proceedings of the New-Moulded Army from the Time They were Brought Together in 1645, till … 1647', in Thomas Carte, *A Collection of Original Letters and Papers*, Vol. I (London: J. Bettenham, 1739), pp. 126–42.

Wolff, Christian, *Grundsätze des Natur- und Völckerrechts* (Halle: Rengerische Buchhandlung, 1754).

Wordsworth, William, *Shorter Poems, 1807–1820 by William Wordsworth*, ed. Carl H. Ketcham (Ithaca, NY, and London: Cornell University Press, 1989).

SECONDARY SOURCES

Aaslestad, Katherine B., *Place and Politics: Local Identity, Civic Culture and German Nationalism in North Germany during the Revolutionary Era* (Leiden: Brill, 2005).

Abell, Francis, *Prisoners of War in Great Britain, 1756–1815* (Oxford: Oxford University Press, 1914).

Aït-el-Djoudi, Dalila, *La guerre d'Algérie vue par l'ALN, 1954–62. L'armée française sous le regard des combattants algériens* (Paris: Autrement, 2007).

Alexander, Don W., *Rod of Iron: French Counter-Insurgency Policy in Aragon during the Peninsular War* (Wilmington, DE: Scholarly Resources, 1985).

Allan, David, *A Nation of Readers: The Lending Library in Georgian England* (London: British Library, 2008).

Anderson, M. S., *War and Society in Europe of the Old Regime, 1618–1789* (London: Fontana, 1988).

Anderson, M. S., *The War of the Austrian Succession, 1740–1748* (London: Longman, 1995).

Anderson, Olive, 'The Impact on the Fleet of the Disposal of Prisoners of War in Distant Waters, 1689–1783', *The Mariner's Mirror* 45 (1959), pp. 243–49.

André, Louis, *Michel Le Tellier et l'organisation de l'armée monarchique* (Paris: Alcan, 1906).

Andrew, D. T., *Philanthropy and Police: London Charity in the Eighteenth Century* (Princeton, NJ: Princeton University Press, 1989).

Applewhite, Harriet B., and Levy, Darline G., eds., *Women and Politics in the Age of the Democratic Revolution* (Ann Arbor, MI: University of Michigan Press, 1990).

Arni, Eric Gruber von, *Hospital Care and the British Standing Army, 1660–1714* (Aldershot: Ashgate, 2006).

Asch, Ronald G., 'Warfare in the Age of the Thirty Years War 1598–1648', in *European Warfare 1453–1815*, ed. Jeremy Black (Basingstoke: Macmillan, 1999), pp. 45–68.

Asche, Matthias, and Schindling, Anton, eds., *Das Strafgericht Gottes* (Münster: Aschendorff, 2002).

Atherton, Herbert M., 'George Townshend, Caricaturist', *Eighteenth-Century Studies* 4 (1971), pp. 437–46.

Atherton, Herbert M., 'George Townshend Revisited: The Politician as Caricaturist', *The Oxford Art Journal* 8 (1985), pp. 3–19.

Avery, Charles, 'The Duke of Marlborough as a Collector and Patron of Sculpture', in *The Evolution of English Collecting: Receptions of Italian Art in the Tudor and Stuart Periods*, ed. Edward Chaney (New Haven, CT: Yale University Press, 2003), pp. 427–64.

Aymes, Jean-René, 'Catéchismes français de la Révolution et catéchismes espagnols de la Guerre d'Indépendance: ébauche d'une comparaison', *La Révolution française: Les catéchismes républicains* (2009), http://lrf.revues.org/index117.html (accessed 16 September 2011).

Bannerman, Gordon E., *Merchants and the Military in Eighteenth-Century Britain: British Army Contracts and Domestic Supply, 1739–1763* (London: Pickering & Chatto, 2008).

Baugh, Daniel A., *British Naval Administration in the Age of Walpole* (Princeton, NJ: Princeton University Press, 1965).

Baumgold, Deborah, *Contract Theory in Historical Context: Essays on Grotius, Hobbes and Locke* (Boston: Brill, 2010).

Baxter, Douglas C., *Servants of the Sword: French Intendants of the Army, 1630–1670* (Urbana, IL: University of Illinois Press, 1976).

Bayley, A. R., *The Great Civil War in Dorset, 1642–1660* (Taunton: Barnicott & Pearce, 1910).

Beckett, Ian, *The Amateur Military Tradition, 1558–1945* (Manchester: Manchester University Press, 1991).

Beckett, Ian F. W., 'Total War', in *War, Peace and Social Change in Twentieth Century Europe*, ed. Clive Emsley, Arthur Marwick and Wendy Simpson (Milton Keynes: Open University Press, 1989), pp. 26–44.

Beckwith, Burnham P., *Total War: The Economic Theory of a War Economy* (Boston: Meador Publishing Company, 1943).

Bell, Christine, 'Transitional Justice, Interdisciplinarity and the State of the "Field" or "Non-Field"', *The International Journal of Transitional Justice* 3 (2009), pp. 5–27.

Bell, David A., *The First Total War: Napoleon's Europe and the Birth of Warfare as We Know It* (Boston: Houghton Mifflin, 2007).

Beller, E. A., *Propaganda in Germany during the Thirty Years War* (Princeton, NJ: Princeton University Press, 1940).

Bély, Lucien, 'L'occupation française dans les Pays-Bas pendant la guerre de Succession d'Autriche', in *Die besetzte res publica: Zum Verhältnis von ziviler Obrigkeit und militärischer Herrschaft in besetzten Gebieten vom Spätmittelalter bis zum 18. Jahrhundert*, ed. Markus Meumann and Jörg Rogge (Berlin: LIT, 2006), pp. 337–50.

Bennett, J., *French Connections: Napoleonic Prisoners of War on Parole in Leek, 1803–1814* (Leek: Churnet Valley Books, 1995).

Berghahn, Volker R., *Militarism. The History of an International Debate, 1861–1979* (Leamington Spa: Berg, 1981).

Bernard, Lénonce, *Les prisonniers de guerre du Premier Empire* (Paris: Editions Christian, 2000).

Best, Geoffrey, *Churchill and War* (London: Hambledon and London, 2005).

Best, Geoffrey, *Humanity in Warfare: The Modern History of the International Law of Armed Conflicts* (London: Weidenfeld and Nicolson, 1980).

Best, Geoffrey, 'The Place of Grotius in the Development of International Humanitarian Law', in *Grotius et l'Ordre Juridique International: Travaux du Colloque Hugo Grotius, Genève, 10–11 Novembre 1983*, ed. Alfred Dufour, Peter Haggenmacher and Jiří Toman (Lausanne: Payot, 1985), pp. 101–07.

Best, Geoffrey, *War and Law since 1945* (Oxford: Clarendon, 1994).

Biddell, Barbara, *Napoleonic Prisoners of War in and around Bishop's Waltham* (Barnham: Two Plus George, 2007).

Black, Jeremy, *European Warfare, 1660–1815* (London: UCL Press, 1994).

Black, Jeremy, 'A Military Revolution? A 1660–1792 Perspective', in *The Military Revolution Debate: Readings on the Military Transformation of Early Modern Europe*, ed. Clifford J. Rogers (Boulder, CO: Westview, 1995), pp. 95–114.

Black, Jeremy, *A Military Revolution? Military Change and European Society, 1550–1800* (Basingstoke: Macmillan, 1991).

Black, Jeremy, 'The Military Revolution II: Eighteenth-Century War', in *The Oxford History of Modern War*, ed. Charles Townshend (Oxford: Oxford University Press, 2000), pp. 40–54.

Black, Jeremy, *War in the Nineteenth Century, 1800–1914* (Cambridge: Polity, 2009).

Blanning, T. C. W., *The French Revolution in Germany. Occupation and Resistance in the Rhineland, 1792–1802* (Oxford: Clarendon Press, 1983).

Blanning, T. C. W., *The French Revolutionary Wars, 1787–1802* (London: Arnold, 1996).

Bluche, François, 'Connétable', 'Connétablie', in *Dictionnaire du Grand Siècle*, ed. François Bluche (Paris: Fayard, 1990), pp. 388–89.

Bodinier, Gilbert, 'Administration militaire', 'Colonel général', 'Conseil de guerre', in *Dictionnaire du Grand Siècle*, ed. François Bluche (Paris: Fayard, 1990), pp. 43–44, 352, 390.

Bodkin, E. H., 'The Minor Poetry of Hugo Grotius', *Transactions of the Grotius Society* 13 (1927), pp. 95–128.

Boemeke, Manfred F., Chickering, Roger, and Förster, Stig, eds., *Anticipating Total War. The German and American Experiences, 1871–1914* (Washington DC: German Historical Institute and Cambridge University Press, 1999).

Boime, Albert, *Art in an Age of Revolution 1750–1800: A Social History of Modern Art* (Chicago: University of Chicago Press, 1987).

Bois, Jean-Pierre, *Les guerres en Europe, 1494–1792* (Paris: Belin, 1993).

Bonehill, John, 'Laying Siege to the Royal Academy: Wright of Derby's View of Gibraltar at Robins's Rooms, Covent Garden, April 1785', *Art History* 30 (2007), pp. 521–44.

Bongie, Laurence L., *David Hume: Prophet of the Counter-Revolution* (Oxford: Clarendon Press, 1965).

Bonin, Pierre, 'L'exercice de la justice par le Colonel Général de l'infanterie française d'après les sources narratives et doctrinales', in *Combattre, gouverner, écrire: études réunies en l'honneur de Jean Chagniot* (Paris: Economica, 2003), pp. 197–216.

Bonney, Richard, ed., *The Rise of the Fiscal State in Europe, c. 1200–1815* (Oxford: Oxford University Press, 1999).

Bothe, Michael, 'Occupation after armistice; Occupation, belligerent; Occupation, pacific', in *Encyclopedia of Public International Law*, Vol. III, ed. Rudolf Bernhardt (Amsterdam: Elsevier, 1997), pp. 761–67.

Bourassin, Emmanuel, *La France anglaise, 1415–1453. Chronique d'une occupation* (Paris: Tallandier, 1981).

Bourke, Joanna, *An Intimate History of Killing: Face-to-Face Killing in Twentieth-Century Warfare* (London: Granta Books, 1999).

Braddick, Michael J., *State Formation in Early Modern England c. 1550–1700* (Cambridge: Cambridge University Press, 2000).

Brett–James, Antony, *Life in Wellington's Army* (London: Allen & Unwin, 1972).

Brewer, John, *The Sinews of Power: War, Money, and the English State, 1688–1783* (London: Routledge, 1989).

Broers, Michael, 'The Concept of "Total War" in the Revolutionary-Napoleonic Period', *War in History* 15 (2008), pp. 247–68.

Broers, Michael, *Napoleon's Other War: Bandits, Rebels and their Pursuers in the Age of Revolutions* (Oxford: Peter Lang, 2010).

Brown, Howard, *Ending the French Revolution: Violence, Justice and Repression from the Terror to Napoleon* (Charlottesville, VA: University of Virginia Press, 2006).

Brumfitt, J. H., 'Scotland and the French Enlightenment', in *The Age of the Enlightenment: Studies Presented to Theodore Besterman*, ed. W. H. Barber (Edinburgh: Oliver & Boyd, 1967), pp. 318–29.

Buckley, John, *Air Power in the Age of Total War* (London: UCL Press, 1999).

Bull, Hedley, 'The Importance of Grotius in the Study of International Relations', in *Hugo Grotius and International Relations*, ed. Hedley Bull, Benedict Kingsbury and Adam Roberts (Oxford: Clarendon Press, 1990), pp. 65–93.

Bull, Hedley, Kingsbury, Benedict, and Roberts, Adam, eds., *Hugo Grotius and International Relations* (Oxford: Clarendon Press, 1990).

Buzard, James, 'The Grand Tour and After (1660–1840)', in *The Cambridge Companion to Travel Writing*, ed. Peter Hulme and Tim Youngs (Cambridge: Cambridge University Press, 2002), pp. 37–52.

Cameron, Joy, *Prisons and Punishment in Scotland from the Middle Ages to the Present* (Edinburgh: Canongate, 1983).

Cardwell, John, *Arts and Arms: Literature, Politics and Patriotism During the Seven Years War* (Manchester: Manchester University Press, 2004).

Carl, Horst, 'Französische Besatzungsherrschaft im Alten Reich: Völkerrechtliche, verwaltungs- und erfahrungsgeschichtliche Kontinuitätslinien französischer Okkupationen am Niederrhein im 17. und 18. Jahrhundert', *Francia* 23 (1996), pp. 33–64.

Carl, Horst, 'Militärische Okkupation im 18. Jahrhundert', in *Die besetzte res publica: Zum Verhältnis von ziviler Obrigkeit und militärischer Herrschaft in besetzten Gebieten vom Spätmittelalter bis zum 18. Jahrhundert*, ed. Markus Meumann and Jörg Rogge (Berlin: LIT, 2006), pp. 351–62.

Carl, Horst, *Okkupation und Regionalismus. Die preußischen Westprovinzen im Siebenjährigen Krieg* (Mainz: Philipp von Zabern, 1993).

Carlton, Charles, *Going to the Wars: The Experience of the British Civil Wars, 1638–1651* (London: Routledge, 1992).

Carlton, Charles, 'The Impact of the Fighting', in *The Impact of the English Civil War*, ed. John Morrill (London: Collins & Brown, 1991), pp. 17–31.

Carlton, Eric, *Occupation: The Policies and Practices of Military Conquerors* (London: Routledge, 1992).

Carter, Philip, 'An "Effeminate" or "Efficient" Nation? Masculinity and Eighteenth-Century Social Documentary', *Textual Practice* 11 (1997), pp. 429–43.

Ceadel, Martin, *The Origins of War Prevention: The British Peace Movement and International Relations, 1730–1854* (Oxford: Oxford University Press, 1996).

Chagniot, Jean, 'Autorité militaire et justice à Paris au XVIIIe siècle', in *L'armée et la ville dans l'Europe du Nord et du Nord-Ouest. Du XVe siècle à nos jours*, ed. Philippe Bragard (Louvain-la-Neuve: Academia Bruylant, 2006), pp. 211–21.

Chagniot, Jean, 'Commissaires des guerres', 'Justice militaire', in *Dictionnaire de l'Ancien Régime*, ed. Lucien Bély (Paris: Presses Universitaires de France, 1996), pp. 295–96, 711–12.

Chagniot, Jean, 'Les progrès de l'administration', in *Histoire Militaire de la France*, Vol. III, ed. Jean Delmas (Paris: Presses Universitaires de France, 1992), pp. 29–54.

Chalklin, C. W., 'South-East', in *The Cambridge Urban History of Britain Vol. II, 1540–1840*, ed. Peter Clark (Cambridge: Cambridge University Press, 2000), pp. 49–66.

Chandler, David, *Marlborough as Military Commander* (London: Batsford, 1973).

Chandos, John, ed., *In God's Name: Examples of Preaching in England from the Act of Supremacy to the Act of Uniformity, 1534–1662* (London: Hutchinson, 1971).

Chet, Guy, *Conquering the American Wilderness: The Triumph of European Warfare in the Colonial Northeast* (Amherst, MA: University of Massachusetts Press, 2003).

Chickering, Roger, 'Total War: The Use and Abuse of a Concept', in *Anticipating Total War: The German and American Experiences, 1871–1914*, ed. Roger Chickering, Stig Förster and Manfred F. Boemeke (Washington DC: Cambridge University Press, 1999), pp. 13–28.

Chickering, Roger, and Förster, Stig, eds., *Great War, Total War: Combat and Mobilization on the Western Front, 1914–1918* (Cambridge: Cambridge University Press, 2000).

Chickering, Roger, and Förster, Stig, eds., *War in an Age of Revolution, 1775–1815* (Cambridge: Cambridge University Press, 2010).

Chickering, Roger, Förster, Stig, and Greiner, Bernd, eds., *A World at Total War: Global Conflict and the Politics of Destruction, 1937–1945* (Washington DC: Cambridge University Press, 2005).

Childs, John, *Armies and Warfare in Europe, 1648–1789* (Manchester: Manchester University Press, 1982).

Childs, John, *The Army of Charles II* (London: Routledge, 1976).

Childs, John, 'The Laws of War in Seventeenth-Century Europe and their Application during the Jacobite War in Ireland, 1688–91', in *Age of Atrocity: Violence and Political Conflict in Early Modern Ireland*, ed. David Edwards, Pádraig Lenihan and Clodagh Tait (Dublin: Four Courts, 2007), pp. 283–300.

Childs, John, *Warfare in the Seventeenth Century* (London: Cassell, 2003).

Churchill, Winston S., *Marlborough: His Life and Times*, Vol. II (London: George G. Harrap & Co., 1934).

Clark, Christopher, *Iron Kingdom: The Rise and Downfall of Prussia, 1600–1947* (London: Allen Lane, 2006).

Clark, Peter, *British Clubs and Societies c.1580–1800: The Origins of an Associational World* (Oxford: Clarendon Press, 2000).

Clay, Stephen, 'Le brigandage en Provence du Directoire au Consulat, 1795–1802', in *Du Directoire au Consulat. 3: Brumaire dans l'histoire du lien politique et de l'État-Nation*, ed. Jean-Pierre Jessenne (Lille: Centre de Recherche sur l'Histoire de l'Europe du Nord-Ouest, 2001), pp. 67–89.

Claydon, Tony, *William III and the Godly Revolution* (Cambridge: Cambridge University Press, 1996).

Clode, Charles M., *The Administration of Justice under Military and Martial Law* (London: John Murray, 1874).

Clode, Charles M., *The Military Forces of the Crown: Their Administration and Government*, 2 vols. (London: John Murray, 1869).

Cogliano, F. D., "'We All Hoisted the American Flag'": National Identity among American Prisoners in Britain during the American Revolution', *Journal of American Studies* 32 (1998), pp. 19–37.

Cohen, Michèle, *Fashioning Masculinity: National Identity and Language in the Eighteenth Century* (London: Routledge, 1996).

Cohen, S. S., *Yankee Sailors in British Gaols: Prisoners of War at Forton and Mill, 1777–1783* (London: Associated University Presses, 1995).

Colclough, Stephen, *Consuming Texts: Readers and Reading Communities, 1695–1870* (Basingstoke: Palgrave Macmillan, 2007).

Colley, Linda, *Britons: Forging the Nation, 1707–1837* (New Haven, CT: Yale University Press, 1992).

Contamine, Philippe, 'The Growth of State Control: Practices of War, 1300–1800: Ransom and Booty', in *War and Competition between States*, ed. Philippe Contamine (Oxford: Clarendon, 2000), pp. 163–93.

Conway, Stephen, *The British Isles and the War of American Independence* (Oxford: Oxford University Press, 2000).

Conway, Stephen, 'British Mobilization in the War of American Independence', *Historical Research* 72 (1999), pp. 58–76.

Conway, Stephen, "'The Great Mischeif Complain'd Of'": Reflections on the Misconduct of British Soldiers in the Revolutionary War', *The William and Mary Quarterly* 47 (1990), pp. 370–90.

Conway, Stephen, "'Like the Irish'? Volunteer Corps and Volunteering in Britain during the American War', in *Britain and America Go to War: The Impact of War and Warfare in Anglo-America, 1754–1815*, ed. Julie Flavell and Stephen Conway (Gainesville, FL: University Press of Florida, 2004), pp. 143–69.

Conway, Stephen, 'Locality, Metropolis, and Nation: The Impact of the Military Camps in England during the American War', *History* 82 (1997), pp. 547–62.

Conway, Stephen, 'The Mobilization of Manpower for Britain's Mid-Eighteenth-Century Wars', *Historical Research* 77 (2004), pp. 377–404.

Conway, Stephen, 'The Politics of British Military and Naval Mobilization, 1775–1783', *English Historical Review* 112 (1997), pp. 1179–1201.

Conway, Stephen, *War, State, and Society in Mid-Eighteenth-Century Britain and Ireland* (Oxford: Oxford University Press, 2006).

Conze, Werner, Stumpf, Reinhard, and Geyer, Michael, 'Militarismus', in *Geschichtliche Grundbegriffe*, Vol. IV, ed. Otto Brunner, Werner Conze and Reinhart Koselleck (Stuttgart: Steiner, 1978), pp. 1–48.

Corfe Castle, Dorset (National Trust, 1999).

Cornette, Joël, *Le roi de guerre: essai sur la souveraineté dans la France du Grand Siècle* (Paris: Payot & Rivages, 1993).

Corvisier, André, *Armies and Societies in Europe, 1494–1789* (London: Indiana University Press, 1979).

Corvisier, André, 'Guerilla Warfare', in *A Dictionary of Military History*, ed. André Corvisier, English edition ed. and rev. John Childs (Oxford: Blackwell, 1994), pp. 337–39.

Corvisier, André, 'Louis XIV, la guerre et la naissance de l'armée moderne', in *Histoire militaire de la France, vol. 1: Des origines à 1715*, ed. Philippe Contamine (Paris: Presses Universitaires de France, 1992), pp. 383–413.

Corvisier, André, 'La paix nécessaire mais incertaine, 1598–1635', in *Histoire militaire de la France, vol. 1: Des origines à 1715*, ed. Philippe Contamine (Paris: Presses Universitaires de France, 1992), pp. 331–51.

Corvisier, André, 'Renouveau militaire et misères de la guerre, 1635–1659', in *Histoire militaire de la France, vol. 1: Des origines à 1715*, ed. Philippe Contamine (Paris: Presses Universitaires de France, 1992), pp. 353–82.

Cramer, Kevin, *The Thirty Years War and German Memory in the Nineteenth Century* (Lincoln, NE: University of Nebraska, 2007).

Crane, Arthur, *Napoleonic Prisoners of War in Ashby de la Zouch* (Ashby-de-la-Zouch: Ashby-de-la-Zouch Museum, 1999).

Craske, Matthew, 'Joseph Wright Scholarship: A Revisionist View', unpublished paper delivered at the Wright of Derby Symposium organised by the Eighteenth-Century Worlds Research Centre (University of Liverpool) & Walker Art Gallery, 16–17 November 2007, Merseyside Maritime Museum, Liverpool.

Crimmin, Patricia K., 'Prisoners of War and British Port Communities, 1793–1815', *The Northern Mariner/Le marin du nord* 6 (1996), pp. 17–27.

Daly, Gavin, 'A Dirty, Indolent, Priest-Ridden City: British Soldiers in Lisbon during the Peninsular War, 1808–1813', *History* 94 (2009), pp. 461–82.

Daly, Gavin, 'Napoleon's Lost Legions: French Prisoners of War in Britain, 1803–1814', *History* 89 (2004), pp. 361–80.

Davis, J. C., *Oliver Cromwell* (London: Arnold, 2001).

Dawson, Deidre, and Morère, Pierre, eds., *Scotland and France in the Enlightenment* (Lewisburg, PA: Bucknell University Press, 2004).

Deinert, Christa, 'Die schwedische Epoche in Franken von 1631–35', unpublished PhD thesis, University of Würzburg, 1966.

Demay, Charles, 'Les volontaires auxerrois de 1792 aux armées de la République', *Bulletin de la Société des sciences historiques et naturelles de l'Yonne* 28 (1874), pp. 523–87.

Denys, Catherine, 'L'occupation hollandaise à Lille de 1708–1713', in *Die besetzte res publica: Zum Verhältnis von ziviler Obrigkeit und militärischer Herrschaft in besetzten Gebieten vom Spätmittelalter bis zum 18. Jahrhundert*, ed. Markus Meumann and Jörg Rogge (Berlin: LIT, 2006), pp. 315–36.

Denys, Catherine, and Paresys, Isabelle, *Les anciens Pays-Bas à l'époque moderne (1404–1815). Belgique, France du Nord, Pays-Bas* (Paris: Ellipses, 2007).

Dickinson, H. T., 'The Earl of Peterborough's Campaign in Valencia, 1706', *Journal of the Society for Army Historical Research* 45 (1967), pp. 35–52.

Diefendorf, Jeffry M., *Businessmen and Politics in the Rhineland, 1789–1834* (Princeton, NJ: Princeton University Press, 1980).

Donagan, Barbara, 'Codes of Conduct in the English Civil War', *Past and Present* 118 (1988), pp. 65–95.

Donagan, Barbara, *War in England, 1642–1649* (Oxford: Oxford University Press, 2008).

Donald, Diana, *The Age of Caricature: Satirical Prints in the Reign of George III* (New Haven, CT: Yale University Press, 1996).

Donald, Diana, '"Calumny and Caricatura": Eighteenth-Century Political Prints and the Case of George Townshend', *Art History* 6 (1983), pp. 44–66.

Dorlan, A., *Notices historiques sur l'Alsace et principalement sur la ville de Schlestadt*, 2 vols. (Sélestat: L. Reiffinger, 1843).

Downing, B. M., *The Military Revolution and Political Change: Origins of Democracy and Autocracy in Early Modern Europe* (Princeton, NJ: Princeton University Press, 1992).

Draper, G. I. A. D., 'Grotius's Place in the Development of Legal Ideas about War', in *Hugo Grotius and International Relations*, ed. Hedley Bull, Benedict Kingsbury and Adam Roberts (Oxford: Clarendon Press, 1990), pp. 177–207.

Dreisziger, N. F., ed., *Mobilization for Total War: The Canadian, American, and British Experience, 1914–1918, 1939–1945* (Waterloo, Ontario: Wilfrid Laurier University Press, 1981).

Drilleau, Bernard, 'La maréchaussée aux XVIIᵉ et XVIIIᵉ siècles', unpublished PhD thesis, on microfiche, University of Rennes, 1985.

Duchhardt, Heinz, *Krieg und Frieden im Zeitalter Ludwigs XIV* (Düsseldorf: Schwann, 1987).

Dudink, Stefan, and Hagemann, Karen, 'Masculinity in Politics and War in the Age of Democratic Revolutions, 1750–1850', in *Masculinities in Politics and War: Gendering Modern History*, ed. Stefan Dudink, Karen Hagemann and John Tosh (Manchester: Manchester University Press, 2004), pp. 3–21.

Duffy, Christopher, *The '45: Bonnie Prince Charlie and the Untold Story of the Jacobite Rising* (London: Cassell, 2003).

Duffy, Christopher, *The Military Experience in the Age of Reason* (London: Routledge and Kegan Paul, 1987).

Duffy, Michael, *The Englishman and the Foreigner* (Cambridge: Chadwyck Healey, 1986).

Dupont, Étienne, *Les prisonniers de guerre anglais en France au XVIIIme siècle d'après des documents originaux inédits* (Paris: Boyveau et Chevillet, 1915).

Egerton, Judy, *Wright of Derby* (London: Tate Gallery, 1990).

Egler, Anna, *Die Spanier in der linksrheinischen Pfalz, 1620–1632: Invasion, Verwaltung, Rekatholisierung* (Mainz: Ges. f. Mittelrhein. Kirchengeschichte, 1971).

Elster, Jon, *Closing the Books: Transitional Justice in Historical Perspective*, (Cambridge: Cambridge University Press, 2004).

Ernstberger, Anton, *Wallenstein als Volkswirt im Herzogtum Friedland* (Reichenbach: Fr. Kraus, 1929).

Esdaile, Charles, *The Peninsular War: A New History* (London: Penguin, 2003).

Esdaile, Charles J., *Fighting Napoleon: Guerrillas, Bandits and Adventurers in Spain, 1808–1814* (New Haven, CT: Yale University Press, 2004).

Esdaile, Charles J., 'Patriots, Partisans and Land Pirates in Retrospect', in *Popular Resistance in the French Wars: Patriots, Partisans and Land Pirates*, ed. Charles J. Esdaile (Basingstoke: Palgrave Macmillan, 2005), pp. 1–24.

Favret, Mary A., 'Coming Home: The Public Spaces of Romantic War', *Studies in Romanticism* 33 (1994), pp. 539–48.

Favret, Mary A., *War at a Distance: Romanticism and the Making of Modern Wartime* (Princeton, NJ: Princeton University Press, 2010).

Fergus, David, 'Frenchmen in the Borders', *Scots Magazine* ns 91 (June, 1969), pp. 278–84.

Fergus, Jan, *Provincial Readers in Eighteenth-Century England* (Oxford: Oxford University Press, 2006).

Fiedler, Siegfried, *Kriegswesen und Kriegführung im Zeitalter der Kabinettskriege* (Koblenz: Bernard & Graefe, 1986).

Figgis, John N., *Political Thought from Gerson to Grotius 1414–1625* (Kitchener, Ontario: Batoche, 1999).

Fisch, Jörg, *Die europäische Expansion und das Völkerrecht* (Stuttgart: Steiner, 1984).

Fleishman, Avrom, *The English Historical Novel: Walter Scott to Virginia Woolf* (Baltimore, MD: Johns Hopkins University Press, 1971).

Förster, Stig, and Nagler, Jörg, eds., *On the Road to Total War: The American Civil War and the*

German Wars of Unification, 1861–1871 (Washington DC: German Historical Institute and Cambridge University Press, 1997).

Forbes, J. Macbeth, 'The French Prisoners of War in the Border Towns, 1811–1814', *Transactions of the Hawick Archaeological Society* (1912), pp. 1–16.

Fordham, Douglas, 'Organizing the Avant-Garde: London Artists and the English Militia in the 1750's', *The European Spectator* 5 (2003), pp. 59–82.

Foreman, Amanda, 'A Politician's Politician: Georgiana, Duchess of Devonshire and the Whig Party', in *Gender in Eighteenth-Century England: Roles, Representations, and Responsibilities*, ed. Hannah Barker and Elaine Chalus (Harlow: Longman, 1997), pp. 179–204.

Forrest, Alan, *Conscripts and Deserters: The Army and French Society during the Revolution and Empire* (Oxford: Oxford University Press, 1989).

Forrest, Alan, *Napoleon's Men: The Soldiers of the Revolution and Empire* (London: Hambledon, 2002).

Forrest, Alan, 'The Nation in Arms I: The French Wars', in *The Oxford History of Modern War*, ed. Charles Townshend (Oxford: Oxford University Press, 2000), pp. 55–73.

Forrest, Alan, *The Revolution in Provincial France: Aquitaine, 1789–1799* (Oxford: Clarendon Press, 1996).

Forrest, Alan, 'The Ubiquitous Brigand: The Politics and Language of Repression', in *Popular Resistance in the French Wars: Patriots, Partisans and Land Pirates*, ed. Charles J. Esdaile (Basingstoke: Palgrave, 2005), pp. 25–43.

Forrest, Alan, Hagemann, Karen, and Rendall, Jane, 'Introduction: Nations in Arms – People at War', in *Soldiers, Citizens, and Civilians: Experiences and Perceptions of the Revolutionary and Napoleonic Wars, 1790–1820*, ed. Alan Forrest, Karen Hagemann and Jane Rendall (Basingstoke: Palgrave Macmillan, 2009), pp. 1–19.

Forrest, Alan, Hagemann, Karen, and Rendall, Jane, eds., *Soldiers, Citizens and Civilians: Experiences and Perceptions of the Revolutionary and Napoleonic Wars, 1790–1820* (Basingstoke: Palgrave Macmillan, 2009).

François, Etienne, 'Die Volksbildung am Mittelrhein in ausgehenden 18. Jahrhundert: Eine Untersuchung über den vermeintlichen "Bildungsrückstand" der katholischen Bevölkerung Deutschlands im Ancien Régime', *Jahrbuch für westdeutsche Landesgeschichte* 3 (1977), pp. 277–304.

Fraser, Ronald, *Napoleon's Cursed War: Spanish Popular Resistance in the Peninsular War, 1808–1814* (London: Verso, 2008).

Friedrichs, Christopher R., *Urban Society in an Age of War: Nördlingen, 1580–1720* (Princeton, NJ: Princeton University Press, 1979).

Fritzsche, Peter, *Stranded in the Present: Modern Time and the Melancholy of History* (Cambridge, MA, and London: Harvard University Press, 2004).

Fuller, J. F. C., *The Conduct of War, 1789–1961: A Study of the Impact of the French, Industrial and Russian Revolutions on War and its Conduct* (London: Eyre & Spottiswoode, 1961).

Furukawa, Terumi, 'Punishment', in *A Normative Approach to War: Peace, War and Justice in Hugo Grotius*, ed. Onuma Yasuaki (Oxford: Clarendon Press, 1993), pp. 221–43.

Gaber, Stéphane, *La Lorraine meurtrie: les malheurs de la Guerre de Trente Ans* (Nancy: Presses Universitaires de Nancy, Editions Serpénoise, 1991).

Gaskill, Howard, ed., *The Reception of Ossian in Europe* (London: Thoemmes Continuum, 2004).

Gentles, Ian, 'The Sales of Crown Lands during the English Revolution', *The Economic History Review* 26 (1973), pp. 614–35.

George, M. Dorothy, *English Political Caricature: A Study of Opinion and Propaganda*, 2 vols. (Oxford: Clarendon Press, 1959).

George, M. Dorothy, *Hogarth to Cruikshank: Social Change in Graphic Satire* (New York: Walker, 1967).

Geyl, Pieter, 'Grotius', *Transactions of the Grotius Society* 12 (1926), pp. 81–97.

Gibson, Charles, ed., *The Black Legend: Anti-Spanish Attitudes in the Old World and the New* (New York: Knopf, 1971).

Giebel, Wieland, *Die Franzosen in Berlin, 1806–1808* (Berlin: Berlin Story Buchandlung & Verlag, 2006).

Gilbert, Arthur N., 'Law and Honour among Eighteenth-Century British Army Officers', *The Historical Journal* 19 (1976), pp. 75–87.

Gildea, Robert, *Marianne in Chains: Daily Life in the Heart of France during the German Occupation* (New York: Metropolitan Books, 2002).

Gillis, John R., ed., *The Militarization of the Western World* (New Brunswick, NJ: Rutgers University Press, 1989).

Gleixner, Ulrike, and Gray, Marion W., eds., *Gender in Transition. Discourse and Practice in German-Speaking Europe, 1750–1830* (Ann Arbor, MI: University of Michigan Press, 2006).

Glete, Jan, *War and the State in Early Modern Europe: Spain, the Dutch Republic and Sweden as Fiscal–Military States, 1500–1660* (London: Routledge, 2002).

Goetze, Sigmund, *Die Politik des Schwedischen Reichskanzlers Axel Oxenstierna gegenüber Kaiser und Reich* (Kiel: Kommissionsverlag Mühlau, 1971).

Goodman, Dena, *Becoming a Woman in the Age of Letters* (Ithaca, NY, and London: Cornell University Press, 2009).

Gorsky, Martin, 'The Growth and Distribution of English Friendly Societies in the Early Nineteenth Century', *Economic History Review* 51 (1998), pp. 489–511.

Gould, Eliga H., 'To Strengthen the King's Hands: Dynastic Legitimacy, Militia Reform, and Ideas of National Unity in England, 1745–1760', *The Historical Journal* 34 (1991), pp. 329–48.

Greaves, Richard L., *Deliver Us From Evil: The Radical Underground in Britain, 1660–1663* (Oxford: Oxford University Press, 1986).

Grenby, Matthew O., *The Anti-Jacobin Novel: British Conservatism and the French Revolution* (Cambridge: Cambridge University Press, 2001).

Grimsley, Mark, and Rogers, Clifford J., eds., *Civilians in the Path of War* (Lincoln, NE: University of Nebraska Press, 2002).

Guiomar, Jean-Yves, *L'invention de la guerre totale: XVIIIe–XXe siècle* (Paris: Le Félin, 2004).

Gunn, Steven, Grummitt, David, and Cools, Hans, 'War and the State in Early Modern Europe: Widening the Debate', *War in History* 15 (2008), pp. 371–88.

Gutmann, Myron P., *War and Rural Life in the Early Modern Low Countries* (Princeton, NJ: Princeton University Press, 1980).

Hagemann, Karen, *"Männlicher Muth und teutsche Ehre". Nation, Militär und Geschlecht zur Zeit der Antinapoleonischen Kriege Preußens* (Paderborn: Schöningh, 2002).

Hagemann, Karen, 'Occupation, Mobilization and Politics: The Anti-Napoleonic Wars in Prussian Experience, Memory and Historiography', *Central European History* 39 (2006), pp. 580–610.

Hagemann, Karen, '"Unimaginable Horror and Misery": The Battle of Leipzig in October 1813 in Civilian Experience and Perception', in *Soldiers, Citizens and Civilians: Experiences and Perceptions of the Revolutionary and Napoleonic Wars, 1790–1820*, ed. Alan Forrest, Karen Hagemann and Jane Rendall (Basingstoke: Palgrave, 2009), pp. 157–78.

Haggenmacher, Peter, 'Grotius and Gentili', in *Hugo Grotius and International Relations*, ed.

Hedley Bull, Benedict Kingsbury and Adam Roberts (Oxford: Clarendon Press, 1990), pp. 133–76.

Haggenmacher, Peter, *Grotius et la doctrine de la guerre juste* (Paris: Presses Universitaires de France, 1983).

Haggenmacher, Peter, 'L'occupation militaire en droit international: genèse et profil d'une institution juridique', *Relations internationales* 79 (1994), pp. 285–301.

Hallett, Mark, *The Spectacle of Difference: Graphic Satire in the Age of Hogarth* (New Haven, CT: Yale University Press, 1999).

Harari, Yuval Noah, *The Ultimate Experience: Battlefield Revelations and the Making of Modern War Culture, 1450–2000* (Basingstoke: Palgrave Macmillan, 2008).

Hardacre, Paul, *The Royalists during the Puritan Revolution* (The Hague: Martinus Nijhoff, 1956).

Harland-Jacobs, Jessica, *Builders of Empire: Freemasonry and British Imperialism, 1717–1927* (Chapel Hill, NC: University of North Carolina Press, 2007).

Harris, Eileen, *The Townshend Album* (London: HMSO, 1974).

Harrison, Ross, *Hobbes, Locke, and Confusion's Masterpiece: An Examination of Seventeenth-Century Political Philosophy* (Cambridge: Cambridge University Press, 2003).

Haythornthwaite, Philip J., *The Armies of Wellington* (London: Brockhampton Press, 1998).

Heering, Jan–Paul, *Hugo Grotius as Apologist for the Christian Religion: A Study of His Work De Veritate Religionis Christianae, 1640*, trans. J. C. Grayson (Leiden: Brill, 2004).

Henderson, Nicholas, *Prince Eugen of Savoy* (London: Weidenfeld and Nicolson, 1964).

Hendrix, Scott, 'In the Army: Women, Camp Followers and Gender Roles in the British Army in the French and Indian Wars, 1755–1765', in *A Soldier and a Woman: Sexual Integration in the Military*, ed. Gerald J. DeGroot and Corinna M. Peniston-Bird (Harlow: Longman, 2000), pp. 33–48.

Hentschel, Uwe, 'Krieg als Unterhaltung in deutschen Reiseberichten über den I. Koalitionskrieg', *Orbis Litterarum* 58 (2003), pp. 335–52.

Herres, Jürgen, '"Und nenne Euch Preußen!" Die Anfänge preußischer Herrschaft am Rhein im 19. Jahrhundert', in *Fremde Herrscher – fremdes Volk. Inklusions- und Exklusionsfiguren bei Herrschaftswechseln in Europa*, ed. Helga Schnabel-Schüle and Andreas Gestrich (Frankfurt am Main and Oxford: Lang, 2006), pp. 103–39.

Hesse, Carla, *Publishing and Cultural Politics in Revolutionary Paris, 1789–1810* (Berkeley, CA: University of California Press, 1991).

Hippel, Wolfgang von, *Das Herzogtum Württemberg zur Zeit des Dreißigjährigen Krieges im Spiegel von Steuer- und Kriegsschadensberichten, 1629–1655* (Stuttgart: Kohlhammer, 2009).

Hobsbawm, E. J., *Bandits* (London: Weidenfeld and Nicolson, 1969).

Hochedlinger, Michael, *Austria's Wars of Emergence: War, State and Society in the Habsburg Monarchy, 1683–1797* (London: Longman, 2003).

Holk, L. E. van, and Roelofsen, C. G., eds., *Grotius Reader: A Reader for Students of International Law and Legal History* (The Hague: T. M. C. Asser Instituut, 1983).

Hook, Andrew, 'The French Taste for Scottish Literary Romanticism', in *Scotland and France in the Enlightenment*, ed. Deidre Dawson and Pierre Morère (Lewisburg, PA: Bucknell University Press, 2004), pp. 90–107.

Hopes, Jeffrey, 'Staging National Identities: The English Theater Viewed from France in the Mid–Eighteenth Century', in *'Better in France?' The Circulation of Ideas Across the Channel in the Eighteenth Century*, ed. Frédéric Ogée (Lewisburg, PA: Bucknell University Press, 2005), pp. 203–30.

Hopkin, David, 'The World Turned Upside Down: Female Soldiers in the French Armies of the Revolutionary and Napoleonic Wars', in *Soldiers, Citizens and Civilians: Experiences and Perceptions of the Revolutionary and Napoleonic Wars, 1790–1820*, ed. Alan Forrest, Karen Hagemann and Jane Rendall (Basingstoke: Palgrave Macmillan, 2009), pp. 77–95.

Hopkin, David, Lagadec, Yann, and Perréon, Stéphane, 'The Experience and Culture of War in the Eighteenth Century: The British Raids on the Breton Coast, 1758', *French Historical Studies* 31 (2008), pp. 193–227.

Houlding, J. A., *Fit for Service: The Training of the British Army, 1715–1795* (Oxford: Clarendon Press, 1981).

Houtte, Hubert van, *Les occupations étrangères en Belgique sous l'ancien régime*, 2 vols. (Ghent: Van Rysselberghe & Rombaut, 1930).

Howard, Michael, Andreopoulos, George J., and Shulman, Mark R., eds., *The Laws of War. Constraints on Warfare in the Western World* (New Haven, CT: Yale University Press, 1994).

Hunt, Tamara, *Defining John Bull: Political Caricature and National Identity in Late Georgian England* (Aldershot: Ashgate, 2003).

Hutton, Ronald, *Charles the Second: King of England, Scotland, and Ireland* (Oxford: Oxford University Press, 1991).

Hutton, Ronald, *The Restoration: A Political and Religious History of England and Wales, 1658–1667* (Oxford: Oxford University Press, 1985).

Innes, Joanna, 'The "Mixed Economy of Welfare" in Early Modern England: Assessments of the Options from Hale to Malthus (c.1683–1803)', in *Charity, Self–Interest and Welfare in the English Past*, ed. Martin Daunton (London: UCL Press, 1996), pp. 139–80.

Jakubowski-Tiessen, Manfred, and Lehmann, Helmut, eds., *Um Himmels Willen: Religion in Katastrophenzeiten* (Göttingen: Vandenhoeck & Ruprecht, 2003).

James, Robert D., 'The Trials of the Regicides: Transitional Justice, Memory, and Law Restoration England', unpublished MPhil dissertation, University of Cambridge, Seeley Library, 2008.

James, Trevor, *Prisoners of War in Dartmoor Towns: French and American Officers on Parole, 1803–1815* (Chudleigh: Orchard Publications, 2000).

Jasanoff, Maya, *Edge of Empire: Conquest and Collecting in the East, 1750–1850* (London: Fourth Estate, 2006).

Jeffery, Renée, *Hugo Grotius in International Thought* (Gordonsville, VA: Palgrave Macmillan, 2006).

Jeismann, Michael, *Das Vaterland der Feinde: Studien zum nationalen Feindbegriff und Selbstverständnis in Deutschland und Frankreich 1792–1918* (Stuttgart: Klett–Cotta, 1992).

Johnson, Hubert C., *Frederick the Great and his Officials* (New Haven, CT: Yale University Press, 1975).

Johnson, Trevor, *Magistrates, Madonnas and Miracles. The Counter Reformation in the Upper Palatinate* (Aldershot: Ashgate, 2009).

Jones, D. W., *War and Economy in the Age of William III and Marlborough* (Oxford: Basil Blackwell, 1988).

Jones, Robert W., 'Notes on *The Camp*: Women, Effeminacy and the Military in Late Eighteenth-Century Literature', *Textual Practice* 11 (1997), pp. 463–76.

Kaiser, Michael, '"Ärger als der Türck": Kriegsgreuel und ihre Funktionalisierung in der Zeit des Dreißigjährigen Kriegs', in *Kriegsgreuel: Die Entgrenzung der Gewalt in kriegerischen Konflikten vom Mittelalter bis ins 20. Jahrhundert*, ed. Sönke Neitzel and Daniel Hohrath (Paderborn: Ferdinand Schöningh, 2008), pp. 155–83.

Kaiser, Michael, 'Maximilian I. von Bayern und der Krieg', *Zeitschrift für bayerische Landesgeschichte* 65 (2002), pp. 69–99.

Kamen, Henry, *Imagining Spain. Historical Myth and National Identity* (New Haven, CT: Yale University Press, 2008).

Kanter, Sanford, 'Exposing the Myth of the Franco-Prussian War', *War and Society* 4 (1986), pp. 13–30.

Kappelhoff, Bernd, *Absolutistisches Regiment oder Ständeherrschaft? Landesherr und Landstände in Ostfriesland im ersten Drittel des 18. Jahrhunderts* (Hildesheim: Lax–Verlag, 1982).

Kasai, Naoya, 'The Laws of War', in *A Normative Approach to War: Peace, War and Justice in Hugo Grotius*, ed. Onuma Yasuaki (Oxford: Clarendon Press, 1993), pp. 244–75.

Keeble, N. H., *The Restoration: England in the 1660s* (Oxford: Blackwell, 2002).

Keen, M. H., *The Laws of War in the Late Middle Ages* (London: Routledge and Kegan Paul, 1965).

Kennedy, Emmet, *A Cultural History of the French Revolution* (New Haven, CT: Yale University Press, 1989).

Kennett, Lee, *The French Armies in the Seven Years' War: A Study in Military Organization and Administration* (Durham, NC: Duke University Press, 1967).

Kenny, Anthony, *Aquinas* (Oxford: Oxford University Press, 1980).

Kinsella, Helen M., 'Gendering Grotius: Sex and Sex Difference in the Laws of War', *Political Theory* 34 (2006), pp. 161–91.

Kintzinger, Martin, 'Der Auftrag der Jungfrau: Das besetzte Frankreich im Hundertjährigen Krieg', in *Die besetzte res publica: Zum Verhältnis von ziviler Obrigkeit und militärischer Herrschaft in besetzten Gebieten vom Spätmittelalter bis zum 18. Jahrhundert*, ed. Markus Meumann and Jörg Rogge (Berlin: LIT, 2006), pp. 63–88.

Kitchen, Martin, *The Silent Dictatorship. The Politics of the German High Command under Hindenburg and Ludendorff, 1916–1918* (London: Croom Helm, 1976).

Klingender, Francis D., *Art and the Industrial Revolution* (London: Carrington, 1947).

Knight, W. S. M., *The Life and Works of Hugo Grotius* (London: Sweet & Maxwell, 1925).

Kroener, Bernhard, *Les routes et les étapes. Die Versorgung der französischen Armeen in Nordostfrankreich (1635–1661). Ein Beitrag zur Verwaltungsgeschichte des Ancien Régime* (Münster: Aschendorff, 1980).

Kühlich, Frank, *Die Deutschen Soldaten im Krieg von 1870–71* (Frankfurt am Main: Lang, 1995).

Kunisch, Johannes, *Der kleine Krieg: Studien zum Heerwesen des Absolutismus* (Wiesbaden: Steiner 1973).

Lacey, Andrew, *The Cult of King Charles the Martyr* (Woodbridge: Boydell Press, 2003).

Lafon, Jean-Marc, *L'Andalousie et Napoléon: contre-insurrection, collaboration et résistances dans le midi de l'Espagne, 1808–1812* (Paris: Nouveau Monde Editions, 2007).

Laidlaw, James, ed., *The Auld Alliance: France and Scotland over 700 Years* (Edinburgh: University of Edinburgh, 1999).

Lambourne, Wendy, 'Transitional Justice and Peacebuilding after Mass Violence', *International Journal of Transitional Justice* 3 (2009), pp. 28–48.

Larrieu, Louis, *Histoire de la maréchaussée et de la gendarmerie des origines à la Quatrième République* (Ivry-sur-Seine: Phénix Éditions, 2002).

Lauterpacht, Hersch, 'The Grotian Tradition in International Law', *British Year Book of International Law* 23 (1946), pp. 1–53.

Lawson, Cecil, *A History of the Uniforms of the British Army*, Vol. II (London: Peter Davies, 1941).

Lee, R. Warden, 'Grotius – the Last Phase, 1635–45', *Transactions of the Grotius Society* 31 (1945), pp. 193–215.

Lee, Wayne E., 'Early American Ways of War: A New Reconnaissance, 1600–1815', *The Historical Journal* 44 (2001), pp. 269–89.

Leebaw, Bronwyn Anne, 'The Irreconcilable Goals of Transitional Justice', *Human Rights Quarterly* 30 (2008), pp. 95–118.

Leggiere, Michael V., *Napoleon and Berlin: The Franco-Prussian War in North Germany, 1813* (Norman, OK: University of Oklahoma Press, 2002).

Lenman, Bruce P., 'The Transition to European Military Ascendancy in India, 1600–1800', in *Tools of War: Instruments, Ideas, and Institutions of Warfare, 1445–1871*, ed. John A. Lynn (Chicago: University of Illinois Press, 1990), pp. 100–30.

Lévy, Jean-Michel, 'La vertu aux armées pendant la Révolution française', *Cahiers d'histoire* 12 (1967), pp. 359–75.

Lieven, Dominic, *Russia against Napoleon. The Battle for Europe, 1807 to 1814* (London: Allen Lane, 2009).

Lindegren, Jan, 'Men, Money and Means', in *War and Competition between States*, ed. Philippe Contamine (Oxford: Clarendon, 2000), pp. 129–62.

Lindegren, Jan, 'The Politics of Expansion in Seventeenth-Century Sweden', in *Spain and Sweden in the Baroque Era (1600–1660)*, ed. Enrique Martínez Ruiz and Magdalena de Pazzis Pi Corrales (Madrid: Fundacion Berndt Wistedt, 2000), pp. 169–94.

Lindsay, Suzanne Glover, 'Mummies and Tombs: Turenne, Napoléon, and Death Ritual', *The Art Bulletin* 82 (2000), pp. 476–502.

Lorenz, Maren, *Das Rad der Gewalt. Militär und Zivilbevölkerung in Norddeutschland nach dem Dreißigjährigen Krieg (1650–1700)* (Cologne: Böhlau, 2007).

Lorgnier, Jacques, *Maréchaussée: histoire d'une révolution judiciaire et administrative, vol. 1: les juges bottés* (Paris: L'Harmattan, 1994).

Lottin, Alain, and Guignet, Philippe, *Histoire des provinces françaises du Nord de Charles Quint à la Révolution Française (1500–1789)* (Arras: Artois Presses Université, 2006).

Lough, John, *An Introduction to Eighteenth Century France* (London: Longman, 1960).

Louthan, Howard, *Converting Bohemia: Force and Persuasion in the Catholic Reformation* (Cambridge: Cambridge University Press, 2009).

Lutz, Ellen, 'Transitional Justice: Lessons Learnt and the Road Ahead', in *Transitional Justice in the Twenty-First Century: Beyond Truth Versus Justice*, ed. Naomi Roht-Arriaza and Javier Mariezcurrena (Cambridge: Cambridge University Press, 2006), pp. 325–41.

Lynn, John A., 'A Brutal Necessity? The Devastation of the Palatinate, 1688–1689', in *Civilians in the Path of War*, ed. Mark Grimsley and Clifford J. Rogers (Lincoln, NE: University of Nebraska Press, 2002), 79–110.

Lynn, John A., *Giant of the Grand Siècle: The French Army, 1610–1715* (Cambridge: Cambridge University Press, 1997).

Lynn, John A., 'How War Fed War: The Tax of Violence and Contributions during the Grand Siècle', *Journal of Modern History* 65 (1993), pp. 286–310.

Lynn, John A., 'Recalculating French Army Growth During the Grand Siècle, 1610–1715', in *The Military Revolution Debate: Readings on the Military Transformation of Early Modern Europe*, ed. Clifford J. Rogers (Boulder, CO: Westview, 1995), pp. 117–47.

Lynn, John A., 'The trace italienne and the Growth of Armies: The French Case', in *The Military Revolution Debate: Readings on the Military Transformation of Early Modern Europe*, ed. Clifford J. Rogers (Boulder, CO: Westview, 1995), pp. 169–99.

Lynn, John A., *The Wars of Louis XIV, 1667–1714* (London: Longman, 1999).

Lynn, John A., *Women, Armies and Warfare in Early Modern Europe* (Cambridge: Cambridge University Press, 2008).

McCormack, Matthew, *The Independent Man: Citizenship and Gender Politics in Georgian England* (Manchester: Manchester University Press, 2005).

McCormack, Matthew, 'The New Militia: War, Politics and Gender in 1750s Britain', *Gender & History* 19 (2007), pp. 483–500.

McCreery, Cindy, 'Breaking All the Rules: The Worsley Affair in Late Eighteenth-Century Britain', in *Orthodoxy and Heresy in Eighteenth-Century Society*, ed. Regina Hewitt and Pat Rogers (Lewisburg, PA: Bucknell University Press, 2002), pp. 69–88.

McCreery, Cindy, 'True Blue and *Black, Brown and Fair*: Prints of British Sailors and their Women during the Revolutionary and Napoleonic Wars', *British Journal for Eighteenth-Century Studies* 23 (2000), pp. 135–52.

Macdonell, John, 'The Influence of Grotius', *Transactions of the Grotius Society* 5 (1919), pp. xvii–xxiii.

MacDougall, Ian, *The Prisoners at Penicuik* (Dalkeith: Midlothian District Council, 1989).

MacHardy, Karin J., *War, Religion and Court Patronage in Habsburg Austria: The Social and Cultural Dimensions of Political Interaction, 1521–1622* (Basingstoke: Palgrave Macmillan, 2003).

Mackenzie–Stuart, Alexander J., *A French King at Holyrood* (Edinburgh: John Donald, 1995).

McKeogh, Colm, *Innocent Civilians: The Morality of Killing in War* (Basingstoke: Palgrave, 2002).

McKibbin, M. A., 'Citizens of Liberty, Agents of Tyranny: The Dual Perception of Allied Prisoners of War during the French Revolution', *Selected Papers – Consortium on Revolutionary Europe, 1750–1850*, 26 (1996), pp. 112–20.

Mackillop, Andrew, 'The Political Culture of the Scottish Highlands from Culloden to Waterloo', *The Historical Journal* 46 (2003), pp. 511–32.

McLay, K. A. J., 'The Blessed Trinity: The Army, the Navy and Providence in the Conduct of Warfare, 1688–1713', in *War and Religion after Westphalia, 1648–1713*, ed. David Onnekink (Farnham: Ashgate, 2009), pp. 103–20.

Martin, Philippe, *Une guerre de trente ans en Lorraine, 1631–1661* (Metz: Serpenoise, 2002).

Marwick, Arthur, *Britain in the Century of Total War: War, Peace and Social Change, 1900–1967* (Harmondsworth: Penguin, 1970).

Marwick, Arthur, ed., *Total War and Social Change* (Basingstoke: Macmillan, 1988).

Masson, Philippe, *Les sépulcres flottants: prisonniers français en Angleterre sous l'Empire* (Rennes: Ouest-France, 1987).

Matikkala, Antti, *The Orders of Knighthood and the Formation of the British Honours System, 1660–1760* (Woodbridge: Boydell, 2008).

Melton, James Van Horn, *The Rise of the Public in Enlightenment Europe* (Cambridge: Cambridge University Press, 2001).

Meumann, Markus, 'Comment les conflits entre militaires et civils étaient-ils réglés au XVIIe siècle? Les exemples du Nord de la France et du Duché de Magdebourg', in *L'armée et la ville dans l'Europe du Nord et du Nord–Ouest. Du XVe siècle à nos jours*, ed. Philippe Bragard (Louvain-la-Neuve: Academia Bruylant, 2006), pp. 89–100.

Meumann, Markus, 'Generalauditeur', in *Handwörterbuch zur deutschen Rechtsgeschichte*, Vol. II, (Berlin: Erich Schmidt, 2nd edn, 2012), cols. 95–96.

Meumann, Markus, 'Die schwedische Herrschaft in den Stiftern Magdeburg und Halberstadt während des Dreißigjährigen Krieges (1631–1635)', in *Die besetzte res publica: Zum Verhältnis von ziviler Obrigkeit und militärischer Herrschaft in besetzten Gebieten vom Spätmittelalter bis zum 18. Jahrhundert*, ed. Markus Meumann and Jörg Rogge (Berlin: LIT, 2006), pp. 239–67.

Meumann, Markus, and Rogge, Jörg, eds., *Die besetzte res publica: Zum Verhältnis von ziviler Obrigkeit und militärischer Herrschaft in besetzten Gebieten vom Spätmittelalter bis zum 18. Jahrhundert* (Berlin: LIT, 2006).

Meyer, Jean, *La France moderne de 1515 à 1789* (Paris: Fayard, 1985).

Middleton, Richard, 'The Recruitment of the British Army, 1755–1762', *Journal of the Society for Army Historical Research* 67 (1989), pp. 226–38.

Miller, John, *After the Civil Wars: English Politics and Government in the Reign of Charles II* (Harlow: Longman, 2000).

Möller, Hans-Michael, *Das Regiment der Landsknechte. Untersuchungen zu Verfassung, Recht und Selbstverständnis in deutschen Söldnerheeren des 16. Jahrhunderts* (Wiesbaden: Steiner, 1976).

Montroussier, Laurence, 'Français et Britanniques dans la Péninsule, 1808–1814: étude de mémoires français et britanniques', *Annales historiques de la Révolution française* 348 (2007), pp. 131–45.

Moran, Daniel, and Waldron, Arthur, eds., *The People in Arms. Military Myth and National Mobilization since the French Revolution* (Cambridge: Cambridge University Press, 2003).

Morieux, Renaud, 'Ordre social versus ordre national: les prisonniers français sur parole et la population anglaise au 18e siècle', *Annales d'histoire économique et sociale* (forthcoming).

Morrill, J. S., and Walter, J. D., 'Order and Disorder in the English Revolution', in *Order and Disorder in Early Modern England*, ed. Anthony Fletcher and John Stevenson (Cambridge: Cambridge University Press, 1985), pp. 137–65.

Morrill, John, 'Cromwell, Oliver (1599–1658)', *Oxford Dictionary of National Biography* (Oxford: Oxford University Press, 2004), http://www.oxforddnb.com/view/article/6765 (accessed 23 February 2010).

Morris, R. J., 'Voluntary Societies and British Urban Elites, 1780–1850', *The Historical Journal* 26 (1983), pp. 95–118.

Müller, Hermann–Dieter, *Der schwedische Staat in Mainz 1631–1636: Einnahme, Verwaltung, Absichten, Restitution* (Mainz: Stadtbibliothek, 1979).

Mulligan, William, 'Review Article: Total War', *War in History* 15 (2008), pp. 211–21.

Münch, Paul, ed., *'Erfahrung' als Kategorie der Frühneuzeitsgeschichte* (Munich: Oldenbourg, 2001).

Münchow–Pohl, Bernd von, *Zwischen Reform und Krieg. Untersuchungen zur Bewußtseinslage in Preußen, 1809–1812* (Göttingen: Vandenhoek, 1987).

Munck, Thomas, *The Enlightenment: A Comparative Social History 1721–1794* (London: Arnold, 2000).

Murdoch, Steve, *Britain, Denmark-Norway and the House of Stuart, 1603–1660* (East Linton: Tuckwell, 2000).

Neely, Jr, Mark E., 'Was the Civil War a Total War?' *Civil War History* 50 (2004), pp. 434–58.

Nicolson, Benedict, *Joseph Wright of Derby: Painter of Light*, 2 vols. (London: Routledge and Kegan Paul, 1968).

Nicholson, Eirwen, 'Consumers and Spectators: The Public of the Political Print in Eighteenth-Century England', *History* 81 (1996), pp. 5–21.

Nowosadtko, Jutta, 'Erfahrung als Methode und als Gegenstand wissenschaftlicher Erkenntnis', in *Die Erfahrung des Krieges: Erfahrungsgeschichtliche Perspektiven von der Französischen Revolution bis zum Zweiten Weltkrieg*, ed. Nikolaus Buschmann and Horst Carl (Paderborn: Ferdinand Schöningh, 2001), pp. 27–50.

Ogée, Frédéric ed., *'Better in France?': The Circulation of Ideas Across the Channel in the Eighteenth Century* (Lewisburg, PA: Bucknell University Press, 2005).

Oman, Charles, *A History of the Peninsular War*, Vols. I, V–VI (London: Greenhill Books, 2004–05).

Oman, Charles, *Wellington's Army, 1809–1814* (London: Greenhill Books, 2006).

Onuma, Yasuaki, ed., *A Normative Approach to War: Peace, War and Justice in Hugo Grotius* (Oxford: Clarendon Press, 1993).

Orgeval, Gabriel Le Barrois d', *La justice militaire sous l'ancien régime: le Tribunal de la connétablie de France, du XIV⁴ siècle à 1790* (Paris: E. de Boccard, 1918).

Ostwald, Jamel, *Vauban under Siege: Engineering Efficiency and Martial Vigor in the War of the Spanish Succession* (Leiden: Brill, 2007).

Pargellis, Stanley, *Lord Loudoun in North America* (New Haven, CT: Yale University Press, 1933).

Parker, Geoffrey, *The Army of Flanders and the Spanish Road, 1567–1659: The Logistics of Spanish Victory and Defeat in the Low Countries' Wars* (Cambridge: Cambridge University Press, 2nd edn, 2004).

Parker, Geoffrey, 'Early Modern Europe', in *The Laws of War: Constraints on Warfare in the Western World*, ed. Michael Howard, George J. Andreopoulos and Mark R. Shulman (New Haven, CT: Yale University Press, 1994), pp. 40–58.

Parker, Geoffrey, *The Military Revolution: Military Innovation and the Rise of the West, 1500–1800* (Cambridge: Cambridge University Press, 1996).

Parker, Geoffrey, 'The "Military Revolution, 1560–1660" – A Myth?', in *The Military Revolution Debate: Readings on the Military Transformation of Early Modern Europe*, ed. Clifford J. Rogers (Boulder, CO: Westview, 1995), pp. 37–54.

Parrott, David, *Richelieu's Army: War, Government and Society in France, 1624–1642* (Cambridge: Cambridge University Press, 2001).

Parrott, David, 'Strategy and Tactics in the Thirty Years' War: The "Military Revolution"', in *The Military Revolution Debate: Readings on the Military Transformation of Early Modern Europe*, ed. Clifford J. Rogers (Boulder, CO: Westview, 1995), pp. 227–51.

Pascoe, Judith, *The Hummingbird Cabinet: A Rare and Curious History of Romantic Collectors* (Ithaca, NY: Cornell University Press, 2006).

Paulson, Ronald, *Representations of Revolution, 1789–1820* (New Haven, CT: Yale University Press, 1983).

Paye, Claudie, '"der französischen Sprache mächtig..." Kommunikation im Spannungsfeld von Sprachen und Kulturen im Königreich Westphalen (1807–1813)', unpublished PhD thesis, University of Saarland, 2007.

Pearce, Susan M., ed., *Interpreting Objects and Collections* (London: Routledge, 1994).

Pearce, Susan M., *On Collecting: An Investigation into Collecting in the European Tradition* (London: Routledge, 1995).

Pepper, Simon, 'Aspects of Operational Art: Communications, Cannon and Small War', in *European Warfare, 1350–1750*, ed. Frank Tallett and D. J. B. Trim (Cambridge: Cambridge University Press, 2010), pp. 181–202.

Philp, Mark, *Resisting Napoleon: The British Response to the Threat of Invasion, 1797–1815* (Aldershot: Ashgate, 2006).

Picaud–Monnerat, Sandrine, *La petite guerre au XVIIIe siècle* (Paris: Economica, 2010).

Pierard, Gabriel, 'Un dépot de prisonniers de guerre anglais de 1798 à 1814', *Annales de la Société royale d'archéologie de Bruxelles* 50 (1961), pp. 174–90.

Planert, Ute, 'From Collaboration to Resistance: Politics, Experience, and Memory of the Revolutionary and Napoleonic Wars in Southern Germany', *Central European History* 39 (2006), pp. 676–705.

Planert, Ute, *Der Mythos vom Befreiungskrieg. Frankreichs Kriege und der deutsche Süden: Alltag–Wahrnehmung–Deutung, 1792–1841* (Paderborn: Schöningh, 2007).

Pocock, J. G. A., *Barbarism and Religion II: Narratives of Civil Government* (Cambridge: Cambridge University Press, 1999).

Poitrineau, Abel, 'Code Michau', in *Dictionnaire du grand siècle* ed. François Bluche (Paris: Fayard, 1990), p. 340.

Pollak, Martha, *Cities at War in Early Modern Europe* (New York: Cambridge University Press, 2010).

Pörtner, Regina, *The Counter Reformation in Central Europe: Styria, 1580–1630* (Oxford: Oxford University Press, 2001).

Price, Munro, *The Perilous Crown: France Between Revolutions, 1814–1848* (London: Macmillan, 2007).

Pritchard, James S., *Louis XV's Navy, 1748–1762: A Study of Organization and Administration* (Kingston: McGill-Queen's University Press, 1987).

Puymège, Gérard de, *Chauvin, le soldat-laboureur. Contribution à l'étude des nationalismes* (Paris: Gallimard, 1993).

Quataert, Jean, *Staging Philanthropy: Patriotic Women and the National Imagination in Dynastic Germany, 1813–1916* (Ann Arbor, MI: University of Michigan Press, 2001).

Ranlet, Philip, 'The British, Their Virginian Prisoners, and Prison Ships of the American Revolution', *The American Neptune* 60 (2000), pp. 253–62.

Rauser, Amelia, 'Hair, Authenticity and the Self–Made Macaroni', *Eighteenth-Century Studies*, 38 (2004), pp. 101–17.

Raven, James, 'Libraries for Sociability: The Advance of the Subscription Library', in *The Cambridge History of Libraries in Britain and Ireland: Volume II 1640–1850*, ed. Giles Mandelbrote and K. A. Manley (Cambridge: Cambridge University Press, 2006), pp. 241–63.

Raven, James, *London Booksellers and American Customers: Transatlantic Literary Community and the Charleston Library Society, 1748–1811* (Columbia, SC: University of South Carolina Press, 2002).

Redlich, Fritz, *De Praeda Militari: Looting and Booty, 1500–1815* (*Vierteljahrschrift für Sozial- und Wirtschaftsgeschichte* Supplement 39) (Wiesbaden: F. Steiner, 1956).

Regan, Patrick M., *Organizing Societies for War: The Process and Consequences of Societal Militarization* (Westport, CT: Praeger 1994).

Remec, Peter Pavel, 'The Position of the Individual in International Law According to Hugo Grotius', in *Grotius Reader: A Reader for Students of International Law and Legal History*, ed. L. E. van Holk and C. G. Roelofsen (The Hague: T. M. C. Asser Instituut, 1983), pp. 241–44.

Rétat, Pierre, 'The Evolution of the Citizen from the Ancien Régime to the Revolution', in *The French Revolution and the Meaning of Citizenship*, ed. Renée Waldinger, Philip Dawson and Isser Woloch (Westport, CT: Greenwood Press, 1993), pp. 3–15.

Ridel, Charles, *Les embusqués* (Paris: Armand Colin, 2007).

Rink, Martin, *Vom "Partheygänger" zum Partisanen: Die Konzeption des kleinen Krieges in Preußen 1740–1813* (Frankfurt am Main: Lang, 1999).

Roberts, Michael, 'The Military Revolution, 1560–1660', in *The Military Revolution Debate: Readings on the Military Transformation of Early Modern Europe*, ed. Clifford J. Rogers (Boulder, CO: Westview, 1995), pp. 13–35.

Robson, Eric, 'The Armed Forces and the Art of War', in *The New Cambridge Modern History: Vol. VII: The Old Regime, 1713–1763*, ed. J. O. Lindsay (Cambridge: Cambridge University Press, 1957), pp. 163–90.

Rogers, Clifford J., ed., *The Military Revolution Debate: Readings on the Military Transformation of Early Modern Europe* (Boulder, CO: Westview, 1995).

Rogge, Jörg, 'Zur Theorie, Praxis und Erfahrung militärischer Besetzung (Okkupation) im späten Mittelalter', in *Die besetzte res publica: Zum Verhältnis von ziviler Obrigkeit und militärischer Herrschaft in besetzten Gebieten vom Spätmittelalter bis zum 18. Jahrhundert*, ed. Markus Meumann and Jörg Rogge (Berlin: LIT, 2006), pp. 119–28.

Roht–Arriaza, Naomi, and Mariezcurrena, Javier, eds., *Transitional Justice in the Twenty–First Century: Beyond Truth Versus Justice* (Cambridge: Cambridge University Press, 2006).

Rooms, Etienne, 'Contributions de guerre', in *La Belgique espagnole et la principauté de Liège 1585–1715, vol. 1: La politique*, ed. Paul Janssens (Luxembourg: Dexia Banque, 2006), pp. 86–87.

Ross, Mary Ellen, 'La femme militaire de la Révolution française: motifs, modèles et tactiques littéraires', in *French and Francophone Women Facing War/Les femmes face à la guerre*, ed. Alison S. Fell (Oxford: Peter Lang; 2009), pp. 47–65.

Roux, Georges, *Napoléon et le guêpier espagnol* (Paris: Flammarion, 1970).

Rowe, Michael, 'Between Empire and Home Town: Napoleonic Rule on the Rhine, 1799–1814', *The Historical Journal* 42 (1999), pp. 643–74.

Rowe, Michael, *From Reich to State: The Rhineland in the Revolutionary Age, 1780–1830* (Cambridge: Cambridge University Press, 2003).

Rowlands, Guy, 'The Capitalisation of Foreign Mercenaries in Louis XIV's France', in *Die Kapitalisierung des Krieges: Kriegsunternehmer im Spätmittelalter und in der Frühen Neuzeit*, ed. Matthias Meinhardt and Markus Meumann (Berlin: LIT, 2011).

Roy, Ian, 'England Turned Germany? The Aftermath of the Civil War in its European Context', *Transactions of the Royal Historical Society*, 5th Series 28 (1978), pp. 127–44.

Rublack, Ulinka, *The Crimes of Women in Early Modern Germany* (Oxford: Clarendon Press, 1999).

Ruggiero, Alain, 'La présence de l'armée et ses conséquences dans le département des Alpes–Maritimes de l'an II à l'an X', in *La Révolution française: la guerre et la frontière* ed. Monique Cubells (Paris: CTHS, 2000), pp. 155–66.

Russell, Gillian, *The Theatres of War: Performance, Politics, and Society, 1793–1815* (Oxford: Clarendon Press, 1995).

Rydberg, O.S., and Hallendorf, Carl, eds., *Sveriges traktater med främmande magter jemte andra dit hörande handlingar*, 5 vols. (Stockholm: Norstedt, 1902–09).

Sampson, Richard, *Escape in America: The British Convention Prisoners 1777–1783* (Chippenham: Picton, 1995).

Satterfield, George, *Princes, Posts, and Partisans: The Army of Louis XIV and Partisan Warfare in the Netherlands (1673–1678)* (Leiden: Brill, 2003).

Saunderson, Barbara, 'English and the French Enlightenment', *Aspects of Education* 47 (1992), pp. 19–37.

Savory, Reginald, 'The Convention of Écluse, 1759–1762: The Treatment of Sick and Wounded Prisoners of War, and Deserters of the British and French Armies during the Seven Years War', *Journal of the Society for Army Historical Research* 42 (1964), pp. 68–77.

Schama, Simon, *Citizens: A Chronicle of the French Revolution* (New York: Alfred A. Knopf, 1989).

Schindling, Anton, 'Krieg und Konfession im Alten Reich. Bedingungen für die Wahrnehmung und Erfahrung des Dreißigjährigen Krieges', in *Zeitenwenden: Herrschaft, Selbstbehauptung und Integration zwischen Reformation und Liberalismus*, ed. Jörg Deventer (Münster: LIT, 2002), pp. 255–71.

Schmitt, Carl, *Der Nomos der Erde im Völkerrecht des Jus Publicum Europaeum* (Cologne: Greven, 1950).

Schneider, Erich, 'Revolutionserlebnis und Frankreichbild zur Zeit des ersten Koalitions-krieges (1792–1795)', *Francia* 8 (1980), pp. 277–393.

Schom, Alan, *Napoleon Bonaparte* (New York: HarperCollins, 1997).

Scott, Jonathan, 'England's Troubles: Exhuming the Popish Plot', in *The Politics of Religion in Restoration England*, ed. Tim Harris, Paul Seaward and Mark Goldie (Oxford: Blackwell, 1990), pp. 107–31.

Scotti-Douglas, Vittorio, 'Regulating the Irregulars: Spanish Legislation on *la guerrilla* during the Peninsular War', in *Popular Resistance in the French Wars: Patriots, Partisans, and Land Pirates*, ed. Charles J. Esdaile (Basingstoke: Palgrave, 2005), pp. 137–60.

Scouller, R. E., *The Armies of Queen Anne* (Oxford: Clarendon Press, 1966).

Seaward, Paul, *The Cavalier Parliament and the Reconstruction of the Old Regime, 1661–1667* (Cambridge: Cambridge University Press, 1989).

Semmel, Stuart, 'Reading the Tangible Past: British Tourism, Collecting, and Memory after Waterloo', *Representations* 69 (2000), pp. 9–37.

Shaw, Malcolm N., *International Law* (Cambridge: Cambridge University Press, 5th edn, 2003).

Shaw, Philip, 'Abjection Sustained: Goya, the Chapman Brothers and the *Disasters of War*', *Art History* 26 (2003), pp. 479–504.

Shaw, Philip, 'Dead Soldiers: Suffering in British Military Art, 1783–1789', *Romanticism* 11 (2005), pp. 55–69.

Sher, Richard B., *Church and University in the Scottish Enlightenment: The Moderate Literati of Edinburgh* (Edinburgh: Edinburgh University Press, 1985).

Showalter, Dennis E., 'The Prusso-German RMA, 1840–1871', in *The Dynamics of Military Revolution, 1300–2050*, ed. MacGregor Knox and Williamson Murray (Cambridge: Cambridge University Press, 2001), pp. 92–113.

Showalter, Dennis E., 'The Retaming of Bellona: Prussia and the Institutionalization of the Napoleonic Legacy, 1815–1876', *Military Affairs* 44 (1980), pp. 57–63.

Skates, John Ray, 'German Prisoners of War in Mississippi, 1943–1946', *Mississippi History Now*, September 2001, http://mshistory.k12.ms.us/index.php?id=233 (accessed 1 October 2010).

Skinner, Quentin, *The Foundations of Modern Political Thought: Vol. 2 The Age of Reformation* (Cambridge: Cambridge University Press, 1978).

Smiley, Marion, 'Review: Democratic Justice in Transition', *Michigan Law Review*, 99 (2001), pp. 1332–47.

Smith, David L., 'The Struggle for New Constitutional and Institutional Forms', in *Revolution and Restoration: England in the 1650s*, ed. John Morrill (London: Collins & Brown, 1992), pp. 15–34.

Spitzer, Alan B., *The French Generation of 1820* (Princeton, NJ: Princeton University Press, 1987).

St Clair, William, *The Reading Nation in the Romantic Period* (Cambridge: Cambridge University Press, 2004).

Steele, I. K., 'Surrendering Rites: Prisoners on Colonial North American Frontiers', in *Hanoverian Britain and Empire: Essays in Memory of Philip Lawson*, ed. Stephen Taylor, Richard Connors and Clyve Jones (Woodbridge: Boydell Press, 1998), pp. 137–57.

Steiger, Heinhard, '"Occupatio bellica" in der Literatur des Völkerrechts der Christenheit (Spätmittelalter bis 18. Jahrhundert)', in *Die besetzte res publica: Zum Verhältnis von ziviler*

Obrigkeit und militärischer Herrschaft in besetzten Gebieten vom Spätmittelalter bis zum 18. Jahrhundert, ed. Markus Meumann and Jörg Rogge (Berlin: LIT, 2006), pp. 201–40.

Stephens, F. G., and George, M. Dorothy, eds, *Catalogue of Political and Personal Satires in the British Museum*, 11 vols. (London: British Museum, 1978).

Steppler, G. A., 'British Military Law, Discipline and the Conduct of Regimental Courts Martial in the Later Eighteenth Century', *English Historical Review* 102 (1987), pp. 859–86.

Stevens, Carol B., *Russia's Wars of Emergence, 1460–1730* (Harlow: Pearson, 2007).

Storrs, Christopher, ed., *The Fiscal-Military State in Eighteenth-Century Europe: Essays in Honour of P. G. M. Dickson* (Farnham: Ashgate, 2009).

Storrs, Christopher, 'Giustizia militare, militari e non militari nell'Europa della prima età moderna', in *Militari e società civile nell'Europa dell'età moderna (secoli XVI–XVIII)*, ed. Claudio Donati and Bernhard R. Kroener (Bologne: Mulino, 2007), pp. 573–609.

Stoyle, Mark, '"Memories of the Maimed": The Testimony of Charles I's Former Soldiers, 1660–1730', *History* 88 (2003), pp. 204–26.

Strachan, Hew, *Carl von Clausewitz's On War: A Biography* (London: Atlantic Books, 2007).

Strachan, Hew, 'On Total War and Modern War', *International History Review* 22 (2000), pp. 341–70.

Strupp, Karl, ed., *Wörterbuch des Völkerrechts: Vol. 2* (Berlin: De Gruyter, 1925).

Sullivan, Michael, 'Restoring the Summer Palace', *Times Literary Supplement*, 24 June 1988.

Tallett, Frank, *War and Society in Early-Modern Europe, 1495–1715* (London: Routledge, 1997).

Tanaka, Tadashi, '*Temperamenta* (Moderation)', in *A Normative Approach to War: Peace, War and Justice in Hugo Grotius*, ed. Onuma Yasuaki (Oxford: Clarendon Press, 1993), pp. 276–307.

Teitel, Ruti, *Transitional Justice* (Oxford: Oxford University Press, 2000).

Teitel, Ruti, 'Transitional Justice Genealogy', *Harvard Human Rights Journal* 16 (2003), pp. 69–94.

Thirsk, Joan, 'The Restoration Land Settlement', *Journal of Modern History* 26 (1954), pp. 315–28.

Thompson, Andrew C., *Britain, Hanover and the Protestant Interest, 1688–1756* (Woodbridge: Boydell Press, 2006).

Thompson, Carl, *The Suffering Traveller and the Romantic Imagination* (Oxford: Clarendon Press, 2007).

Thorp, John T., *French Prisoners' Lodges: A Brief Account of Fifty Lodges and Chapters of Freemasons Established and Conducted by French Prisoners of War in England and Elsewhere, Between 1756 and 1814* (Leicester: Freemasons' Hall, 1935).

Tieghem, Paul van, *Ossian en France* (Paris: F. Rieder, 1917).

Towsey, Mark, 'All Partners May be Enlightened and Improved by Reading Them: The Distribution of Enlightenment Books in Scottish Subscription Library Catalogues, 1750–c.1820', *Journal of Scottish Historical Studies* 28 (2008), pp. 20–43.

Towsey, Mark, 'First Steps in Associational Reading: Book Use and Sociability at the Wigtown Subscription Library, 1795–9', *Papers of the Bibliographical Society of America* 103 (2009), pp. 455–95.

Towsey, Mark, *Reading the Scottish Enlightenment: Books and their Readers in Provincial Scotland, 1750–1820* (Leiden: Brill, 2010).

Trim, D. J. B., 'Huguenot Soldiering c. 1560–1685: The Origins of a Tradition', in *War, Religion and Service: Huguenot Soldiering 1685–1713*, ed. Matthew Glozier and David Onnekink (Aldershot: Ashgate, 2007), pp. 9–30.

Tyson, Peter, 'The Role of Republican and *Patriote* Discourse in the Insurrection of the Vendée', unpublished MA dissertation, University of York, 1994.

Underdown, David, *Pride's Purge: Politics in the Puritan Revolution* (London: Allen & Unwin, 1985).

Urban, Mark, *Wellington's Rifles: Six Years to Waterloo with England's Legendary Sharpshooters* (New York: Walker and Co., 2004).

Van Buskirk, Judith L., *Generous Enemies: Patriots and Loyalists in Revolutionary New York* (Philadelphia: University of Pennsylvania Press, 2002).

Vincent, R. J., 'Grotius, Human Rights, and Intervention', in *Hugo Grotius and International Relations*, ed. Hedley Bull, Benedict Kingsbury and Adam Roberts (Oxford: Clarendon Press, 1990), pp. 241–56.

Wahrman, Dror, *The Making of the Modern Self: Identity and Culture in Eighteenth-Century England* (New Haven, CT: Yale University Press, 2004).

Wallace, Miriam L., *Revolutionary Subjects in the English Jacobin' Novel, 1790–1805* (Lewisburg, PA: Bucknell University Press, 2009).

Walter, Friedrich, *Die Geschichte der österreichischen Zentralverwaltung in der Zeit Maria Theresias (1740–1780)* (Vienna: Holzhausen, 1938).

Walter, John, *Understanding Popular Violence in the English Revolution. The Colchester Plunderers* (Cambridge: Cambridge University Press, 1999).

Walters, J. B., 'General William T. Sherman and Total War', *The Journal of Southern History* 14 (1948), pp. 447–80.

Walzer, Michael, *Just and Unjust Wars: A Moral Argument with Historical Illustrations* (New York: Basic Books, 1977).

Weber, Reinhard, *Würzburg und Bamberg im Dreißigjährigen Krieg* (Würzburg: Echter, 1979).

Wees, Hans van, *Greek Warfare. Myths and Realities* (London: Duckworth, 2004).

Western, J. R., *The English Militia in the Eighteenth Century: The Story of a Political Issue, 1660–1802* (London: Routledge and Keegan Paul, 1965).

Wexler, Victor G., *David Hume and the History of England* (Philadelphia: American Philosophical Society, 1979).

Whigham, Thomas L., and Potthast, Barbara, 'The Paraguayan Rosetta Stone: New Insights into the Demographics of the Paraguayan War 1864–1870', *Latin American Research Review* 34 (1999), pp. 174–86.

Wight, Martin, *International Theory: The Three Traditions*, ed. Gabriele Wight and Brian Porter (London: Leicester University Press, 1994).

Williams, Gwyn, *Goya and the Impossible Revolution* (London: Allen Lane, 1976).

Wilson, Kathleen, *The Sense of the People: Politics, Culture and Imperialism in England, 1715–1785* (Cambridge: Cambridge University Press, 1995).

Wilson, Peter H., 'Atrocities in the Thirty Years War', in *Plantation and Reaction: The 1641 Rebellion*, ed. Jane Ohlmeyer and Michael O'Siochru (Manchester: Manchester University Press, 2011).

Wilson, Peter H., 'The Causes of the Thirty Years War 1618–48', *English Historical Review* 123 (2008), pp. 554–86.

Wilson, Peter H., 'Defining Military Culture', *Journal of Military History* 72 (2008), pp. 11–41.

Wilson, Peter H., *Europe's Tragedy. A History of the Thirty Years War* (London: Allen Lane, 2009).

Wilson, Peter, 'Warfare in the Old Regime, 1648–1789', in *European Warfare, 1453–1815*, ed. Jeremy Black (Basingstoke: Macmillan, 1999), pp. 69–95.

Wilson-Bareau, Juliet, 'Goya: The Disasters of War', in *Disasters of War: Callot, Goya, Dix*, ed. Anthony Griffiths, Juliet Wilson-Bareau and John Willett (London: South Bank Centre Publications, 1998), pp. 28–55.

'Winchester Castle', in *A History of the County of Hampshire*, vol. 5, ed. William Page (Victoria County History) (London: Constable, 1912), pp. 9–12.

Winkelbauer, Thomas, 'Nervus belli Bohemici. Die finanziellen Hintergründe des Scheiterns des Ständeaufstands der Jahre 1618 bis 1620', *Folia Historica Bohemica* 18 (1997), pp. 173–223.

Winkelbauer, Thomas, *Ständefreiheit und Fürstenmacht: Länder und Untertanen des Hauses Habsburg im konfessionellen Zeitalter*, 2 vols. (Vienna: Ueberreuter, 2003).

Withington, Phil, 'Citizens, Soldiers and Urban Culture in Restoration England', *English Historical Review* 123 (2008), pp. 587–610.

Wood, James B., *The King's Army. Warfare, Soldiers and Society during the Wars of Religion in France, 1562–76* (Cambridge: Cambridge University Press, 1996).

Woolf, Stuart, 'French Civilization and Ethnicity in the Napoleonic Empire', *Past and Present* 124 (1989), pp. 96–120.

Woolf, Stuart, *Napoleon's Integration of Europe* (London: Routledge, 1991).

Worthington, David, *Scots in Habsburg Service, 1618–1648* (Leiden: Brill, 2004).

Wright, Gordon, *The Ordeal of Total War, 1939–1945* (New York: Harper & Row, 1968).

Youngman, Fiona, '"Our Dear Mother Stripped": The Experiences of Ejected Clergy and their Families during the English Revolution', unpublished DPhil thesis, University of Oxford, 2008.

Zamoyski, Adam, *Moscow, 1812: Napoleon's Fatal March* (New York: HarperCollins, 2004).

Index